D0960033

# The Devil Inside
# the Beltway

# The Devil Inside
# the Beltway

*The Shocking Exposé of the
US Government's Surveillance and
Overreach into Cybersecurity, Medicine
and Small Business*

## By Michael J. Daugherty

Broadland Press
Atlanta, Georgia

Broadland Press
2030 Powers Ferry Road
Suite 520
Atlanta, GA 30339
www.michaeljdaugherty.com
www.broadlandpress.com
info@broadlandpress.com

Hardcover:
ISBN 13: 978-0-9857422-0-1
ISBN 10: 0-9857422-0-8

Paperback:
ISBN 13: 978-0-9857422-2-5
ISBN 10: 0-9857422-2-4

DISCLAIMER: Memories can't be verified to perfection since the human
mind is faulty, but in telling this story, I have relied upon interviews with my
attorneys, friends, and co-workers, in addition to court documents, emails,
letters, journals, and other research. I have also taken certain liberties such as
dramatizing, compressing, and/or combining events, times, or conversations. In
some cases, names and identifying details have been condensed and/or changed
to avoid unnecessary embarrassment to private individuals. This was done in an
effort to move the story forward and spare readers the mundane, trivial details
not critical to the story. While I may not remember word for word what was said
in the conversations contained in this book, I have done my best to ensure that
they capture my recollections and perceptions of what was discussed. For those
who want more details and facts about the underlying basis for my story and
strong opinions, you will find in the endnotes links to full versions of all documents and emails referenced in this book. In short, this is my story. It is an emotional story of years marred by torment and disgust dealing with the FTC. It is,
ultimately, my personal account about events that have forever changed my life.

Printed in the United States of America

This book is dedicated to all the small business men and women around the world.

From the independent contractor, telecommuter, small medical practice, independent bookseller, part-time mother working during school hours, technology business that builds the magic of tomorrow, to the student working part-time as she puts herself through school, artists creating their masterpieces, housekeeper making her children's lives better than hers, and former corporate players that chucked it all for a small piece of paradise that they can call their own . . . you are my strength and safety. You are not alone. You are the backbone of the world's economy.

# Contents

# Contents

# Acknowledgements

Life is a wild ride sometimes. I would like to thank those that have helped me hold on.

To my parents, Roy and Joan Daugherty, for letting me know I always had a home to come back to. That has always helped me take risks and stare fear in the face.

To my sisters, Christine and Diana, for knowing and believing that I will land on my feet.

And finally, to those too many to mention . . . to friends, employees, managers, bosses, doctors, nurses, technicians, and medical staffs that have stuck with my company, believed in us all, and cheered me on, I can't thank you enough. This book was started long before NSA, Surveillance, and Privacy were top stories in the media. I knew I could attempt to slay the Devil Inside the Beltway because you were standing there beside me when strangers might think I was crazy to attempt such a thing. My heartfelt thanks to you all.

# Who is the Devil Inside the Beltway?

The Devil is a mindset that infiltrates the minds and souls from the weak to the powerful; it hates principle, memory, and truth.

The Devil moves freely among us, numbs our ethics, compromises our moral character, cauterizes our memory, charms us into submission, and convinces us that its carnage is for the betterment of mankind.

The Devil is the master of spin in a world of no up or down, right or wrong, truth or fiction; just a manipulative verbal volleyer always at the ready to spew.

The Devil is seductive in convincing you that you are powerless.

The Devil lives in the silence.

But never forget, knowledge is power. Stare down the Devil Inside the Beltway. Look right into its eyes.

*"Hardships often prepare ordinary people for an extraordinary destiny."*

—C.S. Lewis

# CHAPTER 1
# Breach of Trust

Right now—and completely unknown to them—Americans are sharing sensitive personal data—their bank records, credit card numbers, passwords, tax returns, and letters, to name a few.[1]

*Thomas D. Sydnor, II,*
*Testifying before the US House of Representatives,*
*House Committee on Oversight and Government Reform*
*July 24, 2007*

## The Call—May 13, 2008 Atlanta, Georgia

My nightmare began with a stranger's call from out of the blue. A lightning bolt out of nowhere, I didn't know if it was a random hit or a strike with intent. But until that moment, life was good for me and seemingly for everyone at LabMD.

LabMD is my baby and my life. After being in medical and surgical device sales for over a decade, I built the company from scratch in 1996 using equity lines of credit and charge-card advances. We—and by that I mean myself and current and former physicians, technologists, and employees—built a beautifully run cancer detection facility that focuses on prostate and bladder cancers, as well as almost every other test that may be ordered by a urologist. By May 13, 2008, we were debt free, profitable, and private. I was not looking for a stock run or going public to make a killing. I just wanted to be the best lab possible and to enjoy the meaningful work. That morning there were calm waters all around.

But then everything came to a screeching halt. I was in my office answering e-mails when I looked up and saw Bill Barnett, our VP of Operations and General Manager, standing in front of my desk, typically crisp in his tucked-in shirt, creased pants, and double-knotted shoes. And I saw he had *that* look on his face; I knew that blank look. It came with a pregnant pause that said to me, "Mike, brace yourself, and please don't go ballistic on me." Of course, I always brace myself for the worst. That way, nothing seems so bad when I'm confronted with the words that follow his three seconds of silence.

"We received a phone call from some guy at a data security firm in Pennsylvania," he said monotonously.

"And you are telling me this why . . . ?"

"Well, the guy—some Robert Boback from a company called Tiversa—says he's got a file of ours. He was able to download our data because they perform security intelligence."

Baffled, I fired off questions: "Security intelligence? What the hell is that? For whom? What file is it?"

"He says it's a file containing patient health information."

"That makes no sense at all. Let me get this straight. This guy calls us, says he has *our* file? How did he get it? How does he know it's our file? Have this guy prove what he has in some form of documentation. And please ask for it in writing. This stinks to high heaven. Only communicate in writing."

"Okay." Bill paused. "It doesn't make any sense." Another pause. "I can't wait to find out how this guy got this." We were both on edge, alarmed and mad.

Hearing patient information was in possession of this company set off multiple alarms. I was terrified for our patients. I had a basic instinct to protect them. It was hard to believe it was our file just because this guy said so. I considered LabMD's network security and overall system set-up ahead of the game, especially compared to what I saw on a day-to-day basis in a typical physician's office.

*Slow down*, I coached myself. *This makes no sense. Just gather the info and execute. But if there's patient data out there, then we need all hands on deck.* I needed someone to bounce off my thoughts and get feedback. This called for our lawyer, Evelyn O'Connor.

Good morning, Chairman Waxman, Ranking Member Davis and distinguished members of the committee.

My name is Robert Boback and I am Chief Executive Officer of Tiversa, a Pennsylvania-based company that provides information technology and investigation services that help or protect organizations, government agencies and individual consumers from the disclosure and illicit use of sensitive, confidential, and personal information of peer-to-peer file sharing, or P2P, networks . . . Beginning in 2003, Tiversa has developed systems that monitor and interact with and within P2P networks to search for sensitive information. Where an individual user can only see a portion of a P2P file sharing network, Tiversa can see the whole. It is our belief that no other system has this capability.[1]

*Robert Boback, CEO, Tiversa,*
*Testifying before the US House of Representatives,*
*House Committee on Oversight and*
*Government Reform July 24, 2007*

## May 13, 2008 Atlanta, Georgia

## General Counsel's Advice

Evelyn O'Connor had been LabMD's general counsel since 1996, so by 2008 she and I could finish each other's sentences. Hailing from Oklahoma and having attended law school there, she relocated to Atlanta after graduation. I had met her soon after, when she was dating a friend of mine. That was when I didn't know what it was like to need an attorney, let alone work with one.

Cool and in control, but not icy, the tall, beautiful, well-dressed Evelyn has a disarming manner that makes her easy to get to know. Shrewdly observational, she can be objective when I'm emotional—always a good balance for me. Besides, having the same lawyer for so many years builds up a bank of experience and trust that's invaluable when new alarm bells go off. All the "get to know and trust each other" stuff is behind you. I know Evelyn is trustworthy; she's on our side.

I called her and brought her up to speed on what Bill had just told me.

"He says his firm does security intelligence," I told Evelyn, sarcasm dripping in my voice.

"Mike, our firm gets calls like these from snake oil salesman trying to sell services by instilling fear. Make this guy prove what he says. Make him show you what he's got and disclose how he got it. If there is a problem, identify it and fix it, but have this guy do more than shake his rattle."

As I hung up the phone and returned to my paperwork, I had no clue the next five years of my life would be dramatically changed by what I then thought was just an annoying little fly in the ointment. I had no inkling that this bug was more like a band of locusts that would cost my company at least a half million dollars and countless hours pulled away from our growth and opportunities. And I had no idea I'd encounter federal government officials, US Congressional representatives, bloggers, reporters, underwriters, and a seemingly endless parade of self-righteous lawyers. Little did I know that any scenario I could conjure up could not have possibly been as crazy, unbelievable, or bizarre as what was about to happen.

I did know that letting my emotions create all sorts of stories in my mind was a waste of time, perhaps even damaging. Oblivious to what lay just ahead, I decided not to worry about their claim until we had more information. *I can't assume we have a problem until I know we have a problem. Who the hell is Tiversa and this guy Boback, who has such unmitigated nerve?*

I turned to my computer, fired up my trusty advisor Google, and typed in "Tiversa." Up popped the company's Web site and a stock photo of corporate office buildings (that tells me nothing) and an obvious marketing pitch, "Do you know who is searching for and finding your data on the P2P?" Then, following a quick delay to build the anticipation, two ominous words popped up in yellow: "We do."

*Is that trick supposed to instill fear and make me want to run to this company?*

The message reminded me of aggressive marketing tactics used when the US Department of Health and Human Services (HHS) began its Health Insurance Portability and Accountability Act (HIPAA) patient privacy regulations a decade ago. A week didn't go by without a card in the mail from some "education" company warning me to enroll in their patient privacy course so I wouldn't go to jail.

Bill soon returned with more info. "We just got the file from Boback. It is a financial billing file. It is over 1700 pages long. It contains nine thousand patients' billing information. Thank goodness it did not contain phone numbers or home addresses. It has patient names, social security numbers, insurance company names, and policy numbers, as well as dates of birth and diagnosis codes. It is the summary report of patient accounts that had a balance due to the laboratory. I have no idea how this file could have come into Boback's possession." Bill paused and looked thoughtful. "But, boy, am I ever going to find out."

I was rolling in shock and disbelief. Bill was right there with me.

"Oh my God, ask this guy to give us more information. Remember, please e-mail . . . no phone. Evelyn thinks this is suspicious."


Bill asked Boback for info via e-mail. Then we passed the time, pretending nothing was wrong. Interrupting our anxiety, we received another e-mail forwarded to Bill from Boback right after lunch:

From: Rick Wallace
Sent: Tuesday, May 13, 2008 1:11 PM
To: Robert Boback
Cc: Chris Gormley
Subject: LabMD


Mr. Boback,
Per your request, I checked back against the timeline to see the date that we originally acquired the file pertaining

to LabMD. It appears that we first downloaded the file on 02/05/08 at 3:49PM. Our system shows a record of continued availability for sporadic periods over the past several months but we did not attempt to download it again The system did not auto-record the IP, unfortunately, most likely due to the little amount of criteria indexed against the DSP. We may, however, have the actual source IP address in the data store logs but it was not readily available at this point. If it is there, I should be able to get it but it would take some time.

Please let me know if I can be of further assistance.

Thank you,
Rick Wallace
Forensic Engineer
Global Incident Response Operations Center (GIROC)

I crowed to Bill, "They downloaded this but they don't have any information? Global Incident Response Center? Response for who? This just doesn't add up. Who in-the-know calls a medical facility and says, "Hey, we just found your file with our secret recipe software?"

Bill stood there in stony silence, every bit as dazed and confused as me.

"Okay, we'll just play it very low key and easy with this guy, Bill. We want him to keep talking."

*This is bad news*, kept repeating in my head; I just knew it. *Patient security first, figure out what's going on second*, I repeated in my mind. *And try to stay calm.*

Bill "gets it." All about execution and professionalism, he's any business owner's dream of an operations leader/GM. He nodded and we were immediately on the same page. My experience told me he's better at poker than I am. That made him a good choice for luring Mr. Boback into disclosing what cards he was holding.

"Bill, I think we need to slow things down here. Does this make any sense to you at all?"

"No. He has to cough up way more info."

"I know. We need to not act too hastily here. Let's think of exactly what we want to know from him."

Bill left my office and got to work on formulating a list of what he wanted to know.

Before we got a chance to send another question, Bill returned to my office with another e-mail from Boback. "Oh, you are going to love this first sentence. Check this out."

From: Robert Boback
Sent: Tuesday May 13 2008 14:13:15
To: Bill Barnett
Subject : LabMD

Bill,
We are able to provide investigative and remediation services through our Incident Response team if you are need of their professional assistance. They would locate and identify the precise source of the disclosure. They could also identify additional disclosed files from that source (of which there are most likely additional files since most individuals are sharing an average of over 100 files per PC). They can also perform a Global Spread Analysis to determine severity of the breach. Most importantly, they can work to recover and cleanse the sensitive documents from the P2P. I only mention this because it appeared that there was some confusion about the breach.

If any of these services are of interest to you, please let me know and I will put you in touch with our Operations team to get it started.

Regards,
Robert Boback
CEO Tiversa

"I have your file; do you want to hire me?" is the message I was putting together. My instincts screamed, *Danger!*

I looked at Bill's stunned face and knew we were thinking the same thing as I said, "Yeah, right, we aren't buying this one, buddy. How the hell did this guy get our information? ARGH ... what the hell are we going to do here? Time for the lawyer, dammit."

I want to just disclose now that I am an advisor to Tiversa, and in that role I do have a small equity stake in Tiversa ... The American people would be outraged if they were aware of what is inadvertently shared by Government agencies on P2P networks ... I asked Mr. Boback to search for anything marked classified secret, or secret no-foreign. So he pulled up over 200 classified documents in a few hours running his search engine ... I am a civilian and I am just in business.[1]

*General and former game show host Wesley K. Clark,*
*Testifying before the US House of Representatives,*
*House Committee on Oversight and Government Reform*
*July 24, 2007*

*"America will never be destroyed from the outside. If we falter and lose our freedoms, it will be because we destroyed ourselves."*

—ABRAHAM LINCOLN

# CHAPTER 2
# Blindfolded While Looking for Exits and Answers

Now driven with adrenaline, Bill, Tom—our manager of IT—and I, marched up the stairwell, feet pounding. The echoing sounds fueled our urgency. Within minutes of getting the information from Boback, we blew into the billing manager's office. We surrounded Rebecca, our billing manager, who had no idea what hit her, but she instantly sensed panic and seriousness in the air. No smiles or blinking eyes in sight. We needed to slam this down hard, right now. Tom opened up her desktop and started the hunt.

The file that Tiversa had possession of was found in Rebecca's "My Documents" folder, along with almost 900 music files. Rebecca, in direct violation of policy, was getting music off the web using LimeWire. As we learned, LimeWire was an unruly beast that could also cause her to expose her workstation files without her ever knowing.

### What the Hell is LimeWire?

LimeWire is one of the many free peer to-peer software programs (known as P2P) that are easily accessible online. The programs allow users to download media files such as music, movies, and games using a P2P software client that searches for other connected computers. The "peers" are computer systems that are connected to each other through the Internet. Thus, the only requirements for a computer to join peer-to-peer networks are an Internet connection and P2P software.

"Rebecca, what is this for?" Bill asked, pointing at the files.

"I listen to music. What's going on?" was all he could get out of her before she resumed looking down at the ground in silence.

"We'll have to explain that later. Right now we're trying to answer 'What's going on?' ourselves." Bill and Tom dug a little further.

"So, Rebecca, how did LimeWire get on your computer?" I asked her with zero humor.

"Uh, uh, I don't know... Well, it's always been there." Judging by the look on her face, her muted voice, and her statue-like rigidity, she was stunned. My instincts told me *this makes no sense*; my mind was thinking *are you kidding me? You know better than this! This violates every policy in the book!*

"Okay, Rebecca, we need to review that entire workstation, and audit yours. Save all your work, please. Take your work and go sign on from one of the cubicles. These guys are going to have to dig in here. Stay close to answer questions, please." I was monotone and dead serious. I wasn't in the mood to be anything else.

She looked down at the floor like a scolded child and agreed, saying, "Yes, sir." She looked like she wanted to crawl into the nearest hole. She picked up her work and stepped back as everyone watched in the awkward, seemingly endless silence.

Before Rebecca walked out, I looked at Bill and said, "Okay, do your thing. I won't be much help if I just stand here staring at you. Keep me posted." Not wanting to intensify an already tense situation, I walked back to my office looking straight ahead and stone-faced.

Bill began a deeper examination process and searched all of the applications for other possible vulnerabilities while taking screen shots for later reference.

After saving the file and screenshots on a CD, Bill deleted both the billing file and LimeWire. Then he immediately reviewed every other workstation and server in the company for any evidence of LimeWire—or any other application installed without authorization. He found none. He spent the next three days reviewing the servers again and again. We interviewed employees and grilled Rebecca (to put it mildly), yet everything and everyone else came up clean. That was a relief. We had containment.

The search told us that the only probable way someone could have come into the computer without authorization was through LimeWire. The download occurred through a program that one employee had installed without our authorization or knowledge. A program that didn't appear on the desktop. A program that stayed hidden from our view during inspections. How were we to know or anticipate such intrusions? The questions were endless.

Rebecca insisted she had no idea she could expose sensitive material through her computer. In fact, she said she had no idea anyone could access her computer externally; she believed she was only using the software to listen to music while she worked. Although she signed an employee handbook acknowledging that downloading software was against company policy, I did not believe she would have risked committing career suicide by being careless with patient data.

We would one day learn that more than 450 million other computers in the world were also vulnerable. We now assumed that Rebecca's computer was the gateway Boback used to get the file; it seemed obvious but we had no concrete proof.

So what the hell just happened? We needed answers and we needed them now, so we turned back to Robert Boback to see how many more cards he would show in his quest to "help us out."

Rep. Yarmouth: Do you think that users that download P2P software applications are being tricked into sharing files that they would not ordinarily share?

Sydnor: Yes. They are inadvertently sharing files they do not intend to share. In the report we attempt to explain why, although the user does not intend that result, that result may have been intended by others. That is not a question we purport to be able to answer based on the publicly available data that we were able to review. But the short answer is yes, people are making catastrophic mistakes with these programs . . . That is also a very important part of the problem, and people who do not want to be distributors of pirated goods on these networks should be able to make that choice and have it be very easy, and right now it is simply not.[1]

*Thomas D. Sydnor, II, Testifying before the*
*US House of Representatives,*
*House Committee on Oversight and Government Reform,*
*to Representative John Yarmouth, R–KY.*

*"The most terrifying words in the English language are: I'm from the government and I'm here to help."*

—RONALD REAGAN

# CHAPTER 3
# Post-Traumatic Confusion Syndrome

## May 14, 2008, 4:45 pm, Atlanta, Georgia

I sat in my office alone, needing quiet time to think. Shell-shocked and looking for answers, Bill, Tom, and I all felt confused. Worried and looking for reassurance, I again turned to Evelyn O'Connor, LabMD's lawyer.

"Okay, Evelyn, we found the file, we deleted the file, we closed what we think might be the window, we are researching all workstations, and we are interviewing employees. Nothing else is out of the ordinary. What the hell just happened?"

"That I can't tell you, but do you think the file was out there other than just this one instance? Is there any other evidence?" she asked.

"I don't know yet. The door is shut. How it got out, we're pretty sure we know. But we need more time to find out more."

"This is really odd. I'm going to confirm what you're required to do in this legal gray area."

"I know. It's odd and it's creepy. We have to methodically go through everything and stay focused. Let me know what you find out about the legal angle on your end, and I'll keep you in the loop from the lab."

I hung up the phone. I was pleading to the Gods. *This sort of thing just doesn't happen to us. We don't cut corners or expenses. This just doesn't make sense.* "What is going on?" I said aloud. Then I turned in my chair and called Tom and Bill into my office.

"Please shut the door." The silence was ominous as the door shut and nobody said a word as they took their seats.

"Now, gentlemen, until we get a grip on this, nobody else who doesn't already know learns about Mr. Boback. Understood?"

"Understood."

"Good. Now, what's the plan for tomorrow?"

"Operation: Methodical IT Checklist. We'll make sure every square inch of the place is closed and clean," replied Bill.

## Love my Lawyer, But Here We Go with the Legal Bills

In the meantime, Evelyn started reviewing legislation and legal journals, and looking wherever else lawyers look to find out if we need any additional security requirements according to the current laws in place (in 2008). We weren't sure what to do regarding what *might* have just happened. I say "might" because we still weren't sure what just happened.

Now that we had Rebecca's computer on lockdown, we could move on to the rest the company. We reconfirmed there were no issues or areas of concern. Overall, IT operations looked fine as far as the current status of the company goes. We discovered zero evidence of peer-to-peer (P2P) software anywhere else within the organization, so we moved outside the company to address our next dreaded fear.

What if the file was someplace else? God forbid, but how do we find out if the file has been "taken" before? One obvious person to have the answers was Robert Boback. We had no choice but to contact him. But I don't like verbal conversations with those who have not proven themselves as trustworthy. I prefer written documentation to prevent history from being rewritten.

"Bill, I think we need to keep this guy on a short leash. This guy seems to know everything about this file but has a price tag on the information. Especially since we've been so sideswiped, keep communications in written form so we have documentation. You need to do the talking; I'm likely to get too aggressive because I really want to rock his boat. We need to keep him relaxed so he'll give up as much info about our patients and property as possible."

"Got it. I'll fire off something to him when I get home," Bill responded.

Evidently that meant early the next morning. Bill e-mailed the following to Tiversa:

From: Bill Barnett
Sent: Thursday May 15, 2008 4:34 AM
To: Robert Boback
cc: Michael Daugherty

Could you provide us with the information from the data store logs that Duane mentions below and also did you record the dates when you came across the "sporadic" availability, even though you did not download it again? If we had those dates, we could then cross reference this data to our known data.

Thank you,
Bill W. Barnett
LabMD
VP of Operations and General Manager

May 15, 2008 10:03 AM

Bill,
Per Duane's e-mail below, it would require some time to get to that type of information which would need to be handled through our Incident Response Operation Team and would require a professional services arrangement. As I mentioned in my last e-mail, there are many more necessary benefits to a proper investigation of the disclosure by our team.

Regards,
Robert Boback
Chief Executive Officer
Tiversa, Inc.

*And the penny drops. Charming voice and faux concern aside, Boback wants bucks.*

Apparently Mr. Boback was loath to make any attempts to give us the facts, unless we pay him. My head was swirling in amazement. *Now let me get this straight: You call us up and say you have downloaded a data file that belongs to us, you opened it and read it, knowing it was patient health information. Then you want to sell us your information regarding the circumstances surrounding the file. Your Web site talks about your powerful technology that discovers and knows where the files are. And you want us to pay you for this?* Approximately three and a half years later, my lawyers would sue Tiversa and Dartmouth for computer fraud, computer crimes, conversion, and trespassing. It was already clear to us that Robert Boback wasn't acting like someone calling from a charitable organization; I now viewed him as a smooth operator trying to scare us, his potential client, into purchasing Tiversa's services. *Oh excuse me, sir, you have no idea who you are dealing with.*

The most offensive part of this interaction was Boback cloaking himself as a "concerned citizen." LabMD operates a cancer detection facility. We *totally understand* that patient privacy is of the utmost importance. Our processes fully meet or exceed our industry's standards. We have never taken this responsibility lightly. Nor do we suffer fools gladly.

## Searching for a Needle in Cyberspace that May or May Not Be There

On high alert, Bill continued to manage the search for the file in cyberspace and assigned a tech support person, Elizabeth, the task of working from her home (to be outside of LabMD, as others in cyberspace would be), outside of our office network, looking for any evidence of our file on the Internet. Anywhere.

Elizabeth has a computer science degree from George Washington University. A "full-fledged" computer geek at age 27, she was comfortable playing in cyberspace and looking for evidence. Working from home for this assignment, she searched for any file titled

"LabMD" as well as a myriad of other titles and content suggestions. We had her examine all the known P2P networks in use from 2006 to 2008. No matter where she looked and what she tried, she continually came up empty. As we waited, we were left with time, paranoia, and an uneasy feeling we were being watched.

Something was extremely wrong but until we had everything settled down we couldn't fully analyze everything. Running on pure adrenaline, we saw the to-do list of possible solutions shrinking as we checked off our reviews of all systems. We needed Boback to stop the stalemate and answer our questions.

Thanks to our lack of progress with Boback, back to the lawyer we went—and tick-tock, tick-tock, went the billable time clock. I called Evelyn and brought her up to speed, sharing that we've secured everything that needed securing, that we've spoken to Rebecca, that we emailed Boback, and that Tiversa won't give us additional information until we hire them.

"What to do, what to do, what to do, Evelyn?" I asked. "We think our data is secure and clean. I want documentation from this outfit. Meanwhile, we continue to look out into the cyber-world for any evidence of our file, and we've found nothing."

Evelyn responded, "I researched the state and federal regulations, but because LabMD performs its services solely in Georgia, there are no federal or state statutes requiring any patient notifications by LabMD. I would not notify anyone until we have more accurate and reliable information of what is really going on. More time is warranted to get to the bottom of this."

I chimed in, "We see not one shred of evidence the file is anywhere else, and it seems the group that has our property could well be the group that took it. They have it in safekeeping but won't 'fess up."

By May 22nd, our day-to-day operations were back to normal. Actually, except for the few people in the office who knew about this, medical operations had never changed. Yet we still had the nagging question about what information Tiversa was holding back.

Lo and behold, at 11:22 am, Boback sent Bill this e-mail:

From: Robert Boback
Sent: Thursday May 22, 2008 11:22 AM
To: Bill Barnett

Bill,
I hope this e-mail finds you doing well. We have continued to see people searching for the file in question on the P2P network by searching precisely for the exact file name of the file in question.

They may or may not have been successful in downloading the file, however. Although, our system has also recorded that the file still exists on the network (as of last Friday) although we have not attempted to download another copy. The longer the file resides on the network, the more difficult the remediation tends to be.

Considering the presence of SSNs in the file, this disclosure should be remediated ASAP. Please let me know if you are in need of some assistance in the remediation of this disclosure. We do address this type of activity through our Incident Response Services if you need assistance.

I was in one serious foul mood. I spoke to my computer screen like it was Boback's face and said, "*My employees* are the 'people searching' for the 'exact file name,' you idiot. If you know that people are looking, you would help us out and build your relationship with us and stop dragging us along." I was steaming. I felt his e-mail was patronizing and insulting. I thought, *Look, buddy boy, you're letting me know that you are able to constantly watch our company via cyberspace is giving me the 'big brother' creeps. This 'concern' is in direct conflict with your refusal to cooperate with me.*

As I read the e-mail, the concerned tone hit me as the height of hypocrisy. I was sickened and infuriated. I kept repeating the situation over and over, hoping to wake up from my nightmare. This man would not tell us the most basic information about how he got the file and was holding our *medical information* hostage unless we paid him for an "investigation," yet he is evidently still surveying our network and warning us about downloads as though he's some kind of hero? Calling out of the blue, refusing to provide factual data, asking to be paid, and letting us know he is watching us with this e-mail was hardly the way to build trust. Responding to basic questions, like providing us with an IP address that he already has, do not require an investigation.

I stormed across the hall to Bill's office, stuck only my head through the door, and said, "He isn't going to take no for an answer. He won't tell us a damn thing more until we hire his company. Drag him along. See what he'll tell us about his pricing. I am not happy."

Bill fired back:

From: Bill Barnett
Sent: Thursday May 22, 2008 12:30 PM
To: Robert Boback
Subject: Re: Tiversa/LabMD

I hope you are well also.
What is the remediation cost and timeline?
Thank you for your note.
Bill
LabMD
VP of Operations and General Manager

We were even more resolved to find what happened via our own research, as Tiversa was again proving untrustworthy. Obviously, Boback was looking at our activity and using what he knew to try and close the deal. He's actually surveying our network and the

Internet for any activity regarding our file. If he were performing all this work out of concern for the well-being of patient data, and not a business opportunity, he would eagerly have answered our questions to some degree without the exchange of our personal check.

Within 45 minutes, Bill got this response from Boback:

From: Robert Boback
Sent: Thursday May 22, 2008 1:16 PM
To: Bill Barnett
Subject: Tiversa/LabMD

Bill, our IRC (Incident Response Case) services are billed hourly as it (total time involved) varies case to case for the overall cost. I can have one of our Operations Directors send you the IRC SOW if you are in need of the services. As far as timing, we have a team of forensic professionals that are dedicated to this type of service, therefore we can begin the investigation and remediation immediately after receiving a signed SOW. Typically the total time for the process (start to finish) is about 2 weeks. Please keep in mind that it can vary depending on your needs and the extent of the spread of the file.

Hopefully we will be able to act quickly to avoid further spread. A file of this nature will be highly sought after by ID thieves.

Here is a link to a recent Information Week cover story that further explains the problem.
http://www.informationweek.com/your-data-and-the-p2p-peril/206903416?queryText=206903416

Let me know if you would like to review the SOW and I will have one sent.

Best Regards,
Robert Boback
Tiversa, Inc.

Bill, a man of few words, simply e-mailed Boback: "I would like to receive and review the SOW."

In my 15 years in surgical sales, if I wanted to have a long-term relationship with a physician, I would help him solve his problem as quickly as possible. I would *prove* my value and not just talk about it. I considered being proactive to be in my own self-interest. I'd build trust quickly and the client would be more likely to retain my services. Apparently, Tiversa didn't share this philosophy.

The main point of the service agreement, went like this:

## 8.1 Fees[1]

In consideration of the Incident Response Services, the Customer will pay Tiversa the fees set forth below:

| Description | Fee |
|---|---|
| Incident Response Case Fee – includes all aspects of Activities 1-3 as detailed in Section #2 of this SOW, as well as the following:<br><br>• Eagle Vision™ system configuration, set-up and run time<br>• Database access and runtime fees<br>• Account Manager Professional Services Fee<br>• Cyber Forensic Analyst Professional Services Fee | $475/hr. |
| Fees for Additional Services[1] | $475/hr. |

This was exactly what I expected. High prices and no guarantees, but I only asked for this for documentation purposes. If I was going to hire someone outside of the company to help with this issue, Tiversa was the last company that I would consider. *Funny how they will cough up a price list faster than an answer to our problem.* As far as I was concerned, our Tiversa chapter was over. But on June 6, we received another e-mail from Boback:

From: Robert Boback
Sent: Friday June 6, 2008 11:04:10
To: Bill Barnett
Subject: LabMD

Bill
I hope this e-mail finds you doing well. I wanted to follow up with you as I have not heard anything regarding the disclosure at LabMD. I am not sure if you caught the recent press about Walter Reed Army Medical Center having a disclosure of over 1000 patients SSNs, etc. The story of the disclosure has been picked up by over 200 publications. Since then, we have seen the usual increase in search activity on the P2P (presumably media) in attempt to find this and other information of this type. Given this fact, we should move to remediation very quickly. If you have been able to locate the source of the disclosure internally, that would be helpful. The file, however, will most likely have been already taken by secondary disclosure points, which will need to be found and remediated.
   Please let me know if you need assistance.

Best Regards.
Robert Boback
Chief Executive Officer
Tiversa, Inc.
The Leader in Information Containment Management
144 Emerville Drive, Suite 300
Cranberry Township, Pennsylvania 16066

"Well, Bill, looks to me like old Bob here is trying to turn up the heat with sweet sounding horror stories. Nice try. Please don't respond."

"No problem there."

Not being able to see into the future, I didn't know if we would hear from Boback again or not. We had blissful silence until July 15, 2008, when he tried to turn the thermostat up a few more degrees:

From: Robert Boback
Sent: Tuesday July 15, 2008
To: Bill Barnett
Subject: Breach notification

I wanted to follow-up with you regarding the breach that we discussed several weeks ago. We have continued to see individuals searching for and downloading copies of the file that was provided. The longer the file is allowed to remain available to the public, the more difficult (and costly) the remediation tends to be. 43 of the 50 states have very strict laws requiring the immediate notification of the affected individuals. It is very important that you contact the individuals affected ASAP.

I know that this breach is troubling, however it is important to note that LabMD is not the only company that has been affected by this type of breach. This is a widespread problem that affects tens of thousands of organizations and millions of individuals. I am not sure if you read the *Washington Post*, but there was a front page article last week involving a widely reported file sharing breach of Supreme Court Justice Stephen Breyer's SSN and personal data. Wagner Resources, the investment firm responsible, took immediate action to solve the problem, which resonated with the affected individuals. In fact, many of the individuals whose information was disclosed contacted the owner of the firm to say that HE was the victim of this relatively unknown, although dangerous, security risk.

Here is a link to the article: http://www.washingtonpost.com/wp-dyn/content/article/2008/07/08/AR2008070802997.html

If you need a breakdown of the various state laws regarding breach notification. I can provide one for you.

Sincerely.
Robert Boback
Chief Executive Officer
Tiversa
The Leader in Information Containment Management
144 Emeryville Drive, Suite 300
Cranberry Township, Pennsylvania 16066

I noted the "empathy" he displayed in letting us know we were not alone and that a Supreme Court Justice had also been victimized. Also, he was kind enough to include other horror stories and links to the *Washington Post* so we could read the articles as soon as possible and break a fresh sweat. Bill and I duly noted the longer we waited the more expensive this was going to be. Finally, Boback offered to provide us with a breakdown of state laws regarding notification, just in case we didn't think we could be breaking laws. What went missing was any proof or information about how this may be occurring.

I was not going to dignify his faux concern with a reactive response. The wording needed to be perfect. After a week of slowing down the clock for our eager beaver, Bill fired off this thank you note:

From: Bill Barnett
Sent: Tuesday, July 22, 2008
To: Robert Boback

Thank you for your communications to our organization. Upon further contemplation regarding the seriousness of your endeavors, our attorney would like to further discuss your work with you. In that regard, all future inquiries and communications should only and exclusively be sent to Evelyn O'Connor, Partner, at Owen Gleaton Egan Jones and Sweeney. Her contact info is below. Please send the name of your legal counsel to Mrs. O'Connor as well.

Thank You,
Bill W. Barnett
LabMD
VP of Operations and General Manager

"Okay, Bill, let's see how fast he either runs to or away from Evelyn." After the send button was hit, the silence was deafening. LabMD tried to get back to normal operations. We continued to perform outside searches for the file (for the next year, actually) and repeatedly came up completely empty-handed. We didn't believe anything got out in the first place, but we took no chances, continually looked, and found no trace of a breach. We've not had a single call from a patient or doctor or anyone stating they had any issues, losses, or damages due to this incident. My instincts sensed we were fine.

Tiversa had contacted us, telling us "people" were searching for it when it was LabMD employees searching for it. Due to the way Tiversa was setting this up, if the file searches were coming from a potentially more malicious source, I thought Boback would have thrown in that tidbit as well just to close the deal. He didn't mention anything of the sort.

I was, and am, well aware that instincts aren't enough. But put another way, we had zero evidence the file ever got out in any other fashion than Tiversa locating it via LimeWire with their unique and powerful program—and we had no desire to scare the hell out of patients, clients, and anyone else, based on Tiversa's sabre rattling.

## What Happens to Our Patients' Tissue, Or Yours If It Were You

At 5:30 pm the lid of the box opened and Danny stared down to see what he would be delivering to LabMD that evening. Danny was LabMD's courier. He had his huge specimen bag, which he loaded up with everything he had carefully lifted out of the courier box. Barcoded and already expected in the lab, Danny drove around Atlanta each weeknight from office to office, picking up specimens in the company's Honda Insight. He usually got to the accessioning department at LabMD at 8:30 p.m. each evening.

Thanks to the technology at LabMD that kept all specimens organized and barcoded, each specimen took only seconds to process. As the barcode reader beeped with each entry, Danny entered about 10 specimens per minute, organizing them in stacks based on which department would receive the specimen. Blood tubes and urine cultures went to the clinical lab. Urine cytology and all tissue samples went to the anatomic pathology lab. Kidney stones and some esoteric tests were flown overnight to California. Each bag held a part of a human being. Each bag held a diagnosis someone was anxious to hear. Each bag affected a life.

It was 10:00 p.m. now and Danny was done for the night. The clinical specimens were logged and in the refrigerator. The boxes of biopsy tissue were stacked in the pathology processing room waiting for the 7:00 a.m. staff to arrive the next morning. Danny shut off the lights, locked the door, and drove home for the night. Once FedEx arrived in the morning with the rest of the cases from around the United States, the processing would be repeated, and once all specimens were accounted for, the lab team could get to work.

Seven o'clock sharp the lights flicked on in the laboratory. Mary, who has been at LabMD for six years, picks up where Danny left off, preparing the specimens from the local Atlanta area while she waits for the FedEx shipments to arrive.

Moving the prostate biopsy boxes to her station in the grossing room, she turns on the fan and water that is part of her station. A stainless steel grill lies over the top of the drain so she can document and measure every piece of tissue that arrives. This is for the "description" on the final report, documentation that describes what was received and analyzed. Each specimen is usually around 5 mm long and the width of a fine piece of string.

Once Mary has finished with the measuring, she puts each piece into cassettes for the next stage of processing. Each cassette is color coded per patient to ensure yet another safeguard to prevent confusion. A typical patient, George, had twelve specimen jars, so his case will have twelve cassettes, all the same color. Each cassette will have his unique case number and individual location printed on it; again, yet another safeguard to prevent confusion.

After Mary has finished "grossing" all the prostate tissue for the day, she puts the cassettes in a round rack that will sit inside a large jar. The jar is filled with alcohol, covering the cassettes that hold the tissue, and Mary places the lid on the jar and opens the microwave to "process" the tissue. Today George is sharing the jar with ten other men from around the country.

This microwave is not anything like you'd see at an appliance store. It is a piece of advanced technology costing over $30,000. It regulates time, temperature, and consistency of dehydration throughout the tissues as the microwaves do their dehydration. There are no second chances. Overcooking is not an option.

After approximately thirty minutes, the cassettes are removed from the microwave jar and transferred to the embedding center. Now that the tissue has been dehydrated, hot wax will be poured over the tissue, filling the cassettes, and then the wax is fast cooled to solidify. This embeds the tissue in a block of wax, and once solid and cool, the block is removed from the cassette.

George's tissue is now halfway through its journey to the pathologist. She will diagnose whether or not he has cancer. The blocks of tissue, all twelve of them, are sliced one cell thick and placed ever so gently on a slide. The solid wax provides support around the tissue so that the microtome, the machine that holds the knife that cuts the tissue one cell thick, can cut through without destroying the tissue. The microtome looks like a very fancy meat slicer. Its blade is much smaller and much sharper.

Janet, our experienced histotech who prepares the tissue for the pathologist, uses her gentle hands and keen eye to take the wax block and lock it firmly in place next to the blade. Like a fine cheese slicer, she turns the wheel, lowering the blade through the block, cutting a one-cell thick slice, back and forth for four or five cuts. Each slice, so fine and delicate, will fly away if there is the slightest breeze in the room, so no brisk movements or walking by her stool are allowed while Janet is cutting. All the slices are still connected, as the wax continues to do its job.

Janet takes the "ribbon" of one cell thick wax and tissue and lays it on top of a warm bath of water. Now that the cutting is done, it is time to rehydrate the tissue, preparing it for the next step in the process.

Once the ribbon floats to the top, but before it gets too soggy, Janet takes each slice and places it on a slide. Mary has already helped Janet on the backend by proactively having the glass slides machine labeled with the case number, location, and patient name, again ensuring accuracy and zero chance for error.

As the slides are completed, four or five per location, twelve per case, they are lined up in a holding rack and moved over to the staining room.

The staining room contains chemicals that are applied in a specific order for a specific length of time, removing the wax and treating the tissue so that the visualization of the cells is at an optimal level. The various chemicals are in small tubs inside the stainer. The machine's computer brain records and executes each step of the staining process.

Mary is back in action now entering the data for each case into the stainer and slide cover machine. She taps the monitor keypad to start a process which is truly, a 21st century wonder. She loads the slides and hits the start button. The arm lifts the slide rack, moves it to the proper tub, and slowly and ever so gently sinks the slides into the chemicals. Every movement and time is being watched and recorded by the software inside the stainer. The machine slowly lifts the slides from the tub at exactly the right moment, then stops and patiently waits above it to ensure nothing is left to drip off over the wrong location. Our friendly, beloved robot then moves the slides to the next assigned location. Various beeps ring out as stages are complete or problems are encountered. It is an incredible piece of machinery.

The staining process takes about an hour. The tissue on the slide is covered by the "cover slipper" that is attached to the stainer. The machines are connected and hand-off the slides on their own. Placing a thin film on top of the tissue to secure it in place, while not compromising visualization in any way, the cover slipper does its work and the tissue is nearly ready for the pathologist.

Mary unloads the cases from the cover slipper and opens up a slide holder book. Made of thick cardboard with areas cut out the size of a slide, each patient has their own book of slides that is filled and then moved along with the corresponding paperwork to the corner of the pathologist's desk.

The desk holds a high-resolution monitor, computer connected to the laboratory database, and high- powered microscope. The doctor picks up George's folder and organizes the slides. Starting with the right base slide, she places the slide under the lens and looks into the microscope. This slide is clearly benign. *The stains have really made the characteristics of the cells pop out nicely this morning*, she thinks. *My life is so much easier with technologists who know what they're doing.* She loads the next slide.

Carefully reviewing the entire specimen, the 5 mm pieces of tissue magnified many times over, she works her way through the case, lifting each slide from the left apex and setting it up to read. She writes, "Cancerous cells. Score of Gleason 3 + 3" in the designated area for the transcriptionist to enter.

As she completes the case, she diagnoses George to have prostate cancer in two of the twelve specimens submitted. The locations are near each other in the prostate.

After the transcriptionist has entered the data, the doctor confirms the entries and hits "enter" on the data software. The data travels through the cables over to the other side of the building to the IT server room, resting in the proper location with the server database. George's fate is determined . . . and it's not the news he wants.

The next morning, Jan, the nurse, arrives at the doctor's office at 8:00 a.m., getting ready for the day. One of the first things she does is go to LabMD's secure Web site to connect with the results database. Logging in her restricted-access information, the page opens, showing the data from LabMD. Jan clicks on the icon to print all results entered since her last visit.

Upon looking at George's results, a brief sadness crosses Jan's mind as she thinks, *Shoot. Good thing it looks like an early catch.* She picks up the stack of charts and walks to Dr. Bounds's office, seeing him reviewing something on his workstation.

"Here are your lab reports. Mr. Burke is Gleason 3 + 3."

## November, 2008, Atlanta, Georgia

### A Not-So Thinly Veiled Threat?

Duane Kirkland, a colleague of Evelyn's, said he received a strange call from an attorney for Tiversa named Jim Cook. Cook has been talking to the FTC and alleged there are laws in place regarding leaks of personal information. He claimed Tiversa was concerned about being sued for not reporting the file being in the Public Domain or doing something required under the law.

"You've got to be kidding me. The FTC? Public Domain? This story gets more surreal and it just won't die. Yeah right . . . Who else would believe that a file was in the public domain when it was stored on a private medical facility's computer? I am not buying it. What is motivating him to actually call and tell us this?"

"I have no idea. He did not elaborate and I'm not familiar with what is going on. I told him I would relay the information."

"How much do you want to bet they're throwing us under the bus because I wouldn't hire them? Where is Evelyn?"

"She's out of the office the next couple of days. I wanted to get this info to you," Duane said. "I'm sure you two can touch base shortly."

"If people from the FTC want to take a lead from a company like Tiversa, then they have too much time on their hands. Thanks for the call."

I felt baffled. There seemed to be nothing to actually *do*. I wasn't going to call the FTC and check in. But now I had two things to worry about. Should I waste my valuable time wondering whether or not a file got out when there was no evidence that it did and wait to see if the Federal Trade Commission knocks on our door?

Tiversa—a company that had just become even more soulless to me, if that was possible. *Should I have rolled over? What if the file is sitting out there? I just don't believe it is.*

Boback's persistence while demanding blind trust until he received payment for services yet to be rendered reminded me of the worst kind of televangelist. I knew I wouldn't sell my soul to this particular devil no matter what the consequence. I would take my chances with the unknown. I had faith. I knew my team and trusted each one of them.

*"There are vampires.
They are real, they are of our time, and they are here,
close by, stalking us as we sleep."*

—NICKY RAVEN, *DRACULA*

# CHAPTER 4
# The Calm Before the Storm

## Fall 2008 to December 2009

After withstanding that last salvo of Tiversa's mental abuse, LabMD tried to get back to normal. We had concluded the alleged file incident to be a one-time occurrence or a mistake. We learned a lot about peer-to-peer (P2P) technology. We removed the P2P software and had no evidence that the file was anywhere except at Tiversa.

P2P software does what its name implies—that is, users install a piece of software on their workstations allowing them to communicate with other "peers" over the Internet. But because they're not closed networks, everyone in the world who has that software may become part of the network. To find a file, you have to search for the exact file name. The file has to be open. You can't just go shopping. I don't think it really is a network in that sense. These are not intentionally connected computer networks. That word "network" can be tricky.

With P2P software, in principle, the power of the Internet was handed to individuals—a great idea. "Let freedom ring; let's share and be one big, happy, open society. Thanks for your data and here's mine." Sounds a bit naive *now*, doesn't it?

Our people at LabMD were far from alone in our 2008 naiveté. Through our research, it became clear that the vast majority of computer users didn't understand P2P software or its pitfalls.[1] During the past twenty years, massive numbers of people have become computer users. Most who installed P2P software had no idea how it can mess with the rest of their computers or their private networks. When in the hands of a user with bare-bones knowledge, P2P software is choked with potential pitfalls of unintentional sharing.

How were we supposed to know this back when it was all so new, so harmless, so free? Few can write code, build firewalls, or install basic parts, but almost everyone can turn on a computer and click a mouse. Through the development of "user friendly" applications (operations knowledge not required), the word *inadvertent* sports an entirely new meaning. Who would intentionally install software to listen to music knowing they could be sharing the entire contents of their hard drive with strangers?

With 20/20 hindsight, the so-called "innocent" sharing of music has turned into a stack of powder kegs in a candlelit room. Rebecca likely thought, "This software is great!" Blissfully unaware of the downfalls, the guard had been down for everyone, the US government included. The future looked bright—until the first alarm bells rang. The gongs told us the free joy ride was about to end.

Unfortunately, security wasn't the reason why alarm bells first rang; the anger of the recording industry was. The industry was losing hundreds of millions of dollars in revenue as LimeWire and similar "apps" enabled copyrighted musical property to be shared for free.

With content and bandwidth still small and early in development, the first files had to be small and fast—like audio files. Presto! People around the world could swap music. Anyone could build a library of music and then share it with friends and total strangers. If you wanted a particular song, well, you'd look out to your neighborhood of music libraries and help yourself. No asking required. What was not to like about that?

However, if a newbie user left other files open that might interest "friends," they were free to take more files—without the computer owner even knowing it. These early versions of sharing software were chock-full of security weaknesses. Our nation's trust was blind. Welcome to yet another new headache for the workplace.

The small audio files were the first files that enjoyed a newfound open market for trading. The Recording Industry Association of America (RIAA) didn't like that. The revenue from its marketplace was evaporating. While people might think music is free because they're used to turning on the radio and just listening, the stations and advertisers have footed the bill. If you heard a song on the radio and loved it, you could either buy it at the store or download it at a particular site for a fee. But when downloads became available at *no* cost, what do you think people did?

The RIAA couldn't go after *every* downloading member of the world, although it went after a few kids, trying to kill the practice at its roots.[2] They moved in to nail LimeWire, just as they'd already buried Napster—with the lawyers, money, and survival instincts. The recording industry's arguments against Napster boiled down to this:

- Its users were directly infringing the plaintiffs' copyrights.
- Napster was liable for contributory infringement of the plaintiffs' copyrights.
- Napster was liable for vicarious infringement of the plaintiffs' copyrights.

They went after LimeWire for the same reasons. Everyone lawyered up and marched off to court.

All these changes were coming so fast, how could everyone keep up? Because the Internet and its tentacles sprawled in all directions in a wonderful but messy and disorderly way, dynamic organizations had a tough time keeping up.

The "latest and greatest" security solution could be outdated in a matter of months. Updates were constantly called for. New products were appearing very quickly. Still, the Internet would not cooperate or behave in an orderly, predictable manner, bothering everyone, and making control freaks like me go absolutely nuts.

## Exactly How Much Caution is an Abundance?

Meanwhile, back at LabMD, Bill, Tom, and I believed that we had dislodged Tiversa from our life. Nonetheless, out of an abundance of caution, we kept checking the outside world for any evidence of the file. Everyone in our company was painfully aware that violations of LabMD's computer usage policies would not be tolerated. If we found any pesky insects in our house or in anyone's room, whoever put them there would be shown the door. As a small company with fewer than 30 workstations, we were able to review all servers and computers in short order. Our network remained clean with no P2P software installed anywhere other than that which had been removed from Rebecca's computer.

LabMD employees were aware of the not-new instruction "don't download anything to your workstations." They simply read more blood, analyzed more urine, processed and diagnosed more tissue for cancer, and excelled at what they always did. I kept them blissfully unaware of the threatening world that lurked in the back of my mind.

2009 was a year of planning and trying to lay the groundwork to grow the company. Developing new testing services, hiring more sales reps and managers is a tough job that requires full focus. People who work at small businesses have to wear a lot of hats and be ready to turn on a dime. And despite our efforts to return to "business as usual," Bill, Tom, Elizabeth, and I still couldn't help but keep one eye open at night. We heard the dull whisper in the back of our uneasy minds repeating our fears: *What if our file really did get out? What if we get another phantom phone call? What do we do if the missing file and all its data is out there somewhere . . . multiplying?*

The haunting psychological game had taken a toll. I was worried about the unknown but still had no further evidence that there was anything to be worried about. The checklist in my mind occasionally ran to the obsessive. We had scoured and searched but found nothing. Where was the evidence of a file actually being "out there"? Back in 2008 we knew our searches were hitting the P2P networks because Boback kept e-mailing us. He said "others" were looking for the file when we knew it was *our* Elizabeth doing the searching.

We couldn't prove the file hadn't gotten "out there," but we honestly believed we were right. Call it raw intuition, but it added up. No calls or e-mails were received from anyone else, even in the most remote way. We had concluded there was no "there" out there. But still, I shuddered, what if?

*"I know the price of this to me.*
*I'll light the candle that shines on you.*
*I'll be a slave to the beauty but not the truth."*

—MARY CHAPIN CARPENTER – "SLAVE TO THE BEAUTY"

# CHAPTER 5
# The First Strike

## Early January 2010

Thirteen months had gone by with one eye open at night and still no evidence of our file being out on the loose. Our guard started to fall late in 2009 and we welcomed 2010 with renewed optimism. Something special typically happens the first week of January when everyone gets back from the holidays, rested, ready, and raring to go. People feel they get a fresh start in all things new.

Bill and I eagerly wanted to get back to work. We had a lot to do to grow LabMD. A new sales manager needed to be hired, as well as another person in business development. We had identified big opportunities to expand our services outside of the urology marketplace.

As a private company, we enjoyed the luxury of focusing on execution, even if it took time. Debt-free, profitable, and focused on getting things done right, we were in a good position for expansion. We enjoyed the open road of grabbing opportunity, overcoming challenges, meeting new physicians, and gleaning that sense of satisfaction when successfully completing a complex task. We felt "in the zone" and ready to roll.

One phone call from Washington DC changed all of that. Bill received a call from a man at the Federal Trade Commission named Alain Sheer. The brief call was simply an opportunity for him to tell Bill about a letter he was sending to LabMD concerning a file he had received. Our lawyer had drummed into our brains not to converse with strangers, so Bill didn't banter with Mr. Sheer about the content he allegedly was holding in Washington. Mr. Sheer simply said we'd soon receive a letter asking us questions about the file.

Now, it might seem like we would've panicked with fear and frustration at this new development. Actually, we'd already learned that panicking would be a waste of energy. In fact, we dealt with the federal and state governments all the time. Since our inception, governmental inspection groups have always thought very highly of our lab. The process of annual inspections to update our federal licenses has built a relationship of mutual respect between LabMD and the inspectors so we were naive in our lack of worry about this FTC inquiry. At the time, we didn't consider answering this letter to be that big of a deal—just another task to complete. After Bill and I spoke for a minute, I said, "Okay, we'll deal with what comes, but the FTC is probably just doing its due diligence. Our little friend Boback must not like it when he doesn't get his way."

The next afternoon, as I walked through the administration area to my office, I glanced over to my in-basket and saw a letter with "Federal Trade Commission" stamped in the upper left corner. I quietly picked it up, closed my office door, sat down, and braced myself as I peeled back the lip of the envelope. I wanted to trust and believe what we were taught in high school civics class—that the government was on our side. But this moment marked the beginning of the end of my belief in our Federal Government. "Truth, Justice, and the American Way" followed right out the window.

Right off the bat, the letter's immensity shocked me. This was no little letter. Eleven pages, single-spaced. The first sentence described it as a "non-public inquiry letter."[1] I picked up on their terminology immediately. Why would the FTC describe the letter as "non-public"? The FTC's first thinly veiled threat, duly noted, was to use the term "non-public" as a constant reminder that if it became known we were under a federal inquiry, it wouldn't be good. They didn't have to remind me that our competitors would use this information to cast doubt on our reputation.

## The Stupid Zone

I called this the beginning of my living in the Stupid Zone. Wasn't the FTC simply performing its due diligence? Isn't everyone innocent until proven guilty? I still trusted the process.

However, there wasn't a single direct question within the entire letter, which hinted that government lawyers *think* they speak English. I considered the letter's tone a cross between political correctness and lawyer-speak gone wild. Each indirect question was slightly different and broader than the previous. Each sentence was laced with the intent of boxing in prey.

Right out of the gate we needed a crash course in learning this new language, "FTC Lawyer Speak." Here is a snapshot:[2]

For purposes of this letter: the word "any" shall be construed to include the word "all," and the word "all" shall be construed to include the word "any"; the word "or" shall be construed to include the word "and," and the word "and" shall be construed to include the word "or"; the word "each" shall be construed to include the word "every," and the word "every" shall be construed to include the word "each"; and the term "document" means any preexisting written or pictorial material of any kind, regardless of the medium in which such material was created, and regardless of the method by which it is stored (e.g., computer file, computer disk or tape, microfiche, etc.); obtain, store, maintain, process, transmit, handle, or otherwise use (collectively, "collect and store") in conducting your business, how and where you collect and store the information, and how you use the information. The response should include, but not be limited to: documents sufficient to identify the type(s) of personal information you collect and store, the source(s) of each such type of information (such as consumers, employees, medical providers, healthcare plans, and insurance companies), and the manner by which you collect or obtain the information (such as by paper documents or electronically though a Web site); and documents or a narrative that describe in detail how you use each type of information in conducting your business.

They also are really picky and evidently don't have faith in other government agencies.

Please send all documents and information to: Alain Sheer, Division of Privacy and Identity Protection, Federal Trade Commission, 600 Pennsylvania Ave., NW, Mail Stop NJ-8122, Washington DC 20580. Due to extensive delays resulting from security measures taken to ensure the safety of items sent via the US Postal Service, we would appreciate receiving these materials via Federal Express or a similar delivery service provider, if possible."

I can't make this stuff up.

I hadn't been this confused since Clinton speculated on what the definition of "is" is. Knowing it would take at least one law degree to understand this letter's meaning, I called Evelyn O'Connor, and immediately sent her a copy. As I've learned so many times, when one lawyer throws a big lob to another, the match starts the "legal cost" clock ticking. Having Evelyn just review this one letter cost LabMD nearly $1,000 in legal fees. The FTC showed no respect for the implications of its actions on the businesses they engage; every confusing question requires extensive analysis and, as a result, more huge legal fees.

The option of picking up the phone and asking Mr. Sheer what he really wanted did not seem like a smart idea. He was a lawyer and an investigator on behalf of the US Government. He would probably not answer our questions and perhaps would only try to burrow in deeper. And though our trust took a blow, in our innocence, we didn't want to jump to paranoid conclusions. (Please allow me to save you time and heartache if something similar happens to you. If the FTC comes knockin' at your door, don't answer it. Trust me on this one.)

Still, ever the optimist, I thought, *Pfft. Nothing to be concerned about here. We're so organized, we can knock out this nuisance data request in no time.* Compared to almost every organization we had worked with, including physicians' offices all over the country, our IT department represents a model of efficiency and organization.

So while the FTC's questions were overly broad asking for X, Y, Z, and the kitchen sink, we had everything they asked for; not many businesses could boast that.

Over the next six weeks, we met with Evelyn on three different occasions to make sure we were riding the right track. Evelyn worked on the actual language of the answers, while Bill worked nights and weekends organizing all the documentation. Living in the Stupid Zone, we knew the FTC lawyers would be impressed if we went above and beyond their requests for information. Like putting together a major collegiate term paper, we proactively gave them what they asked for and then some: diagrams, policies, software, server data, backup records, massive amounts of information in thousands of pages. The billing staff suspended their normal operations, which meant no money was being put in the bank, so they could redact all the patient names from the files we were sending to the FTC.

We did all this to show them we're the good guys, and not a cause for concern. We wanted to shine here.

For the final assembly of this masterpiece, Evelyn came to the office and saw the binders and white boards; stuff sprawled over the conference room table plus papers, boxes, disks, and drawings. We ate our sandwiches, swigged our Cokes, and marked off our checklists as we slaved away. We believed LabMD had more than answered the FTC's questions. We felt good.

After about six weeks of this, yes, six weeks, we finally boxed everything. With relief and eagerness to get back to our day jobs, we shipped two boxes of papers and CD-ROMs, approximately 5,000 pages, to the FTC via the US Postal Service. I wanted the best security measures available when shipping to the FTC.

By this point we had spent at least $20,000 on lawyer fees, not counting the value of our employees' time and lost productivity from our core business. This enormous detour of an inquisition forced me to take my eye off the ball of creating new business and networking opportunities for our small business. The FTC was oblivious.

A few days later, after our due date, the FTC called looking for the boxes. We had sent them via the US Postal Service. Continuing to inspire confidence, they asked us if we wouldn't mind resending everything using Federal Express. We had just taken our first giant step leaving the Stupid Zone.

*"We shall go on to the end.*
*We shall fight in France, we shall fight on the*
*seas and oceans,*
*we shall fight with growing confidence and*
*growing strength in the air,*
*we shall defend our island, whatever the*
*cost may be.*
*We shall fight on the beaches, we shall fight on*
*the landing grounds,*
*we shall fight in the fields and in the streets,*
*we shall fight in the hills;*
*we shall never surrender."*

—Winston Churchill

# CHAPTER 6
# Section 5 of the FTC Act—
# The Trap that Congress Laid

**February 2010**

Having sent our homework assignment to Washington DC, we had our first chance to breathe while we waited for the FTC to go through all the documents, data, and details. The piggy bank of the US government was cracked open to pay. There just had to be a connection, right? Now that I had a chance to relax, it dawned on me that maybe I wasn't as calm as I thought I was. Perhaps I was too busy to notice that I wasn't so cool after all.

I was haunted by what had to be a Tiversa/FTC connection.

But at work I had to act like all was right with the world. One thing I've learned from running a company is this: if people think their employer is in trouble, they instinctively worry about themselves and their jobs. I had no reason to alarm them since we had no idea what situation we were in or its consequences. While it is distracting waiting for that knock at the door, letting other people in on the matter would needlessly concern them and create energy-draining diversions. In the end, this was my battle to fight.

I'm sure the employees saw a whole lot of hustle and bustle going on. I probably didn't always have a happy smile on my face, either. Secrets do take their toll—and for that matter, so does being accused of something you know you didn't do. When that accuser is the federal government, surviving that emotional stress requires using your energy to put everything in its proper perspective—all the while complying with their requests and running the business—so for everything else I had no emotional energy. I was numb.

In the meantime, to forward its agenda, it seemed the FTC's primary tactic was to divert our attention away from the day-to-day operations of our medical facility. Their game was coming into focus. "Drain us dry" was their first card laid on the table.

## Why Does the FTC Think This Any of Their Business?

Now that the dust had temporarily settled, I had a chance to reflect. When things like this first happen, your first reactions are shock and denial; so although Evelyn had tried to educate me on the status of the situation, all I heard was legal mumbo jumbo. Now that we had complied with their requests, I devoted time to understanding the laws in place that would allow the FTC to operate as they do.

Finally ready to listen and capable of actually hearing her, I called Evelyn, who had taken the time to research this further. "Evelyn, got a minute?"

"I have about ten."

"Let's get into what people at the FTC are relying on. I need to hear this again. What makes them think they're *allowed* to do all of this? The file was taken. We know where it is without any evidence it's out of control anywhere. There have been no damages to patients. I don't get it."

With surgical precision, she referred to the FTC Web site and read me the following:

The Federal Trade Commission is an independent agency established by Congress in 1914 to enforce the Federal Trade Commission Act ("FTC Act"). Section 5 of the FTC Act prohibits 'unfair methods of competition,' and was amended in 1938 also to prohibit 'unfair or deceptive acts or practices . . .'

Under Section 5, the commission has determined that a representation, omission, or practice is deceptive if it is likely to mislead consumers acting reasonably under the circumstances and it is material that is likely to affect consumers' conduct or decisions with respect to the product at issue. In August of 1994 Congress amended section 5 of the FTC Act to provide that an act or practice is unfair if the injury it causes or is likely to cause to consumers is: (1) substantial; (2) not outweighed by countervailing benefits to consumers or to competition; and (3) not reasonably avoidable by consumers themselves.[1]

Like a broken record I asked Evelyn—using louder decibels with every word—"So what the hell does *that* mean? In two years, we've had no complaints and no indications that files got out anywhere else. Boback calls, says he's got the file, won't tell us a damn thing unless we hire him, nor will he say how he got it other than via his 'patent pending' technology. He calls us back in late 2008, via his lawyer, saying he's giving the case to the Federal Trade Commission, and then does it! By January 2010, 14 months later, the FTC is coming after us! So, Congress made the FTC supreme overlords over technology and data security? When did they have the time to go to MIT?"

At this point, I realized I was back on the gerbil wheel while yelling at Evelyn. Luckily for me, she was rational and objective with a far different temperament than mine. More analytical and detached, she's constantly "at work" staying calm and cool while I rage. Sometimes I joke that I'm paying hourly for psychotherapy instead of legal advice. My frustrated helplessness needed a release.

"So now the FTC is investigating us as if we did something wrong when we're the *victims* and *we know who took the goods*? What do we do?"

Every time I repeated that sentence, Evelyn never changed her answer, "Section Five doesn't have to have actual damages."

She gently, and continually warned me that Section 5 was a quagmire. I just could not comprehend this.

"Section Five was written to give broad powers to an investigative agency. To be in violation of this law, there doesn't have to be any actual harm."

"Tell me again so it will sink in."

"Section Five can be 'enforced' if injury is 'reasonably' possible."

"Reasonably possible? What's the legal definition of *that*? Loose legal definitions like these openly invite abuse of power." I was getting angrier by the second. "There *must* be a way out of this; deception isn't on the table. That is impossible. We don't see the patients and we don't even have brochures; we don't have *any* means by which to be deceptive! The phrase 'likely to cause injury' is a loophole the FTC is trying to stretch wide open. 'Likely to cause' doesn't mean you have to cause it to violate the statute? This is nuts! Evelyn, tell me, why are they knocking on our door?"

"Mike, I don't know. I can't understand it, either. But I do think it's important to cooperate so they don't create more problems by saying that LabMD is uncooperative."

I hated that comment. I knew she had to say it. With another step away from The Stupid Zone, it vaguely dawned on me, *Hey, is this about power and not truth? Ya think?* I rubbed my hands over my face and eyes, trying to push back the headache I knew was minutes away. Evelyn felt confused, too. She didn't know what to do except repeat the facts.

"Mike, Section Five is based on two mandates that the FTC was given by Congress. They are charged with protecting consumers from deception, statements that aren't true and are meant to deceive the consumer, and reasonable practices. Reasonable, as a legal term, can be quite controversial. The FTC wants to look at LabMD's data security practices and decide if they were reasonable and/or deceptive. There doesn't have to be damages or an actual loss of data to violate Section Five, in the FTC's opinion. Even though you're sure nothing got out, the FTC wants to look around anyway."

"And that will cost a damn fortune. Where do life-long government lawyers get their expertise in technology to even judge?"

"It makes no sense to me, either, Mike. I don't see the rationale in choosing to go after LabMD here. Until we really know what they're up to, we give them exactly what they want, no more, no less, and we answer their questions."

Hearing the facts delivered dispassionately and analytically overwhelmed me with frustration. No matter how much I would rail about this to Evelyn, she didn't have the answers I wanted to hear. Learning about Section 5 and coming to terms with it felt as if I was going through Elizabeth Kubler Ross's *Five Stages of Death and Dying*. I kept swinging back between "No way" and "That's not possible" to "This is damn ridiculous."

"Could I go to jail?" I asked Evelyn.

"They're not going to put you in jail," Evelyn replied. "At this point, those types of things occur only with flagrant disregard of the courts. There aren't even civil charges here. Don't get ahead of yourself. We sent them loads of information and answered their questions. They might just go away satisfied you have all these procedures and safeguards in place."

"I know that seemed like a stupid question, Evelyn, but now that I see Congress has shredded the Bill of Rights by creating these animals, I guess anything is possible. I really hate it that Boback turned this over to the FTC. I feel like we're being punished for not hiring Tiversa." *If I had paid Tiversa, would the company have protected me and not thrown our file in front of the FTC?* Was it just me, or did something stink? I didn't expect my lawyer to dive into it, but I was resolute.

My mind wandered, not really hearing what Evelyn was saying. I did not understand how much power Congress has given to government administrative agencies. It was shocking. I had a hard time getting my head around it, so far away was this new reality from my assumptions about the Feds. *Can the US government even be given such power by Congress, circumventing the concept of innocence until proven guilty?* My eyes were opening to the realization that government agencies can wreak havoc on whomever they choose . . . and the legislative and judicial branches seem to be just fine with that. I would have never thought this had the tree not fallen down on me.

Maybe Congress did not intend to let these lions off the chain, but they are off the chain nonetheless, with many government lawyers posing as kings of the jungle, chasing whomever they want, chewing them up and asking for forgiveness later. Most little animals seem to adopt a healthy respect for their power to avoid being killed because there isn't enough blood or money to even survive the fight. *Survival trumps justice in this new world.*

I came back in focus as Evelyn again mentioned she was baffled about why the FTC was using their limited resources to climb all over LabMD. "I find it hard to believe they are going to keep at this."

I calmed myself, rationalizing that the odds of the FTC continuing to dig after all the information we'd just turned in were slim. Besides, this was early on. I had no reason to upset myself for a long-shot, Hail Mary "what if." There was no handbook out there on what to do in this situation. I was flying by the seat of my pants while seated in the Fed's dark room. Passivity and patience are not my specialties. I wanted to swing a bat.

Quite successfully, however, I went back to my normal routine while still waiting to hear back from the FTC. The crust on my American pie was thick, and most of the time I still continued to believe that truth and justice would somehow win out. Eventually these accusers would come to their senses, see it our way, and move on, right?

Evelyn wasn't exactly having a good time. She seemed to be outside of her comfort zone, having had little experience dealing with the FTC. Her law practice had moved more toward heavy automotive representation. Dealing with the behavior of a government branch is every bit political as it is legal. That's why nobody wants to walk onto the center stage of the FTC without experience. Fear of the unknown. Evelyn takes defending her clients very seriously and she doesn't like to lose, so I sensed that her lack of direct experience with these agency lions was leaving her a bit uneasy.

But I wanted her right at my side. I had total faith in her abilities. It's a choice between having 15 years of trust built with one lawyer versus learning as you go with someone new. At this point in time, I wasn't willing to risk starting a new "marriage" that might also result in games of over-billing, lack of communication, never being available by phone, and other tricks some lawyers masterfully play. And although Evelyn may not be experienced in this area, she's no fool. She knows how to play the game. I decided to keep on our steady course, even though I thought that, if given the chance, Evelyn would be happier not embroiled in this situation. I also knew she would never abandon her client.

The FTC's Alain Sheer got in touch with Evelyn and asked us to get together the week of March 8, 2010. Due to various conflicts and travel schedules, we couldn't free up a date until March 16. By then, the FTC had been in possession of its box of goodies from us for weeks. I was intensely curious. *What did their people have to say?* The magic day, March 16, Bill and I drove to Evelyn's law office, parked, took the elevator to the second floor, walked across the courtyard, and entered the tall, midtown Atlanta skyscraper. I nervously sat on the couch and pretended to read the latest edition of the *Fulton County Daily Report* until Evelyn came to greet us. We felt both curious and anxious for the FTC to finally "get to the point" and/ or go away.

The three of us settled into the firm's familiar conference room. Evelyn pulled up the telephone and dialed the FTC.

Mr. Sheer answered the phone in a tone of formality. He exhibited the icy, cordial professionalism of a government lawyer investigating someone for supposedly outrageous acts that warrant spending tax-payer money. On the one hand, they cloak themselves in a broadly written law protecting the consumer while hovering over us with squinted eyes. On the other hand, they tell us to have a nice day.

"Hi, Mr. Sheer. How are you? This is Evelyn O'Connor."

"Hi, Evelyn. Thanks for calling. I'm fine, thanks. You?"

Evelyn kept the banter going with "Great! So we're here to discuss our submissions to you . . ."

Alain interrupted, "Yes, I have with me Ruth Yodaiken, who's also working with me on this case."

"Hi, Ruth."

"Hi, Evelyn."

Friendly greetings amongst attorneys. So nicey nicey I wanted to puke.

The stark yet obvious realization had hit me; they're all just doing their jobs—my lawyer included. I was the only person whose head could end up on the block. *This makes no sense. This cannot be happening. I'm in a movie.*

As the conversation started, they smacked me right across the face. They insisted we hadn't answered their questions fully! At the same time, this pair seemed like they weren't familiar with all of the material. *How can they send us an 11-page letter, turn my management team upside down, up-end the company, grind our growth plans to a screeching halt, and then say we didn't answer them fully?* They told us we sent information that wasn't how they wanted it, saying "we don't see that our questions have been answered completely" and "You have submitted paperwork with un-redacted patient information." I thought to myself, *"This can't be. I know the billing department blacked out all the patient information so it could not be seen."* But I kept my mouth shut so I didn't look combative. I had no idea what we were dealing with.

Now, knowing Evelyn like I do, she reliably reads sentences line by line and answers them literally. She pays close attention to every word. Highly detailed, she's the last person to make mistakes.

We answered every damn FTC request thoroughly. But guess who had the bigger club and was holding it over our heads? They were a humorless team somewhat lacking in social skills. I swallowed my fury and took another sip of the Kool-Aid, agreeing it was best to be as cooperative as possible and give them everything they wanted and more, hoping they'd finally go away.

It wasn't long before we muted the phone to discuss what was coming out of their mouths. They were all over the place. I looked at Evelyn and asked what the hell they were talking about. Evelyn said, "I have no idea; we better get everything they say in writing."

"No kidding! I don't believe a word they're saying," I chortled. *This is going to keep costing a fortune. Nobody is going to believe this.*

Sounding compliant and conciliatory, Evelyn unmuted the phone and said, "Alain, just to make sure we're all on the same page, would you be so kind as to put in writing exactly what you're looking for? I don't want to waste time for either party here."

A full two-second pause followed.

"Yes. I'll send you a follow-up." This verbal commitment was delivered in a slightly perturbed tone of voice that indicated Alain would comply, but not with pleasure.

Asking the FTC to put its requests in writing was our first dare, which is ridiculous, but true. New lesson noted: Best to piss them off and get it in writing than trust them with verbal agreements.

After we realized we would have to reinvent the wheel with another submission, Alain suggested we take a look at the Nutter agreement.[2]

"Nutter agreement? What's the Nutter agreement?" Evelyn asked.

"It is a consent decree that Nutter entered into with the Federal Trade Commission," Alain replied. "That decree will demonstrate a template of the type of solutions that the FTC often offers." Keeping our cards close, Evelyn briefly thanked him for the information without engaging in idle chatter.

After Evelyn hung up the phone, we looked at each other momentarily and made a few bland utterances like "interesting" and "hmmmm." The FTC people had a way of making us feel completely insignificant and powerless and the center of attention, all at the same time. This call shed zero light on why we found ourselves in the middle of this situation.

My fantasy of this nightmare being over was crushed. That was certainly going on in my head at this point—confusion—but I have to say, the FTC's shocking laziness, if nothing else, pulled my head out of the clouds. *How confusing was that call! Answer questions? We answered them. Redacted info? We had the billing department work for hours blacking everything out. Who is Nutter? It wasn't the FTC that had their files taken. The fact that the FTC doesn't care about that elephant in the room evaporates any respect I have for its people. Something is very wrong here. Oh my God, this nightmare isn't over!*

Sending us to research the Nutter agreement consent decree continued Mr. Sheer's game. No straight shooter, he suggested we pull settlements so we could figure it out ourselves—another torture trick for FTC "jollies." His cryptic message was his way of showing us what was in store for LabMD. I was learning how to speak "Alain."

## Who is Nutter and What is an FTC Consent Decree?

I drove back to our office with one big question: What exactly is an FTC consent decree?[3] As stated in Wikipedia:

> A consent decree (also referred to as a consent order or stipulated judgment or agreed judgment) is a final, binding judicial decree or judgment memorializing a voluntary agreement between parties to a suit in return for withdrawal of a criminal charge or an end to a civil litigation. In a typical consent decree, the defendant has already ceased or agrees to cease the conduct alleged by the plaintiff to be illegal and consents to a court injunction barring the conduct in the future.

Within 48 hours, Evelyn had pulled up the Nutter agreement and called me to explain. "Nutter agreed that they would admit no wrongdoing and sign a consent decree that they agreed to work with the FTC over a ten-year period to bring their security policies and procedures up to snuff. They also agreed to annual audits. As an additional bonus, there would be a '30-Day Notice' posted on the FTC Web site letting the public know the FTC had once again saved the day."

I fired off expletives while Evelyn sat silently on the other end of the phone. She'd become my federal government punching bag, God bless her. My rant continued.

"The FTC likes to seduce you into thinking this is no big deal. There's no admission of guilt. You simply 'sign right here and it won't be that big of a deal at all.' Yeah right, like we're buying that one. The Internet is forever, so this posting for thirty days is ironic. Don't the cyber-investigators get that the Internet is forever? And of course, when people learn that a corporation made no admission of guilt, they'll certainly believe that."

By now, the sarcasm was forming small pools around me.

"So when our competitors run to our doctors and imply that LabMD may have lost patient data but they don't give them any other information, the doctors will stop and give us the benefit of the doubt while they research these allegations. Sure, that's exactly how it happens! Like physicians have so much extra time these days. We all cooperate and then go skipping happily along the way. The lawyer gets paid. Alain Sheer gets to hold us up as another example for London's Prisoner Parade. Congress is none the wiser. And another small business, namely LabMD, bites the dust. Over my dead body." I was just getting started.

"We can chalk up the ability to create such perverse stretching of the Fourth Amendment to the United States Constitution as another one of Congress's many talents. They created this monster as they look the other way." I was screaming inside. *This is not happening! This is a nightmare. How does the Constitution and Bill of Rights go up in a ball of flames? There's nothing we've done differently from 2006 to 2008 compared to any other organization in the country, including the federal government. And now I'm surrounded by government lawyers and attorneys? I can't sign anything like that decree! It's corporate suicide.*

Evelyn's level-headedness took over. Looking carefully, we noted a few glaring differences between our situation and the Nutter agreement.

- Number one, our security measures were up to date; Nutter had out-of-date data security.
- Number two, Tiversa came in with "unique" technology. We don't believe there are patient damages or uncontrolled data; Nutter's poor security allowed a breach.

- Number three, the company that took the file refused to give us information unless we paid for it; Nutter had no third party either demanding funds or handing data over to the FTC.

## Waiting for the Other Shoe to Drop

No word from the FTC; they were keeping us in the dark as they loomed overhead, judging. They were masters of the slow emergency. I couldn't sit around waiting for the next shoe to drop and I couldn't just sit around angry. I had to do something. So I said to Bill, "I think we should call someone to look over everything just in case surprises are lurking in our system. I want to do it with an abundance of caution and for peace of mind. I think the FTC is fishing around looking for anything that will work and they haven't found it yet, so I want to make sure there isn't anything hanging out there. Who can we contact to give us a checkup and, I hope, a clean bill of health?"

"Let me make some calls and I'll get back to you, Mike." This was code from Bill that I could expect a detailed spreadsheet and industry analysis. He is so good at what I am not.

Within a few days, Bill had contacted several vendors to analyze our network. Just as we suspected, all their fees were through the roof. They normally worked with much larger companies that had much larger budgets. Typically, they'd dive into sales mode to up-sell us. Bill firmly told them all we wanted was a penetration test to see if and where vulnerabilities were—that's it, period. Still, they tried to tip over the apple cart looking for sales opportunities while fulfilling our request. Many had no idea about being in a medical facility; they could pull the entire network down. Most of all, I didn't feel comfortable telling an outside company how our entire software solution was built.

"Bill, why don't I call Henry Kensington? He has a heavy medical client base."

"I suppose that's fine. At least we know him."

When our appointment day arrived, I found Henry was waiting in the foyer. After general business niceties and some light banter about our families, I dove in.

"Henry, we're being investigated by the FTC for data security practices."

"What? Jesus! Why? What?"

"Yeah, that was our first response as well. We don't believe for one second we've done anything wrong. We're cooperating fully, hoping they'll go away. I need your complete confidentiality. Nobody knows, and I don't want anyone to know. This type of misunderstanding could destroy our reputation."

"Well, yes, completely," he said, still dazed in disbelief. Nevertheless, I had the sense that Henry was all business and he smelled blood.

"So what we need is a data analysis to show the FTC we have a sturdy, safe, and secure network."

"Well, all sorts of issues could come up. We'll have to understand the entire system."

"Of course. I need to impress upon you that Bill and Tom are up to speed. If you come in and don't take their lead, you'll lose their cooperation. Please don't come in like a savior trying to sell us every toy in the store. Bill is the boss and decision maker, not me. He has all the specifics. We keep our company tightly locked down for a reason. The laboratory software is unique and proprietary. This issue came up on the billing side, and that department isn't even on the same servers as the laboratory information system."

"Well, what happened?"

"We aren't totally sure. It looks like an employee put LimeWire on one workstation and one file was taken. It was on no other computer in the company, neither the software nor the file. It was never on a single server, just one workstation. That's it. But that's what happened, we think. Now, we know who has the file, and we also firmly believe it hasn't spread. I can't discuss anything more. I just want your testing services."

"What does the FTC want?"

"They want to ask questions forever, making sure our practices were, and are, up to standard. However, there's no standard that they're citing, so that will be for a later battle. We're trying to go along for now, thinking it's the easiest way out of this mess."

"Holy cow, how did you get *into* this mess? Why did they pick *you?*"

"Bad luck. Who knows? I just have to get out of this corner. Can you help?"

"Sure. We can review the network, do a penetration test and some analytics, and let you know what needs improvement. What's the FTC trying to get at?" Henry asked again.

"I wish I knew. I think they' are making things up as they go along because they always get away with it. We don't know if this will satisfy them, but I'm not looking to bring in one of the "tower-of-power" data companies that just overcharge and inspire fear."

"Frankly, I think for some reason the FTC people have deemed us guilty from day one, and nothing will shake them off. Now they're building a case to justify their verdict, so I'm not going to drain the bank. All jury without a trial, these people. Anyway, we need penetration and network security testing from an outside party. So contact Bill and let's set it up."

"Mike, your life is so boring!"

"Yeah . . . isn't it, though? We're all guilty until proven innocent. Okay, enough of that."

Henry and I finished our evening talking about lighter topics. I found that talking about my ordeal felt strange and I preferred to keep it under wraps. But I made a resolve. *The Feds were going to get as little blood out of me as possible.*

## Leaks in the System?

After Bill met with Henry's team a week later, they decided to do the analysis during the weekend, when all was quiet and nothing could be disturbed. Henry would run his analytic software in our network and spit out data for analysis. Then we set an appointment to review the data on May 14, 2010.

That day arrived in no time flat.

I walked into the already darkened conference room where we could see the results projected on the screen. Henry and Bill stood waiting.

"Sorry I'm late . . . crazy day."

"No problem," Henry said. "We just got started."

"So what did you find?"

"Well, there are four ranges of potential severity here."

"Okay—hold on—let's cut to the chase before we go for words like 'potential.' Are there any problems that will freak out the FTC or open doors that we've left open?"

"No."

"Good. Now I can pay attention without anxiety. Explain."

"Okay, Mike. There are four ranges of potential risk, most of them minor, very minor. There are a few open ports that appear vulnerable," Henry said.

Bill jumped in. "Those are *not* vulnerable. They're open for the lab software to communicate with outside clients. They're protected."

"So which is it? Where is the data giving specifics of all this?" I asked.

"Well, I didn't bring the exact info. I'm just looking at this now as it goes up on the screen."

After 5 minutes of hearing nothing but banter, the silence was getting to me. Bill and I quickly glanced at each other, mirroring what we were both thinking: *Just give us the data, and we'll take it from here.*

Trying to hurry this along, I asked Henry, "So, how can we make sense out of all of this? Looks like overkill to me. What's there to be concerned about as far as any type of security risk?"

"Well, these bars indicated in red are open ports. Do they need to be open?" Henry asked.

"*Absolutely.* They need to be open for communication. *And* they're protected. We have the router and firewalls," Bill answered.

"Okay, you can review this and see if there's anything that isn't as it should be. We can run this as often as you like. We'd prefer to handle this for you and keep a twenty-four seven watch on everything."

"How are you able to watch twenty-four seven?"

"We have software and notification pushes that come to us in the event of any irregularity."

"We have that internally as well, Henry. Bill's team is also on notification watch. We like to keep things centralized and internal. Otherwise, we're dealing with too many cooks in the kitchen."

"But our surveillance software is much stronger than what you'd probably have for a company this small. You'd have the benefit of that." Henry was rolling into selling mode without a full analysis.

*They just can't help themselves, can they? It's in their DNA. Build doubt, sow anxiety, keep you stupid, and close the deal. This drives me crazy.*

"Henry, we're only here to discuss the report. Bill has to look it over and then we'll get back together since you haven't looked at it, either. We want to run it again. How long will it take you?"

"Overnight, usually."

"So it could be done over a weekend?"

"Right."

"Okay, we'll review the data and get back together." I excused myself and left Bill to finish up.

Sure, we got Henry's report, but we weren't going to sit around for a sales pitch when *he* hadn't even read the report. Our message was, "If you want to get other services, execute the one we asked for first and we might just stick around." It's a classic example of why we prefer to keep our services in-house.

There were no surprises in our system's security. I knew that, but the government would only be happy if we could hand over a formal, third-party report. The FTC doesn't look at price tags or perform a cost/benefit analysis. Why would they bother to do that?

## Another Swing at the Ball

In May 2010, we had to turn in our "homework" again. But I was unnerved by my quandary. I couldn't let government employees cloaked in the American flag turn their hypocrisy on me by seducing me into an "easier route" by signing a decree. Some battles aren't worth taking on—I get that. But these people wanted me to declare to the world that my company was lax in security. *This would forever mar our medical facility and invite these robots into my life for years to come. That ain't gonna happen.*

In my imagination, I saw two FTC lawyers looming over my desk as I signed page after page of an agreement—one that would submit my company to their whims over the next two decades. Then they'd take the agreement, shoving it in their briefcases chock-full of decrees and squeeze the lid shut. Indifferent to what had just transpired, they'd look at each other as they walked out the door saying, "Let's go for a latte." Then, as their backs are turned, I notice their red tails poking out the back of their suit jackets.

I played the same vow over and over: *I am not signing a consent decree . . . no way . . . never.*

*"Government is like a baby.*
*An alimentary canal with a big appetite at one end*
*and no sense of responsibility at the other."*

—RONALD REAGAN

# CHAPTER 7
# The FTC Goes Fishing and Throws Back the Catch

We decided to do nothing until Alain Sheer's letter arrived with his written version of what he asked for in our recent phone call. As we waited for Mr. Postman—oops, I mean the letter to arrive via any means other than the US Postal Service—Evelyn dug into FTC history to look for clues on how this "animal" typically behaves.

About a week after our conference call with the FTC, Evelyn called me with another educational installment from "Dealing with the FTC 101." She said when it comes to data security issues, consent decrees seemed to be the FTC's favorite "solution." As it turned out, we learned that the road the FTC was trying to walk down could be summed up like this: The FTC finds an example of a data security problem, calls you in to have a "friendly chat" with the guards, and promises to go away in exchange for signing a document that lets them check in on you for the next 10 to 20 years.

My eyes were starting to stay open now. I didn't fail to notice the FTC's version of clanking chains, damp cells, and scaffold being built outside our window. Today, this is better known as reputation assassination. Draining all your money with expensive lawyers, and exhausting you with a long fight, and keeping you in suspended investigation animation are just a few of their other methods of making you agree that signing isn't that bad. The FTC's victims get to admit no wrongdoing (and you know everyone will believe that, so no harm done!). Plus you're required to hire an outside party to submit reports to the FTC every year or two (and we all know how cheap those consultants can be). As a bonus, the FTC will post the information on its Web site for "only" 30 days, which is irrelevant, as the Internet is forever.

I launched into my next round of venting with Evelyn poised behind the plate ready to catch the next stream of fastballs.

"What fool believes something stays online for only 30 days? This is straight out of the textbook on what drives people nuts about the Feds. They're trying to regulate the Internet and they don't even understand it. Tell me, Evelyn, are any of the other consent decree victims medical?"

"No," she said.

"Small companies?"

"No."

"Any circumstances like a security firm swiping our stuff and then turning it in to the FTC?"

"No."

"Lovely. I can play the game, but I'm *not* having our name out there in cyberspace for the world to believe we're slack in our IT practices. I will not do it."

Without much more to say, Evelyn moved on to the next teaspoon of castor oil and described the FTC's business guide: "The business guide was posted in 2009 as an educational piece to inform businesses of best business practices today. Its main focus . . ."

Interrupting her reading, I jumped in. "Is a business guide a *law*?"

"No."

"Is 2009 the same as 2008?"

"No." She chuckled.

"Good. I just want to make sure I'm not losing my mind. A 2009 guide is worthless when examining 2008 practices."

"True. But I'm still going to e-mail this guide to you and Bill. It serves as the best template of what I see the Feds shooting for. To me, it's the best evidence for knowing how they define 'good enough.' It's a slick marketing piece we should regard as their 'wish list.' For now, it's as good as we're going to get."

I repeated the main points: A business guide is not a law and *this* business guide wasn't around in 2008. How can they apply this to us? *Oh yeah, I'd better suspend logic because it hasn't been on the table here for quite some time.* Evelyn, grasping for a response, couldn't do much more than empathize and agree. She didn't even have to say it; I knew what she was thinking: *These are the cards we've been dealt, so let's just play them.*

I sat in silence at my desk, perplexing thoughts running through my head. *The FTC's trying to catch light in a jar. Their actions were saying they wanted to examine our practices and see if we violated Section 5. But they weren't saying what standards applied or even exist in this exploding cloud of cyberspace. Nor did they say how the statute itself applied. I see, the FTC believes they're entitled to make up the rules as they go along.*

Evelyn, my tether and balance, took my silence as her cue and said, "Based on our interactions with the FTC so far, the political underbelly may be more telling than what is on the face of this government agency at this point. Mike, listen, the business guide is the best template from which we can glean how the FTC defines a standard."

"Yes," I replied coolly. "When you're kept in the dark, you aren't capable of finding the exit easily. How can a business guide be considered a standard?"

"Good question. What's so perplexing is why they choose to put so much time, money, and effort into this guide. Perhaps the people at the FTC consider guides like this to be examples of what's reasonable as stated in Section 5. Can they get away with this or not? I know that finding out would cost a pretty penny. Obviously, they think they're on solid ground here." There was a slight pause before Evelyn added: "I'm sure others would beg to differ."

Reviewing this business practice guide, we noted that the FTC wanted documentation, education, written practices, and accountability. We had no problem complying with all of that. As a matter of fact, we felt confident that, given the standards at the time, LabMD was comfortably ahead of the curve.

As we continued our FTC 101 course, we saw many more examples where this agency had been given broad enforcement powers by

Congress through the aforementioned Section 5. We also learned that the FTC enforced these powers by creating an uphill battle of work, investigation, litigation, and bureaucracy to which most companies would ultimately succumb. Debating the FTC is a hugely expensive endeavor. With its army of lawyers, lengthy history of enforcement, and a chairman who sleeps in superman pajamas and cape, even thinking of taking on this organization gives one reason to pause. But consider the consequences for LabMD. The fight would be cheaper than the damage created if our doctors doubted our ability to protect patient information from leaking into cyber-eternity. Our choice became painfully and expensively clear: LabMD had no choice but to fight. It boiled down to death or chronic illness. Two lousy choices, but really only one choice if I wanted the company to live.

## Two Weeks of Mundane Bliss

The waiting game provided me with two full weeks to get back to my core business and daily routine. Wake up, take out the dogs, work out early at the gym, call my sister, answer e-mails, arrive at the office by 10, knock out the mail, meet with Bill, have lunch with Mary, deal with the issues of the day, visit Dr. Martin, Dr. Bounds (our local clients), grab a meal on the run, get home by 7 or 8, hit the sack by 11, and wake up and start the day over. Oh, how I had come to take for granted the joy of the mundane.

Two weeks later, buried in the moment, I looked up at my computer's e-mail message screen to note a rude interruption. Sure enough, the FTC letter[1] had arrived, bursting our brief bubble of peace. It was sent via e-mail and fax to Evelyn's office, successfully avoiding the US Postal Service once again. Like my clients' patients waiting for their test results, I felt that pause of anxiety before clicking on the e-mail. *Would what the FTC sent in writing be so different from what was said on our conference call? Would the process drain us financially? Were the players going to be logical or unreasonable?*

I opened the letter in my e-mail and found they didn't even spell my name right.

I laughed out loud, "Jesus . . . it's *Daugherty*, not *Dougherty*. I mean, if you expect perfection, boys, you'd better practice what you preach!"

The second and third sentences, equally amusing, stated, "In general, we found the company's response to be inadequate, both in the narrative descriptions in the letter and the documents that were supplied with it. We ask that the company respond fully to the access letter." I roared out loud.

"How the hell can over five thousand pages be inadequate, especially when the narrative descriptions pointed you to the documents?"

Like any lawyer, Alain Sheer refused to say anything absolute in writing, leaving himself an escape hatch. On the one hand, he had the nerve to ask us for all this documentation; on the other hand, we sent it and he then stated that he wants it numbered. We redacted our tails off—all 5,000 pages, mind you—but Sheer wanted them Bates labeled (meaning every page have a unique number so the FTC can keep it organized). *What's he talking about? And, please Mr. Sheer, you are doing the investigating, so I think the FTC should number the pages.* Now he wants us to cut his meat for him so he can eat us for lunch.

Recalling our conference call, as far as I could tell, the FTC's problems with our first "cargo shipment" were three things: incomplete answers; non-redacted personal patient information; and documents weren't numbered. Now with this letter, Sheer opened the door of wonder even wider, using broader terms but few specifics.

A few examples: "Our Request Nine, for example, generally asks for documents describing in detail LabMD's security practices." *Classic. The FTC wants detail. Define detail. We must be speaking a different language. Wait, forget that, God only knows what you will say.* Another favorite, "Similarly, Request Ten seeks information about risk assessments, including copies of assessments and documents that detail how assessments were conducted." *Holy cow, we sent them tons of diagrams and reports. Didn't they read everything? I guess they require everything boxed up with a bow on it.*

I pulled out my BlackBerry and called Evelyn. She knew exactly who was calling.

"Do you believe this?" I blurted out. "I knew we'd get another broad response. If this guy had to be specific he would break out in a rash."

Evelyn laughed and then got down to work.

"I know. He wants supporting documents and details." She sounded resigned. "We'll look closely at what they state they want. I think we already gave them the kitchen sink."

"Yeah, but we don't want to tick him off because, as you know, in the real world, junior man loses. We can't call them up and ask what they're talking about. We have to remember the goal: Do what we have to do to make them go away. Being cooperative makes it way more likely they'll go away, so let's just make them think that *we* think they're being reasonable and go along with their game for now. I think the Kool-Aid must be working on me today."

Evelyn replied with more of the same. "I know, I know, I know."

Although the letter didn't shed light on specifically what the FTC wanted, it certainly shed light on their tone. If we tried to pin them down to specifics, we got more generalities. Alain Sheer wouldn't let us box him in. He's the face of the federal government looking down at us. Looming, sniffing, smiling, and acting *as if* he's in a dialogue, but he's clearly not.

I was viewing Sheer in my mind as one cool, calculating cat who enjoyed toying with his prey and justifying his behavior with the words "consumer protection." I imagined he saw us as villains who deserved to get caught. I kept forgetting we were *under a non-public inquiry.* The FTC's behavior was the last thing that should be kept non-public.

*How do we deal with this new development?* Evelyn and I came to the only strategy we knew was possible: roll over, give up all the documentation again, and forget saying everything was all there in the first place. Like a screaming baby, the Feds wouldn't tell us what we could give them to make them shut up. They had made their move, looming over little LabMD, threatening to knock us off the chessboard, bishop to pawn.

The January 2010 FTC letter had said to submit items only from 2007 forward, but we decided to bag that requirement in favor of showing how this whole issue evolved. The Internet is a new tool, the world evolves, the law lags behind, the FTC chases its tail, and we get caught in the crosswind of this whirling dervish. We at LabMD did nothing wrong; we operated like everyone else, if not better. But for now, we still had to play along.

Using the FTC business guide as a template, we went back through the history of the company for physical evidence of having the stated requirements in place. This meant reviewing our servers and workstations for any and all application history. It meant reviewing all employee policy manuals and training materials. It meant stopping all other management activities and solely focusing on this, then getting it back to Evelyn as soon as possible for her review. Our approach might have been overkill, but we felt defensive, confused, and still in the dark. We were throwing it all against the wall, hoping something would stick.

Only managers in the company plus our lawyer knew about this investigation. Gathering all of this information again fell squarely on Bill's back. A huge haystack of years of data stored on servers needed to be retrieved. Bill reviewed and documented everything possible, pulling out whatever was relevant. He spent 20 hours a day for three days doing this. After getting everything organized, he handed it to Tom.

Tom, a 73-year old, highly experienced Medical IT industry veteran, took seven days (including the weekend) to clean it up, organize it, and put it in a logical and chronological order. We were reshuffling the same old cards for a new round of the same game. Baffled and still believing that they had all their answers in the first round, we tried our best to make them happy, but their first hand had all the answers. None of this was going to make a difference.

We continued to cooperate with the FTC while still dumbfounded by their methods. True investigators would be finding evidence themselves, not having it organized and carted out to them by their suspect. *What type of organism had the United States Congress created?* That question rolled through my brain daily.

## Time to Submit Our Response

After two weeks of culling and organizing, Evelyn had to review everything one last time. We were required to boil down this mountain of data into a comprehensible document that would give the Feds what they wanted—or what we thought they wanted. Mr. Sheer, in keeping with his propensity to be frustratingly ambiguous, said he expected to hear back from LabMD "soon."

During the next two weeks, Evelyn logged 35.1 hours of billable time. I can only imagine how painful that must have been—almost as painful as it was for me when I opened her invoice. She certainly deserved payment, but still, this FTC nightmare was draining LabMD of valuable capital. The monotony was taking its toll on everyone.

The documentation we submitted was good, given the circumstances. However, as a medical facility, we believed the United States Department of Health and Human Services (HHS) was the regulatory body to which we were beholden. Of course, in this real world we found ourselves in, the only way to get that decided was to spend a fortune getting to the courts. Reading HHS publications and looking at their positions made our situation with the FTC even more puzzling. The March 2007 HIPAA Security Series, Security 101 for Covered Entities, mentions the challenges of absolutely securing data:

> The security requirements were designed to be technology neutral and scalable from the very largest of health plans to the very smallest of provider practices. Covered entities will find that compliance with the

Security Rule will require an evaluation of what security measures are currently in place, an accurate and thorough risk analysis, and a series of documented solutions derived from a number of complex factors unique to each organization. HHS recognizes that each covered entity is unique and varies in size and resources, *and that there is no totally secure system.*[2] (author's italics)

LabMD absolutely was within (if not beyond) industry practices, even though no exact standards had been around at the time.

This document was our attempt to throw everything against the wall and see what would stick. We sent it off to the FTC on June 4, 2010 via FedEx ground, as the FTC continued to remind us that they don't like the US Postal Service. I'm not sure if we crossed our fingers or threw flowers, but I know we said prayers: "Please, dear Lord, we've been good. Make these people go away."

*"You see, boys forget what their country means by
just reading The Land of the Free
in history books. When they get to be men
they forget even more.
Liberty's too precious a thing to be buried in books,
Miss Saunders.
Men should hold it up in front of them every single
day of their lives and say:
I'm free to think and to speak.
My ancestors couldn't, I can, and my children will.
Boys ought to grow up remembering that."*

—JEFFERSON SMITH, *MR. SMITH GOES
TO WASHINGTON*

# CHAPTER 8
# Mr. Daugherty Goes to Washington—It Isn't a Wonderful Life

## Early June 2010

I have often thought that, when used appropriately, denial has its benefits. We had sent off everything on June 4th to Washington DC, with nothing more to do until the FTC responded. We didn't expect a fast turnaround. We had a business to run.

Bill gets in around seven in the morning to beat Atlanta traffic and get ready for the day's operations. He plans the day and prepares for the arrival of employees and for receiving patients' specimens, knowing exactly what's arriving from where before it hits our doors. Our ordering system may show, for example, 10 biopsy cases from Phoenix with 30 vials of blood. Local biopsies picked up the evening before from Atlanta may have with them 15 cytologies (urine to be examined for cancerous cells indicating bladder cancer), 60 tubes of blood, and 14 urine cultures (urine to be examined for bacteria, after which we need to identify what drugs will kill the infection). These come from various states ranging from California to South Carolina, down to Florida and over to Missouri.

If anything is going to be late, Bill determines if the lateness will affect the stability of the specimen's ordered test. Some tests can be run after seven days, while others are toast after 24 hours. These are among the checks and balances constantly reviewed at LabMD to make sure everything runs smoothly.

In our world, patients come in the door only via tubes and vials. Holding a stranger's blood in our hands constantly reminds us we have a duty to be at the top of our game.

Bill and I complement each other well. He is Mr. Day-to-Day Detail and I am Mr. Big Picture. I typically arrive well after the rush-hour traffic around 10:30 a.m. after going to the gym and returning home to get ready. That can be a plate-spinning, multitasking scene that often annoys people at the gym who believe I'm on my BlackBerry *all the time*. You could say I start work the second my eyes open. If I wake up in the middle of the night, I try to get back to sleep ASAP just so my work brain won't kick in.

Thanks to our well-tested, state of the art system, we could afford to have our attention temporarily diverted by the FTC without anything imploding. What really got socked were our plans for business growth and future operations. All the money spent on lawyers and senior management addressing this issue came straight out of the time and money piggy bank that was initially meant for business development.

## Invited to FTC Headquarters

After we sent the documentation to the FTC, I spent the first week at work getting my bearings. By the second week of June 2010, we were back in the saddle without the FTC. It was delightful to say, "Hey, I haven't thought of these guys in days!" We hoped the FTC would fade into the background.

So much for that! On July 1, 2010—a Thursday—we were all looking forward to the Fourth of July weekend. Friday was a holiday. In what would turn out to be a perverse pattern which the FTC would call a series of coincidences, Alain Sheer contacted us on the eve of the holiday weekend to let Evelyn know we were being invited to Washington DC. She had the unenviable task of giving me the bad news when we were winding down to celebrate our country's birthday. My first knee-jerk, unfiltered comment, spoken ever so softly but firmly, was "that son of a bitch." I expressed it with the deepest of sincerity.

Two seconds seemed like three minutes as my shelter of denial crumbled. My head dropped and I took a deep breath. I felt numb, tingly, and perplexed.

"Evelyn, what in the hell did he say?"

Calmly, she replied, "He didn't say much. He is not Mr. Conversation. He said he wanted a company representative to come to Washington and for us to schedule time over the next few weeks so we "could discuss the matter further." He also said he'd like to see what further security safeguards we have taken to ensure improvement in our security practices. There wasn't much else. It looks like we need to make another submission to show him what additional steps we've taken in securing the organization since January. He's expecting that before we go up to DC."

"Do you think they want to come here instead? We have absolutely nothing to hide. We just need to get this over with. Ask them to come to Atlanta and see our facility."

Evelyn said she'd contact them after the holiday to make that proposal.

At this point, I'd gotten used to swallowing my emotions while pushing the FTC people to the back of my mind. I turned my attention to Destin, Florida, for a urology meeting. All weekend, I was entertaining clients and having a big party overlooking the beautiful Destin Harbor—always a good time. I needed that pendulum swing of being surrounded by good people to give me perspective and keep me from overreacting. *This was still probably nothing, so why waste pointless energy dwelling on what was highly unlikely to occur?*

As we grilled hot dogs and hamburgers, put the beers and sodas in the cooler, and laid out enough food for a small army, I had a relaxing, fun time unwinding with this intelligent and passionate group of professionals. As the fireworks lit up the evening sky, I harbored this thought: *Boy, if I told these people what was going down right now, they wouldn't even believe me. Happy Fourth of July! God bless America.*

## Operation: Make These People Go Away

Back in the office after the long holiday weekend, I heard the phone ring. Evelyn.

"The FTC has no interest in coming to Atlanta. They want us in Washington DC within two weeks. You, Bill, and me."

"Okay then, it looks like it's a hot summer in DC!" I said sarcastically. "Which days can you go, Evelyn? And where do they want to meet first? The Lincoln Memorial or Arlington Cemetery?"

We picked July 23, 2010. I booked our tickets to get the cheapest fare possible and called Evelyn to let her know. We needed to set our pre-meeting meeting and selected Wednesday, July 14th. That day, as Evelyn arrived at our office for the lunch meeting, Bill, Tom (our IT manager), and I were waiting in the conference room.

A striking woman, whenever she shows up at our office, heads turn. Over the last three years, two of her visits were to terminate high-level employees. Coincidently, she wore the same cutting-edge, fashion-house dark pink dress on these two termination visits. Remembering those days, we reminded her to never wear the pink dress to our office again.

On this day, thankfully, Evelyn arrived in dark blue. A total professional, Evelyn was always smiling and easy to approach. Nevertheless, our people had, well, let's call it a healthy respect for her.

After the greetings and niceties, none of us wanted to beat around the bush. This was Operation: Make These People Go Away. How could we do that?

Because we've received no requirements from them, anything we did was nothing short of a shot in the dark. We still ran with the same game plan; be proactive and show them who we were and what we've done.

Since January 2010, Evelyn often played devil's advocate repeating, "But the file got out, but the file got out, but the file got out." This was the FTC's main concern. Today, she grilled us again. "What if the file got out over and over? What if the file has been replicated thousands of times? What have we done and how do we know? After it was taken, it could have been replicated a million times. We have no idea."

I retorted, "Nor do we know if a tree fell in the woods and we weren't there, would it make a sound? But I get it. They're running toward potentially the worst case scenario and want to grill us for it. We have zero evidence that any of that happened and, believe me, if they know that, we would not be stuck on this slow moving train. We have looked and found nothing, zero, nada—not one patient phone call, not one credit card complaint, not one doctor call, and not one file found out in cyberspace. The bottom line is where are the evidence, rules, and standards? They can't make them up as they go along!"

"Okay," I said, "you may recall that we hired Henry to do a full analysis of security vulnerabilities within our network. This produced another few thousand pages. We went over the top, but since the FTC is going over the top, we had to go overboard. Do you think they will shoot us if we don't put a Sherman tank outside our server room?"

Evelyn cracked up and replied, "I haven't read anything about Sherman tanks in Section 5, but let's not give the FTC any ideas."

## Preparation Time

By now, we'd done so much research we could have submitted an application for Doctoral degrees in computer science. We loaded down Evelyn with network status reports and checklists for her to review. She spent the entire next day reviewing them to prepare an additional submission to the Federal Trade Commission. These two days alone resulted in 10 hours of billable time. As the dollars flew out the door, once again our attention got diverted from our core business of providing top-notch laboratory services helping doctors and their patients diagnose life-altering conditions.

As Evelyn reviewed thousands of pages of supplemental documentation from our outside party's risk assessment, we had multiple telephone conferences with her. She worked on her final correspondence to the FTC before her flight to Washington DC. All I could think was, *There is nothing wrong here. There is no honest investigation going on. Bye-bye profit margin. Bye-bye future plans.* We couldn't afford raises that year, and worse yet, couldn't disclose why to our staff; the FTC domino effect.

The next day Evelyn could work on this analysis was July 21st. By this point, she had turned her attention to reviewing the law, specifically discussing with me the benchmark language in the pertinent statute regarding substantial harm versus acts that *could have* caused substantial harm. She spent two half-days prepping for this conversation, finalizing the submission and letter, as well as researching the law at a deep level. The afternoon of the 22nd—the end of the day before we were leaving for Washington DC—Evelyn was ready. She let me know that, due to her research, it wouldn't surprise her, at all, if Alain Sheer handed us a consent decree as soon as we sat down.

She said, "Why they're going after this one-off mistake with no evidence of damage is beyond me, but they are. They're not backing off. And based on how they're behaving and what I've seen in previous actions, I believe they're going to hand us a consent decree. Don't be surprised if this meeting is real quick."

I replied in no uncertain terms, "I'm not signing anything. We don't have to sign anything right there, do we?"

"No."

"Good, because I'm not signing a thing. Let's get on with it already!"

"And you don't have to," she said. "Just be aware there is a pretty good possibility."

## My Resolve

To describe me as feeling completely frustrated would have been an understatement. I needed to get my anger under control. It had taken me a long time to realize that lawyers don't like emotion. I had every right to get mad, but they just back off and get quiet; that ticks me off even more. They're supposed to stay removed and objective, but sometimes I don't buy it. I haven't met people who are highly successful and not passionate about what they do. *For the sake of everyone's sanity, I have to keep my hot temper and cutting tongue in check.*

Was I really flying to Washington DC to talk to the Federal Trade Commission? The more this dragged on the less respect I had for the agency. At an instinctive level—at the core of my being and intellect—I believed this entire thing was a farce. If I became a notch on the belts of these government automatons, I wouldn't be able to live with myself. I was hell-bent on not trading my integrity and honesty for their perverted justice. If I buckled under these guys, I'd be a broken man.

"No!" I kept saying out loud in the car, in the shower, and at the mirror like some bad-ass tough guy. "I ain't signing shit!"

Rarely did I ever make that comment to Evelyn without getting silence in return. I may be wrong—who knows what other people's silence means?—but I can tell you I took it as if she thought the FTC wasn't going to go away. I was being so loud and forceful, it was better for her to lie low until my hurricane of anger passed by than to say, "Oh, sure. You say that now." My reaction to the silence or subject changing was simply, "Whatever." Anyone who knows me well knows I'm not afraid to be the only one going against the tide. But I also let some battles go by, turn the other cheek, and ignore insignificant consequences of wrongdoings, if that's the smarter move and the stakes are too low.

The stakes here couldn't be higher. This ordeal was going into overtime and we were starting to feel the effects. The company was not growing, but I would *not sign anything* that would result in a public innuendo or decree that would potentially taint my company with falsehoods. *We haven't compromised on this. Now is not the time to start.*

## On Board for Washington

Evelyn, Bill, and I didn't meet until I'd reached the Delta gate. I'd actually overslept! I flew to the airport, blasted through security, texted them my whereabouts, and arrived at the gate as everyone was boarding.

Because I practically live on Delta, I was upgraded while Evelyn and Bill each had their own rows in the back. We didn't have much to say anyway on the short trip to Washington's Reagan Airport. In the taxi, we arrived at 600 Pennsylvania Avenue, missing the morning rush hour.

We walked into the nondescript foyer with its standard security mini-airport setup. After clearing security, we watched a guard phone to announce our arrival. Then we took the elevator to the third floor. Alain was there to greet us.

*This is Alain? Middle aged, middle height, and middle weight. Not physically imposing at all. Almost disarming. If we hadn't had all this back and forth already, I would consider his appearance non-threatening and trustworthy. Fine, he doesn't look imposing, big deal. It's his conniving brain that is my big concern.*

Suddenly, I felt like a straight-A student who's still confused about why he got called into the principal's office. *So we finally get to meet Mr. Alain Sheer—that pain in my ass who's "just doing his job." What does one say to one's potential executioner upon first meeting? Hello, nice axe you have. And by the way, old chap, no hard feelings, I know you're just doing your job.*

We got past the sternly professional hellos and walked the 50 feet to the conference room. All I remember is smoked glass and steel; it was a sterile environment. I don't remember pictures on the wall. I don't remember seeing other people. The three of us sat down on one side of a long table trying to be cordial and relaxed. I took off my jacket. Then I told Alain I had to run to the restroom. He *personally* escorted me to the men's room—this guy I had been calling a pain in my side. *Isn't that nice? Maybe he's a nice man.* I was grasping for hope. Then I came to my senses. *Wake up, Mike. This is Big Boy time.*

Here I was, trying to be polite and seeking to impress him as a hard-working American guy just doing the best I can. No harm, no foul. But underneath my faux politeness was a nagging anxiety.

I wanted to scream, "We are good people, we work hard, we work in medicine, we assist in diagnosing cancer, we take care of people. Nothing bad happened here. You are wasting your time and taxpayer money. We don't belong here. Get off our backs. Go away!"

And then it hit me, *I wonder if that damned other shoe, the dreaded consent decree, is about to drop?*

I walked out of the restroom and my "guard" Alain was nowhere to be found. It gave me hope that somehow our presence—finally seeing us in person—would get through to him. But my naiveté soon came crashing down.

Ruth Yodaiken, the other lawyer on Team FTC vs LabMD, was also in the room. Probably 50 years old, 5'5", plain brown hair, non-descript and quiet, she was as matter of fact as matter of fact could get. I think there was a pulse. She seemed nice. I don't get it with me sometimes. I wanted to like her.

The meeting finally began.

Alain's tone—deftly soft, measured, and monotone—gave me chills. So calm and indifferent he was as he flipped our world upside down like an omelet in a pan. He explained the meeting was requested because the FTC still had questions regarding LabMD's responses to its inquiry and "concerns" about LabMD's security practices. My stone-cold expression covered my stunned feelings on the inside. *Concerns? Oh, that's rich. I have "concerns" about what you're trying to get at. I have "concerns" about your having no standards and crushing the Constitution. I have "concerns" about how to get out of this mess. Yeah, we all have concerns.* Now every time I hear the word "concerns," a rash breaks out.

Alain continued to identify six areas of "concern": (1) training; (2) scope of written policies; (3) measures used to enforce policies; (4) methods used to avoid, discover, and assess risks; (5) circumstances surrounding the LimeWire P2P installation; and (6) definition of the word "customer." As I listened to his summary, I couldn't get over the shock of our presence in the first place—like suspects in a CSI crime show who didn't know why they were surrounded by worked-up investigators.

To me, everything had been so obvious in our first submission to the FTC, I concluded an unknown agenda must be at play. *What was this guy really after?* I grasped in the dark for reasons. *Ah, they want to see us in person to know what type of people we are—the only logical reason. We'd already given them everything they requested and more. Now it must be a game of asking the same question repeatedly in different ways. Did we slip up or are they trying to slip us up?*

As Evelyn took copious notes and handled the interaction, Bill and I observed.

Evelyn's response to Alain's question about the LimeWire P2P installation was saying it was at worse and perhaps a one-time mistake by an employee who's no longer with our organization. The software had been isolated and removed. LabMD moved on. I saw Alain and Ruth blink their eyes twice then resume the questioning. Their silent responses to our answers were deafening. *This is a chess game cloaked as a friendly conversation.*

Alain definitely led the moves by asking most of the questions. His were broad in nature while Ruth asked more about specifics. I suspected she took on the role of worker bee in subordination to his supervisory role.

When Evelyn answered questions by pointing to our previous submissions, Alain flipped through his manual as if unfamiliar with the details. *How do you like that? He's cracking us over the head but can't keep things straight. Typical government efficiency fiasco. This is not happening.*

In effect, their disorganization confirmed my suspicion they hadn't dug deeply into any of our previous submissions. Otherwise, they wouldn't ask the questions they did. *Are they winging their questions or aiming to trip us up by intentionally repeating themselves?*

Either way, I was mentally shaking my head in disgust. *Look at them*, I thought. *These two are so out of touch with the real world. They have spent so much time in this building that they truly believe that the center of the universe is right here in Washington DC. How are they going to know about technology? They're government lawyers. They have no standards. They have bare bones technology knowledge. But they have power. Lots of it.* I kept my mouth locked shut and listened with razor sharp hearing to every word and nuance. I sat in my chair with perfect posture and at full attention, as I was sure these power mongers enjoyed victim submission.

About midway through the meeting, Alain gave us a homework list of more items to retrieve, including documentation of LabMD's employee training practices during the period in question. Then it dawned on me. *What, no consent decree? I don't think he is going to close this up and give us that consent decree. Evelyn had prepared me for a consent decree. Where is it so I can tell Alain to shove it? Don't tell me these turtles will keep dragging this out!*

But drag it out they did. Alain and Ruth requested documentation related to how we manage responses related to employee training on the subject of data security. That would include the protection of data that's stored, collected, transferred, maintained, and transmitted by LabMD. Here's a sampling of questions and requests that came our way:

For written policies: What written policies were in effect when the LimeWire incident occurred? State how current versions differ from prior versions. Provide a previous version of each written policy and what time frame each was in effect concerning policies related specifically to data security. If no written policy existed in 2007-2008, then state that.

For measures used to enforce policies: How did managers know what to tell employees during a training session and, specifically, about LabMD's data security practices? How did LabMD confirm the content of the manager's discussions with training? How did the trainers cover ways in which personal information could be exposed or lost? How were they told to protect that information? How did LabMD enforce its policies and procedures during the period in question? How does LabMD enforce its policies and procedures now? Is there a policy regarding enforcement?

I braced myself for the next probable question, something like, "Where is your policy book on writing policies?"

No more jitters here, everyone settled into the game of rehashing everything. I silently cheered on Evelyn when she coolly, yet politely, peppered her responses with "we put that in the submission last April" or "that was sent to you already for this meeting." These remarks sent Alain flipping through his notes again. *They're dispassionately going through the motions before they cook our goose. And so far, I still don't see a consent decree.*

My ears pricked up when they moved on to discussing the LimeWire incident.

How does LabMD know that no other files were shared? Did LabMD confirm that no other files were shared?

I wanted to shout, "Alain, haven't you paid attention to anything?" Instead, I kept my mouth shut and let our lawyer talk. Evelyn calmly explained that, upon its discovery, we immediately tore the whole network apart reviewing every file on that computer and the entire system with a fine-toothed comb. I seethed inside. *You know that stuff we previously submitted to you, Alain? Did you even read it or didn't it have the hook you need?*

Cool as a cucumber, Evelyn answered more questions as if she'd never been asked them before. As she navigated their dance, I worked hard to stay emotionless and expressionless. Focusing on my breathing became my full-time job, yet my thoughts made my blood boil. *This really is our government at work. This makes me sick.*

After about 45 minutes of rehashing information they already had in their possession, Alain asked about our staff's and management's access to workstations. A lull followed as he swung ever so slightly in his chair. He cracked the silence by calmly inquiring, "Can just anyone install software on the workstations there?" Five full seconds passed. Then Bill replied, "No, only managers can do that." Five more heavy seconds passed. Alain's chair come to a halt, then his body steadied. He leaned forward and looked Bill straight in the eye, picked up his tone of voice and asked him, "So you let managers install whatever software they want without any supervision?"

Alarms rang in my head. *Game over! He's trying to entrap us. Wake up, Mike, this guy thinks he is so good and he's so bad. This is not a game; this is a nightmare. Get out. Get out. Get out.*

From that moment on, I saw lips moving but couldn't hear a word. *Yes, all the pieces of the puzzle are coming together. Boback, the President of Tiversa, calls and says they have our file but won't say how that file got to the company. To get information, we had to retain Tiversa. We search extensively and find no evidence of our file being "out there" in cyberspace. Boback sends a one-sided, ridiculously expensive agreement to start an investigation—without guaranteed results. Feeling manipulated, we walk away. Boback keeps contacting us. We tell him to call our lawyer, then his lawyer calls our lawyer to say Tiversa is turning LabMD's property over to the FTC. Nobody will believe this farce.*

*Yet here I am with Alain Sheer playing the one-two entrapment strategy—a government fishing expedition. Knowing that the first one who speaks loses, I won't take the bait.*

Like ice water thrown in my face, I finally woke up and embraced the truth. *Mike, this is real. These guys are after us and they won't go away. This passive crap ain't gonna cut it.*

I looked around the room, first to my lawyer. She was doing a good job but felt just as baffled as we did. Second, I looked at Bill, who still thinks being a Boy Scout will work with these people—that fair and square will win the day. Then I looked at Ruth, seemingly a hard-working, go-through-the-motions, worker bee lawyer. And then I turned to Alain—presumably the cunning one, the dangerous one, the strategist.

Alain's smooth game was beginning to show as he tried to gently open us and then go in for the kill. Why hasn't he mentioned Tiversa? I didn't believe for one second he didn't know who Tiversa was, how Tiversa got the file, or that Tiversa didn't give it to the FTC. His silence was not building any trust.

I felt disgusted that the FTC would offer no information to help us solve any problem (if there even was one) but, on the other hand, would drill down on us as if we'd committed a felony. We had found no evidence of our file getting past Tiversa. If the FTC agents knew otherwise, they should cough it up. *But they must have nothing more; their case has got to be weak. If they could hang us with anything worse than this, they would have already brought out the rope.*

Alain Sheer represented the loaded gun of the towering and huge federal government. He had no time for listening, petty details, or insignificant roadblocks. I had to get over the fact we'd been plucked out of obscurity and were now the subject of an interrogation by the United States Federal Trade Commission. I had to get over the fact that none of these facts mattered to FTC agents. They didn't have the time or interest to look closely at the details. So they kept on walking, trying to crush us under their boots in a self-righteous pursuit of what they considered justice. They wanted us to sign a little piece of paper that would shred our own reputation with innuendo, require 20 years of expensive audits, and open us to years of potential fines and government blood-letting. Because they were blasé about proportionality, overreach, facts, destruction, and fairness, their indifference sickened me. I kept my face blank. I didn't want the Devil to know I wasn't drinking the Kool-Aid.

*I'm a lousy follower.* It was almost a relief to finally realize that if anyone was going to get us out of this corner, it was going to have to be me. I could not afford a lawyer to do it. If we got into the FTC's kangaroo regulatory judicial bureaucracy, we would be there for a very long time, coming out with a tainted reputation, or worse yet, dead due to bankruptcy. No, I was going to have to come to my own rescue using strategy, patience, and cunning. My mind made up, I watched their lips move and their faces come back into focus, and I could start to hear their voices again. War.

I had mentally returned around wrap up time. From what I could gather, they were discussing the definition of customer. Alain just confirmed that our patients may in fact be characterized as Lab-MD's customers. This was the ass-covering portion of our discussion where "Alain the lawyer" was letting us know his legal justification, considering that patients never enter our facility. He said that, because we rely on our patients for payment and we may have direct contact with them for bill-paying purposes to the extent there may be no insurance coverage or insurance fails to pay, they can be categorized as customers. He could now check that off his list.

Then came another attempt at throwing a noose to hang ourselves. He asked whether we had made any representations to customers regarding the security of data and personal information. Of course, we answered no, but what he was actually asking, being the self-taught law student I was rapidly becoming, pertained to whether we've violated the deceptive practices aspect of Section 5. Looks like Alain will have to rely on the legal argument of what is "reasonable" in our security practices. "Reasonable" is the last word I would use to describe any aspect of this charade of justice. It was an insult to the United States Constitution.

Finally, as Alain concluded their "meeting" with us, he asked if we had any final questions. At this point, Bill said, "Yes. Can you explain . . ." Evelyn and I must have been on the exact same wavelength, which was "we need to get the hell out of here and keep our mouths shut." We both looked at him, aghast. Picking up on this in milliseconds, Bill quickly changed his mind about having any further discussion. "Well, uh, no, forget it. I think I have what I need." After the awkwardness of those few seconds, we stood up and said our goodbyes.

With our plastic smiles still intact after shaking hands, we walked out of the conference room—quietly but intently—making our way straight to the elevator. All I could hear were Evelyn's high heels clicking along the linoleum floor at breakneck speed. After what seemed like an agonizing five minutes, the elevator finally came and we got in. The millisecond the door closed, I turned to Bill and jumped right down his throat, "What the hell were you thinking about asking them? Are you crazy? Those people are dangerous. Let's not say anything until we are out of here and in the taxicab." I thought, *Okay, Mike. That was uncalled for. Chill out and get out.*

Not another word was spoken as we got to the ground floor. The doors opened. I reminded myself that running out of the building might not look too good. At this point, we would have believed the entire building was bugged. At this point, we might have believed the entire city was bugged. In my opinion, we'd just exited a bureaucratic version of Hell.

Getting a taxi was easy before lunch. The plastic looks on our faces faded quickly as we slammed the taxi doors. Evelyn and I looked at each other. I said, "That guy is dangerous—a snake, snake, snake—and being there was bone chilling."

Evelyn confirmed, "Oh man, you're not kidding. Talk about a preconceived agenda. He won't let this thing go and I don't know why."

"Some of those questions he was asking they were just like guilty till proven innocent. Do you always let managers install what they want? Are you kidding me? Oh my God, this guy won't go away. Oh yeah, driver, we're going to Reagan Airport."

I had just been immersed in unethical filth and needed a spiritual shower. The Mike Daugherty that arrived in DC that morning was not the same one that left. I was finally awake.

*"You are braver than you believe, stronger than you seem, and smarter than you think."*

—Christopher Robin

# CHAPTER 9
# Trying to Lower Our Coffin into the Ground

## July 23, 2010

After an explosion like we've just experienced, there comes a quiet time that one should use to reflect on what just happened. And that's exactly why we were all pretty quiet on the way to the airport. We each took our own breather to get back to some sense of normal reality. It may seem strange, but I don't think any of us wanted to talk about what just happened. We needed a moment to gather ourselves. I dialed Delta Air Lines and booked an earlier flight. We rode to the airport, got through security, and ate lunch. Evelyn was going to summarize the day's events on paper. We would be back in Atlanta by mid-afternoon.

Nothing like staring at puffy clouds from 37,000 feet to put me into my own world. My overwhelming thought was: *Something's wrong here. Very wrong.* I had just countered the immoral, perverse, and evil.

I knew if I said that to others they'd cut it in half and chalk it up to drama or, worse yet, ignorant paranoia. I felt alone, deep in my thoughts, but rock solid calm. This was a new beginning. They had gotten my full attention now. I was ready.

The first big lesson I'd learned owning and operating my own company was to gather lots of information, but also listen carefully to my instincts. Whenever I'd stray from them, I'd get burned. Dealing with the FTC would mean using all my resources, all my brainpower, all my life experience and, most important, all the trust in what my gut was telling me.

Dealing in any profession requires a quick mind, acute observations, and constant adjustments. In a rapid state of change, one learns to navigate the inevitable challenges and surprises of life. I learned this from playing tennis. As a teenager back in the 1970s, I never connected to the typical sports of baseball, football, and basketball. But in the spring of 1974—after tennis exploded into the national consciousness thanks to Billie Jean King and Bobby Riggs—I picked up my mother's old tennis racket and bought a can of tennis balls for $1.99. I'd play in the street with my sister or neighbor using an imaginary net. Then I advanced to an actual court. I'd ride my bike down the dirt road to the courts at the local junior high school. By constantly hitting the ball against the wall, I found a connection. I liked pounding it hard and hearing the sound of the ball against the strings and the wall; I loved it. Even though I could never beat that damn wall, I kept trying and would never stop.

I recalled our spring vacation to Florida that year—the kind of trip every Michigan family was eager to take. During the cold winter we counted the days until spring and fantasized about getting to Florida. On a trip to the mall one day in the spring of 1974, I used my paper route money to buy a book, *Tennis to Win*. It came with us on vacation, along with my new metal racquet—a Wilson T-2000.

Once we got to Florida, the rest of my family scampered off to the beach. I hated the beach. I never understood the concept of lying around. Instead I looked for the nearest tennis court. I found one: the most beat-up piece of cement in Daytona Beach. Not a soul in sight, hot as hell, weeds growing up the side of the poles holding up the net. Why not? I opened my book, broke the spine so it would lie open, and set it on the ground four feet behind the baseline. I studied the illustrations for a correct service motion and I mimicked the technique as best I could. Then I hit tennis balls over and over and over. I loved the peace and quiet. I loved the feeling of getting it over the net. I loved the learning. I loved tennis. I was hooked.

My game was lacking for quite a while, but I couldn't get enough of the sport. Improving my skills felt extremely satisfying. In tennis, everything starts with the feet. Baby steps and moving your feet quickly to get to the ball provides a lot of time to execute the shot.

And no two shots are alike. Each shot requires processing new data in milliseconds. Decide, commit, and adjust with no two shots the same. That's tennis!

Playing tennis has taught me the importance of constant adjustment, something that is serving me well in this current quagmire. Repetition isn't boring; no two situations are alike; similarities between situations help me build on experience and improve; successful execution results from constant changes that are made in rapid-fire baby steps based on constant new incoming information. Above all else, I learned to never, ever quit. I learned to continue until the fat lady sang, and when she finally did, I pretended to be deaf.

As I simmered looking out the window, staring down 37,000 feet to what must have been more than a few tennis courts in my field of vision, I took all that wisdom from my heroes—Lendl (work ethic), King (leadership), Ashe (intellect), Evert (mental toughness), and Borg (relentless)—and applied it to the FTC. I'm alone here on my side of the net and I need to gather information quickly, intensely, and deeply on what the next return will do. When I figure that out, I'll take that ball and hit it back at a hundred miles an hour. I'll let it all hang out, because if the FTC doesn't deserve a hard shot right at them, nobody does.

After what I'd experienced that morning in our nation's capital, I suspected the FTC was brimming with hypocrites, carrying out their duties while simultaneously cloaking themselves in the American flag and trampling the ideals of our Founding Fathers. That suspicion sparked a slow burning fire that became my constant companion. That light, that buzz, and that constant energy started someplace over the Carolinas—and became a cocktail of fury, duty, self-defense, principle, and quiet determination. It was confidence in truth and faith in everything I'd believed this country was about. In my heart, I knew if I rolled over at this pivotal crossroad due to a politically correct strategy or lawyerly advice, I'd be haunted with regret forever. That would be worse than anything these guys could do to me. There had to be a way to win without hurting the company and employees. I just had to keep hitting the ball against the wall until I figured it out.

## Time for Silence, Reflection, and Research

This was Friday afternoon, July 23rd. Upon landing in Atlanta, Evelyn, Bill, and I gathered at the gate area. It felt like we had just returned from a convention. We were just glad that was over. In our lighthearted mood and with easy conversation, we tore through the concourse, walked past baggage claim, found our cars, and said, "Have a good weekend." It was good I had a vacation scheduled for the next week. It was also good that, in spite of the FTC's "house-on-fire" attitude, the agency moved at a snail's pace.

*What angle of attack should I take to get rid of these people? What about jurisdiction?*

LabMD is a federally regulated clinical and anatomic medical laboratory. We adhere to federal guidelines and regulations called CLIA (Clinical Laboratory Improvement Amendments) and undergo an annual CLIA inspection to keep us in compliance. *How could the FTC find that we were unreasonable if the CLIA inspectors approved us? They have more direct control over our laboratory and said we were fine.* To do my own research on the regulations, I needed copies of our previous inspections. The reports would show that communication practices were part of it and that LabMD had passed with an inspector *physically* present.

First thing Monday morning before leaving for vacation, I looked at the inspection reports. *If they signed off on everything and they had been physically on site, how could the FTC argue with their findings?* In our most recent inspection, only weeks before, we came up with a perfect score; not one single deficiency.

Within the reports, I wanted to find the specific language to throw back at the FTC lawyers. I reasoned that throwing logic or morality or common sense at a lawyer is a waste of time; throwing another law at them was at least speaking their language. I gathered all the pertinent information and e-mailed it to Evelyn.

Of course, I knew that trying only one thing at a time wouldn't work. While our first pitch at the batter gave them everything they wanted, this now appeared to be just the first few innings of what would be a very long game.

The challenge to come up with effective strategies seemed overwhelming. I felt like I was standing at the base of a mountain without a map, looking straight up but unable to see the top. *Might as well get started anyway.*

## Pilot Camp: A Total Blast

I do my best work after I have time to simmer and calm down. Because I'm a licensed pilot, I find no place more fun and relaxing than to be surrounded by hundreds of other pilots and planes. I packed my bags and flew to AirVenture[1] in Oshkosh, Wisconsin, which I refer to as "pilot camp." It's the largest general aviation show in the world. There was no better place for me to enjoy a mental break.

I enjoy many great things about being a pilot, but I especially enjoy the freedom and being with other pilots. To be a pilot requires discipline and lifelong learning. Pilots come from a plethora of diverse backgrounds, professions, and interests, and this visit represented a much needed head change from where my mind had been with the FTC.

I checked into the dormitory at the University of Wisconsin for the $50 a night special—a single room with a single cot in a cinderblock dormitory with no air-conditioning. (I brought a fan for the window.) I watched aviation lovers from all over the world check into this Disneyland for flight geeks, a refreshing change from the beings in DC. Everyone in Wisconsin is just so nice.

When I got to the airfield, the toughest thing was deciding what to do first. Usually, I'd hit the vendors to shop for deals on oil and supplies and see what's new. Then I'd look at all the planes and jets and drool all over the new toys. The Federal Aviation Administration (FAA) always has great courses going on and the forums have endless courses from industry pros (wow . . . nice job, Feds . . . see, I just knew you had it in ya!) This year I sprang for the $125 entrance fee for the Aviator's Club tent, an air-conditioned venue with an all-you-can-eat breakfast, lunch, snacks, ice cream, and drinks (non-alcoholic). When the skies opened up, I knew I had gotten my money's worth. All this made for a short week. The FTC was a faded memory . . . but not for long.

## Recap of Our Washington Trip

By the time I returned from Wisconsin, I was tanned, cheesed-up, and relaxed. Unfortunately, my newly found rejuvenation was needed right away. Evelyn and I had touched base about debriefing and planning our responses from our meeting in Washington. On August 10th, I received her summary of our visit to Washington, DC For the most part, it read:

> Alain explained that the meeting was requested because the FTC had questions regarding LabMD's responses to the FTC inquiry and concerns about LabMD's security practices. He identified five general areas: (1) training; (2) scope of written policies; (3) measures used to enforce policies; (4) methods used to avoid, discover, and assess risks; (5) circumstances surrounding the LimeWire P2P breach; and (6) definition of "customer."
>
> Alain began the meeting by explaining that the FTC wants to ensure that LabMD has implemented reasonable security measures that take into consideration the highly sensitive nature of the information handled. He categorized the data handled by LabMD as being on the "high end of sensitivity." The granular detail was excruciating and aimless. I will footnote the specific document but must give you a taste via Item 8:
>
> Provide documents sufficient to identify the policies, procedures, and practices you have used on each network identified in the response to Request 6 to prevent unauthorized access to personal information

collected and stored on the network, as well as the time period during which such policies, procedures, and practices were written and implemented. The response should include, but not be limited to, documents that concern, reflect, or are related to: controls on direct or remote access to personal information (such as a firewall policy or a password policy); controls on accessing and/or downloading personal information without authorization; the lifecycle of personal information, including maintaining, storing, using and/or destroying the information; controls on the installation of programs or applications on computers or work stations on the network by employees or others; limits on the transmission of personal information within the network and between the network and other (internal and external) networks; logging network activity and reviewing the logs; secure application and Web site development; employee training; and plans for responding to security incidents.[2]

This from an agency with "Broad Powers" but no standards.

The FTC requested to receive LabMD's supplemental documents and information discussed during the July 23rd meeting no later than the end of August 2010. With another to-do list from our Federal Leviathan, the plates at LabMD were again overflowing with things to do. The entire management team at LabMD was getting deeply angry at this ignorant obstacle course that the US Congress was turning into a marathon: And the irony of the FTC acting as if there were standards and laws back then when there were no standards . . . and they knew that.

While this summary from Evelyn is a testament to her note-taking skills, it made my mind brew with this constant thought: *They can't look at the first submission and figure it out for themselves? After that first meeting, isn't this all just a formality? Why don't they get this information gathering game over with and drop the axe so I can tell them I'm not signing anything? They must still be fishing.*

On August 11th, Evelyn, Bill, and I met for five hours regarding the FTC probe and to review the collection of pertinent supplemental documents and information. *No one* was having a good time.

The first part involved reviewing everything yet again. Then we looked at all the practices that weren't in writing and memorialize them per the FTC's request. This was the *physical* evidence piece of the game, not the *psychological*. This time Alain had given us a specific hard date to respond by—the end of August. Already near the middle of August, we had to repackage things once again. Bill sounded exasperated when he asked, "I wonder if they're going to actually dig into it this time."

We felt that the FTC wanted us to, in essence, take everything we'd submitted already and reorganize it for them. I know they were packaging their request to look like they wanted more, but it struck us as laziness

"Do you always allow managers to install whatever software they like?" Alain had asked. He used the sinister tone of a policeman asking a suspect. He might as well have asked, "Do you always let your children play with loaded guns while you're out drinking at the corner bar?"

I looked up from the summary list. "Evelyn, we know we're being sat on by an elephant, so we'll continue with our original plan of patience and submission. Maybe he'll eventually lose interest and find new, unfortunate victims to torment."

"I find it hard to believe they don't have better things to do," Evelyn replied.

Feeling more jaded, I responded, "Oh, after what I saw in DC, don't bet on it. The FTC is in cybersecurity panic. The Feds want to control the masses by playing 'Put A Head on A Spike' and the head they want to spike is LabMD's. That will *not* be happening. Even on a spike, this head has a fully functional, moving mouth."

After our mini-gripe session, we affirmed we would, once again, get back on the gerbil wheel. We'd supply the FTC with supplemental responses regarding LabMD's training, scope of written policies and measures used to enforce policies, and methods employed to avoid, discover, and assess risks. As far as the CLIA submissions were concerned, Evelyn said, "While it's great LabMD scores consistently well on inspections, at this point I don't think this information will do much good. The FTC guys think it's their chalkboard to write on, so CLIA inspection results won't matter to them. I say we restrict our responses to only what they ask for."

With that, Evelyn again mentioned finding a lawyer whose main career experience lies in dealing with the Federal Trade Commission.

"Mike, this is getting deeper and deeper. It's not my area of expertise. We need someone who's worked with these people, so we can figure out why they're so perplexing."

Evelyn seemed to want to bolt for the door when actually *I* was the one trying to beat her to the exit. In my heart, I didn't want to hear this counsel from my counsel, but I knew she was right. After our "seeing is believing" experience in Washington DC, I was beginning to understand her position. "Okay. I'll make some calls and see who's out there."

## Onward with the Action Items

I had to start looking for another lawyer. *Lawyers. Some of them cause nothing but trouble when you hire them to solve your problems. How can I find a lawyer who knows what to do in this situation and isn't going to take advantage of the company?* At the moment, that seemed like a task taller than making the FTC go away.

Here we were confounded by the FTC's persistent presence, working with an attorney who felt this case was quickly expanding beyond her expertise, and hearing zombies at the front door banging to get in. I didn't want to fight. I just wanted them to go away—but not if it meant sucking the lifeblood out of my company or hearing lawyers and judges drone on endlessly about the subjective definition of "reasonable" and "unfairness" as the company gasped for air. *If it came down to war, war it would be. Like Goliath staring down at small David and his little slingshot, this giant, too, has no idea what's in store.*

It was getting more difficult to keep those thoughts to myself and continue down our genteel path.

The LabMD team began to gather the data for Evelyn to organize our response. With the summary and game plan now decided, we split into two teams. Bill would gather all the data and assemble it for Evelyn to reduce it to writing and get our 5,000 pages and two boxes of information down to a little package. Then the poor, overworked lawyers at the FTC wouldn't have to break a sweat. Meanwhile, I would recruit a lawyer to our team.

I also assigned myself the unspoken task of digging up who Tiversa and the FTC really were. *This stinks. Okay, it's not a legal term, but I know stink when I smell it. Evelyn won't be able to get rid of the smell; she'll work within the law. Discovering the truth behind this seedy underbelly crap is going to be my contribution to the cause.*

I put on two hats that afternoon. I wore one hat to find another lawyer and a bigger hat to turn myself into a private investigator representing myself and all the souls who worked at LabMD. *Go home and start digging in one direction or another. Just do something.* So that's what I did.

I fired up my laptop and started with LimeWire. So much came up I didn't know where to begin. Read this, read that. Blah blah blah. Before long I felt depressed, overwhelmed, and hopeless. Not quite thinking straight, I played around a bit longer but came up empty. I threw in the towel for the night.

## Fair?

I woke up Friday morning, August 12th, feeling lower than low. I recalled my high school civics teacher, Mrs. Lewandowski, who told the class there were only two types of fair in life: taxi fare and the fair that had fun rides. If we believed any other type of fair existed, we would experience a lot of disappointment. I pondered that as I stood in the shower and felt the spray of water run down my back. *Am I being too stubborn? Too unrealistic? Maybe they really will go away. If they put out an announcement about a decree, our competitors will be on us like vultures. We'll have an indelible mark on our foreheads. We could be ruined.*

It seemed like my brain was in a dark room feeling around for the light switch. I had to do more research to know who the true enemy or enemies were. I decided to start with something easy; I'd Google FTC lawyers and make a few calls. While this wasn't fun, it was relatively mindless. Ring ... leave a message. Ring ... voicemail. Ring ... "Hello?"

"Hi ... This is Michael Daugherty. Is this Mr. X? (He will remain nameless here for the legal reasons.)

"Yes."

"I'm calling about your experience in dealing with the FTC and defending those under investigation."

"What type of investigation?"

"We got a letter about a non-public inquiry regarding data security."

"Are you currently represented by counsel?"

"Yes, but we've decided to seek an attorney who has direct experience dealing with the FTC."

"Oh, are you getting a fine?"

"No. They keep asking for more info and we've already given them a ton. We've been very cooperative. This all started when someone took one of our data files and then turned it over to the FTC."

(Silence)

"So ... uh ... we locked everything down ages ago and it was a fluke. But the FTC guys don't seem to care and this is getting serious. They showed us a consent decree that they worked out with another company but, unlike that company, we did nothing wrong."

I hated saying the words "we did nothing wrong." I shouldn't have to deny anything. I felt like a demoralized criminal pleading in vain to the judge after being sentenced.

I continued.

"My current lawyer thought the FTC would present the evidence to us, but their people just asked for more info. We flew all the way up there a few weeks back and faced a strange rehash."

He chimed in. "The FTC is going to want that decree and fighting to get rid of it will be worse than signing it."

"Well, I won't let them say we did something wrong when we didn't. Did you work for the FTC at one time?"

"No, but I've been in front of them many times. There's no way to get around those people."

I was at a loss for words. *What does one say? Are you good—as if anyone would say no?* Then I cut to the chase.

"Well, to be upfront, I don't want to waste your time, so would you send me an engagement letter with your fees and I'll get back to you?" This was the only way to get out of the call that came to mind.

As we exchanged information, I felt like I was rolling the dice in Vegas. Already he didn't sound like Mr. Positive, and I had no clue what he could do. I have the utmost contempt for lawyers until they personally prove themselves otherwise. Right now, I had dim hopes.

I made two more similar calls. The common thread through them all was painfully direct. They all said things like this: "The FTC is no fun and fighting is expensive. If you aren't going to court or being fined a bunch of money, just take your licks and go home. Move on . . . it isn't worth it. They will make your life a living hell."

With that, I quit. It was Friday. I left for home before rush hour and pretended none of this was happening. When I got there, I threw off my tie, opened the windows, and played a CD as loud as I could tolerate (*Tim McGraw Greatest Hits*). How could I disappear? I played this denial game for the next 48 hours as my sense of injustice grew. Withdrawing into myself allowed me to calculate a way to navigate the waters. But I needed more knowledge. I also needed a break so I could stay sharp, but I could not think of anything else.

I went to dinner with friends and put on my game face. I'd become used to keeping quiet about this in public, my little secret. With one hand resting on my chin and a beer in the other, I looked somewhat interested in the conversation, yet my mind floated elsewhere. *Should I attempt to top the conversation by saying, "Well, I'm sorry your relationship is going south, but I have the FEDERAL GOVERNMENT crawling down my back*"? Everyone was in such a carefree mood, who was I to spoil the evening? I sucked it up and sipped my beer.

I took Saturday for myself. On Sunday morning, I felt like I might be my old self again, so I putzed around, went to the gym and the coffee shop, met some friends, and didn't watch the clock. After cleaning up every detail on my personal to-do list, I ended up back at my house, plopped on the couch, my remote control in hand and two wonderful and loyal Golden Retrievers at my feet. What could be better than that?

The ghost in the room was not leaving regardless of how much I tried to ignore it.

I reached for my laptop, booted up, and checked my e-mail. Then I hit Google and effortlessly, almost accidentally, fell into my first meaningful discovery. I typed in the word LimeWire, but this time my brain was calm enough to patiently wade through the data bombarding me. The first thing that jumped out was an announcement that, four days before on August 11, 2010, the recording industry won its copyright piracy lawsuit against LimeWire for inducement of copyright infringement, common law copyright infringement, and unfair competition.[3]

With focused interest, I read the court found "failure to utilize existing technology to create meaningful barriers against infringement" was a strong indicator of intent to foster infringement. Did that mean LimeWire would be responsible for damages that occurred to anyone who suffered a data loss due to the nature of its software? At no time did anyone at LabMD intentionally or knowingly use the LimeWire software to violate any regulations. *Could this be a way out?*

I forwarded the article to Evelyn and surprisingly got a response within five minutes. It was 3:40 PM on Sunday, August 15th. In her e-mail, she wrote that it was a great legal decision by the court and wondered if the copyright issue would apply to LabMD.

*Okay, I'm feeling lucky. Let's see what happens when I check out our friends at Tiversa.* So I Googled Tiversa and clicked on the link to its home page. *My, these guys are proud of themselves. Oh my God! They're bragging that Robert Boback testified before Congress. The guy on the phone is in front of Congress? This I have to see.* I opened the most relieving, exciting, validating, and infuriating revelation ... and I had hit pay dirt.

I dove into the testimony given by Robert Boback, CEO, Tiversa before the House Committee on Oversight and Government Reform dated July 29, 2009. I stared at the text that started out, "Good morning Chairman Towns, ranking member ISA and distinguished members of the committee."[4]

Boback went on to give background on peer-to-peer networks, which have provided a gateway for users around the world to share digital content, most notably music, movies, and software. However, he said that over time it had been used not only for planned file sharing—its intended use—but for unintended uses of searching for malicious content and/or distributing and sharing illegal information. He said millions of documents that weren't intended to be shared with others were made available on these networks.

He went on to discuss Social Security numbers and Medicare fraud, pointing out an increased awareness of the problem. He said that even on the FTC's Web site—and this is in 2009, after Tiversa took possession of our property, mind you—there's not a single mention of P2P or file sharing as an avenue for criminals to gain access to consumers' personal information.

*How amusing that Mr. Hyde likes to sit in front of Congress playing Dr. Jekyll. I'm not surprised that the FTC is trying to rewrite history here. The FTC guys were as clueless as everyone else in 2008 and earlier.*

Returning to Tiversa's home page, I found more, such as the testimony Robert Boback, Tiversa CEO, gave before the House Subcommittee on Commerce, Trade and Consumer Protection, May 4, 2009. This testimony started, "Good afternoon Chairman Rush, ranking member Radanovich, and distinguished members of the subcommittee." More of the same, blah, blah, blah. So I flipped to page 4, then to page 6, and then I saw the words in bold: "Examples to follow on subsequent pages." I got hit with the biggest ball of adrenaline I've ever felt. When I looked at page 9, I saw OUR file. LabMD's file.[5] Right there in black and white.

Shock and awe. *I knew I wasn't nuts.* I was staring at a partially redacted page of our file that Tiversa had in its possession. It still had exposed dates of birth, first names, and CPT codes sitting there for the entire world to see—right in the Congressional Record. That unforgettable moment knocked the wind out of me. Feeling mortified, vindicated, and excited, all at the same time, I yelled at the monitor, "I bet he threw us under the bus because we wouldn't sign his services agreement! I wonder if any examples that he put up for the world to see were his clients."

I couldn't wait to tell Evelyn. I cut and pasted the testimony's link into an e-mail to her and wrote only three words: "The penny drops." Then I hit Send, still fuming with rage. *That hypocrite showed our file to Congress! He has the nerve to try to get us to pay him $40,000 and then sits in front of those representatives like he's a saint?*

As if I'd won the lottery, I danced around my living room. "I knew it in my gut . . . I knew it!" I said to my two bewildered Golden Retrievers, who weren't quite sure if this performance was resulting from a mistake on their part or not. "I was never crazy. When the FTC guys find out about this terrible behavior, they'll let us off the hook!"

After realizing it was good nobody was watching, I plopped back on the couch and was suddenly brought back to reality. My entire world had changed in a flash but the house was still filled with Sunday afternoon silence.

## Tiversa's Reach

I returned to the laptop to reread Boback's shocking testimony from both the hearings. All I could think was, "This is so awesome, now people will believe it." He talked more about inadvertent file disclosure in which users mistakenly share more files than they had intended. "User error" happens when users download a P2P software program without fully understanding the security implications of the selections they make. He also said that today's existing safeguards, such as data loss prevention, firewalls, encryption, port scanning, policies, and so on simply don't mitigate P2P file-sharing risk effectively.

Boback referred to testimony he gave before the House that said most consumers and security experts at corporations worldwide have little understanding of the information security risks caused by P2P. Most corporations believe current policies and existing security measures will protect their information—but they won't. Then the words "today we will provide the committee with concrete examples that show the extent of the security problems that exist on the P2P networks" jumped off the page. *What does that mean?*

Bragging about his company's technology and developments, he said Tiversa can see and track all the previously untraceable activity on P2P networks in one place. Whereas an individual user can see only a small portion of the P2P file-sharing network, their people can analyze broader searches. Tiversa can see the P2P network in its entirety and in real time. He compared his company to Google, saying Tiversa can process 1.6 billion searches per day. He boasted that his company located and downloaded tax returns in one brief search. He later stated that increased awareness is required to deal with the problem. As an example, he pointed out that the Federal Trade Commission's Web site still doesn't have a single mention of P2P or file sharing as an avenue for criminal access. Of the six methods identified on the FTC's Web site in May 2009, very few, if any, could ever result in the consistent production, let alone the magnitude of the P2P networks. In conclusion, he said that the inadvertent file sharing on P2P file-sharing networks is highly pervasive and large in magnitude because it affects consumers, corporations, and government agencies. Existing policies and IT measures simply haven't been effective in curbing *inadvertent (author italics)* sharing.

*Boback certainly came across like a Boy Scout, so concerned with his fellow man. Such a concerned citizen, so believable, so credible. But how did he get in front of Congress, anyway? Who does this guy know? And how did little old LabMD, minding our own business down here in Atlanta, Georgia, end up on Tiversa's radar?*

On a roll, I went back to Tiversa's home page. *Man, you guys are way more important than I thought.* After reading the typical company stuff, I clicked on the About Us tab and saw the company's Advisory Board.[6] Staring at me was a photo of General Wesley Clark. *What? A military general? So this is who introduces them to the boys inside the Beltway? Looks like some big-boy hitters are involved with this company.* We had used the terms "hustler" and "oily salesman" to describe this man. Now, it appeared, he had been dancing with the stars. Scrolling down the "About Us" page, I saw Dr. Larry Ponemon, who's with a think tank. Bearing a stellar résumé, Ponemon had been recently appointed by the White House to the Department of Homeland Security. Would he be less than pleased about the machinations going on behind the scenes? Maybe or maybe not.

And then, lo and behold, another big hitter, Howard Schmidt. It appeared that Mr. Schmidt was also with Homeland Security. He worked with eBay and Microsoft, and was at the White House during the Bush administration. This guy has had a long and distinguished career in defense, law enforcement, and corporate security spanning almost 40 years; most impressive. *Holy crony. He is Obama's Cyber Security Chief!*

Obviously, these big boys on this advisory board could open doors—eBay, Microsoft, the White House, Homeland Security, the FBI, Stanford were just a few top organizations with which this Tiversa team had connections. Getting Robert Boback in front of Congress must have been as easy as calling the concierge to book lunch.

I imagined it going down something like this: "Hey, Congressman Towns, Howard Schmidt here. Yeah, wife and grandkids are fine. You? Glad to hear it. Hey there, Ed, got a favor to ask. We want to chat you guys up on data security. You'll look real pro on national defense by letting my boy in Pennsylvania clue you in on some technology threats to the country. Let's get a hearing on data security and we can show our stuff. Call in the FTC. They'll eat this up. Good. Thanks. See ya soon!"

## What You Know and Whom

As the shock drained away, reality knocked out my sense of humor. To this heavyweight team that was steeped in self-importance, I was nothing more than a speck of dandruff they flicked off before walking into the office. They can't possibly know, can they? Or is this how things always get done inside the Beltway? Do they all scratch each other's backs like they're at the country club closing deals over a round of golf? Are they deaf and dumb but wanting to be a part of the deal so they can hit it rich if Tiversa goes public?

Either way, it looks like it's all about relationships—who you know and what you know. Regardless of any of that, I was sure of one thing. Tiversa presented a different face to the House of Representatives than they did to LabMD. Boback would only provide us with specific details of how they got our file *if* we signed a contract and handed over money. While the members of that subcommittee might have believed Boback cared about the good of the country, I simmered with fury. To Tiversa, LabMD was just another sales call. While acting like Paul Revere yelling that the British are coming, it looked to me like he was simply calling his government client to sell more services. *What is in it for all the industry cronies? Who'd have thought these technology geeks would embrace crony capitalism with such fervor? Don't most of them live near San Francisco?*

Although it's easy to fool the uneducated, it's probably not so smart to confuse Congress. Based on what was happening to LabMD, it became crystal clear this House subcommittee had bought Boback's pitch, hook, line, and sinker.

*"Always eyes watching you and the voice enveloping you.
Asleep or awake, indoors or out of doors,
in the bath or bed—no escape.
Nothing was your own except the few cubic
centimeters in your skull."*

—GEORGE ORWELL, *1984*

# CHAPTER 10
# Big Brother is NOT Family

## August 2010

Two years of scrounging around in the dark came to a screeching halt within one hour. The lights were getting so bright so fast, my eyes could barely adjust. Congressional testimony, finding our file published in the Congressional Record, big shots on the Tiversa board deeply involved in the White House, the Pentagon, Congress, and then the FTC running at us and threatening reputation assassination? It made my head spin with sensory overload. And after what I've been through so far, I believed every word that was burning my eyes.

I reminded myself: We are a small medical laboratory diagnosing cancer and disease. We are a small business. After our last tour of the nation's capital, I knew these FTC empty suits with attitude were dead serious. I recalled my father's words when I was in college about lawyers. He said the first year of law school was when "first they kill your conscience then they kill your logic." As my father was a homicide detective with a load of experience, I never forgot his words. My hope for finding any conscience or logic was growing dimmer.

*What were we doing that differed from every other computer-using business and government agency? Wasn't it a rampant problem for the entire free enterprise system? Yet we were the ones with our head in the FTC's crosshairs. How do I fight these sanctimonious government-lifer lawyers?* We weren't just dealing with one vampire outside our door. It seemed like Frankenstein, the Mummy, and a few werewolves had all joined Dracula in hot pursuit and out for blood. In my head, I yelled to them, *"Boys, boys, boys, . . . calm down! There's no big treasure inside the castle. We're NOT that important. Now go back to your lair and regroup. Someone has gotten you all worked up over nothing and you're looking, well, not to be harsh, but you're all looking SO DUMB."*

Then my humor turned somber. *These people are so out of touch with reality. They have no respect for those they represent, wasting our money like this. The FTC is a dangerous animal and logic will not kill the beast.*

I snapped out of the dramatic movie playing in my mind. Except for my dogs on the floor, I was alone in my house. It was Sunday, August 15, 2010. My laptop was on my stomach as I lay on my couch. There was calm in Atlanta, my neighborhood, and my house—in stark contrast to the deafening roar blazing away in my head. Deep in thought and out of touch with my surroundings, I kept going back to my dramatic discovery. I had to reread the testimony several times to make sure it sunk in.

*Yep, no need to pinch myself; this is real. Wow. I can't believe this. I guess this has always been there in the public record, but who thinks to go checking the Congressional Record for any mention of their property?* If I had mentioned this to anyone without direct evidence in hand, they would have thought me a conspiracy theorist gone off the deep end.

I got in my car and drove to Starbucks for an infusion of obscurity. I got in line and took in the packed room of book lovers, coffee drinkers, laptop users, and various friends chatting. "Venti skinny decaf latté, please—thanks." I paid and stood waiting. *I want to know more. I want to know how these players connect to each other. I want to know how it all happened. I want to know if the FTC gives a rat's ass.*

Most important, to get anywhere, I knew it was time to dismiss any lingering patriotic belief that my government had my back. The FTC's actions had already demolished my faith in government agencies. Mission accomplished—the puzzle was starting to come together.

I picked up my latté, drove home, sat on the floor of my living room, and woke up my laptop, ready for round two of my investigation.

The ever-growing stink had started with Robert Boback, followed by Tiversa this and Tiversa that, P2P speeches, and alarm bells. I had seen variations of all this before. Besides Tiversa, I had no idea what I was looking for, so I read down the list of options: Health care. Data hemorrhages. Peer-to-Peer networks. Dartmouth. *Hmmm. What does Dartmouth have to do with this?* I clicked on a link from *Wired Magazine.* The page downloaded and opened up to this title: "Academic Claims to Find Sensitive Medical Info Exposed on Peer-to-Peer Networks."[1]

Right before my eyes I saw page one of our file, this time with the protected health information redacted out in bright red. The same one that's in the Congressional Record. I felt like a bomb had gone off. I was getting used to this feeling.

I went numb as I read the first sentence: "Academic says he found thousands of sensitive medical records leaked over peer-to-peer networks, computers in hospitals, clinics and elsewhere." This came from M. Eric Johnson, the director of the Center for Digital Strategies at Dartmouth College. *Here we go now with an arrogant academic out to save the world, like he knows so much . . . and there the readers are, getting one side of the story, just lapping it up. Disgusting. Dartmouth and Tiversa had taken our file and published it in a magazine. Who the hell is THIS guy and what's he doing with our property?*

Not only was I getting fed up and fired up, I felt duped. This piece was published in 2009 and I was just now seeing it in August of 2010. These arrogant bastards were using me as an unwitting public whipping boy. Bypassing my shock, I moved on to pure rage while trying to concentrate on what was in front of me. *You boys want to play hardball with my patient's info, huh? I have to stop being surprised by all of this.*

The first page of the article gave background information, stating his report came on the trail of news that a file containing sensitive information about the presidential helicopter was leaked from a government contractor's computer over a P2P network. Two paragraphs down, I got closer to infamy when it referred to a 1,718-page document that had been obtained from a medical testing laboratory. It included Social Security numbers, dates of birth, insurance information, and treatment codes. The article states that Johnson doesn't identify any of the "leakers." *Leakers? Did Johnson just insinuate we are "leakers"? Nice spin, sleezeball. Oh, the self-righteous are so proud of themselves.*

At the end of the discussion about LabMD, Johnson talked about an Adobe form that could be used for writing drug prescriptions. It's a digital document that includes a physician's signature and information that could be used by thieves to blackmail patients or to sell celebrity information to a tabloid. The author wrote that "it's important to note all of these files were found without extraordinary effort and certainly far less effort than criminals might be economically consented to undertake." *Oh really. Well, I guess you haven't read the US Congressional Record to learn about Tiversa's super duper unique and all powerful technology there, Superman. So which is it, boys? Hi-tech snooping technology or low-hanging fruit?*

Before I could digest Mr. Johnson's surprising opinion, he dropped another tidbit of information that further validated my suspicions. He said the study was partially funded by a grant from the Department of Homeland Security.

## Welcome to the Club

"Homeland Security?" I screamed. *All of this makes perfect sense now. Dartmouth and Johnson just joined the "club."* Eric Johnson at Dartmouth, Homeland Security, US Congress, Tiversa, the Federal Trade Commission, White House appointees, and various other self-appointed "extremely important" people. How could they not be connected? Boy oh boy, Paul Revere's poor horse must be tired with so many hitchhikers riding on its back. *This fit together like the last piece of a puzzle. Everything made sense. I didn't like what I saw, but it all fit.*

Then I clicked to the next page and, to no surprise, I saw Tiversa's name highlighted in blue, billing itself as a P2P intelligence service that helps companies and government agencies uncover the source of sensitive files leaked to P2P networks. Sarcastically, I crowed, "I wonder if Tiversa registered with the Internal Revenue Service as a charitable organization?" *Calm down, Mike ... read on.*

Mr. Johnson's detailed article explained that over a two-week term in January 2008, Tiversa collected (a.k.a. took with surveillance software) more than 3,000 files. After "winnowing out" duplicate irrelevant files, the company had pared down the data to 161 files containing sensitive information that could be used to commit medical or financial identity theft.

*Medical? They went looking for medical? How many terrorists get through medical school? Entitled bastards.*

The article concluded with scare tactics mentioned in a Tiversa 2007 visit to the US House Oversight Committee. Tiversa had reported inadvertent leaks over peer-to-peer networks and claimed to find more than 200 classified documents in just a few hours of searching. These documents allegedly included one from a contractor working in Iraq. The report detailed the radio frequency the military used to defuse improvised explosive devices. Another search uncovered sensitive but not classified information: A detailed diagram of the Pentagon's secret backbone network with server and IP addresses; password transcripts for the Pentagon's secret network servers; contact information for Department of Defense employees; certificates that allow someone to gain access to a contractor's network.

According to testimony, the Defense Department traced the latter link to someone with a top-secret security clearance who worked for a Department of Defense contractor. She had P2P software on her home computer, onto which she apparently also loaded the sensitive work files. That was the last word of the article. Game, Set, Match ... Team Paranoia.

I sat back and breathed for a minute and then sighed heavily. I looked over to my prized painting of George Washington by Steve Penley, searching for inspiration. *What will I do? This is all so sensationalistic and scary. Thank God this is in writing because nobody would believe me if it weren't. Let me get this straight, the US government is funding a private company to pursue and retain this highly classified and sensitive information? What if China shows up and makes an offer to buy Tiversa? What happens then? Is there anyone that is actually thinking over there?*

*George just stared back at me. No help there.*

I reread the article once, twice, and a third time. Not much more jumped out at me, except one brief statement I thought would slip by anyone who didn't work in medicine: an innocent comment that President Obama had allocated $19 billion to help build a nationwide health information network. This would help convert all patient medical records to a digital format by 2014. Even a common fool with a little medical experience would know that converting all patient medical records by 2014 is as possible as counting every grain of sand on the beach. *Oh yeah, that'll solve the problem. Just throw money at an issue, bark off an order, and tell them to call you when they're done. Classic!* It's like one of my favorite lines from the movie *Dangerous Liaisons*, where Glenn Close, as the countess, says, "Like most intelligent people, they are incredibly stupid."

I reread Johnson's article, *Data Hemorrhages in the Health-Care Sector,*[2] to let it sink in. Some of his admissions floored me even more.

- To collect a sample of leaked data, we initially focused on Fortune Magazine's list of the top ten publicly traded health-care firms.
- To gather relevant files, we developed a digital footprint for each health-care institution.
- With the help of Tiversa Inc., we searched P2P networks using our digital signature over a 2-week period (in January, 2008) and randomly gathered a sample of shared files related to health care and these institutions. Tiversa's servers and software allowed us to sample in the four most popular networks.
- As a second stage of our analysis, we then moved from sampling with a large net to more specific and intentional searches.

- One of the features enabled by LimeWire and other sharing clients is the ability to examine all the shared files of a particular user (sometimes called "browse host"). Over the next six months, we periodically examined hosts that appeared promising for shared files. Using this approach, we uncovered far more disturbing files. For a medical testing laboratory, we found a 1,718-page document containing patient Social Security numbers, insurance information, and treatment codes for thousands of patients. Figure 4 shows a redacted excerpt of just a single page of the insurance aging report containing patient name, Social Security number, date of birth, insurer, group number, and identification number. All together, almost 9,000 patient identities were exposed in a single file, easily downloaded from a P2P network.

Nice picture of our file you put in your academic paper there, buddy boy. This guy is talking about my company in a research paper and letting everyone know that he can see all files of a particular user. What did he mean by "user"? Did he mean workstation? And if so, does that mean they came in and looked at everything on that workstation and downloaded what they were hired by the Feds to download?

This whole thing just killed me. "Oh yeah, we went out looking for medical files, tra-la-la. I wanted to find out exactly what Mr. Johnson meant by using the words "leaked data," because by now, my understanding of P2P technology was that you still had to go into a workstation and get it. It wasn't like we fired the file out into the world for everyone to pick up. It's one thing to drive by my house and take a picture. It's another to stand outside with binoculars and look through the windows like a cyber peeping tom.

*Wow. So let me get this straight. This gets blasted all over Congress and magazines but you won't tell us how you got it unless we pay you?* I was beyond furious and frustrated, yet this may seem odd, but by late afternoon, I felt good—relieved actually. I was *finally* starting to understand *who* was attacking my company and also starting to understand *why*. I saw new puzzle pieces appear before my eyes that fit together. Logically. Finally I understood. I was on cloud nine.

I stopped my research, ending on a high note, then went to dinner with friends at Osteria 832, an amazing pizza and pasta place in the Virginia Highlands neighborhood in Atlanta. My dinner companions joked about my good mood. I had to laugh it off and keep my secret—something I hate because keeping secrets is so much work. I cracked the case. The puzzle was almost complete. Now what?

## Sharing the New Discoveries

The next morning, I felt eager to get to the office and share my discoveries with Bill. I walked into his office, copies of the articles in hand. I laid out my points, bullet after bullet. Bill was stunned. He needed time to process this information so there was practically no conversation. Deep down, I think Bill felt somehow responsible for much of this. IT functions and management within the company came under his operational umbrella. This entire situation nagged at him every bit as much as it nagged at me ... perhaps more; he was always just so stoic about it. The missing facts and data the FTC was failing to give us had frustrated him the most. People with power, but lacking knowledge, can be especially dangerous.

Bill was deeply and morally offended that the FTC was conducting this witch hunt and thus diverting our attention away from running a cancer detection facility. He had yet to join me in the subsequent realization that explaining this to the Feds was going to get us nowhere.

I left Bill alone to give him the space he needed, then I called Evelyn from my office.

"Hello, Mahesha. It's Mike Daugherty. Is Evelyn in?"

"No, she's in conference preparing for mediation. She won't be around the next few days."

"Oh. That's too bad. Okay, I'll e-mail her."

I knew when Evelyn was prepping for trial or in mediation she went into radio silence. I understood. At the same time, I couldn't wait to talk to her about this game-changing information. She replied to my first e-mail Sunday afternoon, but not after that. However, just as I had forgiven her absence, the phone rang. Evelyn.

"Hey, I'm so glad you called," I said.

"Yeah, Mike, I'm about to become MIA. I'm getting ready for another client event this week, but I read your stuff. Wow. I really *don't* understand the FTC guys now. They've got to know this is happening, so I don't understand why they're still pursuing us."

"I know. It's fantastic and shocking all at the same time. Can the FTC hold us accountable and responsible when we can show them we're the *victims?*"

"Well, I hate to break it to you," Evelyn answered, "but while all this new info connects the dots for us, I don't believe it will move the FTC. It's probably not news to them. It doesn't take a rocket scientist to figure out the FTC got our file from Tiversa. It doesn't change anything regarding what we had to submit to them. We still have to move forward with gathering the information they requested and summarizing what our policies were by what we're memorializing now in writing. I'm sorry, Mike. I know you don't want to hear this, but I don't see how this will get us off the hook."

"Look, dammit. We haven't done anything wrong. There's got to be a way out of this." She no doubt heard the frustration in my voice.

"Well, we don't know what they'll do when we make this next submission," she replied. "It will show them the lab's data security practices were tight. It's a frustrating process. I think you should find a lawyer who has more experience in this than I do. Right now, all I know is to comply with their requests and see what move they make. We're not yet ready to rock the boat."

"I hear you, Evelyn. I'm just tired of this lumbering giant casting his long, overbearing shadow over us. These guys are so lethargic and robotic and emotionless and slow, slow, slow. All right, I'll let you get back to your mediation prep. Thanks for the call. Bye."

"Hang in there, Mike. Bye."

If I still hadn't cracked the safe that only meant I had more digging to do. I understood Evelyn's legal logic, but I did not care what everyone said. Yet it was becoming ever clearer that we couldn't solve this with only the cards we held in our hands—a deflating thought that came too quickly.

I was so relieved to have this valuable information that I mistook it for a win. My lawyer pulled me back to reality. We may have won a game in this set, but the match was far from over. Still, my "never ever never ever quit" character kept kicking in. I tried to concentrate on something else. That something else worked until the middle of the afternoon when the ghost of the FTC popped into my mind. I went back and hit Google. I simmered all afternoon. *There's got to be somebody, somewhere, somehow who has actually dealt with these bastards and won.* I returned to Google.

Every time I put in "fight FTC" or "fight with the FTC" or "defeat FTC" or anything like that, it kept showing how the FTC came out on top one way or the other. Then, I entered something like "FTC data security consent decree." A new link popped up, buried pages deep in the Google listing, referencing a man named Ben Wright who wrote a blog entry with the headline "FTC treats TJX Unfairly." When I clicked on the link, I knew I'd found another soul who thought the FTC was full of crap.

Another ray of light came shining down into our pit.

*"Whatever you do in life, surround yourself with smart people who'll argue with you."*

—John Wooden

# CHAPTER 11
# Finding Mr. Wright

## August 18, 2010

Ben Wright's blog[1] was the only Internet site I could find that criticized the FTC's data security enforcement behavior. While looking for a needle in an online haystack, I stumbled on his commentary from the spring of 2008, which argued that the FTC unfairly treated TJX, the parent company which owns T.J. Maxx, Marshall's, and other off-price retailers. Watching the huge shadow of the US federal government spread, this article was my first sip of water since being abandoned in the desert.

According to Ben, the FTC alleged that TJX engaged in "unfair" practices in violation of Section 5. The unfairness, as stated by the FTC, was that TJX collected private credit card information from consumers, but failed to use adequate security procedures to protect that information. Here's what happened:

On January 17, 2007, TJX announced it had fallen victim to an unauthorized computer systems intrusion. In mid-December 2006, TJX discovered its computer systems were compromised and customer data had been stolen. The hackers accessed a system that stores data on credit card, debit card, check, and returned merchandise transactions. The intrusion was kept confidential, as requested by law enforcement. TJX said it was working with General Dynamics, IBM, and Deloitte to upgrade computer security. By the end of March 2007, the number of affected customers had reached 45.7 million and has since prompted credit bureaus to seek legislation requiring retailers to be responsible for compromised customer information saved in their systems.[2]

As Ben Wright went on to opine, "By declaring TJX was unfair, the FTC implied TJX had been bad." So the FTC found the TJX incident to be much more than unfortunate or embarrassing for

TJX and resulted in its punishable culpability. It's important to note that the FTC did not allege that TJX engaged in a "deceptive" trade practice violating Section 5. An example of "deception," according to the FTC, is when an enterprise tells individuals it will secure their data and then fails to do so. Instead, the FTC essentially said TJX was "unfair" because it was not "secure enough." Not "secure enough" to defeat the sophisticated criminal organization that achieved the break-in. The FTC said the remedy for this "unfairness" was that TJX should implement security controls, more or less like the payment card industry data security standard; however, that standard itself was questionable, shaky at best. The implication: If a merchant follows the payment card industry data security standard, then it has achieved "fairness." The FTC said TJX was unfair because it couldn't keep up with the hackers. But by that standard, according to Mr. Wright, "Is not the entire credit card system unfair? TJX wasn't unfair. It was unlucky."

*Oh my God! Out of the wilderness comes the voice of reason. Who is this guy?* Well, it turns out Benjamin Wright was an attorney, author, and LabMD's potential knight in shining armor. His Web site bio stated he's the author of several technology law, business, and computer security books published by the SANS Institute, the premiere educator for IT professionals. With 25 years in private law practice, he has advised many organizations, large and small, private and public, on privacy, computer security, records management, and e-discovery. He has been quoted in publications from *The Wall Street Journal* to *The Sydney Morning Herald*. He teaches the law of data security and investigations at the SANS Institute and maintains popular blogs accessible at benjaminwright.us.

I whacked my knee on the corner of the table running to get my cell phone. I didn't even notice the pain as I dialed Ben. His phone rang about five times.

"Hello?"

"Is this Ben Wright?"

"Speaking."

"Mr. Wright. Hi. This is Mike Daugherty. I'm the President and CEO of a medical laboratory in Atlanta, Georgia, called LabMD. I was looking at your blog and got excited to see what you're saying about the FTC. I need to talk about it. The first concern I need to address with you is that you, as a lawyer, have no conflicts, because I'm working *against* the FTC."

"Oh, I can clearly say I have no conflicts regarding working against the Federal Trade Commission."

Such a wonderful ironic tone . . . a kindred spirit. "Have you ever represented a company called Tiversa or Dartmouth University?"

"Not that I can recall, no. What's going on?"

"Well, let me boil this down for you. Feel free to jump in if I stray or become confusing. I founded my company in 1996. We have forty employees and we test any type of specimen that comes out of the urologist's office—prostate tissue, blood, urine, kidney stones, and so on. In 2008, our phone rang and a man named Robert Boback said he was the president of a data security company in Pennsylvania named Tiversa. He told me someone there had downloaded a confidential file of ours off a P2P network. He tried to get us to hire him on several occasions over the next few months and we resisted. But he wouldn't give any information about the circumstances surrounding how he obtained our file. About a year later, we got a phone call from Boback's lawyer saying that his client, Mr. Boback and Tiversa, was giving the file to the Federal Trade Commission. Lo and behold, last January, the Federal Trade Commission called us and has been investigating us ever since." I didn't say it, but I thought it might be time to join forces with Ben.

"And let me guess. The Federal Trade Commission wants you to sign a consent decree basically admitting your security standards aren't up to snuff."

*Oh my God, this guy already gets it. Mike . . . don't sound too excited or you'll come across like a nutcase.*

I said, "Well, that seems to be where they're going, but they move like molasses in winter. If it comes to that, I won't sign anything.

However, the FTC isn't going away. As a matter fact, their people are driving us crazy because they're just—I don't know—persistent. We've been totally transparent, we've sent them boxes and binders and CDs full of information. We don't believe it's ever been examined properly. They keep saying we didn't give them enough or it's not the right stuff. In effect, they're side-slamming my company.

"And you won't believe what I just found out this weekend; I am *not* making this up. Boback and Tiversa somehow got *in front of Congress* discussing P2P network security and how organizations are behind the times in securing themselves, including the FTC. Then Boback published our file during the hearing and it ended up in the Congressional Record. I mean our file is in the *Congressional Record!*"

"Wow. This I have to see."

"And it gets worse. I found out that Dartmouth University has been working with Tiversa performing a study which was partially underwritten by the Department of Homeland Security. That study is how Dartmouth got the file. I just recently learned all of this, even though it's been going on for two years. The FTC isn't saying *anything* to me. Its silent stare makes me feel like I'm being chastised by my upset grandmother.

"I don't mean to ramble, but I read your blog about TJX. I want to know what you think about this so far and see if you can help us out." I paused to hear what Ben had to say.

"Wow. Let's take a breather here. As far as taking the case and going up against the FTC, I haven't handled this type of legal activity before, but I do believe the FTC reps are wrong in what they're doing. This is amazing stuff; it sounds like a movie. I think the FTC is way off base using these methods. It can't stop data loss by running around chasing companies and firing off consent decrees."

"What is the focus of your legal practice? Are you admitted into the DC bar?"

"I'm not a member of the DC bar. I'm only admitted to the Texas bar. However, I can certainly help your team. And I have a lot of specific knowledge of this. I'm the legal instructor at the SANS Institute, and as you read, I'm quite up to date on this topic. I feel strongly that the FTC's tactics are absolutely wrong regardless of whether they think they're right or not."

"That's music to my ears, Ben. What is SANS?"

"SANS is well-known in the information technology community and stands for SysAdmin, Audit, Network and Security," he explained. "It's the leading organization that participates in information security training and security certification. It develops research documents on various aspects of information security and it operates the Internet Storm Center, which is the Internet's early warning system. Basically, SANS is the 'go to' organization for Internet training and security."

"Well, what do you think about what I've told you so far?" I leaned into the phone for his answer.

"Of course, I have to look into it further, and I need to get more information. But none of this surprises me."

For the first time over the past two long years of doubt and confusion, I felt I'd found someone who understood both the law and how cybersecurity worked.

"Ben, this is such a relief. You're the first lawyer I've spoken to who doesn't feel chained to Section 5 or stop at 'the file got out, you're toast, write the checks, sign the decree, and best of luck.' None of them have sufficient knowledge of cybersecurity to be credible in arguing anything technical. I feel like I'm being placated as the stubborn client who won't accept his fate."

Ben responded. "Guilt isn't the issue for many of these data security lawyers. The universal chorus coming from these lawyers is that, 'in the real world, unless you really want to take on this huge agency, the FTC can do whatever it wants.' Due to their sheer size and resources, most people don't fight back. When and if you fight the FTC, you'd better be prepared to lose a leg. So you need to ask yourself, 'am I better off fighting them and maybe losing, or am I better off rolling over and withdrawing from this battle?'

"'I think you're better off getting it behind you so you can get back to focusing on your business' is the DC lawyer speak."

As I talked to Ben Wright—a lawyer who totally gets IT issues—I realized he had the necessary information and technology education to argue these points with credibility. I felt a twinge of disappointment that he didn't handle cases before the FTC. "Nevertheless," I continued, "you're the only lawyer I've spoken to who comprehends the legal and technical side of this, so I can't let you get away from me. I need you to speak to my outside counsel and my VP of operations. This is a big deal. Can we get you to Atlanta soon?"

"Yes, I can be there. What did you have in mind?"

"Well, I think you need to look at our computer security system. It's easier to have your brain and eyeballs here with us so we can all go through it together. I'll check with Bill and Evelyn about their schedules, but I'd like to get you to Atlanta—as soon as possible. Can you please e-mail me your schedule and rates?"

"Yes, I'd be happy to."

Things were beginning to look promising.

I immediately called Evelyn and reached her voicemail. I told her what had happened and that I needed her availability for the next week. Then I called Bill and asked for the same thing. *Finally, an educated lawyer who understood technology and didn't think I was rolling a giant boulder uphill.* I drove home feeling optimistic again, although still a bit cautious. Another good night's sleep followed.

The next day was the usual routine: up early, gym, coffee, shower, get the dogs ready. (about three days a week the dogs come with me to the office; needless to say, they don't go near the laboratory.)

I walked into the office and immediately told Bill about the conversation. "Okay . . . ," he said cautiously.

"Bill, this guy sounds great. I think we'll get our first mesh of law and the real world of technology here."

"I hope so, Mike. I really do. I just haven't met him yet." I understood Bill's skepticism. A reserved and analytical type, he wouldn't get fired up until he'd spent time with Ben himself.

Evelyn e-mailed me about talking the next day, so we set a time. Still looming over us was an end-of-August deadline for the FTC. The best thing I could do was to stay out of the way. Bill, with his proclivity for detective work, would gather the hard evidence. Then I could spend my time proactively searching for out-of-the-box solutions to save the company from unwarranted embarrassment, bad press, and whatever might follow.

## Lawyer Games

Coincidentally, that afternoon I received a letter from a DC attorney I'd previously contacted about joining our legal team. The first thing that struck me in his correspondence was the words "consulting agreement" rather than "engagement letter." Another hot tip: When you hire a lawyer to consult, that is less involved than to be engaged. If there is a future problem, the lawyer will try to get off the hook by saying they were just "consulting." I was still in the first paragraph and this guy had already lost credibility. I had no time for lawyer semantic games. You're either in, or you're out.

In paragraph four, line three, he called our "incident" a release to a third party of "certain types of personal information." *Okay. Mr. Leapfrog-straight-over-the-alleged-issue-with-a-cute-label. Sounds as if he thinks we did something by accident.* Then I looked at the last page and saw a release of liability. I stopped reading, shoved it in the file, where, as far as I was concerned, it could stay unsigned for years to come. Because Evelyn and I were scheduled to speak the next day, I didn't pressure myself. *I'll find a good lawyer later. Right now this is too arduous a process.*

Several aspects of the lawyerly point of view represented by this letter amused me. Number one, lawyers all seemed to be saying the same thing: "The FTC is tough, your file somehow got out, you're cooked, yada yada yada." This classic lawyer faux concern was hiding their real intent, which was to lay down the tracks covering their tails, lower expectations, and not get emotionally invested—probably what they learned to say in their legal malpractice insurance classes.

Number two, a favorite line out of the mysterious "How to Handle Clients" handbook is this: "It's just best to get this over with and put it all behind you." Tell me: How can I get *anything* behind me if I have to sign an FTC agreement to be audited for the next two decades? Twenty years of hanging out with the FTC was hardly putting anything "behind me." Allowing the FTC to come in and audit us—especially given how those people treated us with their silence, contempt, and belief they rule the world—well, you can forget that option. It sounded like community service, if not a prison sentence. It sounded about as invasive as a patient on the table with Dr. Bounds.

Then imagine this: Suppose the FTC hires a third-party company that becomes yet another villain who overcharges and exploits our anxieties. A whole new Pandora's Box of hopelessness would open. Plus with this kind of access, the FTC would then have the right to sanction and fine us.

Additionally, I'd have to deal with the damaging innuendo. To sell the company or get a loan would require me to acknowledge and discuss the decree. Really, why would anyone want to buy, invest in, or loan money to my company once they hear that the FTC rolls in like a hurricane every 12-24 months? Any lawyer who calls a 20-year consent decree a "light slap on the wrist" is someone who sleeps like a baby while his innocent clients languish in prison. Not interested. Facing that outcome, I'd close the corporation. However, without my signing that decree, the FTC simply doesn't have the power. *I will take my battle all up front, please.*

Finally, number three, the most important point: We didn't do anything wrong; no crime was committed, there is no proof that the file is anywhere but at Tiversa, Dartmouth, Congress and the FTC. I believed this now more than ever. Regarding the lawyers (possibly with the exception of Ben Wright), I felt they would bide their time and wait for the storm to pass, all the while thinking, "*Sure,* you didn't do it. That really is irrelevant when dealing with a government agency." Why would I pay boatloads of cash to lawyers who call their lack of engagement "being objective" and justify their lack of empathy as "critical to maintaining that objectivity?"

Right out of the gate, all of the lawyers I spoke to leap-frogged over my point that we'd done nothing wrong. Regardless if their shingle said "data security practice," it seemed they didn't understand nearly enough about IT or cybersecurity. Add to that most lawyers I know think getting to the truth isn't what's actually happening in a courtroom. They have a point; they want to figure out what the worst-case scenario is they have to argue, but they're simply not concerned with *my* truth.

With each lawyer I spoke to, my exasperation got deeper and the mountain in front of me got higher. As if the FTC weren't bad enough, I was fit to be tied dealing with these "say anything, spin everything" attorneys.

*"Learn from yesterday, live for today, hope for tomorrow. The important thing is not to stop questioning."*

—ALBERT EINSTEIN

# CHAPTER 12
# Patience, Perseverance, and Hope

### August 20, 2010

Evelyn called me late in the morning, her mind focused on the upcoming status report. We had about a week and a half before we needed to have everything to the FTC.

"Evelyn, I may have a possible game changer here."

I recounted the entire conversation with Ben Wright. I didn't ask Evelyn, but rather told her: "I'll be flying him in next week and would like you to attend for a half-day afternoon session. The plan is to pick him up and take him to dinner. The next morning, Bill will download all the technical information for him. His brain will be full of information from a thorough overview. After that, we'll have a conference meeting and Ben will share his observations, insights, and suggestions."

"Okay, I'm available August 25th."

Like Bill, she didn't sound nearly as excited as I was. Evelyn can be a tough read.

I couldn't wait for Ben to get to Atlanta. Evelyn had always been the first to acknowledge she didn't have enough expertise in this area—a sign she was a good lawyer. I also thought she couldn't wait to get away from the FTC. How I envied she had that option. I needed a break.

On Friday, August 21st, my dad was turning 81, so I hopped a flight to Detroit and soaked up the relaxation that seeped into my body as the Delta jet climbed up and away from Atlanta. Nothing was better for my mental state than an idyllic Michigan summer, with late setting suns, warm days, and cool nights. I was happy I couldn't discuss this case with anyone in my family, even though I knew they wanted to hear about my life.

My father, a retired Detroit homicide detective, was suffering from prostate cancer, so I didn't need to load him up with anything else to worry about. My mother, also a former Detroit police officer and school teacher, would have worried and wanted to know more. If they knew this situation, their questions would cause me to lose my patience and frustrate me. Then they'd hover with pained looks on their faces like parents watching from the stands as their kid played a close tennis match.

I arrived at Detroit Metro Airport feeling 21 again. My family peppered me with questions: "How's it going; how's the business; how are the dogs?" I small-talked until I could finally crawl into bed. The next morning, I slept in until 9:30 or 10:00 and then went over to see my sister, brother-in-law, niece, and nephew, who lived only a mile away. But most of the time I did what I needed to do—absolutely nothing. No plans, no goals, no pressure. I loved celebrating my dad's birthday, not only because he'd made it to his 81st year, but because all the attention was on him. What a welcome change of pace.

As we sat around the dining room table, my eyes scanned past everyone in the room. Feeling like an outside observer, I realized I was holding myself back because I was clutching a big secret, which was not my nature. I needed to slip away and visit my safe haven and foundation— University of Michigan in Ann Arbor.

I had learned how to think at Michigan. Nothing outside of my family has impacted me more than my time at U of M. When I visit campus, it seems no time has passed. Most of the buildings and trees are still there. When I walk through the campus, I mentally go back to an innocent time when my life loomed large in front of me and everything was possible. I remember being the only person in my freshman composition class who didn't raise a hand when asked who had been a valedictorian or salutatorian. Suffice it to say, the other students kicked my ass academically that first year. But from that experience, I learned two brutal lessons: 1) I had to study, and 2) I wasn't special. That hurt. I didn't want to go back after my first term.

My mother did the best thing she could have ever done for me. As I was packing my clothes the Sunday night of Thanksgiving weekend, I told her I didn't want to return to Ann Arbor. Expecting a torrent of empathy, instead she said brusquely, "Too bad. You are going to get a college education and you are going back to Michigan. Work harder." Here I was, looking for an ounce of sympathy and I got a pound of intensity. She forced me to shut up, suck it up, and deal with it.

Academics didn't come easy for me, and especially not in the intensely academic competitive environment of Ann Arbor. I simply didn't know how to study. I had to hyper-organize myself, reach out to professors, and live in the library. I listened to classical music while I studied. The music kept me in the chair for more than 30 minutes. By settling into this, I discovered entire new worlds of people, thoughts, and ideas. Ann Arbor has become my touchstone— the place where I earned a sense of achievement and where I return for grounding and perspective.

The morning after Dad's birthday party, I told my family I was meeting a friend for breakfast. Instead, I parked in central campus and walked around. As I sat in the grass behind Mason Hall, the campus reminded me that a worthwhile endeavor isn't easy and I am part of a greater community. I have to give back by returning the opportunities afforded me and standing up. This government behemoth can't quash those less powerful or fortunate.

No matter what comes of this moral injustice perpetrated by these government and private industry rogues, I knew I could always come back here, heal my wounds, count the scars, and start over. More important, Congress, cybersecurity, the FTC, and this Goliath of the Federal Government have given me an opportunity to fight. With the support I had around me, it was important not to break in two but to stand up and challenge the process. I could do it. I had the money. I had the means. In my mind, I had no other choice. In fact, the manner in which the FTC was walking all over me made me pity those who didn't have my resources or determination.

As I sat on the grass feeling recharged, rejuvenated, and refocused, I decided I'd drag this out to see what the future held. Embracing the struggle as the thrill of the unknown, I was ready to see this adventure to the end.

## Mr. Wright's Arrival

Back in Atlanta, my mental break continued until Ben Wright's arrival from Dallas the evening of Tuesday, August 24th. In the meantime, Bill and Evelyn were doing the final gathering of documents to submit to the FTC—due in exactly one week. As I drove through downtown Atlanta en route to Hartsfield-Jackson International Airport to pick up Ben, I tried to put out of my mind how much money the company was spending on this governmental game of dodge ball. It only strengthened my resolve. I was so ready to greet the stranger I hoped would show us the way out of this mess. *No pressure, Ben!*

On our first phone meeting, Ben had come across as likeable and smart. When I picked him up, it felt as if we'd known each other for years. Because he was one of only six people on the planet who knew about what was going on (other than the US government and Tiversa, of course), we easily fell into conversation. I found him quick, intelligent, and refreshingly well-versed on the topic. No need to explain the FTC or Section 5 to Ben.

We chatted on our way to the beautiful restaurant Canoe, which sits on the Chattahoochee River in the Vinings area of Atlanta. Over salad, I chatted about LabMD. "You know we're a small company. That's the way I planned it. I didn't want lawyers, bankers, investors, or tons of middle managers running around. I just wanted it to be a quality place that has a rock solid base of business. Some people hear our name and think WebMD, but unlike that company with its many employees, we have only forty."

"It's a fascinating business you're in, Mike. How did you start your company?"

"Well, I had always worked as a technical sales rep in the surgical arena at Mentor Corporation, so I got to know the surgeons well. I learned surgery through training and osmosis. After being with the same company for almost fourteen years, I sensed it was time to go. My last three years there, from '95 to '98, were terrible. Those on the management team showed more interest in politics and looking good than executing their work. Before long, they outnumbered me. It was time to go, even though I didn't want to.

"A friend of mine kept poking me in the arm telling me, 'It's not *your* company.' His words sunk in. I resolved not to build my house on someone else's property ever again. So I changed the services I offered. The surgeons gave me access to their needs and I responded with a product and service mix that filled a niche. LabMD took off. I still can't believe I employ forty people, Sometimes I think we should be at least twice that size by now. This whole ordeal has side-tracked growing the business."

"What about you, Ben? I read on your bio that you went to Georgetown University."

"I'm a native Texan and went back home after Georgetown. I was interested in computers early in my career. In the late 1980s, I started writing books about technology law and electronic commerce law. In the 1990s, I wrote about transactions over the Internet. In the 2000s, I started working in security law and found a niche. Security became a big deal in the early 2000s. As this was happening, I was aware of SANS and told this association we should do a book and a course on computer security law. I have blogged a lot about it ever since. I guess that's how you found me," he said with a smile.

I smiled back broadly, my eyebrows raised. I said excitedly, "Exactly! And isn't it *amazing* that five days ago I had no idea you were on the planet. Now here you are. Isn't that incredible?"

"Yes, the Internet has flattened the world. Mike, you have a lot of enthusiasm about this. So many companies I've worked with don't have your attitude. You have a different personality than the typical corporate type. Most corporations don't take on the FTC; they just roll over, making it a business decision. That's what strikes me as different about you and this situation. I look forward to seeing the lab in the morning. This will be very interesting."

I loved Ben's insight and intensity. He knew his stuff *and* the law. Meeting this lawyer who was engaged, passionate, and knowledgeable about IT filled me with hope.

"I'm excited you're here, too. Tomorrow morning, you'll start with a tour of the company to get a feel for who we are and how we operate. The blood and tissue will be in by eight-thirty, so you can see the operation from the beginning. Then the rest of the morning, you'll be with Bill, my VP of Operations and General Manager. He'll have you reviewing the specifics of our IT department—taking a deep dive into what we have, what we do, and what we've shown the FTC. Please do *not* sugarcoat anything. We believe we met *all* the operation customs in the industry at the time. However, if what we have is crap, I expect you to tell us so. We believe we have done *nothing* wrong, but I need an expert to review things and be honest with me about where we stand.

"These damn FTC lawyers we're dealing with could not be less interested in what effect they're having on LabMD. They refuse to let us know what the hell is going on. I'm at my wit's end. The Beltway lawyers I have interviewed to defend us are worse. All I have to say is "FTC," and their ears shut as their mouths open and say, 'Roll over. Truth is irrelevant.' Evelyn, our outside counsel, will join us after lunch." After I took a swig of my water, I continued. "Evelyn has provided me with rock solid legal counsel for years, but she feels like we need someone with more experience in this area than she brings. I don't blame her, but I trust her. I don't trust many lawyers, so I'm afraid to let her go. Again, pull no punches. If you see we're sunk, we're sunk. If not, then we'll discuss how to hit back."

"I look forward to tomorrow, Mike," Ben said calmly.

"So do I, Ben."

I paid the check, got the car, and dropped Ben off at the Marriott, wishing him a good night's rest. I drove home with a glimmer of hope. But hopeful or not, my conviction never wavered. I wouldn't give these dogs a single bone before I got to the bottom of this.

## Prepping for Battle

We'd made arrangements for Ben to meet Bill in the morning and receive a full explanation of our IT system, together with a blow-by-blow account of our experience with Tiversa. Once I arrived in the office, I had no reason to press my ear against the door or breathe over their shoulders as they were doing their review. We'd debrief at lunch and then Evelyn would join us to dive into Ben's findings.

To avoid wasting time, I had food brought in. I planned to suck Ben's brain dry and make this day a bargain. Every dollar I spent and every moment of productivity and focus on patient care this torture took from LabMD increased my resolve and determination. In fact, I saw this meeting as prepping for battle before we went to war.

Bill and Ben met me in our conference room with its 20-foot-long black granite conference table and matching black leather chairs. Ben exclaimed, "Wow, this is nice." His comment prompted me to confess that we'd bought it on Craigslist for $1,700 from a law firm on the brink.

After my bragging about my thrifty buying skills, I dove in, "Okay Ben, your turn. What are your impressions?"

"Well, I have to say, this is unlike anything I've seen before. Your laboratory is impressive. Your experience with Tiversa is very unusual.

"Regarding your IT security practices, I also don't see anything out of industry norms for 2006 to 2008. As a matter of fact, I'll probably shock you by saying I don't even think there's proof that LabMD has suffered a patient data security breach. The fact that the file 'got out,' as they like to say, isn't proof of a breach. Tiversa states it has unique abilities. Tiversa's people admit, even boast, that their software is potentially stronger than Google. So this event that has occurred is not a typical compromise of patient or consumer data security.

"The information we have is incomplete. However, the only credible information we have about the patient file being someplace where it is not supposed to be is that it is in the hands of Tiversa, Dartmouth, and the US government. In their hands, you can bet it's safe, not out of control, and under lock and key. That is not a breach."

This was too big a statement to take in quickly. What an incredible statement coming from an expert in law and technology—someone who had no skin in this game, less than 24 hours on the scene. That's what astounded me. I'd been so desensitized by Section 5's definitions of "reasonable" and "unfair" that I didn't know how to react to Ben's 180-degree turn. "There was no breach? Was this even going to matter?" *It seems so outlandish to the uneducated ear. Because I considered the FTC an uneducated ear, I imagined the FTC, and I found myself smirking.*

Ben continued, "The most important point is, though, that the FTC is trying to hold LabMD to a standard of data protection perfection (though FTC alleges its standard is reasonableness). The FTC should not hold any company to a standard of perfection. Perfection isn't a standard. It isn't even possible. A standard of perfection is irrational in law, just as it is in medicine and IT. The concept of 'reasonableness,' which the FTC likes to argue, is off base and won't get them where they want to go.

"Furthermore, a standard of perfection fails to give companies like LabMD incentive to strive for good security.

"The FTC doesn't understand what it is doing. If it really wants to tighten up the Internet for consumers, punishing LabMD is *not* the way to do it. Quite frankly, going after LabMD and not Tiversa, the *real* culprit here, is an outrage. *You* are the *victim.*"

I was curious how our rational, reserved, austere Evelyn would react to this point of view. And how would these two lawyers mix? She and Ben constituted a study in contrast. Evelyn is six feet tall and dresses like a fashion model. She is a fighter, a trial lawyer, and knows too well that injustice is just part of the risk, but she is not a technology or FTC expert. Ben is about five-ten and slender at about 160 pounds—open and passionate. As a private company, we enjoyed the luxury of focusing on execution even if it took time. He knows technology and the law, but he is not a litigator with Evelyn's experience in front of a jury.

"Well," I said to Ben, "have you ever tried to get statues to smile? I have low expectations of the FTC. Evelyn will be here any minute. You'll have to 'hit' her with this more than once. It's not about logic; it's about the law. Section Five is like a huge net that allows these professional bullies to pull in as many fish as they can handle. How will your opinion get us out of their net? That's the challenge."

"I'm not afraid of the FTC," Ben said bluntly.

I *loved* that he said that. He was the first person I'd met who wasn't afraid of the FTC.

When Evelyn and Ben met, I chose to play mediator while mostly preparing myself to change Evelyn's point-of-view. This would be a challenge for me because my nature is to make a decision and take control early. Here, I had to lay back and let the intellectual debate expand. What a juicy day this was so far. If I wasn't so pissed off at the financial and opportunity cost this was exacting, I might have even called it fun.

We ate our lunch, waiting for Evelyn so we could continue the discussion. My cell phone rang, announcing Evelyn's arrival.

## Did He Really Say That?

After a few formalities, the three of us sat down and Ben started his summary.

"I see nothing amiss in this company's procedures," he said. "You have nothing to be ashamed of. LabMD has taken steps in line with everyone else's across all industries during the time in question. P2P vulnerabilities have caught governments and businesses off guard. There is no such thing as perfect security, no matter what. Your policies and procedures are right in line with everyone else's. The FTC guys are living in a fantasy world. They can't get what they want the way they're going about it."

Evelyn hit back with the Devil's position. "The pit of quicksand about Section Five is that Congress has laid out the law so the FTC gets broad powers and an elastic definition of the word 'reasonable.' To date, the FTC guys aren't even saying what they consider to be 'reasonable.' They're just asking questions," she declared with uncompromising candor.

I jumped in and added, "However, after our trip to DC, we got loud and clear that these 'questions' aren't exactly forthright. We answer them and they ask the same thing again. They're toying with us.

"So, in taking Section Five at face value," I continued, "I don't see how we can create an argument until we're told exactly what they'll do—and why. Alain and Ruth still appear to be moving forward toward a consent decree, but we can't be sure. Why they didn't dump it on the table last month, I don't know. The more we encounter the FTC, the more mysterious their actions are. We've been nothing but cooperative, while they've been nothing but perplexing, contradictory, and slow. However, they have a lot of power, and playing along to get rid of them seems like the smarter first move."

"And that's ridiculous and unfair," Ben interrupted. I liked his passion. "There was *no* breach of patient data security. We have no credible information that the file has ever been unsafe."

*Oh Lord, he didn't just say that so early, did he? Yep, he said it! How will Evelyn take that?*

I wasn't sure if Ben was playing the role of great defense attorney or if he really meant it. Not many lawyers lead with their personal opinions. Plus this was so far off what anyone else had said, I was unsure it would fly. That being said, I was ready to argue it until the cows came home.

I looked over at Evelyn for a pulse.

"Really? How can you say that?" She remained composed and skeptical.

Then I jumped in, also playing the Devil, with "Yeah . . . really? Why? How so?" I wanted to test the firmness of Ben's opinion.

Ben continued. "Looks to me like Tiversa took the file with its super-powerful technology that's not available to other people, as Tiversa said in congressional testimony. Then, after Tiversa used this technology to snatch the file, they kept the file safe and secure, as did the US Government and Dartmouth University. When a file containing patient data comes into the hands of security people who are cooperating with government, no patient data security breach has occurred.

"From the evidence we have, there was no breach. Honestly. I am dead serious here. LabMD was the *victim* here. LabMD was not the wrong-doer."

*She'll never buy this!*

But given the recipient of the news was the master of calm and objectivity, no change in Evelyn's pulse occurred. She listened and observed like a great judge. If I could get her to believe that there had been no breach and why, we had a shot at her "getting it" and laying the ground game for seeing Section 5 as a gaping congressional black hole that sucks in the innocent. She would be better equipped to build the ground game to fight back the Devil.

"LabMD did not give Tiversa permission to do anything. Tiversa did not have authority or permission to look for, take, or interrogate the file. Cyberspace is not a geographic place. To be "in cyberspace" is an unclear and controversial abstraction. But what is clear is that the file was LabMD's property, and Tiversa knew that it was LabMD's property.

"Tiversa intentionally set out to find sensitive property that did not belong to Tiversa. Tiversa's used the property to advance Tiversa's interests to the detriment of LabMD. We aren't sure how the file was retrieved at this point. Tiversa knows. Tiversa and Dartmouth have the answers. If these guys were on an academic study, then there should be protocols in place. There should be controls."

Ben continued. "If the FTC guys want to argue that LabMD had unreasonable security, they'll have one tough argument. The likelihood that the patients were ever at risk of harm is very, very low. The FTC is aiming for perfection, but won't admit it. There are no damages to patients here.

Although the FTC's people are are well-intentioned, they do not understand the topic. They have not carefully studied the application of Section 5's reasonableness requirement to data security. Not only is the FTC misguided, but what the FTC's trying to do won't solve the problem its trying to solve.

"Let me get this straight," I said. "Tiversa used its software to find and take the file. They won't tell us about the circumstances because we won't hire them, and then ..."

"They're putting on a 'good guy face' for the US Congress," interrupted Ben. But they *aren't* looking like good guys to me."

"The fact that you're confirming what I've been thinking from the beginning is surreal to me," I replied. "Until now I felt totally alone, but my instincts would not let me surrender."

I always felt Evelyn didn't take me seriously when I went "there" with my conspiracy theories. Perhaps she did, but didn't see the relevance. I hardly believed it myself, so I never held this against her. But because Ben's point wasn't sinking in, I had to hear it from him more than once. Without hard proof, I would be dismissed as paranoid, over-reactive, or just plain nuts. Finally, I had that proof in writing and Ben was making it a reality.

I harbored no hope of the FTC ever admitting being wrong or that LabMD was actually the victim here. The FTC guys believe they're doing the Lord's work, but somehow I'd lost the lottery and become their target: *Let's make an example of these saps at LabMD so everyone else will straighten up.* This had to be one of their favorite tricks. As a result of their contemptible view of American business, they stretched the law, justifying their behavior and congratulating themselves in their attempt to save the world.

Then I reminded myself I'd only met Ben the night before. Was he being sincere or acting like a "say anything" defense lawyer to sell us something? I needed to test him, especially because others would be doing the same. The truth didn't matter to the FTC. We wanted to make them go away.

*Is this the truth? Would this convince the US government?*

I probed further, challenging Ben by saying, "Okay, Ben. Who will believe Tiversa took our file and then turned it in to Congress? We don't want to look like fools—and we certainly don't want to piss off either the FTC or the well-placed kingpins connected to Tiversa."

"Why not? I'm not afraid of the FTC," Ben answered firmly.

"Really? Seriously? Look at them! The FTC is at the 2007 Congressional hearing with Dartmouth, Wesley Clark, and Tiversa's CEO Bob Boback. *They were all at the table together.* Presto, months later, Boback calls with our file, it gets opened, placed in the record, and then it gets to the FTC. They *all* stink! The hearing was a glorified sales call. They're making my life hell, and they seem to have only just begun. No wonder people roll over."

"Mike, they're *wrong.* They don't understand how untenable their behavior and positions are. I'm not afraid of them."

Assessing the opposing team, I was thinking of all the time and money it would cost more than the fear.

"I get it. I know that. And I'm relieved by what you're saying, but I just don't know what to do about it. I mean, look at these guys! Congress? Dartmouth?"

"All those guys on the board . . . Schmidt is in the White House, for God's sake! The FTC probably got its marching orders from Congress. It all lines up, but I can't prove the connection. I can smell the stink, but I can't see the skunk."

*It doesn't look like being* right *matters,* I thought, discouraged. *The agency is dragging me into a losing battle. No wonder I'm frustrated, shocked, and angry.*

"This is so wrong," I said as I rolled my head to loosen the tension building in my neck and shoulders. Ben was giving me good ammo for the fight. I paused and the room quieted down for maybe 10 seconds. *How do I make the mighty fall? It has been known to happen.*

Evelyn broke the silence. "Well, true or not, and I'm not saying it's *not* true, but we just need more info. How are we going to prove this? And I hate to point this out, but will the FTC even care? The FTC's people may not be interested in *how the file got out.* More likely, they care about *why the file got out.* They're trying to pin the tail on LabMD by using the broad interpretation of Section Five and saying that LabMD was not 'tight enough.'"

"Ugh! I'm so sick of this crap," I retorted. "This investigation comes from a group of people who live in a bubble, never having had any technology training. Their opinions are not true just because they say so. They stretch the law like they're jamming their size 11 feet into size 9 shoes. I won't let them ram this down my throat just because they have a huge shadow and a big stick. Our situation is *not* like anything else we've read about or other actions they've taken. I'm not rolling over because they say so."

"And, Mike, I'm not saying to roll over," Evelyn replied. "I'm just saying it's what their agenda seems to be. Of course, playing so close to the vest, everything is a risk calculation. I still don't understand why the government is expending so much time, money, and resources on this and on us. It doesn't make sense."

"They're not the government; they are the *enemy*," I declared. "Actually, they're nothing more than a bunch of lawyer bureaucrats who report to the FTC, a bunch of self-righteous zealots with power but no knowledge. They've grown up in the bubbles of academia and government. They have power because Congress is asleep at the wheel. President Obama appointed these zealots and everyone accused rolls over because spending money dealing with these fools is bad business."

Suddenly, I felt Ben and Evelyn's eyes on me as if I were a hurricane they wanted to pass quickly. I shut up. I had a flashback to one of my old bosses. He had seemed so amused by my passionate rants, he'd wait with a smirk on his face and stare patiently, waiting for me to end my speech. When I was finally done, he'd say, "Feel better now?" And we'd burst out laughing.

To lighten the mood I said, "I know. It's George Bush's fault. Everything else is!"

Nevertheless, my rant turned on a light. *What was I doing, expecting my lawyers to take over and come to my rescue? I had to take control and call the shots; it was my money and my company. Wake up, Mike! You're the CEO. Be the CEO.*

I took a few deep breaths and closed my eyes.

"Okay. What do we know? Let's break it down. We know we have a file that came into Tiversa's possession. We know that file then got to Dartmouth, to the US Congress, and to the FTC."

Ben stepped in, "And we do not know how it got out. They know something and I strongly suspect they know a lot. We have no evidence of a breach because we know where the file is and we know that it is, and has been, secure. We have no credible evidence that patients were at risk of harm. Therefore, this is not a patient data breach. The FTC will have difficulty accepting what I am about to say, but controlled custody is not a patient data security breach.

"Tiversa and Dartmouth are not identity thieves. They are not trying to hurt the patients identified in the file. They were institutions, acting with the support of the US Department of Homeland Security."

I looked at Evelyn for any clues she might be buying in.

"So? What do you think?"

"Well, I think this entire event doesn't make sense, so we have to do something other than roll over or keep answering their questions. Let's see where we go."

Her response was good enough for me. Better than waiting around for more of the FTC's painfully slow chess moves. "Okay, so in tennis when I'm getting my ass kicked, my coach says to break it down, go back to the beginning, and take smaller steps. How about this? If Tiversa, Dartmouth, and the FTC know things, then let's ask them.

This will show the FTC we can dig into what happened as well. And this will put Tiversa and Dartmouth on notice and on the spot. It's time to start strategizing.

"Let's brainstorm what we want to know and maybe we end up sending an inquiry to these guys. I mean, if these self-proclaimed heroes care so much about the truth and the patient, then let them step up to the plate and give us information—and answers. Not that I have any hope they will, but it starts a paper trail and puts them on notice. Let's pull our enemies close."

I didn't wait for affirmation. I was asking rhetorically. We were doing it.

I grabbed my BlackBerry like I was calling 911.

"Mary, will you please bring in the whiteboard and markers from my library to the conference room." As I hung up, I said, "Let's take ten and start brainstorming on what we want to know and let's ask the boys who know it."

I walked to my office with quite the quick step, feeling like a lion in a cage eager to get out. I was fed up with having our backs to the wall while the FTC guys scratched their chins deciding what torture device to use next. I was eager to start turning the tables.

So far today, I think Ben put a crack in Evelyn's argument that the "the file got out, so it's a breach." I just don't think she believed that it was going to matter. Yet Ben was the first expert in both law and technology with whom we'd spoken. With the crew in line, we needed to move forward, turning the ship around little by little.

Evelyn acted as stenographer, then Ben, Evelyn, and I brainstormed for at least an hour, writing our questions and thoughts on jumbo 24" × 36" Post-It notes. As we tore off each page and lined the walls of the conference room, we had the following list of what we called "the investigation questions."

With these questions we intended to obtain information that LabMD, the owner of the patient file, legitimately needed to know to fulfill its responsibilities.

## Investigation Questions for Dartmouth and Tiversa

- What method, manner, services, technologies, and/or parties were utilized to access and obtain possession of LabMD's property?
- Have you shared LabMD's property with anyone, redacted or not? If so, with whom and under what circumstances?
- Do you have a financial or business relationship with Dartmouth College or the US Federal Trade Commission (FTC) that would be relevant to LabMD's property and/or your access and/or possession of LabMD's property?
- To your knowledge, what are and have been the financial, business, or other relationships between you and/or Dartmouth College and/or the FTC?
- Please identify all records and data you possess that belong to LabMD or pertain to LabMD.
- Please identify any and all records and data belonging or pertaining to LabMD that you have accessed or reviewed, whether currently in your possession or not.
- Please identify and disclose the identity of any, and all communications you have had with Dartmouth College, the FTC, or any other individual or party regarding LabMD or its property.
- If you have engaged in communications with anyone regarding LabMD or its property, whether specifically naming LabMD or not, please state the purpose and content of any such communications.
- Please provide the dates and forms of any communications listed in response to items above.
- What was your justification for accessing, taking possession of, processing, storing, and/or examining LabMD's property?
- Please provide a full explanation of how you examined, interrogated, changed, processed, stored, and/or transmitted LabMD's property.
- What was your justification for opening any file considered LabMD's property?
- Please provide a full explanation of the security you have and are now applying to any and all property belonging to LabMD.
- Have you destroyed any records related to your acquisition, processing, or possession of LabMD's property or records? If so, please provide a full explanation.

- If you have destroyed any such records referenced above, please identify each record and the date each record was destroyed.
- Were you involved in, or have you witnessed on the part of any other recipients to this letter, a pattern of conduct involving taking property like LabMD's property in connection with attempts to solicit the property owners as clients, threats to expose the property to authorities, and/or efforts to reap benefits from the property?

Each was a sincere question that we were sure they would ignore. Therefore, each was also laced with intent to expose their hypocrisy. I could just see them flipping through their policy manuals on what to do with this move. Of course, I would be blown off my chair if they actually *did* care about business and the patient/consumer. If this turned out to be so, then we'd have valuable information to help us correct anything that might actually be wrong. Then we needed to break this travesty down and gather information to help define and defend what is "reasonable."

As we reviewed the questions, the breeze of the AC system broke the silence. "I can't think of anything else to possibly include in this, can you?" I asked after we reviewed the questions.

After pondering a bit, Evelyn responded, "This is pretty comprehensive."

"Okay, so here's the big question: do we send this to the FTC people (in addition to Tiversa and Dartmouth) and ask them the same questions, or do we let that dog sleep?"

Ben cut in with "Send it. They need to be held accountable, too."

I said sarcastically, "Like they're going to answer. You can't expect reason from the unreasonable. But this at least puts them on notice; lets them know we're playing a different game from here."

Evelyn calmly said, "I don't know what good will come from asking the FTC these questions, except to show them you're chasing the perpetrator. However, we all know they already know who got the file and gave it to them. The FTC was right there with Dartmouth and Tiversa in front of Congress in 2007."

"Let's leave the FTC on the mailing list for now," I said, "and I'll chew this over. I *love* these questions. If anyone replies, it will be Dartmouth. Tiversa will not reply. Evelyn, if you got a letter like this, what would you do?"

"Ignore it. In the context of the conversation, Evelyn's statement wasn't to be taken literally. She was speaking sardonically. She knew that the recipients of the letter should respond quickly, truthfully and completely. But given the performance of the recipients to date, she had good reason to believe they would ignore it.

"Exactly. But then you would know that we know. That's what I want! If they reply, then it's a bonus. But they're so damn busted, they won't reply in a million years. This is to show them we are demanding to know and they should tell us.

"Now, Dartmouth is another story. This needs to get out of [professor] Johnson's sphere and into the administrative area. College administration won't be happy about this. They might even do the right thing and answer. I doubt it, but they need to know what Johnson and Tiversa have been doing. Sending this letter to the FTC people only shows them we're looking. So far, talking to the FTC has been like talking to the wall. But if the FTC folks know things that will help us protect patients, they must cough it up.

"You think the FTC guys don't know how Tiversa got this? *Of course they know,*" I said. And they know to keep their mouths shut, too. Silence is the mother's skirt they all hide behind."

Suddenly I felt the air thin on top of my soapbox again. Being the end of the day, it was time to stop the billing clock and let my expensive guests go home.

"Okay, it is four-twenty," I pointed out. "Evelyn needs to get out to beat Atlanta traffic and Ben, we need to get you to the airport."

Evelyn said, "I will get this all cleaned up and e-mailed to you when I get to the office. Ben, it was great to meet you. I enjoyed our time together today."

"Nice to meet you as well," Ben said. "What a fascinating series of events." He smiled.

We stacked our papers and stuffed our briefcases. I called for Ben's transportation and said goodbye to Evelyn. Ben and I both took an e-mail break and when I returned to the room, he sat there patiently, ready to leave. He stood up when I walked in. As I shook his hand, I said, "Ben, I can't thank you enough. I feel so relieved that I'm not nuts. I need time to let this sink in and decide what to do next."

"They're wrong, Mike," he repeated.

"I know, but that seems to have little to do with how they operate. A battle will be expensive. Maybe they will quit; I have no idea. But I'm certainly more convinced than ever of our innocence. I'm not signing anything. I can't. I'd be flipping the switch at my own execution."

As we walked down the hall toward Ben's taxi, we said our goodbyes. Then I turned around and drew a deep breath. This was a lot to take in. *What a great day.*

*"Never argue with an idiot.
They will only bring you down to their level and
beat you with experience."*

—GEORGE CARLIN

# CHAPTER 13
# Simmering with a White Elephant

## August 25, 2010

After every byte of data downloads into my brain, I chew it around for a while. This time was no different. I drove home feeling eerily calm and centered. I was actually glad to be sitting in a classic Atlanta traffic jam so I could have some time to digest this latest episode.

*No breach? Seriously? Who's going to believe that?* "The file got out," as Evelyn would say. My mind flashed back to that scene from *The Silence of the Lambs* when Hannibal Lecter got frustrated with Agent Starling about obvious clues. "First principles, Clarice. Simplicity. Read Marcus Aurelius. Of each particular thing ask: What is it in itself? What is its nature? What does he do, this man you seek?"

What do I know versus what do I assume? I know Tiversa, Dartmouth, and the FTC have our data file, but I don't know how they got it. I assume Rebecca's LimeWire account created a path that left it vulnerable, allowing them to come in, poke around, find it, and take it. We were in such a panic to clean up that we erased the file of the workstation and unwittingly destroyed potentially helpful information.

I know Tiversa has patent-pending, super powerful technology. I know that Dartmouth and Tiversa worked together to download it. Did the FTC either ask for it after Boback offered it up in front of Congress with the FTC sitting right there, or did Boback and his attorney just send it to the FTC, as they said they would, to save themselves from a potential lawsuit? Did Boback give up LabMD to the Feds rather than use any files owned by his paying customers? Had we allowed ourselves to be manipulated, would I be sitting here thinking about this right now?

Ben says it appears there has never been a loss of control of the file. I know that everything is vulnerable. EVERYTHING. Leaving something vulnerable does not make a breach, especially from a legal perspective. That is not the definition of a breach. A breach goes to an untrusted source . . . and the US Government is who funded Tiversa and Dartmouth to search for and download our file. None of them let it go flying around cyberspace. They are trusted . . . but not liked at all. However, the layperson may think this, because all files around cyberspace are vulnerable to some degree. But experts know files can be vulnerable to malware, hardware, and even some power strips.[1] In the *National Interest: Cybersecurity Pipe Dreams*, Jorge Benitez and Jason Healey wrote:

> There is a popular misconception that perfect cybersecurity is obtainable if you invest in sufficient defenses and practice reasonable access procedures. The cold, hard truth is that we live in an age where cyber-offensive capabilities are dominant. For example, specialists who test the vulnerabilities of our nation's computer systems said in private conversations that their success rate is nearly 99 percent—and that penetrating that remaining 1 percent is primarily a question of investing additional time and money. Policy makers must understand this distinction: Complete cybersecurity is a myth, but cyber resiliency is obtainable and worthwhile.[2]

We know who has it, and it has always been contained—something I never thought of. Kill logic, kill conscience . . . what does the law say?

Did Evelyn buy Ben's opinions? I bet she's only concerned with what the FTC will buy. Ben is our expert witness who's also our lawyer. He thinks the FTC people don't understand or have the knowledge to judge. I feel like I'm trapped under a building after an earthquake. I need help lifting.

Panicking won't set me free; I have to think and be sharp. I like Ben. He has a soul. He gets personally involved. One of the good guys. The FTC is a stale house of self-righteous incompetence, a lumbering bureaucracy that can't keep up with the speed of technological change. I'm dying to tell this to a judge. Will we get to a judge? Or maybe the FTC will just go away now . . . When will the government snooping end?

The next thing I knew, I'd arrived at my exit. I drove the last mile and pulled into my driveway, then shut off the car and my brain. I had earned the break.

By the time I got to the gym the next morning, I was in full rearview mirror mode as I did my 30 minutes of cardio on the step machine. I stayed inside my head.

The same question kept coming up—*now what?* What do I do with this deeper information? I won't go knocking on the Devil's door. What would I say to Alain Sheer? The FTC would just turn it around against me. We had abandoned all trust in the agency long before this.

Besides, because we'd built up experience with the FTC, we understood this animal better. Speed and efficiency was not its motto, so the odds were big we'd have a long wait. I could use that to the company's advantage. I was still in the dark. I didn't know if we were in store for an FTC diagnosis of remission, cure, or death. The FTC does seem to enjoy their petty torments, keeping a bag over our heads and making us wonder. I have to learn to live in the gray zone, not knowing anything until the FTC contacts us.

In no time flat, the 30-minute cardio was up—time for my trainer to kick my ass with the weights. I quickly checked my BlackBerry. Evelyn had e-mailed the investigation letter we assembled yesterday. *Fast!* I got ready to turn off my brain and work out to keep my sanity.

After my workout, I met my friend Nadia Bilchik, an executive producer at CNN during the week and on-air talent during the weekend. From South Africa, Nadia has lived in the United States since 1998. That gives her what I call a "world view;" she's never boring and isn't afraid of strong opinions, thankfully, including mine.

We got our coffee and oatmeal and sat in big, cushy, brown leather chairs. Swallowing what was actually going on, I talked in half-truths, leaving her with the false impression that she was getting the full pie instead of a slice. Best to keep it that way so I could have a release from the FTC situation. I realized I worked to keep this FTC fiasco a secret. The point is I wasn't going to allow the FTC to infiltrate my entire life. They've done plenty of damage to my business life already.

Now it was time to get to the office and talk to Bill. He likes his alone time in the morning to get all his ducks in a row, so I left him alone until about ten o'clock. I walked into his office and sat in front of his perfectly organized desk, then quickly launched into conversation.

"Ben thinks there isn't a breach and the FTC has no right to be in this game. Tiversa and Dartmouth have our property so we'll be sending them each a list of questions. Their silence will speak volumes." After we kicked the can around, Bill and I concluded that we couldn't see the future, but we could deal with what we knew. We set out to summarize the letter of investigation we wrote.

"I just got it from Evelyn." I found it on my BlackBerry, forwarded it to Bill, and kept talking.

"Anyway, the point is to put Boback and Tiversa, Johnson and Dartmouth, on notice and see if anyone will cough up any info. If they're so 'concerned,' they should be more than willing to answer these questions. I have little hope, but I like the paper trail it starts. I can't decide if the FTC should receive a letter or not. Then the guys will see we're chasing the culprits, but since they already know the culprits, it could be a waste of time. We may risk pissing them off."

"Well, we wouldn't want to piss them off!" Bill said sarcastically.

As Bill read through the letter of investigation, my thoughts went back to how our company's growth opportunities were being wasted while we stayed so deep in this rabbit hole. *I really have to try to suppress my disgust. Success is the best revenge. I may settle for survival.*

"This looks really good!" he said.

"Yeah. Ben and Evelyn brought up good points yesterday. I was ready to FedEx it down the FTC's throat last night, but that would only have awakened the beast. It may be smarter to leave the FTC out of this for now. Let's see if we get any response from Tiversa or Dartmouth. We'll play 'good dog' while I figure a way out of this that won't break us. Where are we with finishing up the docs for what goes to the FTC next week?" I asked, changing the subject.

"We've sent everything to Evelyn. Remember, she wants to talk this afternoon," Bill responded.

"Oh yeah, I forgot. What time?"

"Two."

"She's still wrapping all the info in a nice bow for Alain. Okay, I have to run to St. Joe and USOA. I'll be back by one, I hope." USOA was Urology Specialists of Atlanta, a long-time client of LabMD.

## Window to the Urologist's World

Unlike working in a big company, job descriptions are dynamic in a small business. When I visited USOA, my CEO hat came off and sales rep hat went on. I've known most of the Atlanta urologists since 1987 so we're way past formalities. Not only did I love working with them, but I could also keep my fingers on the pulse of the market. USOA was my window to the real world of a urologist's office.

I walked in. "Hey Beth, is Brenda back there?"

"I think so."

"Okay, thanks. Hey, Danitra. How are ya?"

I could have stayed all day shooting the bull with everyone, but I had to wade past the fun and check out things in the surgery center to make sure that all was well with our servicing their needs.

"Hello, Brenda!"

"Hey, honey! How are ya?"

"Cool. The usual twenty-eight hours a day needed with only twenty-four hours allowed. How're you?"

"I'm fine. I need to add a new nurse in your lab system and make sure all employees have new passwords."

"Okay. Where can I get a list of names and what they want their user ID to be? Can you e-mail that to me? I can send it to IT, and Brandon can set you up in a matter of minutes."

"Okay. Will do. Oh yeah, while you're here, Dr. Bounds told me he wants a second opinion on a case that came back this morning. He's in room five, so when he steps out, can you get the patient's name and get that off to Johns Hopkins hospital? It's a prostate case."

"Okay, I'm on it. Thanks."

After I took care of these items, Brenda and I chit-chatted about her son, the summer, her vacation, my dogs, etcetera. I like coming here. I get a lot of business, personal, and community satisfaction all rolled into one. A salesman at heart, I love the field, the marketplace, and my clients. Plus I know that because the doctors and nurses are so busy, if they call me, it's a *big* problem. By dropping in, I can catch any issues while they're still smoke rather than a four-alarm fire. And what I learn through casual conversation can be golden—full of competitive market knowledge and countless other types of feed-back. It's a win-win.

That day, a pharmaceutical rep had brought lunch (always a spread), so I pinched half a sandwich and completed my rounds, then fired off the requests for USOA and left, thinking about my call with Bill and Evelyn.

Only a week away from having to send our third submission to the FTC, we were no longer in the dark about their machinations. We fully expected them to review it, find something missing, and then either give us another assignment or pull the trigger on a con-sent decree. Since we still didn't want to disturb the sleeping giant, we quietly climbed the FTC beanstalk and entertained the requests.

Again, we were to "memorialize" any policies we had in place that weren't in writing. In the real world a small company doesn't write down everything. Unlike the government, we can't take our sweet time and ignore costs.

Memorializing whatever wasn't in writing exemplified the type of frustration I'd have to constantly swallow while dealing with the Feds. I felt as if I'd get blank stares if I told them we didn't perform bomb sweeps of our cars before sending employees out to pick-up lunch. Their response would probably be something like,

"So, evidently you have inadequate safety procedures and disdain for your employees. May we see your transportation policies and travel logs? We will pay particular attention to your safety videos on seat belt use. What do you mean you don't have a safety video on seat belt use? I see . . ." Then they'd jot down something on legal pads, followed by the coldness of cuffs they'd lock around my wrists. Why not skip to the cuffs, so we could go to court and get it over with?

Instead, my team and I mentally drown in the painstaking process and constant threat of reputation assassination. In their quest to "help the consumer," the Feds hurt our company by diverting our attentions away from more pressing matters, like our core business of diagnosing illness and helping people get the treatment they need to survive. If we just got to a judge, we could duke it out on a level playing field—assuming that even exists. Who knew the level field was on the top of a mountain?

When I got back to the office, I dropped everything, texted Bill to meet me in the conference room, and dialed Evelyn's number. As Bill walked in, I already had Evelyn on speakerphone.

"Okay. Here's Bill."

"Hi, Bill."

"Hello, Evelyn."

"What did you think about Ben?" Bill asked Evelyn.

"Oh, Ben has great ideas and shed light on things we needed to know. How the FTC deals with that is another question. This doesn't change much in the short run. Let's give them what they want and see what they do. When and if the battles start, Ben has given great suggestions."

I piped in. "I decided I'm *not* going to send the investigation letter to the FTC. I slept on it. I believe the Feds knew Tiversa and Dartmouth's role even before they contacted us. Obviously, they don't care. Let them keep the belief they're dealing with an uninformed, small-scale, Southern company that will roll over. I still put my money on them making an example of us versus dropping their inquiry.

"Evelyn, where are you in organizing the stack of hay Bill dropped on your desk?"

We all chuckled, then I left Bill and Evelyn to have their question-and-answer time. They seemed to be on track.

After meeting with Evelyn and Ben, I recognized my stubbornness to hire an attorney who had experience dealing with the FTC. I was slow to go into this battle without Evelyn at my side and Ben didn't handle direct battles either. It made me feel alone and vulnerable. My first round of cold calls to FTC lawyers in the DC area confirmed these suspicions.

With tones of indifference and loath to give any opinions (they were as afraid of me as I was of them), first-round discussions proved the same as my earlier calls. None of them knew anything about data security, but they all knew the FTC was a royal pain. Straight out of the playbook, their advice was universal: "Justice is expensive. You have no idea what will happen. The FTC has an army of attorneys and unlimited resources. Just admit you're trumped and negotiate the best you can. Staff members have short memories, so after you sign the decree, the scuttlebutt is that the FTC doesn't pay attention."

Although reticent with their opinions, these lawyers still showed a willingness to defend LabMD and handle the interaction at rates no lower than $450 an hour. *What could they do for me that Evelyn could not?* I felt more lost than ever.

But now, with Ben lighting a fire by stating the FTC doesn't have factual power, I realized I didn't need just *any* lawyer. I needed a lawyer like Ben who knew technology *and* law *and* the FTC. While Bill continued assembling policy documentation and Evelyn kept organizing and preparing, I fired up my computer and went to Google.

## Lisa Sotto

Many of my discoveries to date—like the Tiversa, Dartmouth, US Congress, White House, and *Wired Magazine* connection—made me frustrated I didn't unveil key facts sooner. This time, I found an article titled "How to Survive an FTC Investigation" by Lisa Sotto.[3] I called her. It rolled to voicemail, so I left a general message then researched her name online. She had quite the pedigree: Homeland Security Data Security, Lead Advisor, DataGuidance US Panel of Experts Member, Law and Ethics Advisory Board, SAI Global, vice-chair US Department of Homeland Security's Data Privacy and Integrity Advisory Committee, and the list goes on. She would know how the enemy thinks.

The next day, the phone rang. Ms. Sotto. She spoke quickly, her voice coming across firm and professional.

I gave her the customary lowdown on the bind I found myself in, but this time I said it with greater understanding and clear-headedness than ever.

"First of all, I apologize for starting this way, but based on my experiences with others in your profession, I must be clear that I consider this a no-charge consultation. If that isn't your understanding, then we have to deal with that first."

"I can have a brief general conversation with you about the situation to see if we can work together. I'm not going to give you any specific advice, as I haven't reviewed anything yet."

"Fair enough. The FTC has opened a 'non-public' investigation into our data security practices to discern whether or not they consider them 'reasonable.' A company called Tiversa took a file containing patient information, and alleged that we had a problem. We wouldn't pay this company for assistance in solving the alleged problem. Tiversa then gave the file to the FTC. I think it's bogus that Tiversa can take a file from us but it's our company that's now feeling the heat from the FTC."

"Doesn't matter."

"Excuse me?"

"Doesn't matter."

"But they took medical files without authorization."

"Doesn't matter. The FTC doesn't care how your file got out. All they care about is that it got out."

I could feel my temperature rising.

*Geez*, I thought, *could we please have a trial before the jury comes marching out with a verdict?* Most lawyers I've encountered are terrified to speak in absolutes in any way, shape, or form. That's why I like it when a lawyer isn't afraid to voice an opinion. Out of the gate, I sensed this woman was unafraid of a good debate. However, I did think there were some valid points still to be made.

"Okay, this frustrates me, Lisa. How can they *not* care? Tiversa takes our file, their CEO wants us to hire them, and when we don't, he turns our file over the FTC. Then the FTC investigates my company! We don't know what the FTC guys are doing, where they're going, or what they're planning to do. Cryptically, they tell us to read consent decrees."

"Have you been presented with a consent decree?"

"No."

"Well, then, you're way ahead of yourself. Don't panic. You have lots of time. The game doesn't even start until they propose negotiations about a consent decree. *Then* you start going back and forth about what will be in the consent decree. The FTC is *slooow* and may even walk away. But—and don't get upset when I tell you this—a consent decree isn't the worst thing in the world. It isn't *that* bad."

"Oh really? First of all, I'm more concerned about my competition and reputation than the decree, but that decree simply isn't okay with me. I don't want to go through the next ten to twenty years with these bureaucrats sniffing over my shoulder. Still, half of them may be dead by then, God willing!"

Lisa laughed. Good. She had a sense of humor. And I got her message that it "wasn't that bad." However, for *my* company, I was sure it would be.

"Lisa, I'm *not* running the risk, and I'm *not* signing anything."

"Well, you still don't know what they'll do. Once the negotiations start, it could take months. Nothing happens fast. You have time."

"What about other states? Have you alerted the patients that their data got out?" she asked me.

"No, we had no laws broken and there aren't any requirements. We have no evidence it is 'out there' to report. The government, Tiversa, and Dartmouth have it."

"I disagree. There are laws out there …"

"Well, I can only rely on our lawyer and she researched every damn state," I protested.

"You have disclosure laws that were in effect in 2008," she countered.

"Well, I'll let our lawyer know, but she's no dope. The issue is all testing was done in Georgia. There were no tests or services performed outside of Atlanta. So, where do we go from here? How do you charge? Please forgive my bluntness, but I like everything upfront. I want us to be fair and transparent with each other."

"My hourly rate is $895. I have other lawyers and paralegals at the firm who will also work on the project at a lower rate. I'll get out an engagement letter and then, of course, I'll have to review your materials before I can specifically say what steps to take next."

I pretended that the wind had not been knocked out of me. Not wanting to be rude, I told her that was fine and gave her my contact information. We hung up.

I liked her but this conversation unsettled me. She seemed perfectly professional and razor sharp, but her disregard of how Tiversa accessed and downloaded medical data stored on a private computer bugged me. *How could I get any of these lawyers to see the Tiversa issue? Fighting it seemed to make them categorize me as stubborn and delusional. Changing lawyers' minds is tough. They usually keep their opinions to themselves. At least Lisa let it all hang out.*

This conversation exemplifies what I went through every time I interviewed a lawyer. I thought Lisa Sotto would be different. Arguably the top lawyer in the country on data security, she was taking the "doesn't matter, suck it up and cross your fingers" stance, which made the situation all the more deflating. I felt alone in the world but not wrong.

Because hers was the same speech I'd gotten from the $350 an hour lawyers, I didn't see what more I'd get for my money.

I sat in the silence of my office, hearing the clock ticking. This outreach had left me feeling steamrolled and dismissed. Are there any FTC expert lawyers in the world who aren't voting for a roll-over? I suppose it's easy to get cocky when pulling in almost a grand an hour. Clearly, I didn't want to write the checks and commission my own steamroller. Sharp as she was, I knew I wouldn't be calling Ms. Sotto back.

That's when my anger swelled. I damn well was concerned that something was up and wondered if all these high-powered lawyers, FTC investigators, Congressmen, and security companies were really interested in security. The lawyers get their money no matter what. Many of them live on billing quotas like car salesmen. The FTC investigators have fairy tale beliefs of actually helping in the cybersecurity war. The Congressmen pretend to help while not rocking boats in fear of losing the next election. And Tiversa and Boback join the fear industry by creating a new vertical market ending in high service fees for them and an advisory board of well-placed cronies to keep the fear-factor high and the business flowing.

The evil they represented wasn't nearly as annoying as the utter hypocrisy. That's what I concluded after talking to the lawyers— especially those who doubt the story, rip into the client like raw meat, send a fat bill, and feel no obligation to gather relevant information before rendering an opinion. Most lawyers will never open themselves to that type of risk. After being brainwashed by their malpractice carriers and managing partners, they only take a stand after hours of billable, tail-covering work wrapped in a bow called "research."

If you're hiring a lawyer, beware. Their engagement letters are one-sided contracts in which another lawyer deals with your lawyer (ironic). The games and pressures their managing partners place on them at your expense (it's all about the money) is kept from you; silence is their favorite noun. Most won't be held accountable.

Remember, when seeking justice, the web of confusion you enter can be perilous. Take your time, do your homework, educate yourself.

The next day, I turned my attention to the completion of our third round of submissions for the FTC. We had only four days left to submit our latest volley. Two stone-faced FTC lawyers were asking questions and making demands; I didn't have any choice but to go along. They believed they were consumer protection masters of the cyber universe—complete with cape and tights—but that didn't mean they knew what they were talking about.

*There's people running 'round loose*
*In the world*
*Ain't got nothing better to do*
*Than make a meal of some*
*Bright eyed kid*
*You need someone looking after you*

—"Stop Draggin My Heart Around"
by Michael W. Campbell & Tom Petty

# CHAPTER 14
# Round Four of Kissing Their Ass

## August 2010

Alain Sheer wanted this root canal drilled a bit deeper. We had to assemble and memorialize all policies and further information, which meant weeks of additional work placed on the backs of an IT department that was already busy supporting a medical facility. My ever-filling tank of anger had to be converted to motivation to keep everything running at LabMD while balancing this extra plate the FTC handed me, all the while keeping a smile on my face. It was hard for me to believe that the FTC wasn't trying to make us trip and fall so we might break the law.

I took a deep breath and walked into Bill's office. He had everything in perfect stacks on his desk, eagerly awaiting my arrival. His crisp organization skills, among others, made me truly appreciate his presence in the company.

"So, what do we have so far? Looks like quite a bit."

"I have all the policies and proof of measures we took, listed in chronological order all the way back to 2001."

I picked up the paper-clipped stack, thumbed through about 20 pages, quickly confirming that the history did indeed go all the way back to 2001.

I said to Bill, "Well, that's going overboard, but why not? They said 2007, but we might as well show them how we've improved as the technology has changed. What do you need from me, Bill?"

"I need you to tell me if it seems anything's missing from before I joined the company in 2006—when you were running everything."

"Well, everything was on that original server, the Dell backup, and the antivirus software. Did you get everything off of there?"

"Everything we could, Mike. Some of the antivirus reports were set to overwrite, so the history isn't there, but you can see the installation date."

"I got ya. That's logical. We had no idea back then we'd be expected to meet the burden of proof as if this was a murder investigation. Okay, this looks complete to me. Do you see any holes, Bill?"

"Well, I don't know what Pat or Jeremy recorded, but I have nothing from them."

Pat and Jeremy were two former IT employees from 2003-2007.

"No gaps in the timeline?"

"None that I see, no." Bill picked up the stack and flipped through to the chronological timeline to show what he was referring to.

"Okay, this looks good. Plus, they only asked for 2007 to present. Going back further should resolve any concerns about our patterns. This clearly shows adaptability and our upgrading efforts over time. I will review this with Evelyn and see what she has to say. Looks great. Please e-mail it to Evelyn and copy me. Thanks a lot."

I walked to my desk and e-mailed Evelyn to call me after she had reviewed the document, still haunted by its irrelevant requirements.

*What the hell did Rebecca really do? Anything? How did we get plucked out of obscurity? Why won't the Feds be more specific? They're not laying any cards on the table. Are they a rubber bullet or an incoming scud missile?*

Then Evelyn called.

"Hi, Mike. I'm condensing all this information into something contained and focused. I'll get it to you tomorrow. Have you seen what Bill sent me?"

"The summary, not all the raw data. No reason for me to go through every field of data; I'd be reading for years."

"I just need to make sure you concur before we move forward."

"It's all there in painstaking detail and if something's there they don't like or is missing, I'd like to know what it is. Nothing changes the fact that Tiversa accessed and downloaded the damn file. I think they're just gauging whether or not to let us off the hook or hang us on the rack. Either way, it's not earth shattering—just reshuffled evidence that our security practices were, at the least, in line with every other entity we encountered."

With dry sarcasm I added, "I'm so sorry we didn't write down and video every move we made. Working here should have been like a reality show with cameramen hovering over everyone at all times. That would have worked wonders for employee retention and morale. And it would have been cheaper to produce, too."

"Yes, and maybe you could've been a television star, too!"

"Great . . . no thanks."

We both chuckled. Then I confirmed, "Is the next step for you to send me the draft submission?"

"Yes, I should have something to you tomorrow. I expect no more than forty pages."

"Okay. One more time for good measure."

I hung up and rubbed my face. Every round of my fury was going into a stockpile for a counterattack to come later. I was becoming a baseball catcher who digs his cleats into the ground, readying himself for fastballs. I swore I'd turn the tables; it was just a matter of when.

The FTC definitely deserved a special response. *One day I'll shine a light so bright on these regulatory robots their masks of concern will melt right off.* I saw Michael Corleone of *The Godfather* planning the murders of the heads of the five families. "But I'm gonna wait until after the baptism. I've decided to be godfather to Connie's baby. And then I meet the Don Barzini and Tattaglias—all the heads of the Five Families." That phrase "I'm gonna wait" sent chills up my spine and fired me up. Oh baby, I was going to wait, all right. *I'm going to let these bastards continue to drop their arrogant cards on the table. Lights on and let the court of public opinion decide. We have a cancer in America. Agencies of the government can't take the law into their own hands simply because they're of the opinion that Congress hasn't created the laws they want.*

*I need to let the world know, make sure the FTC can't blindside other businesses and get my money back. Somehow, when this is over, I have to put the company in a position where we're better off. But how do I do that?*

Two days later, Bill and I reviewed the fourth submission to the FTC, but without the original level of tension. Why should there be? Our naive beliefs of honesty and communication had been blown to bits by their cannons of silence and intransigence. Without discussion, we decided and understood that we'd cooperate until the FTC asked me to sign anything that even slightly hinted at any wrongdoing.

"I don't know how we could do a better job describing and memorializing what typically went down around here, unless they also wanted to know the housekeeping and pest control schedules," I said snippily.

I looked through the various sections:

- LabMD Policy Manual
- IT Staff Walkaround Checklist
- IT Staff Walkaround confirmatory e-mails
- Zyxel firewall documentation
- Trend Micro reports (175 pages)

"Well, that should cover that. Has any of this ever been sent to the FTC before?"

"The walkarounds are new."

"Did we tell the FTC about them before?"

"Yes, but they wanted documented details this time."

"I don't know what can possibly be the point of all this. They seem to be focusing on a half-empty glass. This submission won't do a thing. We walked around and didn't find any problems. Did we miss one aspect of a file-sharing application on a workstation? What should we have done differently? A weekly workstation tear down? I believed the file got out because of Tiversa's unique software. I'm not aware of any evidence that it was otherwise available. Hell, he said so right in front of Congress. Just bring on the consent decree and then we can start the fight. They are just running us into the ground with their sinister game."

"While this data is impressive, it's not perfect," I added. "But they can cast the first stone. Mail it. I'm done. I'll e-mail Evelyn and tell her it's ready for final assembly and letter for my approval to send up to the morons on the mountaintop."

With my final words, Bill left my office. He knew I didn't like to have my rage at the FTC inflicted on anyone, but sometimes he takes the heat. Sure, I can yell at a mirror and plot their doom on my own. And it's not good for staff members to see their CEO slugging a punching bag and screaming expletives. But, I'm human . . . I can't always hold it in!

Like preparing for college exams, last-minute high adrenaline cram sessions took place with Evelyn working on billable time and me waiting, sitting in the stands for her results. She didn't disappoint. What a professional!

August 30, 2010

**VIA FEDERAL EXPRESS**[1]

Alain Sheer, Esq.
Division of Privacy and Identity Protection
Federal Trade Commission
600 Pennsylvania Ave., N.W.
Mail Stop NJ-8122
Washington, D.C. 20580

Re: LabMD, Inc.

Dear Alain:

On behalf of our client, LabMD, Inc. (hereafter "LabMD"), we are providing additional information and documentation to supplement

LabMD's responses and documents previously submitted to the FTC on February 24, 2010, June 4, 2010, and July 16, 2010. This supplemental information pertains to the following areas: (1) LabMD's training, scope of written policies, and measures used to enforce policies; and (2) methods employed to avoid, discover, and assess risks. As you requested in our meeting at your office on July 23, 2010, these supplemental responses cover the 2007–2008 time period.

Off it went and back to our world we returned, except for the big, silent government presence in our front yard, sitting there saying nothing, blocking the sun, sucking the attention away from management.

Unnerving at first, but step by step, inch by inch, we were getting used to working in the presence of the big oaf. Besides, we couldn't stay tense forever and ignore other duties. The mystery would have to come to an end at some point. And regardless of what it was, knowing would take a huge burden off our organization's shoulders. As old pros dealing with the lumbering agency, we knew it could take months before we heard a peep. We took a deep breath and got back to our real jobs. The last thing we wanted to do was talk about the FTC. We needed routine, silence, peace, quiet, and time.

It was a beautiful fall in Atlanta with vacations ending, schools back in session, and temperatures dropping. For us, it was time to get back to the business. I had goals from the beginning of the year I hadn't even started yet. We weren't interested in crunching out mass volumes of patient results and trading quality for profits. Instead, we wanted to find other marketplaces to succeed in. Just having my mind free to explore those options felt joyful.

Yet the coast wasn't clear. Our biggest worry regarding this FTC investigation was having our competitors leverage this salacious information to their advantage, creating doubt, innuendo, and fear of the unknown. In turn, this would make our clients' imaginations run wild with frothy anxiety. Perception is reality in the mind of any client.

Destroying a company's reputation is a misfortune the FTC couldn't care less about. Its agenda is to control the business masses by punishing the few to control the many—wearing them down, breaking their backs and eliciting false confessions. FTC people spew their propaganda via press releases and visits to Congress; plus we can't overlook its annual yearbook.[2] The fine print conveniently doesn't mention broken laws or admission of guilt.

Finally recognizing their patterns, I knew I must expose the FTC's game, flip the board upside down, let the pieces hit the floor and watch them break them into a million shards. To accomplish that, I had to focus on planning, strategy, intentional silence, and timing every move carefully.

The FTC was on my mind at all hours of the day. If I was up in the middle of the night to use the restroom, I thought of the FTC. If I drove down the road to work, I thought of the FTC. The FTC was like a team of chess players; each one of their moves made painstaking slow, allowing me months to ponder and agonize over what their moves would or wouldn't include. The game itself was a form of torture and their slowness and silence were tools in their arsenal. At least chess has the clock to keep the game moving.

## Damning Data Disclosures from WikiLeaks

On October 23, 2010—a peaceful Saturday—I was catching up on work, barely listening to the TV news in the background. All of a sudden, the current events caught my attention. *WikiLeaks*. I kept hearing that word over and over again. *WikiLeaks. What the hell is WikiLeaks?*

I opened my browser to my home page and Whoa! The headlines screamed "WikiLeaks." Apparently, this WikiLeaks outfit was tearing the mask off the US government—like Will Smith in the movie *Men in Black* when he said, "Well, well, well. Big bad bug got himself a soft spot!" *This should keep them busy. Maybe they'll drop us from their jaws like a panting dog and run after the bigger, juicier bone.*

*Had the government put their limited resources in this direction and been more "reasonable" in their security practices, this national security crisis could've been avoided.*

Reading further, I couldn't wait to talk to Bill and Evelyn about this. *How in the hell did this guy Julian Assange—the head of WikiLeaks—catch the government with its pants so far down? I'm not in the least bit surprised. This is terrible. Government heal thyself.*

In all the research we did responding to the FTC, I tried to learn what data security standards existed and which were mandatory. The only standards that existed were government standards for the government itself. Boy oh boy, government agencies sure weren't practicing what they were preaching.

In July 2010, WikiLeaks released close to 77,000 documents on the Afghanistan War—a dress rehearsal for what would come later, which was 400,000 documents called the Iraq War Logs. Clearly, this group was on a mission; its timeline was jaw dropping.[3]

**Dec. 2007:** WikiLeaks officially launches its Web site.

**Sept. 2008:** Anonymous hackers access Republican vice-presidential candidate Sarah Palin's Yahoo! Account during the presidential campaign. Her e-mails are then published by WikiLeaks.

**April 2010:** WikiLeaks publishes video ("Collateral Murder") of a 2007 helicopter attack in Baghdad that killed Iraqi civilians and two Reuters journalists.

**May 2010:** US Army soldier Bradley Manning is arrested on suspicion of providing WikiLeaks with classified material.

**July 2010:** WikiLeaks publishes 77,000 documents on US involvement in Afghanistan.

**Aug. 2010:** Sweden issues an arrest warrant for Assange on one rape allegation and one molestation allegation.

**Oct. 2010:** WikiLeaks publishes the Iraq War Logs—400,000 classified US documents on the Iraq war from 2004 to 2009.

Why on earth are these smirking lawyers breathing down my back when this espionage is happening right under their noses? Who is manufacturing the software that makes this possible? I guess the FTC only plays junior varsity.

The American public soon would no longer be so shocked by these types of disclosures and data losses. This was good news for LabMD. People would become more immune to these occurrences; they wouldn't be so "surprised" by "what happened." The "National Enquirer factor" would soon subside. Cooler heads would prevail and draconian images of our servers being left open to the world wouldn't be as likely to dance in our heads given the news: The head of WikiLeaks, Julian Assange, for example, was threatening the US government—and was now facing bigger problems than ever.

My own worst case scenario didn't appear so bad anymore. The FTC now had submission number four, WikiLeaks was hitting the press, the American public was learning about cyberspace risks, and we had peace and quiet from the FTC. In my mind, the likelihood of never hearing from Team FTC just went up. *How can the FTC have time for a small brush fire when Rome is burning?*

For the first time in 2010, the big bad wolf didn't look so frightening. He might have even left the building.

I simmered as that condescendingly controlling vocal tone of Alain Sheer still rang in my head. Their patronizing shell game needs to be reserved for people who actually break laws, not a hard working medical facility that diagnoses cancer. The FTC was trying to bail water out of the boat one cup at a time, when they didn't see the tidal wave rising right behind them.

*"The caged bird sings with fearful trill
of the things unknown but longed for still
and his tune is heard on the distant hill
for the caged bird sings of freedom."*

—MAYA ANGELOU

# CHAPTER 15
# Getting Back to the New Normal

## Fall 2010 through Early 2011

As we healed our wounds during the fall of 2010, LabMD experienced no additional interruptions from the FTC. We had one eye looking over our shoulder for any sign of the FTC and the other focused straight ahead on running the company. As the media filled with stories of WikiLeaks, the worsening economy, and the Obama administration getting its tail kicked in the mid-term elections, we believed we were out of the woods. With all these sharks swimming in the water, how could the federal government have time for a little fish like us?

The financial hit from the investigation made me feel as if I was running uphill with a tractor tire chained to my waist. The cost of dealing with the FTC was draining our profits—profits intended for new investments, new jobs, new markets, and new equipment. None of that was happening with the FTC sprawled across our doorstep.

With no time or money to achieve our new goals, the company was forced into hibernation. Luckily, I'd built LabMD so we could tread water. We had grown slowly, making sure each area was performing solidly before we moved on to a new market. Debt free and profitable, my rainy-day financial strategy was paying off. LabMD could hunker down and endure. Goliath never did take David seriously and we would use that to our advantage. And how much time did I have to work on our small business before Alain Sheer darkened our doorstep yet again?

By the end of October, we had a wall full of goals on 8.5 × 11 papers, each with a topic and projected completion date. This got our people moving forward. We then all got together in an open group and discussed everything on the wall. The goal was to uncover who needed help, provide cross training, build teamwork, and ferret out any problems. It would become quickly obvious if any of them lived in a bunker.

I was excited to see all the goals lined up and the timelines adjusted. It meant we were growing, moving, learning, and changing. When someone projected December for a completion date and then realized March was more realistic, that was okay with me. I just wanted our goals and tasks to move from Never Never Land into Realityville, or at least one of its suburbs. If someone was truly overwhelmed in his or her job, we'd find out. Many employees can be terrified to ask for help. At this juncture, I couldn't risk the company's health to protect individual egos.

December arrived too soon. We held our annual office holiday party Sunday night at Maggiano's, a family style Italian restaurant that never leaves you hungry. The Friday before, I ran to Costco for a fun-filled shopping spree to get gifts for the employee drawing. I filled the shopping cart with wine glasses, a set of bowls, pretty candles, DVD players, gift cards for movies, and more. I stored them in my office and my assistant played Santa's helper wrapping them. With the price of flat screen TVs falling through the floor, I bought three 21-inch Panasonic TVs for my grand prizes. The evening's loot was ready.

People arrived late to Sunday's party because Peachtree Road in front of Lenox Mall was backlogged with Christmas shoppers. We had an open bar cocktail hour with hors d'oeuvres of crab cakes and calamari. Most of the time, our people wear lab jackets and scrubs, so it was fun to watch everyone "ooh" and "ah" over each other sporting their holiday finest—the Patti Labelle hair, the hot dresses, the stiletto heels, the suits and ties, and even a few cuff links. They'd come to party.

As host, I stood back and made the rounds, enjoying the chemistry in the room. I consider it one of the perks of being CEO. Before we took our seats at the dining tables, I clapped and yelled, "Can I have everyone's attention, please? Welcome to the LabMD 2010 Christmas party. I'll spare you the long formal speech so you can all get back to having fun. I'd like to take a moment to thank you for everything you've done this year. As I say every year, at LabMD the patients come first. But tonight, *you* come first. So please, enjoy this time with your colleagues, family, and friends, and talk with someone you don't work with every day. Merry Christmas. Happy Hanukkah. Happy Holidays. Everyone have a safe and enjoyable night!"

Maggiano's waiters served us a family-style buffet big enough for a small army. Conversations flourished as people passed around the delicious plates of food. After the main course, we moved onto dessert and coffee: chocolate zuccotto cake and profiteroles with vanilla bean ice cream and hot fudge. We'd consumed so much food we couldn't move, so we recovered by drawing for gifts. Everyone except the managers pulled tickets to win prizes. Then came time for playing prize bingo—a first for the company Christmas party. I was surprised at the number of people who'd never played bingo. People were helping each other and competing at the same time. I yelled out the numbers: B-15 B-23 N-7 O-54 G-10. The tension built as people only needed a few numbers to win one of the coveted flat screen TV sets.

My favorite moment of the party happened when quiet, mellow Sherry, who performs dictation for the doctors, filled her bingo card to win one of the flat screen TVs. "Whoooo! I won! Yeah!" Sherry jumped out of her seat, ran to the front, held the flat panel TV over her head, and jogged the entire outer ring of the dinner tables, high-fiving everyone like she'd won a gold medal. With Sinatra crooning carols in the background, everyone enjoyed Sherry's Christmas lottery joy.

As Christmas rolled into New Years, January 2011 brought a much-needed fresh start, not just for me but also for LabMD. As a small company, we have very few formal meetings. Our ability to have face-to-face, spur of the moment conversations with each other keeps things open and transparent. Bill and I typically keep each other informed on a variety of topics, relying on our mutual trust.

However, at times, the noise of day-to-day operations has to be quieted in favor of formal meetings to address questions like where have we been, how far off course are we and why, where are we going and how will we get there? We discuss big picture planning, what new or expanded markets we're considering, what departments need shifting, if any, and so on. During 2010, Hurricane FTC had blown our plans from a year ago out the window. To regroup, I scheduled our 2011 Strategic Planning Manager's Meeting for Tuesday, January 4, 2011.

"So, let's review where we are and where we've been. Last quarter showed great progress in documenting goals, discovering challenges, and cross department training. We did this so we could coordinate our efforts to move the company forward. I'm happy with the increased level of awareness this has created," I said to the seven managers who gathered.

"As far as the FTC goes, Bill has been debriefing you over the past year on the general movements of the beast. I don't know what these guys have in store for us. Part of my job is to protect the company. So, to be cautious, we're keeping our IT infrastructure under constant scrutiny. The FTC has provided no clear standards, so we have to aim high and hope for the best. This, to say the least, has been a frustrating challenge. Thanks for keeping this close to your chest. Now, Bill, over to you."

"Okay, thanks. The last nine months have been spent upgrading our IT infrastructure to state of the art. To upgrade our software, we contacted several software vendors. This industry has not developed product lines for companies as small as us. They came up with special quotes for us."

"After extensive analysis, we've decided to contract with Websense and have budgeted a large chunk of our 2011 IT budget for purchasing and implementing its cutting-edge software package. This process will take four to six months. Specifically, it's designed to protect confidential information, restrict inbound and outbound web access, fight spam and malicious links, protect networks from spyware, prevent the viewing of inappropriate or harmful content, and so on.

"We'll also be contracting with our friends at an Oklahoma-based data intelligence company to execute this project. When we're done, we'll be more state-of-the-art than any of our customers' IT environments."

As Bill continued speaking over the heads of most in the room, I saw dollar signs flying out the door. *No standards, so no choice. Have to aim over the top. If we spend all this time and money on IT and the FTC doesn't get off our backs, I'm going to lose it.*

As the planning day ended, January 2011 was looking the same as January 2010, still dealing with the government's red-hot poker between our shoulder blades. Yet it had been months since we'd heard from the agency. Since then, WikiLeaks news had been all over the press and the populace was becoming more aware of buzz-words like "data theft, hacking, breach, and cybersecurity." When I watched the TV news, I'd often shout at the screen: "Oh, come on! With national security compromises left and right, why are the Feds worrying about *us?* They have to move on to bigger issues!"

Most of the time, though, the entire issue had slipped from my consciousness and I focused on the day-to-day operations of LabMD and rarely looked over my shoulder for the looming presence of the FTC.

Then on February 10, my BlackBerry rang.

"Hello?"

"Hi, Mike. It's Evelyn. I just got off the phone with Alain Sheer."

*"Freedom of speech means nothing to a people who are too weak in their own convictions to speak out against the evil that is eating at the heart of the nation like a cancer."*

—BILLY GRAHAM

# CHAPTER 16
# Remission is Over

By mid-afternoon, all the life had drained out of my body. Feeling numb, I sat in my chair, closed my eyes, and laid back my head, ready for my next hit.

"Well, what does he want now?" I asked Evelyn.

"He wants testimony from a LabMD IT employee, or employees, who performed the walkarounds," Evelyn said dispassionately.

"What?"

She repeated herself in the same tone to help it sink in. I wanted my life to go back to an hour ago when I was blissfully unaware of the FTC's return.

"Testimony? As in under oath?"

"Yes."

"As in this person needs to go to Washington?"

"Yes."

Evelyn was waiting for me to lose my cool. I wouldn't disappoint.

"Oh, you've *got* to be kidding me. Why doesn't he just shoot us now and get it over with? This sadist probably gets all excited when he pulls the wings off a butterfly."

I paused to find my thoughts through the rage I felt.

"Okay. So, do we get to pick who goes to this meeting?" I asked.

"Well, not exactly. It has to be someone from IT who actually did the walkarounds. Mike, when we start talking 'sworn testimony,' it's serious. We need to find an attorney who has FTC experience because I can't figure out why they're digging so deeply. Of course, given Alain's history, I asked for a memorializing of this request in writing to avoid any misunderstandings."

"Good move. Well, it has to be Peter, even though he left the company four years ago to go back to school; or Jeremy. I'll have to check Jeremy's employment dates. Peter probably did all of the walkarounds, anyway. He's a Boy Scout. I bet they'll scare the hell out of this poor kid." (Peter was a young IT desk support guy that came over from Home Depot. He was a great kid to work with. Jeremy, too, was IT desk support who worked with us while he was in school and stayed on after he earned his degree.)

"Because he worked for LabMD, I can represent him and we can meet with him. Will he meet with us?" Evelyn said.

"I'm sure he will. He's a good, honest kid. Can you imagine being in your mid-twenties and getting a call to fly up to DC to testify in front of the FTC? How can I best explain this to him?"

"We won't explain anything except tell him to recall what he remembers and advise him to tell the truth."

"When is the 'Star Council' going to convene?" I said. Sarcasm was helping me cope.

"You know, Alain didn't say. He just wanted me to check with you and then we'd move forward. That tells me he hasn't got a subpoena. Basically, he's seeing if we'll cooperate."

"Oh, I'll save my fury for Alain when the real dance begins. Okay, I'll call Peter or have Bill call him. No, I'll call him."

"Mike, just tell him enough to get him to agree to come in, no more. Until we see him in person, don't mention the FTC or specifics. Say we have a legal situation, we're required to have someone who worked at the company testify, and he might get subpoenaed. I can handle it from there. And Mike, we have to look for a lawyer to take over this entire FTC interrogation. We have got to find someone who has worked with these people. I can't figure out what is driving them."

"Oh, great," I moaned. "I haven't liked anyone I've spoken with. Lawyers don't listen."

"Well, Sheer is sending me that letter. You know it won't arrive tomorrow, so let's lie low until we get it. In the meantime, try to find Peter. He'll definitely need to be interviewed."

"Okay," I replied. Then in my most sarcastic voice, I chuckled and added, "Have a nice day and *thanks* for calling!" *It must be hard to have to call me with crappy news like this. When I react like this, my employees call me Mikezilla, which I find hilariously accurate.*

I got up and walked to Bill's office. Not there. I reached him on his cell phone and said, "The FTC just called."

"Oh, great," Bill's tone of voice fell. In a matter of seconds he appeared, then closed the door behind him.

"The FTC wants to interview the employee who did the walkarounds. See if you can find Peter's contact info. I need to go cool off."

"Okay. Just let me know if you need anything more." *How lucky I was have to have Bill. Because of him, I trusted the company would operate well while continuing to fight these bullies.*

Seeking perspective, I got in my car and drove around Atlanta with my phone off and classical music on. The lush, thick, magnificent trees hung over the streets as if I were driving in a small town, not a major city. In this bubble of safety, my mind calmed down so I could build a kind of mental checklist.

*Will I survive this? Yes.*

*Will the company fail because of this? It could.*

*How quickly might that happen? It can endure a lot.*

*Who can help? Nobody. It's up to me.*

*How can I win? By thinking outside the box.*

*Will I fight back? Yes, but I'm not sure how or when. The time to turn the tables hasn't come yet.*

*Can Peter's testimony hurt the company? No.*

*Will it stop the FTC guys? I doubt it. They aren't about to stop. They'll keep digging and digging until they think they have enough.*

*What's the conclusion? Prepare for war. I have time. I have to control costs. Stealth planning. Look for their weakness. Whether we win or lose the battles, I won't lose the war. But how? How?*

*By making this fun. I can't control whether or not this war will happen, but I'm a man with free will. So I'll make this a fun, educational, positive experience.*

*What will make it fun? Winning will make it fun. Teaching the FTC a lesson will make it fun. Educating the public. Being better off than before. All that will make it fun.*

*How do I prevent us from bleeding to death financially? I could call Phil Carpenter. He's a lawyer who's dropped the hint he wants to work at LabMD full time. If it comes to war, I can't afford to hire a big law firm to drop the bombs. I don't believe they're effective, anyway. Instead, I need nimble dancing around the giant's toes with a lawyer who can lie in wait and fire with careful, steady aim. That's it. Have an in-house legal department.*

*What's next? Have faith and move forward. Call Phil. Get it going.*

Back at the office, I still had to pretend nothing was happening. Only four people in the building knew about the FTC. To fight this battle, I'd have to add a fifth person. But silence would prevail. Why whip up an emotional frenzy and waste energy?

## Legal Help on Board

Phil Carpenter specialized in real estate issues and had a great deal of litigation experience. I'd hired him in 2004 and we won a zoning case against the City of Atlanta. Although he was a partner at his firm, he now works independently and would typically spend about 15 hours a week at the office. I'd go to him when Evelyn had conflicts or was busy with other matters.

Like a man on a mission, I strode into Phil's office and sat down.

"I need to tell you something, Phil."

Nonplussed, Phil sat back in his chair. "What, Mike?"

"We have a non-public inquiry going on with the Federal Trade Commission. The Feds have been breathing down our necks for over a year."

Phil's face showed he needed a moment to take in what I'd just said.

"The FTC? As in the FTC in Washington DC? Why?

"They're asking about our data security practices. Let me start at the beginning, which was in 2008."

I hadn't told this story to anyone from beginning to end before. The story shocked Phil; it still shocked me.

"Well, things are never boring around here, are they?" he responded.

"No, they aren't, I'm afraid. What I wouldn't give for some old-fashioned boredom right now," I laughed.

"This interests me, Mike. And you know I really want to work for you full time. I'd love to focus on one client. I'll be reasonable with my compensation."

And with that, LabMD gave birth to its first in-house legal department to battle with the FTC.

The next morning, Bill and I called Evelyn to rehash a few items.

"Good morning, Evelyn. Mike and Bill here."

"Good morning."

"Okay. Since we're required to be under oath, I want to review our previous submissions. Not that I think we have to, but I want to be prepared."

"Good idea. We should file an amendment. Better to do that now than later."

"So Bill and I will read them independently and get back to you. I can't think of anyone who did walkarounds except Peter and Jeremy. They were long gone by 2007. So, what do we do about that?

"We wait for Alain's letter. If history is any guide, it won't mirror what we recall him saying. So it's best to just wait."

Within a few days, Bill had reached Peter, who was happy to meet with us. Peter was generous in spirit and a pleasure to be around. We scheduled the meeting at Evelyn's office for Thursday, March 3rd. This development especially was taking a mental toll on me, knowing the FTC would be pulling in a 20-something kid and cooking him. More than that, all of the agency's intrusive and seemingly aimless requests agitated me. Tired of overplaying the "nicey nicey" card, I was itching to turn into Mikezilla and hit back.

Two weeks later—on February 23rd—Evelyn received the awaited letter from Alain Sheer and sent it to me via e-mail at 11 p.m. *Evelyn, what are you doing sending me this as I'm about to go to bed? Keep bad news away from me until the morning.*

Dear Evelyn:

This note memorializes our telephone conversation of February 9, 2011, as you requested. As we explained, we would like to conduct an investigational hearing to obtain additional information about the information security policies, procedures, and practices (collectively, "security practices") LabMD implemented between January 1, 2007 and August 30, 2010, including, but not limited to, informal practices and changes in the practices. We believe a hearing will provide information relevant to our investigation into whether the company's handling of sensitive information violated Section 5 of the FTC Act.

FTC investigational hearings are conducted pursuant to Commission rules, including being recorded by a court reporter. *See* 16. C.F.R. §§ 2.7 - 2.9. As we explained, we could proceed by asking the Commission to issue a Civil Investigative Demand ("CID") directing LabMD to make available a person able and competent to testify about the company's security practices. However, if LabMD is amenable, we could forego the need to issue a CID by agreeing, in writing, to conduct the hearing pursuant to Commission rules as though a CID had been issued. *See* 16. C.F.R. §§ 2.4, and 2.7 - 2.9.

You noted that you would talk to your client about proceeding by agreement and identifying a LabMD employee able to testify about the company's security practices during the time period at issue. You can contact either one of us to let us know the response.

Sincerely,
Alain Sheer
Division of Privacy and Identity Protection[1]

My translation: *We at the FTC want to interview your people under oath. We are specifically looking for chinks in your armor and want to know if you are lying in any way, shape, or form so we can beat you down into submission. After all, this is a matter of my not embarrassing myself to the boss, er, I mean national security. We could issue a CID for this, which would make this public if you want to start fighting back. Or else you can cooperate with us and keep us happy. We may get upset if you make us do any extra work, but exactly what we'll do, we'll leave that up to your vivid imagination. As you may have already noticed, fear is one of our favorite tools.*

*Because we will win no matter what, do you want to do this the easy way or the hard way? Please check with your client and let us know if he prefers a slow-burning stake or a fast-firing squad. Of course, we say all of this in a calm tone and polite manner, but don't let that fool you. We are not interested in being nice or getting along. Thank you so very much, and please make it a great day.*

*Sincerely,*
*King Alain Sheer*
*Federal Employee of the Month*

I noted with interest how the FTC kept expanding the timeline. As if I needed any more motivation to refuse to sign a consent decree, this stiffened my resolve even more. The line about conducting "an investigational hearing to obtain additional information about the information security policies, procedures, and practices LabMD implemented between January 1, 2007 and August 30, 2010" was lawyer speak for "we want to dig and dig and dig so we can find the right piece of evidence that will fry your ass." The next step would be "if you decide this is all too much for your company mentally, financially, and operationally, we'll have all the paperwork 'at the ready' for you to sign." Taken literally, it means the FTC is reserving the right to interview everyone under oath. No way, Jose!

The next morning I called Evelyn at 9 a.m. "Evelyn, dear friend and favorite of favorites, please don't send me those e-mails before I hit the sack. My brain went on overdrive and I barely slept. You know that sometimes my crackberry addiction gets the best of me and I can't help myself!"

"Uh, sorry. I didn't think you'd be awake!"

"If you're awake, I'm probably awake. The way I read this letter versus what I understood him to say is that he wants *one* employee, not more than one. The only person able to discuss this in its entirety is Bill, who's been at LabMD the whole time."

"Exactly. But Alain hasn't set a date for the interview, Mike, so let's buy time. Let's break down the facts and think this over. Like you said, there's nothing to hide. Let's . . ."

I interrupted her. "I don't understand why they don't get on with it. We know LimeWire was on the computer. Do they have any evidence the file got out aside from Tiversa? If they do, why won't they tell us? You remember Ben Wright's argument? No breach. The entire world didn't know of the security risks that P2P software created at that time. It seems the Feds aren't feeling too confident right now or they would have handed over the consent decree already."

Evelyn turned the conversation back to the issue at hand.

"We don't have to reply to Alain right now, Mike. I'll tell him I'll be in touch. He hasn't proposed any dates for a testimony and I won't propose any. Let's run the clock, speak to Peter first, and see what we have. As annoying as this is, the FTC still might go away."

"Yes, let's use logic when dealing with the illogical. That is what is so crazymaking about all of this. One day I'll shine a bright light on this crap."

Silence. I pondered if there was anything else to say. There wasn't. So I ended with "All right, let's interview Peter on the third. Call me if the King makes any more moves."

"Okay, will do. Now get back to focusing on the lab, Mike."

*I knew what she meant. "Don't let this consume me." Yet any action by the FTC was a direct hit of false propaganda by the US government to destroy our company's reputation. Who would work with a lab that's slack on patient data? Still, the smartest tool was patience. People think because I'm Type A personality, I have no patience. Partially true. But when patience is needed, I'm good at waiting for the perfect moment.*

## Big Name Law Firm

About 5:30 a.m. on March 1st, I read Evelyn's latest e-mail. At that early hour, she was awake watching C-SPAN; I was awake poking needles into my FTC doll. Specifically, she was watching a security hearing from a few days ago involving the FTC. A lawyer named Jodie Bernstein was about to testify. Evelyn caught the name of Jodie's legal firm, Kelley Drye, and excitedly noted it would be a great fit for our team. I was more impressed that she was awake and watching C-SPAN. The mother of twins, she has a ridiculously busy legal career.

Once I worked out and dragged my grumpy butt into the office, I left a voicemail for Jodie Bernstein per Evelyn's recommendation. The thought of having to hire a law firm with its big names and big invoices to ward off the FTC left me feeling anything but excited. Brand-name law firms can scheme money right out of your wallet. If you don't have a lot of cash and don't fit the pro bono criteria (most don't), you're invisible. But with the clock ticking to prepare for the next FTC hearing, I'd have to hire this firm no matter what.

By March 3rd, I hadn't heard back from Ms. Bernstein. Never mind. We still had to meet with Peter at Evelyn's office. Bill and I arrived at the high rise on the corner of Peachtree and 14th promptly at 9 a.m., took the elevator, and walked into a friendly and familiar place. We made our way to the firm's conference room. As Peter walked in a few minutes later, I noted he hadn't changed a bit. Quiet, professional, serious, and a model person—the kind of guy who lives with his grandmother so he can take care of her. What a credible witness.

After greetings and catch up, I laid out the situation. "Peter, it's been alleged that LabMD had an employee place unauthorized software on her computer. Now, the government is snooping around wondering how this happened. Because you were the primary IT support employee who performed the walkarounds and reviewed the workstations during this time, we need to discuss what you documented, recall, performed, and so on."

Peter looked perplexed. "Uh, well, okay. I don't know what I can recall, but I'll try."

"I bet once we start showing you your reports, your memory will bounce back. Evelyn will be asking the questions, and I may chime in here and there. But I want to assure you, there's no right or wrong here. Just answer the questions as honestly as you can." He agreed.

Evelyn started, "The policies were ironclad regarding LimeWire. I call Rebecca's infraction as an aberration. It's one of those things that just happened despite all of the good measures we had in place ..."

For the next hour, Peter answered questions with credibility and honesty. He repeatedly said he hadn't seen LimeWire on any desktop, including Rebecca's. If he had, he assured us, he would have taken action. Then he described his routine, documentation, job description, and credentials. To sum it up, we had no concerns about Peter saying anything that would hurt the company.

After Peter left, the three of us scattered to check our voicemails and e-mails. To get a signal on my phone, I had to walk to the end of the hall and press myself against the glass so I could retrieve my messages—including one from Jodi. It said: "Hi, Mike. This is Jodie Bernstein[2] with Kelley Drye. I'm sorry I didn't get back to you sooner, but I haven't been in the office. Please give me a call when it's best for you."

I walked into a private office because it had better reception and reached Jodie, who sounded kind and professional. In four uneventful minutes I gave her a quick rundown. Then, with sweetness and light, she promptly handed me off to someone else. *Welcome to Big Law Firm 101. Today's subject will be lead generation and retention.* Meanwhile, the clock is ticking and I have no more time to find a "fit."

"Mike, I'll have my associate Dana Rosenfeld get in touch with you, hopefully this afternoon. She's excellent and has years of experience with the FTC. She's recently joined the firm," she said.

Not happy, I hung up and walked down to the conference room where Bill and Evelyn had reconvened. I reported my call with Jodie Bernstein.

"Well, Jodie is super cordial and empathetic on the phone, but that doesn't mean much. Probably I'll never speak to her again. Her associate Dana Rosenfeld will call me later today. I'll let you know how it goes. By the way, I thought Peter did great, didn't you?"

"Yeah," Evelyn agreed, "he was right in line with what we've been saying all along, especially the part about not seeing anything on Rebecca's desktop or the start menu for months. And he looked at her desktop at least once a month."

At least I was happy with Peter; so was Bill.

"We'll document all this and then what, Evelyn?"

"I haven't set any dates with Alain, Mike. Let's see if Kelley Drye can join the team. If we add a lawyer into the mix, we can ask the FTC for time to get that person up to speed."

"Okay, I'll let you know."

Bill and I walked out and waited for the elevator to take us on a 33-story ride down to the main level. *How can I keep this big law firm from billing us into a financial crisis?*

*"The child has grown
The dream is gone
And I have become
Comfortably numb."*

—PINK FLOYD, "COMFORTABLY NUMB"

# CHAPTER 17
# Oil meets Water

Later that afternoon, around three o'clock, my cell phone rang with an unknown DC area code on the screen.

"Hello?"

"Mr. Daugherty, this is Dana Rosenfeld with Kelley Drye."

"Oh, hello, Dana. Thanks for calling so quickly."

"My pleasure. Jodi Bernstein gave me some background from your brief conversation. Why don't you give me the specifics of what's going on and bring me up to speed?"

"That would be great. First of all, please don't think me rude, but I must make sure we're on the same page regarding a few items. I want to make sure the time we spend now, discussing if, when, and how we'll work together, isn't billable time. I haven't yet engaged your firm. I've been invoiced in the past for these conversations, so I must be crystal clear on this."

"That's fine, as long as this doesn't turn into an excessive amount of time."

"Good. In return, I won't abuse the call and ask for free work."

"Fair enough."

Right away, Dana seemed quick minded, with fast responses and a solid demeanor. I started my standard bring-the-lawyer-up-to-speed speech, except this time I didn't believe I had a hiring choice. The FTC wanted to interview LabMD employees under oath, so the clock was ticking. Finally, here was a lawyer who'd worked at the FTC for years before going into private practice.

Dana's credentials looked good on paper. A partner in the firm's Washington DC office and chair of its Privacy and Information Security practice, she'd been an assistant director of the FTC's Bureau of Consumer Protection from August 1998 to October 2001. Her current practice focused on all facets of privacy and data security, advertising, and consumer financial issues at both the federal and state levels. I also assumed Dana did litigation; the firm's Web site stated she was Vice Chair of the American Bar Association Committee on Private Advertising Litigation. Clearly, she knew how things ticked at the FTC and I was interested in establishing a positive relationship with her firm. I also wanted to ensure my previous negative experiences with lawyers didn't crop up.

"Dana, it always frustrates me that I have to be this abrupt, but I need to put down a few ground rules. First, I'm not a 'surprise' guy and I'd like us to be direct. That doesn't mean rude, but know that, when you're in my inner circle, I don't hold back my passion. And if you have something to say, please say it."

"Second, regarding billing, I won't sign a two-tenths of an hour minimum. One tenth is more than fair. I see no reason to bill a hundred-dollar minimum for what could be a three-minute phone call or a quick e-mail. Your billing needs to be clear, easy to understand, prompt, and the descriptions need to stand on their own."

"Most important, I'm running a small business in an extremely precarious situation. We need your specific experience with the FTC but we have work that other counsel has already performed. We don't need to support this work. I'm not trying to tie your hands and legs and then make you run. But you can't conduct any research without my express permission; I don't allow law firms to educate themselves at my expense. The reason I am willing to pay these high prices is for the years of expertise. If a lot of research is required to achieve our goals, I may conclude that I made a bad choice in hiring a firm that has to return to the drawing board so many times. What I believe I'm buying for the firm's high price is experience. We'll give you what you need to get you up to speed, and you can let me know if you need more, but we're not starting over. Our lawyer, Evelyn, has done a load of work, and we've submitted thousands of pages to the FTC. I need to know what you think is reasonable, so we can agree beforehand. I'm not speaking about an exact to-the-minute quote beforehand, but you certainly have a general idea. This goes back to what I said about surprises. I don't want surprise invoices, and if I get one, we'll have a frank discussion about it."

No high-powered attorney, especially one who loves the law, likes money lectures or giving up control. Because I wasn't comfortable saying what I just said, I'm sure Dana wasn't enjoying it either. However, due to so many law firms willing to drain me dry, I felt compelled to send the message.

Dana's response had a slightly tense, professional tone.

"Mike, while I certainly understand your point, I can't let you know where this is going until I delve into the case. Hours will be needed for us to get into the game. I'll have my associate, probably Kristin, assist as much as possible to keep the costs in line."

"What's your hourly rate?"

"It's $545 an hour, but I can offer a ten percent discount."

I prepped myself for a high number when I asked, "And how much is Kristin's time?"

"She's $390 an hour."

"Okay, let's discuss what's going on with the FTC so you can wrap your arms around this." And I launched into a cliff note version of where we were to date.

Aggressive, clear, controlled, Dana Rosenfeld could clearly stand on her own two feet. I'm not a pushover either, so this had the potential to go either really well or really poorly.

*Does she understand that I mean what I say? I feel a kind of disconnect. I feel like she is rolling her eyes and losing her patience. Am I just being unreasonable? I feel uneasy but I have to move forward. The FTC has started the clock on getting an employee in to interview under oath. I am under the gun. I have to make this work.*

"The FTC people don't care how the file got out," she stated with complete confidence and authority. "They only care that it *did* get out. How it got out is a separate issue. They're only concerned with the adequacy of your security practices. They're willing to consider many options when deciding what to do, from the sensitivity of the data to the size of the company," she said with firm clarity, drawing a line in the sand.

*I was feeling like I had to make the best out of working with Dana as I was out of time. I had no clue if she would be good or not and words alone would never convince me.* I came back with equal force.

"Well, that may be all fine and dandy, but something has stunk from the beginning. Phone calls out of nowhere, Tiversa's CEO refusing to give critical information unless we hired his company, and then we find the same guy is testifying in front of Congress along with Dartmouth and the FTC. Something is *weird.*" Silence from Dana.

I continued. "That's why I'm not signing anything put in front of me by the FTC until I believe this was all legal and above board. I know you'll probably laugh—and it was a stretch for Evelyn as well—but I have a lawyer and technology expert named Ben Wright with the SANS Institute who insists no breach occurred. Ben graduated Georgetown Law."

I intentionally injected that fact to beef up Ben's credentials.

Then I added, "The FTC got the file from a security company that has no authorization to possess it, but I'll hold this story for later. Suffice it to say, I have no intention of signing anything. I don't trust this connection or what really went down. They can tell it to the judge."

"Well, how the FTC got the file isn't relevant at this point, anyway," replied Dana. "I can assure you the FTC doesn't play those types of games. You haven't even been presented with a consent decree, and they're just now asking to get sworn testimony. You're not going to get a decree tomorrow, obviously. We recently took over a case in which the client had already been presented with a consent decree and we got it turned around, so I wouldn't be so sure that a decree is about to happen. I'm not saying this will happen in your situation, but the best thing to do is be cooperative."

"But before I can say anything further, I have to review the materials. Until then, this isn't a productive use of time. However, after reviewing the materials, I'll probably be able to go to the FTC and meet with the people face to face. Let's see if we can buy time and get them to back off on the testimony. First, let's get the engagement letter taken care of. For this type of case we require a retainer of five thousand dollars. Then upon receipt of the letter and funds, we'll start reviewing the situation."

I liked that Dana wasn't afraid to take control. *If we could get on the same wavelength, this should work out well, however, when she assured me the FTC doesn't play "those games," I didn't believe that for a second. I hope she comprehended that I wasn't signing a consent decree.*

"Sounds good," I said. Thanks for the time. Let's set up a call with Evelyn O'Connor, I look forward to working together." I really didn't mean what I said, but I didn't want to be rude. The clock had run down to the bottom of the ninth before we were going to have Peter up against the FTC under oath. I had no time to search for a better fit. She used to work there, she seems tough, so I have to make this work. If she shows behavior that is classic big firm billing issues, Phil will have to rein her in.

*I hung up feeling totally clueless and free-falling. She said '$545 an hour' and 'the FTC doesn't play that way'—what? Something in her manner bothered me. Plus she jumped in milliseconds before I'd finished making my points. She wasn't considering my point of view enough it seemed to me. No time to worry about these things.*

I shook off my concern and called Evelyn. "Evelyn, I just spoke to Dana Rosenfeld at Kelley Drye."

"How was that?"

"I don't know. We'll see when I get the engagement letter. I can't tell if a lawyer is good or not from a phone conversation, anyway. I told her how I work, and she didn't seem to have an issue, but I don't know. Time will tell.

"Dana's nobody's fool, that's for sure. She doesn't have any fear of the FTC people, so that's good. She used to work there. She doesn't seem to hate their guts. I'm not swept off my feet. I don't think she took my points about Tiversa being relevant to this seriously, but she doesn't know me.

"About fees. She has a junior associate who bills out at $390 an hour and Dana's 'discounting' her own rate to $495 an hour. Isn't that nice of her?"

"Wow, that's a lot, Mike."

"Yep, she'd better jump over small buildings in a single bound. Anyway, let's get you two together to see what you think."

"I'm going to be in DC in two weeks, Mike. I have a couple of mornings open if you want to do a face-to-face with Dana while I'm in DC."

"Okay, I'll keep that in mind. I just want to slow the game way, way down. Let's talk next Thursday and then get you and Dana together somehow."

"Okay, Mike. Have a good weekend."

*What a stroke of luck. Evelyn will already be in DC. We can both meet Dana and Kirsten face to face.*

In the meantime, I had four days to shift my focus. Good thing I have a shower, step mill, and television in my office because I was basically living there. In this small window of time, I could focus on the company's to-do list:

- Complete a contract template for our new physician joining the company.
- Go over a contract proposal with the lawyer.
- Research "frivolous lawsuit motion" attorney fees and costs for a thrown-out case (a medical malpractice lawyer tried to corner us with innuendo. The court awarded us almost $60,000 in 2012).

Thursday, March 10th finally rolled around. After my morning ritual of early wake-up, workout, and field a boatload of e-mails, I drove down Piedmont Avenue taking in the beautiful bloom encasing Piedmont Park. As I turned down 14th Street, the scene changed from flora and fauna to high-rise condominiums and office buildings. I love both, and I love how Atlanta combines the two.

As I pulled into the parking garage, I was looking forward to my quarterly meeting and lunch with Evelyn. I didn't want to let her off this FTC issue. I still wanted Evelyn's presence, but logic and the size of the Feds scared me into agreeing to also retain an expensive expert with FTC experience.

Our agenda today was the new physician agreement, the FTC strategy, the Kelley Drye potential engagement, and other miscellaneous legal items. Evelyn came in with the files and folders, and we got down to work.

"Okay, let's start with the hot item first: the FTC and Kelley Drye," she began.

"I don't get why the FTC wants to interview anyone under oath," I said, jumping in. "What do they expect to find? This is a straight-up, clear-cut one-off and they have thousands of pages of data to prove it."

"Which is all the more reason to find a lawyer who has experience with how these people think and operate."

"They want to hold us up by the scruff of the neck, yell Bad Dog, and show everyone what happens to 'bad dogs.' What do we hope to get out of Kelley Drye?"

"Experience and strategy that will make the FTC go away."

"I spoke to Dana Rosenfeld after Jodi Bernstein did the hand off. I want you to talk to Dana, Evelyn. She won't commit to us yet, of course, until she gets more information. First see what you think and then we can meet her in DC."

"Okay."

We finished our agenda on a good note, but I had a doom-and-gloom feeling like I was about to drift into a dark cave on my own raft while Evelyn got to pull away from the FTC.

Driving back to my office, I called Dana. Voicemail.

"Dana, Mike Daugherty here. I would like you to speak with our lawyer, Evelyn O'Connor, for a brief review of her take on where we are and schedule a time for us all to meet in DC. Luckily, Evelyn will be there in two weeks and has the morning of March 22nd open. Are you available to meet us then? Please let me know. Thanks. Bye."

Getting two lawyers on the same schedule, I've learned, takes patience. Most, but not all, go along with the legal process dragging on for months, even years. I had to unlearn my "let's do it now" attitude when dealing with any part of the judicial or legislative branch. They are so used to this, it's so industry engrained, my clock is what was going to have to adjust. *It may take quite a while to set up, but if patience is all that's going to work, then patience is what I'll have.*

Dana responded to my call late Friday afternoon. Playing the role of a bouncing tennis ball between law firms, I contacted Evelyn. She could only do Monday afternoon, so we worked it out. I sent out the conference call number and everyone dialed in.

This call proved to be a tire-kicking exercise about where we've been, what the FTC has done, and how Dana's firm works. Dana seemed completely in command by being informative, polite, and eager, but I still looked at her with a cautious eye. I was worried that she had not comprehended my points from our last call and I wasn't convinced she was concerned about it. I had to suppress the voice in my head because there was no time left on the clock. Despite my hesitation, I drank my poison and told her I would be signing the engagement letter. Not long after we hung up, a bullet came from Dana via e-mail.

Starting our "put it in writing" relationship, Dana sent this:

From: Dana Rosenfeld
Sent: Monday, March 14, 2011 5:32 PM
To: Michael Daugherty
Subject: LabMD Mike Daugherty

Mike,

Thanks for setting up the call today. I enjoyed talking to you and Evelyn and look forward to meeting you both in person.

In terms of next steps, I understand that you will be sending me correspondence with the FTC and related documents to review. Please note that we do need to have an agreement in place before we spend time reviewing these materials and meeting with you and Evelyn to discuss strategy. As I mentioned earlier, since we've not done any work before for LabMD, I will be requesting a retainer. How much that will be will depend on the role you'd like us to play.

Thanks,
Dana

*Boy, I thought I could strike a ball flat and hard. This one is good.* When receiving a big power serve, I was taught to return it with the same intensity; I immediately hit back with the following e-mail:

From: Mike Daugherty
Sent: Tuesday March 15, 2011 7:10 AM
To: Dana Rosenfeld
Subject: RE: LabMD Mike Daugherty

I would like an engagement letter for the review of the materials up to and including our meeting on Tuesday. After we meet, I will decide about moving forward. As we discussed, you mentioned a junior associate would be reviewing these. We are a privately owned medical facility so we watch our costs with a keen eye at all times in this health care cost crunch. We would request all communications be electronic to save on copy costs and hope your minimum increments are .1 rather than .2 hours. Please advise.

Regards,
Mike Daugherty
LabMD

I was feeling uneasy and perplexed. Why did I feel like I was already on opposite sides with Dana? Her manner? Her tone of voice? Something subtle I couldn't put my finger on . . . This big dog in a big town in a big law firm didn't seem to sympathize with my situation. I don't have to like her if she does her job. *If she doesn't believe that LabMD doesn't deserve to be in this situation, can she defend us?*

In dealing with lawyers and law firms, I don't care what comes out of their mouths; I assume it's cover their ass first, client needs second. Many have been over coached by their malpractice carriers and never give a straight answer without an asterisk. They rarely give realistic odds, which isn't their fault. They believe, and they're right, that the judges and juries are so unpredictable; the theme song for the justice system should be "What's Truth Got to Do with It?"

This is why I scoffed at the FTC's banter about "protecting the consumer." It was more like "building careers in government so we can keep working." The more victims snared, the more job security, but where does truth fit in? The lawyers who work in these agencies decade after decade want examples to scare the masses. Their job security is secure by creating problems to solve and consumers to save.

*Funny. Because Dana worked at the FTC, I should save my opinion of it being an ineffective and damaging farce until we got to know each other. Still, if she can't supply the underbelly navigation, hiring her will be worthless.*

By that afternoon I had received Dana's engagement letter. (Anything to do with engagement letters runs at a law firm's top efficiency; that amuses me.) Her e-mail said:

From: Dana Rosenfeld
Sent: Tuesday March 15, 2011 12:05 PM
To: Michael Daugherty
Subject: RE: LabMD Mike Daugherty

Mike,

Since I don't know how many documents we may be required to review, an estimate on time is a bit difficult right now. So I propose instead that you send us a retainer of $5,000 for the initial review and meeting. We bill in .10 hour increments and are fine with electronic communications. My hourly rate is $545, and my associate's rate is $390. I would discount the rates by 10%. If you decide after our meeting not to proceed with the engagement, I will refund any amount in excess of our accrued fees.

In the event that you decide to proceed, we can discuss at that time a more long-term arrangement. I would suggest, however, that if you decide to retain us, you have us actively participate in the matter together with Evelyn. One of the reasons to use experienced FTC counsel is to receive the benefits of our relationships with the staff. Although I don't know Alain well, I have known him for a long time, and he's well aware of our experience and relationships with his managers and the FTC Commissioners.

Please let me know if the retainer agreement set out above is acceptable. If so, I will send you a formal engagement letter for your consideration and signature.

Best regards,
Dana

*Wow. Five thousand dollars and we aren't even married yet. And did she just cyber lecture me about how important existing relationships are with the FTC? That makes sense to me. So far, straight shooting and transparency haven't done the trick. I hope this ends up being more substantial than just managing old friendships. If this is all about "who ya know" and it works, I'll be more upset with "the system." Time will tell.*

As I painfully whipped out my checkbook, I sent the letter to Phil Carpenter for his review.

A few minutes later, Carpenter read the letter and walked into my office.

"I can't let this stay in here. What are they trying to pull?"

"What do you mean?"

"There is a line in the proposal letter that says they can work with others who have been in opposition to LabMD. Forget that."

"Call her up and tell her no way," I said. He quickly returned to his office and I turned back around to my desk.

Phil called Dana and she immediately pulled the language about the law firm being able to represent other future cases that may be adversarial to LabMD's interests. In all fairness, items like these come from the firm's policy, not from Dana as an individual.

I signed it on March 17th, 2011, and sent it Federal Express. Dana had made it abundantly clear the money needed to be in hand before a finger was lifted.

## Machinations of Law Firms and Courts

*Law firms. Here we go again.* I'm tempted to cross out the words "engagement letter" and replace them with "ways our firm protects itself at your expense, even though we have an implicit duty to defend." After all these years, I've learned to be on high alert for the following law firm machinations:

- Circle and confuse commentary. If you're scratching your head with what they just said, you're a victim.
- They only communicate with you verbally. That way when their prior comments conflict, it's your word against theirs because you can't prove it. (Fire this type ASAP.)
- Change the subject or patronize when in a disagreement.
- Confusing objectivity and intelligent dispassion with not being engaged in client defense.
- Two for the price of two when you only need one. You are not going to be notified that several lawyers are working with each other, so take that hourly rate and double it.

- Shock and Awe Invoices that arrive late.
- Total personality changes when discussing invoices that inspire shock and awe
- Going missing in action when it's critical to speak to them
- Never answering the phone. They're practiced at the fine art of hiding.
- Cutting you off at the knees with fear tactics for every legal move you want to make under the guise they're giving you advice when they are really covering their ass.
- Bait-and-switch dump tactics when a new associate you don't know suddenly starts working on your case. It might be in the agreement but not getting your permission is rude.
- Compensation models in which the partners and associates are on a collections scheme. This usually happens when bonuses are based on increased billable hours based on client-paid invoices instead of outstanding invoices. It creates a high-pressure "get-the-money" environment in which lawyers invoice like crazy to "make their numbers." At fiscal year end, they act like a used car dealership that's short of making its sales quota. Thus client needs become secondary during this "money panic" period. Good luck finding this out in advance.

Once you're deep into the game, it won't be easy taking on a legal issue and simultaneously trying to hold a bad lawyer accountable. Lawyers know that few people fight back, so they play the odds and usually win. When they screw you, you can always fire them, but you can't get back your time and money—and suing them is expensive because they don't have to spend $600 an hour fighting legal battles and they get their lawyers wholesale. Complaining to the state bar could be a tactic. Your arguments must be presented factually and professionally. However, as the bar is also lawyers, it's like a lamb finking on a lion to the local lion council.

That's only lawyers and law firms. Then there are the courts.

- You may lose the judge lottery and get a senior status judge who takes his or her sweet time—or is bored or biased or whatever. They have a part time job with a full time paycheck. Some are great. Do your homework. At their age their reputation is pretty on the money.

- Judges may be burned out or numb to the realities of the lives they affect. They may be snuggled in just for their cushy paycheck. Some are just lazy and don't want to work.
- Judges may be taking campaign contributions from law firms and lawyers who argue in their courtroom but they won't remove themselves from presiding over cases from these firms and lawyers. While this activity is legal in some states, it's completely immoral.
- The administrative bodies that supervise judges and lawyers are—you guessed it— other judges and lawyers, so don't expect more than a hand slap. Accountability within the legal system can be a travesty.
- Members of the juries expect to review as much detail as they find on TV crime shows, complete with DNA testing and convenient videotaping. That's not the real world.
- Transcriptionists can be spotty. Bring your own or record every word. You would be shocked what can go missing.

Here's the dirty little secret about the legal system: Injustice is just another day at the office, just like death is another day at the hospital. Not everyone experiences injustice and not everyone dies in the hospital, but it happens more often than you want to know; and you *should* know that. The smart money stays away from this massive meat grinder. Laws, ethics, promises, and policies get broken all day long, so think long and hard before seeking justice through the courts—an expensive gamble with many unpredictable and silent moving parts. Tread carefully amongst the vampires and wolves in search of the good ones. When you find them, cherish them, and throw the other ones out the door. Keep your weapons handy.

## Meeting with Kelley Drye Lawyers

On Monday evening, I flew Delta to Reagan Airport, stayed in Georgetown, got a solid night's rest, and woke up feeling like I was going to the dentist. It suddenly hit me. *Should the room be chock-full of lawyers, this meeting would cost several thousand dollars. That can't happen; I'd better head that off at the pass.* At 6:30 a.m. I sent a text to Dana with the following message:

> Dana, as this is an intro meeting, I want to have only you and Evelyn in the room. Paying for more than two lawyers is not necessary this a.m. Please confirm.

The reply arrived within 15 minutes. In reference to the room being chock-full of lawyers, Dana wrote:

> In a situation such as yours, that's how I work, so if it's not acceptable to you, then you are welcome to come pick up your retainer check.

This pulled the pin right out of the grenade. Five seconds after reading it, I blew a gasket. *Come get my check? Is she serious? Here I am, vulnerable and paying money, and this is the crap I get?*

This her way or the highway without justification was not going to fly with me. I wondered if I was out of line being so furious.

With that thought, I forwarded the e-mail to Evelyn and two high-powered lawyer friends who work in huge firms. I needed feedback from people who could pull me out of the trees. After all, I was already in DC and with the FTC breathing down our back, there was no time to find someone else. I needed some fast feedback.

Within 30 minutes, I'd received unanimous thumbs down for Dana's behavior. *This validates my intuition she's simply waiting for me to stop talking rather than listening to me and following my requests.*

I fired off a quick text telling her "not to go all hardball." Then she backed off and apologized. With that, I decided to go forward with the meeting because I was boxed in. *I hope that was more about her needing her morning coffee and not her normal behavior.*

First, as planned, I had to meet Evelyn for breakfast at the Four Seasons. Strolling up to the table where Evelyn was enjoying her coffee and newspaper, I smirked and grunted. She knew exactly what that meant.

"Nice exchange this morning, don't you think?" I started. "Dana couldn't be playing me more wrong. I feel like I've been brought to DC on false pretenses."

"I'm not really sure what to say about that," Evelyn replied, as baffled as I was.

I swallowed my anger, not wanting to ruin breakfast by bitching about this in the middle of the restaurant. "I'll suck it up and be completely professional, but don't think for one second I think what she did is okay. She's on probation."

"I'm shocked myself, Mike. Totally uncalled for."

After enjoying our breakfast, we jumped a cab and reached the cold, contemporary offices of Kelley Drye. As we waited in the lobby, out strolled a brown-haired, middle-aged woman in a dark blue executive suit and thick high-heels—about 5' 5". Trying to salvage the morning's bad beginning, I greeted her cordially and professionally.

"Hello, Mike. Dana Rosenfeld," she responded.

"Nice to meet you, Dana. This is Evelyn O'Connor."

"Great to finally meet you both. Kristin will join us in a moment. Let's go down to the conference room. Right this way."

Once in the room, we took our places around the table. As I sat down in the chair, Kristin came in and introduced herself. She was a beautiful Asian woman, probably in her early 30s. She sat to my right, Dana across from her, and Evelyn across from me next to Dana.

I wanted to set the tone with background, plus I wanted Kristin to hear our story directly from me. Knowing I'd be paying roughly $1,000 an hour, I spoke fast.

"The first thing I want to point out is that we've worked with Evelyn for over fourteen years. We work well together. Evelyn keeps a firm, objective perspective, and I know she has the company's back." I paused, waiting for acknowledgment but could barely sense a pulse.

"We're perplexed by the FTC animal we're dealing with. We're constantly confused by the agents' seeming lack of knowledge of what's in our submissions, yet we don't want to anger them. We've sent them thousands of documents, but in my opinion, they don't want to break a sweat reviewing them. To top it off, they keep moving the target of what they want. Alain Sheer . . . we don't get him at all. We require everything in writing because he mails letters that are much broader in meaning than what he says—and what he says constantly changes. We've stopped relying on anything that comes out of his mouth."

Dana responded, "Well, I know Alain, but not well, but he can be a bit aloof, I suppose. I think we just need to get an overview from you, hear you out, and see where to go from here." Dana and Kristin flashed that insider's smirk at each other as if they knew everyone there—a good thing. *We'll get their side of the story and see what they think. This sounded like a good first move to me. Always good to take a temperature before making a plan. I'm still ticked about this morning, but I'm willing to keep an open mind. Like I have a choice.*

Without bringing in prior events, Evelyn started out with the chronological timeline starting January 10, 2010. She kept peppering the conversation with statements like "LabMD had adequate policies and procedures in place. This was a one-time error by an unthinking employee and the situation was resolved. There is no evidence of damages."

Kristin was pleasant enough, but I failed to see why she had to be in the room. *I get this game. The queen bee oversees the hive and Kristin does all the work. Ca-Ching.*

I thought I'd taken care of this by being completely impossible to misunderstand, but I was wrong. *I know where this is going and I doubt I can stop it. Damn . . . if it weren't for this pending testimony burning at our backs, I may not be sitting here. Like I have time to manage another beast.*

Like an observer in the stands, I looked around the room as the three of them examined the main points of the timeline. *The information we were dumping probably wouldn't matter a flip until Dana found out what the FTC wanted to know. Could she find out?*

Dana was in complete control. "Okay, here's what we propose. By the end of the day, I'll follow up with a list of what we need from these previous submissions. I'll also call Alain and Ruth, introduce Kristin and me, propose a face-to-face meeting, and see if they'll back off on the testimony. If we can get to the bottom of what they need, maybe we can hold them off from having to interview your employees under oath."

"That sounds fine," I replied.

"Well, we'll find out what they're digging for, we hope. Sometimes they just want things in a certain way," Dana said.

"It was nice to meet you, and we'll wait for your summary," said Evelyn. "Then Mike and I will get you what you need."

"It won't take long. We're very organized. Thanks for your time."

Smiles flew all around the room and handshakes were quickly offered. I walked out the door with a forced smile on my face. *Well, there goes about two thousand dollars.* I felt like I was there solely to pay the bill.

Evelyn and I walked out of the building into a beautiful DC day.

"I don't think Dana gives a flip about the submissions we made to the FTC until she hears what the agents have to say," I said.

"True. She needs the basics, and this may also be political, anyway. They may change their tune because she used to work there. She knows how they think and act better than we do, so that's fine for now."

I grabbed a cab back to Reagan while Evelyn headed toward her hotel on foot. As my taxi pulled away down K Street, I looked back at her walking up the brick-paved sidewalk. On this beautiful sunny day, she strolled at a relaxed, comfortable pace—not only walking away from my taxi, but from the whole FTC situation.

I suddenly felt very alone, but that was an ultimate truth, anyway. *Evelyn has taken me as far as she could.*

THE LAWYERS KNOW TOO MUCH
—CARL SANDBURG (1878—1967)

The lawyers, Bob, know too much.
They are chums of the books of old John Marshall.
They know it all, what a dead hand wrote,
A stiff dead hand and its knuckles crumbling,
The bones of the fingers a thin white ash.
　The lawyers know
　a dead man's thoughts too well.

In the heels of the higgling lawyers, Bob,
Too many slippery ifs and buts and howevers,
Too much hereinbefore provided whereas,
Too many doors to go in and out of.

　When the lawyers are through
　What is there left, Bob?
　Can a mouse nibble at it
　And find enough to fasten a tooth in?

　Why is there always a secret singing
　When a lawyer cashes in?
　Why does a hearse horse snicker
　Hauling a lawyer away?

The work of a bricklayer goes to the blue.
The knack of a mason outlasts a moon.
The hands of a plasterer hold a room together.
The land of a farmer wishes him back again.
Singers of songs and dreamers of plays
Build a house no wind blows over.
The lawyers—tell me why a hearse horse snickers
　hauling a lawyer's bones.

# CHAPTER 18
# We Have Only Just Begun

I was back in Atlanta and in my office by 3 p.m. Around 4:50 p.m., I received an e-mail from Dana. It read:

From: Dana Rosenfeld
Sent: Tuesday March 22, 2011 4:51 PM
To: Michael Daugherty, Evelyn O'Connor
Subject: LabMD: List of requested items

Mike and Evelyn,
Thanks for coming in today to visit with us. As we discussed, we have a few follow-up items that we'd appreciate receiving copies of (to the extent they exist). The items include:

- Documents dates labeled (automatic consecutive numbering) LabMD 0618 0925 (attachments to August 30, 2010 letter)
- Any documentation available regarding system checks from pre-breach to present, including Elizabeth's search for LabMD's files after the breach was discovered
- ProviDyn security reports (other than those provided in the 7/6/10 response)
- Internal logs from 7/10 forward tracking monthly sniffer and penetration testing
- Annual inspection reports from Georgia Department of Human Resources from 2004 to present
- Recommendations and information from industry groups regarding data security best practices
- Number of patients in LabMD servers at time of breach and at present
- Documentation of current efforts to install content filtering hardware/software

I will reach out to Alain next week and report in. In the meantime, please let me know if you have any questions regarding these items.

Best regards,
Dana

Breach? She actually typed the word *breach*. I was pissed and my trust had been violated. I contained my fury and replied:

"Okay, but breach? What breach? Thanks! Mike Daugherty."

It wasn't 60 seconds before she fired back.

"Sorry! How about 'incident'?"

I was really concerned by this slip-up; this wasn't just a battle over words. One person's accidental death is another person's murder and the defense lawyer better well believe this was accidental. "Oops, sorry, didn't mean to call it murder. Jury, please disregard!" *This was no small issue. Is she just giving me lip service?*

I didn't want her to just say it; I wanted her to believe it. When you bill over $450 per hour you better be on top of your game.

"Keep a constant eye on this one. I don't think she believes us," I mumbled to my computer monitor.

A lawyer who doesn't believe you but will still argue your point isn't as effective as a lawyer who believes you and believes *in* you. It's like the difference between a fake smile and a real one—you can tell the difference. If you don't believe your client and you are taking this much money, get off the stage and let your client find a lawyer who will actually defend from the heart and mind. Going through the motions never beats passion and conviction in anything. In my experience, some lawyers will cover up their lack of passion and conviction with a tail-covering speech about their being objective. Objectivity does not mean staying emotionless as you witness an injustice. The judge is to be objective. A jury is to be objective. But if your defense attorneys standing on the sidelines remain "objective" but don't keep their facts straight and just go through the motions, that's not a good thing.

As I looked through her list, I figured it would be easy enough to gather what she wanted, but I was going to have to slow down the financial bleeding. Evelyn was passing the baton to Dana, and I had Carpenter in the office part-time. I had to make him the company's guard dog watching these new lawyers.

I walked into Phil's office, frustrated and animated.

"Okay, did you read that e-mail exchange?"

"No, what did it say?" he asked.

"Pull it up."

Once he pulled up his e-mail, he started reading.

"See, here we go again. Her slip is showing. First the 'come get your check if you don't like it' and now she calls it a breach. She'd better not screw this up."

"As long as she doesn't say that to the FTC, it should be okay," Carpenter said.

"I'm concerned. I don't need to have my defense lawyer think I'm guilty when I'm not. There's no time for a change. We're under the gun. You're going to have to help me keep her in check. I think she thinks 'I've got this—just go sit over there in the corner, you amateur, I know what I'm doing.'"

"I know."

"I'm not sending Kelley Drye a thing until we have a meeting scheduled with the FTC. The lawyers there will have plenty of time to review, but I'm not opening up a vein just to pump out more money."

## Pulling in the Reins

I can't for the life of me remember why, but Dana didn't reach out to the FTC for a whole week. On March 29, Dana called and had a conversation with Alain, letting him know they were now on the team and they wanted to discuss what was going on. She e-mailed Evelyn and me the following:

From: Dana Rosenfeld
Sent: Tuesday March 29, 2011 4:16 PM
To: Michael Daugherty, Evelyn O'Connor

Mike and Evelyn,
I spoke this afternoon to Alain Sheer, and explained that we were recently retained to represent LabMD. I told him that I would greatly appreciate the chance to meet with him to get

his views on the investigation. He readily agreed, and we are tentatively scheduled for next Thursday at 11 a.m. I will keep you posted.

Best Regards,
Dana

We were on for Thursday, April 7, 2011. By this time, it had been 15 months since the first eight-page, single-spaced letter. My expectations were low and nothing would surprise me. *Let's see what magic Dana can pull out of her hat.*

We'd planned to start pulling information right away, and then Carpenter came down with the classic Atlanta spring allergy attack. (This is the price we sometimes pay for our beautiful azaleas and dogwoods in the South.) To keep the reins on costs, I resorted to holding off on sending Dana and Kristin anything right away but still planned on giving them more than enough time to review the materials. I won't allow lawyers to research the entire ocean looking for a goldfish.

Dana sent an e-mail asking for materials on April 5. We got everything to her the evening before their meeting. She e-mailed me the following, which was just what I was thinking:

From: Dana Rosenfeld
Sent: Wednesday April 6, 2011
To: Michael Daugherty
CC: Kristin A. McPartland
Subject: Re: LabMD: List of requested items

If you could overnight the material for early delivery, that would be great. But it's not essential for us to receive them before the meeting if it will cause you to work into the night. Our goal for tomorrow is to get information from Alain, not to give it.

Dana

Through our cryptic communications, I was realizing she thought she spoke the FTC language. She wanted to repackage our submissions in a manner the FTC would prefer. I took this to mean that if the FTC guys wanted their meat cut for them, she was ready with a knife and fork. I was okay with this for one—and exclusively one—reason, which was, as Dana would often put it, "to make them go away." Already on my last nerve, I growled and grimaced as I played along. *Who knows, maybe they'll back off because they all know each other. Whatever works.*

Evelyn was speaking at a conference in New Orleans the day of Dana's meeting with the FTC. We scheduled a conference call for 2:30 p.m. to debrief. For reasons still unclear to me, Kristin had to go to the meeting as well. *Ca-ching.* Again, these associate attorneys seem like personal assistants to me. *What is this? At more than $500 per hour, does Dana have a memory problem or does she get scared riding in cabs by herself?* I was tired of getting run over by the 'We Play Deaf' Lawyers Association of DC.

The conference call began.

"Hello, everyone."

"Hi, Dana," Evelyn and I chimed in.

"Well, I think the call went well in the sense that we got them to back off their idea of having an IT employee come up and testify. That's been put on the back burner for now."

"Wow, that's a relief. Good job! That's GREAT!" I happily said.

"Thank you. I think they were glad to have someone local so they could get this moving and cleared up, one way or another."

"Okay. So what else happened?"

"They're still focused on what practices were in place at the time that allowed this situation to manifest in the first place."

"It's all in the earlier submissions."

Evelyn agreed, "Yes, there isn't anything that isn't in those submissions; they're exhaustive."

"Well, they've given us a chance to take another bite of the apple and show them what was going on in the company. We're to provide a roadmap and outline in a supplemental response to the FTC. Additionally, I think it best that LabMD contact several monitoring companies. The FTC likes outside analysis, so I strongly urge you to hire an outside company to submit an opinion."

"Uh, that sounds expensive. They have to have medical experience. Consulting firms, regardless of their specialty, are not high on my list of effective solutions. Technology is especially suspect. They capitalize on and exploit technical ignorance. The bills are outrageous and typically not coupled with accountability and guarantees. And will the FTC pay attention to the opinion, anyway?"

"I know of firms the FTC prefers and trusts. Someone with a fresh opinion who has never worked with LabMD would have the greatest impact. They'd probably find their conclusions compelling."

I almost choked with laughter. That's a classic point of view from a bureaucrat/academic who thinks we're writing a research paper. Never mind that these so-called "third-party" companies are far from "objective." From my experience, they were Geiger counters looking for gold.

"Dana, I have two huge concerns. One is medical background. You don't hire a tax lawyer to deal with a divorce, and I don't want to hire an expensive, analytical giant with no medical experience. Secondly, I'm concerned about money. These groups tend to be expensive. They capitalize on your fear and pad the bill. Since the FTC has no set standards, this is a free-for-all. There have to be controls."

I sensed these points *again* went in one ear and out the other as Dana continued, "They also asked us to go back and show how the company has responded and changed their practices since the incident occurred. They will consider all of these variables, once submitted, in their decision of whether or not they'll move for a consent decree. We need to have something to them by May 8th. We want to put our best foot forward to make them just go away."

"Okay. Today is April 7th. That's only a month away. Fine. Phil Carpenter will be assisting in this. It sounds like we're just reinventing the wheel and repackaging this. There's nothing new here. Isn't that the case?"

"We're outlining and summarizing to present a big picture of progress and reasonable practices over time. We'll go back further in time and bring them to your current status. As new practices emerge, we want to show a constant self-awareness as well as improvements in data security practices."

We quickly wrapped up the call. Evelyn and I were ready to try anything, but she was on the way out. I felt like I was about to pay for a final round of negotiations with a new general before going to war. If the negotiations made the FTC go away, I would be forever grateful and grovel for doubting Dana. I gave it a 25% shot. I knew I had to try it. After all, logic would indicate that the FTC will drop this against a small company that is a cancer detection facility. Unfortunately, my intuition was screaming that this was not going to matter a lick. Intuitions are not facts. I kept my mouth shut and surrendered the reins to Dana.

Within a week, we'd sent everything up to DC for our new firm to do God only knows what. What more could the FTC possibly want? I felt completely out of control. I could choose to do it their way for only so long.

We assumed that Dana and Kristin, being experienced with the FTC and having worked there, would know how to take the information and repackage it. I had no reason to be excited about this, though, because when dealing with a monolithic government agency, outcomes are a crapshoot. This didn't reflect my opinion of Kelley Drye; it showed my lack of respect for the FTC.

## The Fear Industry

Because we had everything organized and computerized from previous submissions, it wasn't difficult to get our new team members what they needed to kiss the hand of the King. But Dana begged to differ. She repeated her earlier opinion that the FTC likes to see third-party companies perform the analysis. She knew companies the FTC liked to deal with, that the FTC agents had faith in the opinions these vendors reported. Then she offered to contact them. I felt conflicted. Part of me said, "Give it a shot" while the other part said, "This is all a sham."

The FTC, the lawyers, the consulting companies, the tech salesmen, the political campaigners—they're all part of what I call the Fear Industry. The Fear Industry consists of anyone who pours gas on someone's fire to raise anxiety that something bad is happening, then uses that fear to close a deal. The data analysis firms, for example, capitalize on a person's lack of education in computer engineering, all frosted with woulda coulda shoulda and, buried in the fine print of the agreement is a release of liability, promises, and an indemnification added in to boot.

With the way the FTC had already dismissed what we submitted, why would I spend thousands of dollars on more research they'd continue to ignore? This was all a game, but since Dana demonstrated a severe lack of listening skills, I wasn't about to continue an endless debate.

True to form, she did it her way. Acting like she knew better than I did—and on my dime—she called a few "data security companies" for "analysis." On April 12th at 8:30 a.m., I received the following e-mail:

From: Dana Rosenfeld
Sent: Tuesday April 12, 2011 8:30 AM
To: Michael Daugherty
Subject: FW: Questions for client

Mike
This is a follow-up to a conversation I had yesterday with an IT forensic firm called Trustwave. Please let me know how best to answer the questions below so that we can obtain an estimate from the firm. It also would be helpful if I could get a copy of the proposal/scope of work prepared by the Oklahoma firm you are currently working with.

Thanks,
Dana

Within 10 minutes I replied:

From: Michael Daugherty
Sent: Tuesday April 12, 2011 8:45 AM
To: Dana Rosenfeld
Subject: RE: Questions for client

Dana
My first qualifying question will be how much medical experience they have. I will call them tomorrow. Thanks,

Mike
Sent via BlackBerry

Dana replied:

From: Dana Rosenfeld
Sent: Tuesday April 12, 2011 7:56 AM
To: Michael Daugherty
Subject: RE: Questions for client

Mike—It's important that Evelyn or I am on the call to preserve privilege. Please do not make the call alone. We can talk to them about medical experience. I believe Chris is very experienced in this area.
Dana

At this point, Phil Carpenter intervened and said he'd be on the call with me. In the meantime, I had Carpenter slow Dana down in writing. Why have "Ms. $450 an hour" on the phone when my in-house counsel, who is cheaper and local, can handle it just as well? Carpenter sent the following:

From: Phil Carpenter
Sent: Tuesday April 12, 2011 9:34 AM
To: Dana Rosenfeld
Subject: RE: Questions for client

Dana
Can you send us the names of the contacts you have? I will initi-
ate the conversation with them to discuss this matter. We really
need to be sensitive to costs and I can do much of this work,
especially since we have made no decision about going down
this road at this point. It was my understanding that you would
send us the names and we would make the initial investigation.

Thanks,
Phil

She responded with this:

From: Dana Rosenfeld
Sent: Tuesday April 12, 2011
To: Phil Carpenter
CC: Michael Daugherty, Bill Barnet, Kristin A. McPartland,
Evelyn O'Connor
Subject: RE: Questions for client

Privileged and Confidential Attorney Client Communication
   My understanding is that you all wanted to be in the calls
but that was not to be a substitute for outside counsel. I don't
have a problem with you reaching out to the firms to determine their level of sophistication in the healthcare arena. I
would not, however, want you to talk about the FTC investigation or what we want them to do. That is something I need
to be involved in because we need to direct them to address
what I believe will be useful to the FTC. If that's a problem for
you, please let me know immediately.

Dana

"If that's a problem for you." The last time she got this aggressive
was when she told me I could come get my retainer check. Again,
she wasn't hearing me. *Plus the FTC seems to have barely read what we
sent so far. Why would this be any different?*

Plus she didn't send the company contacts we'd requested. More of "her way or the highway." She just kicked the ball back to us if we dared stop playing her game. I could foresee that if we unsuccessfully averted "negotiations," the blame would fall squarely on our lack of doing it "her way." It felt like Dana thought I didn't get it and was saying something like "Here are the Inside-the-Beltway rules in dealing with FTC people that you don't get, Mike":

1. Don't piss them off.
2. Take them seriously.
3. Respond in a timely manner.
4. I am your lawyer and I know what I'm doing, so just let me do it, carte blanche.
5. Remember they have huge resources and they *are* the Federal Government.
6. Again, I repeat, don't piss them off.
7. Let me spend your money, speaking their language, and I'll tell you about it later.
8. The fact is the FTC could not care less about you, and LabMD is expendable. Just do as you're told.
9. No guarantees.
10. If you would just shut up and cooperate, things would be so much easier. The only way out of this is to roll over and hope for the best.

This entire line of thinking mocks the very rights we have as citizens. The agents interpret their power as all-encompassing and are so lawyered-up they just go where they want and apologize later if anyone dares question them. The odds of them being taken on are slim. Time and experience has made them full of themselves while they have run roughshod over whomever they deem suspect.

My thoughts raced. The FTC doesn't have the expertise, the standards, or the knowledge to make any informed decisions, but they *do* have the power. Right now, they can't do much financial damage if I exclude the crazy costs of this sociopathic information-gathering expedition. But if I sign away my rights, the costs can only get worse. Regardless of how much I was itching to fight with them, trying to get them to leave was the smarter move.

However, my patience could only last so long before I turned the tables on them with guns blazing. I hated the illusion of cooperating with these terrorists.

As we waited to resubmit something for the FTC yet again, two new agenda items came to mind—to get Dana under control and to share the following vision:

- Keep Kelley Drye on a short leash by using in-house counsel so the lawyers wouldn't break the bank.
- Try to convince Dana Rosenfeld there wasn't a violation of Section 5 because there was no definition of "reasonable" and no standards to go against. To make this argument, I would show her, not just tell her, the opinions of an expert in the field, namely Ben Wright.

## Challenging the FTC's Jurisdiction

Next, on April 12th, I had a brief conversation with Dana about forwarding a letter from Ben Wright challenging the jurisdiction of the FTC. Surely another lawyer could at least *start* to change her mind. Perhaps this Hail Mary pass would work.

"Dana, I'm sending you the summary letter from Ben Wright. You remember Ben? He's the Georgetown Law School lawyer who lives in Dallas and analyzed our situation last year."

"Okay, I'll look at it."

"Please keep an open mind. Ben is an out-of-the-box thinker, a lawyer, and a classic IT guy. It took Evelyn time to warm up to his ideas, but she did. She just doesn't know if the FTC will be moved at all, as the FTC thinks that Section Five is theirs to make up as they go along. Remember, I'm not signing any consent decree. We did nothing wrong and the file didn't get out to insecure parties.

We see no evidence of LabMD electronic property being anywhere other than government-funded entities. There was not a breach."

I could feel Dana's silence. To me, it didn't indicate agreement, merely tolerance.

On April 13th, I didn't get time to review an e-mail Dana sent early that morning. It contained these questions from one of the data security analysis companies she'd contacted:

1. How big is the company in terms of employees?
2. How many of the following types of servers does it operate?
   a) File/print
   b) E-mail
   c) Web
   d) Database or application
3. Are we only reviewing the breached systems or the whole network?
4. Does the company outsource its IT functions?
5. If so, to whom?
6. If not, how many in its IT department?
7. Would we be asked to perform any types of the following tests/reviews?
   a) Penetration testing. If so, against how many hosts?
   b) Code review
   c) Log analysis
   d) Physical security (e.g., guards and gates)
8. What kinds of policies and regulations should be considered – HIPAA, PCI, etc.?

Question 3 irked me: ". . . reviewing only the breached system or the whole network?" I choked with fury and frustration. *Why in God's name is that word breach coming up again? What exactly do I have to do to get them to agree? This is happening all too often. These high paid prima donna consultants are going to dismiss me as well. Dana will dismiss me as I am not a lawyer in DC. The security company will dismiss me because I am not a computer science specialist. They will, however, run to the bank to cash the check.*

I quickly e-mailed her the following:

From: Michael Daugherty
Sent: Wednesday April 13, 2011 5:01 PM
To: Dana Rosenfeld
Subject: RE: FW: Questions for client

Dana
What's up with this question? "Are we only reviewing the breached system or the whole network?"

Mike Daugherty

To which she quickly and dismissively replied:
"That's the way IT guys talk about 'incidents.' It's just shorthand."
Within five minutes, I responded to Dana with the following:

From: Michael Daugherty
Sent: Wednesday April 13, 2011 5:06 PM
To: Dana Rosenfeld
Subject: Ben Wright, Esq, profile and response. Fwd: LabMD

See below from Ben Wright, who has been retained by LabMD for about a year.
   Here is a link about Ben: http://www.sans.org/security-training/instructors/Benjamin-Wright
   The course he is teaching several times this year:
   http://www.sans.org/security-west-2011/description.php?tid=4572

Mike:
I want to be careful not to run up your bill, but what I am going to say here is helpful to you and LabMD as we assess what to do. LabMD has a whole host of strong arguments that it did not violate Section 5 of the FTC Act. However, it may take a lot of time and effort to make the arguments,

and it may take a lot (such as a lawsuit and/or an investigation by authorities in Georgia) to get all the good evidence to support the arguments. Here are examples (using general summary, imprecise language) of the arguments to be made:

Twenty-seven minutes later, Dana replied with the following:

From: Dana Rosenfeld
Sent: Wednesday April 13, 2011 5:32 PM
To: Michael Daugherty
Subject: Ben Wright, Esq, profile and response. Fwd: LabMD

Evelyn was right. I can assure you that "government agents," i.e., the FTC, did not use surveillance methods to gather the data. In addition, there is no disputing that the file contains LabMD's internal data, which means the burden is on LabMD to either show that its actions did not cause the incident, or that the incident was a limited occurrence. My recommendation is to not have any further conversations with Mr. Wright on this topic.

Dana

As I sat in stunned silence, I felt the fury build inside me. I stormed into Bill's office, my face red with anger.

"Dana Rosenfeld is blowing off Ben Wright. He's a key witness for our defense. He's an expert! She had the nerve to tell me to have no further conversations with him. We have to keep this woman on a tight leash. Now I have to fight Tiversa, the FTC, and our own lawyer. Where's Carpenter? I have to find him."

Bill shook his head in agreement as I vented my steam.

*How can she just dismiss such a well-educated Georgetown lawyer who teaches the Law of Data Security and Investigations at the SANS Institute?*

I stomped back to my office and fired off this reply:

From: Michael Daugherty
Sent: Wednesday, April 13, 2011
To: Dana Rosenfeld
CC: Kristin A. McPartland, Phil Carpenter
Subject: Re: Ben Wright, Esq., profile and response Fwd: LabMD

I just knew you would love Ben.

And THAT argument regarding limited occurrence can be found in the congressional testimony of the CEO of Tiversa. "This unique technology has led some industry experts (*Information Week*) to refer to Tiversa as the 'Google of P2P.'"

It wasn't reasonable technology that gained access to that file or else the entire US government is also right under the bus. But try to overlook the paranoia and don't throw the baby out with the bathwater regarding Ben. The FTC got this from Tiversa and Tiversa has our property and won't give it back. Tiversa used very sophisticated technology to get the file and the FTC thinks it was just "sitting there" for two years. We beg to differ.

In the meantime, we have spent $200,000+ to tighten up holes through which water never leaked . . . and one day I will live to tell this story . . . loudly.

Seven minutes later, disregarding the main body of my response yet again, she retorted:

From: Dana Rosenfeld
Sent: Wednesday April 13 2011 5:20 PM
To: Michael Daugherty
Subject: Ben Wright, Esq, profile and response. Fwd: LabMD

Mike,
If we have a way of showing that the file was not "sitting there" for two years, I'm all ears. I imagine that would be difficult if not impossible to prove, however. But probably more

productive to demonstrate what the $200,000 has bought in the way of added protections.

Dana

I replied with zero hope of getting through to her, so I changed the subject:

From: Michael Daugherty
Sent: Wednesday April 13, 2011 5:55 P.M.
To: Dana Rosenfeld
CC: Kristin A. McPartland, Phil Carpenter
Subject: Re: Ben Wright, Esq., profile and response Fwd: LabMD

Actually, that was something you said in the conference call that Bill thinks he can work on . . . so we are on that . . . have been since the call . . .

Mike

By this time in our relationship I realized that Dana was not buying into this Tiversa argument as relevant to the FTC matter. Boy, did I ever beg to differ. I was in a corner, knew I could not change her mind, and had not time to find another lawyer. I, once again, just kept my mouth shut. Nothing was going to change her mind, so why fight for the sake of fighting? Dana Rosenfeld was the toughest sale I had ever had.

After that exchange, I was done for the day. I threw my jacket and briefcase in the car then slammed the door. I didn't burn rubber as I left, but I sure felt like it. The intellectual arrogance of my legal representative was astounding. I felt trapped. I wanted to fire her right then and there. I felt like she was being disrespectful and not defending us. I couldn't believe she was dismissing experts, and all this with a FTC deadline looming in just a few weeks, I was sure she felt like she was doing this for my own good.

The next morning, I got to work and felt calm to the point of actually being able to have civil conversations. I was still furious, but at least I could speak in a normal tone and had a normal heart rate.

I walked into Carpenter's office and sat in the chair in front of his desk.

"So, did you see those e-mails from Dana?"

"Yes," he replied.

"Man, did I get mad. Ben could run rings around Dana with his technology knowledge. What kind of Congress built these loopholes that allow these agencies to get away with abuse and overreach until someone speaks out? Does anyone there have a conscience? Has anyone ever taken a civics class? They are burning my business down and Congress is so clueless they think the smell is from burning leaves. Unbelievable!"

"Phil, you're now in charge of this outside firm and keeping Dana on a tight leash. I don't trust her an inch."

"But we have to get something to the FTC sometime next month."

"I know. Let's keep the Kelley Drye lawyers on ice. We'll have to write the requested letter of response, and they'll have to approve it."

"Right. I'll let them know," Phil said.

*"In my many years, I have come to a conclusion that
one useless man is a shame,
two is a law firm, and three or more is a congress."*

—JOHN ADAMS

# CHAPTER 19
# Quicksand

On April 15, 2011, at 12:38 p.m., my team and I received an e-mail from Dana. The Kelley Drye lawyers had finished the outline of what they required so we would perform most of the groundwork in-house—my intent all along so LabMD could keep costs under control and survive while taking on this battle. The plan was to look at the outline provided, fill in the gaps, and resubmit the letter for the lawyers' approval. Seemed simple enough.

Dana's e-mail of instruction read:

> From Dana Rosenfeld
> Sent: Friday April 15, 2011 12:38 PM
> To: Michael Daugherty
>
> Mike,
> I attach a draft letter containing a list of questions that are intended to elicit the information we need to provide to the FTC. At your request, we did not go through your prior submissions to glean the answers to these questions. Instead we pose questions that we believe the FTC would like addressed. I will be traveling next week (and checking e-mails), but Kristin will be available to assist as needed.
> Please let me know if you have any questions.
>
> Dana

I didn't like the word "elicit." The word sounded like information was to be pulled out of us without our realizing what was happening. Perhaps my trouble with the word was a projection of my distrust of this entire situation.

The list was exhausting to take in, let alone answer, and yet the Federal courts allow this type of fishing expedition when it comes to Federal agency investigations. The FTC's plan is to defeat via relentless pursuit. Congress created these beasts, and our current and former Congresses and Presidents, regardless of party, have allowed them to grow. I include this in its entirety specifically not to entertain, but to educate and demonstrate the government's wide breadth of questioning and lack of boundaries in this, so far, "non-public inquiry." Our lawyer, once again, wanted us to open our veins in a last ditch hope to make the FTC go away.

The first outline of our fifth submission was as follows. We were to fill it in by answering her questions.

KDW DRAFT—Privileged and Confidential Attorney Client Communication[1]

April __, 2011

VIA HAND DELIVERY

Alain Sheer
Division of Privacy and Identity Protection
Federal Trade Commission
600 Pennsylvania Ave., NW
Mail Stop NJ-8122
Washington, DC 20580

Re: LabMD, Inc.

Dear Alain:

We write in response to your ongoing correspondence with LabMD, Inc. regarding the non-public inquiry into LabMD, Inc.'s compliance with federal law governing information security, and as follow-up to our discussion on April 7, 2011. We provide the following information for your reference:

LabMD is a small, privately held medical services company providing uro-pathology and microbiology laboratory services to approximately 100 physician customers. Founded in 1996 by Michael J. Daugherty, President and CEO and 100% corporate shareholder, LabMD operates in a small, specialized medical testing market. The company started in Savannah, Georgia as Southern Diagnostics & Treatment, Inc. and later moved its operations to Atlanta. In 2003, it changed its name to LabMD. [Please provide a rough timeline of employee growth from 1996 to present—in particular, if most growth has occurred in the past few years, we'd like to state so.] In 2004, LabMD had just seven employees; in 2010, it had approximately 33 employees; and currently, LabMD has approximately 40 employees.

Prior to founding LabMD, Mr. Daugherty worked for 13 years in the hospital and healthcare field as part of Mentor Corporation. [Please describe knowledge of industry and any prior training on data security that you may have received at Mentor. Please also add descriptions for any employees integral to the start-up of LabMD and, specifically, its data security procedures.]

LabMD's primary business is to provide testing of blood, urine, and tissue for physicians. It currently employs [x] number of people in its laboratories. To support this main function, LabMD currently employs [x] number of personnel in its IT department and [x] number in its billing department. In 2005, LabMD employed [x] number of personnel in its IT department.

## Size of LabMD

- On 10/31/05, how many employees (in total) and how many IT employees did LabMD have, and how many computers were in use at LabMD? On 5/13/08, how many employees (in total) and how many IT employees did LabMD have, and how many computers were in use at LabMD?
- Presently, how many employees (in total) and how many IT employees does LabMD have, and how many computers are in use at LabMD?
- LabMD was notified by Tiversa, a private company, on May 13, 2008 that a file appearing to contain LabMD patient information was available on the P2P file sharing site, LimeWire. LabMD immediately launched an investigation into its infrastructure and

data security safeguards, and learned that LimeWire file sharing software had been installed on a Billing Manager's computer on October 31, 2005. The current Billing Manager was using a legacy machine and the software apparently had been installed by an employee no longer employed at LabMD.

## Incident Description

- What can we say about how the file appeared on LimeWire? What evidence do we have that it was or was not a result of the software installed on Rebecca's computer?
- Do we have any evidence of the period of time the file was available on LimeWire?
- Who was in charge of IT security during 2005? You have identified Russ Kirkman from Oct 2006 until April 2009 and Tom Metz from April 2009 to present.
- What was the role of Rebecca Morton, the former employee who installed LimeWire? What types of activities was she performing between 10/31/05 and her departure?
- Can we provide signed Confidentiality Agreements for Rebecca Morton, the billing manager?
- Did these two employees receive and initial the Acceptable Use and Security Policy (in place as of 2nd Quarter 2004) and sign the Acknowledgement Form? If so, please provide copies.
- Was the computer in question used by anyone other than Rebecca Morton?
- Describe in detail the walkarounds during the 2005-2008 time period. Were they done when employees were present at their workstations or at night or early morning hours? What review was done of the employee's computer during the walkaround?
- How did LabMD decide which security measures to implement before and after the incident was discovered? Who was in charge of deciding what security would be in place in 2005?
- Were there any security measures in place in 2005 other than walkarounds to prevent the unauthorized installation of file-sharing software? If so, please describe with specificity. At what point were such measures put into place? Describe with specificity.

- What research did LabMD conduct or what advice was sought to determine an appropriate response after learning of the incident in 2008? Specifically, why was it decided that an employee would search P2P networks from her home computer? What documentation exists of the process she followed to search the networks? Did she rely on the advice of an IT professional in conducting the searches? If so, please identify this person.

## LabMD's Computer Network and Security

LabMD utilizes a single network system with three servers.

- On 10/31/05, 5/13/08, and currently: What did LabMD's network look like—how many servers, how much information, what specific types of security features did it have? Provide a detailed description of what each security feature was intended to address?
- For example, the 2/14/10 response describes intrusion protection of the router/firewall, software monitoring of the server cluster, and individual software protections for each server. Please provide specifics on each point for the 2005 period and presently. In particular, describe what the monitoring is intended for and what the protections actually accomplish.
- Identify which employees (by position, not by name) who have access to private patient information currently. What security restrictions are in place to limit access to patient information? Describe in detail.
- What processes were in place on 10/31/05 and 5/13/08, and are in place currently to avoid P2P software from being downloaded onto employee computers? Describe these processes with specificity and explain why they will prevent the unauthorized release of patient information.
- Itemize training and data usage policies in place in 2005, 2008, and presently. Are there any training records or proof of attending training or receipt of employee materials (such as the Handbook, Code of Conduct, and Compliance materials at time of hiring) with data security provisions?

- Please provide copies of the risk assessment performed in May 2008. Was that the first risk assessment performed? Please provide all copies of any risk assessments from 2005 to present (including the audits to be conducted quarterly starting in 2nd Quarter 2010).
- For the policies identified in Evelyn's letter to the FTC dated 6/4/10, please provide all versions of each policy or state if the policy has not been revised since its adoption date.
- Please provide all versions of the Policy Manual (version in force from 2007 to 2008 and current version already provided. Are there earlier versions?).
- Please provide summary of security features in place to prevent third-party intrusion and/or employee theft of data from 2003 forward (5/08 through 7/15/10 is covered by Evelyn's letter to the FTC dated 7/16/10).
- Describe in detail (or provide documentation) of the current security upgrades now in progress and what they are designed to address. Provide the timeline for these upgrades.
- Match LabMD's security measures to current industry standards for health care information ISO 27799,[2] the HIPAA Security Rule, and other applicable industry standards.

I walked into Bill's office with a stony look on my face and closed the door.

"You were copied on Dana's e-mail. Have you read it yet?"

"Yes. Interesting." This was Bill's safe way of saying he didn't like something.

"Interesting how, Bill?"

"It looks like she wants us to answer all these questions when the FTC *already* has all the answers. They could just look through everything we gave them. I don't understand what's new here. This is just more rearranging the chairs on the *Titanic*."

"Exactly. Except she wants receipts and documentation to such a level that I'm not sure we're convincing only the FTC anymore. I feel like we also have to convince *her*. For example, Ruth told us they wanted documentation from 2007 forward, and Dana is going back to 2003. I guess she wants to go above and beyond their requests to show them a pattern of normal growth and change as the technology grew and changed."

"I see that some of these bullet points are vague and broad. It's like she's the investigator doing her old job at the FTC and repackaging it in the way the FTC thinks. I'm okay with this if it works, but we need to perform the groundwork here and the outside lawyers can approve the presentation. Every recent move has seemed like a battle with Dana. She blows off Ben Wright, wants outside analysis, and now she's going back to 2003. I only get a good read of her by observation. Looking at most of this, let's pull the answers out of the prior submissions and reorganize them. Dana wants to be cooperative and play nice in hopes that the FTC will just back off. I can see that as one option. I don't like that she dismisses Ben Wright, but I'm willing to try this one more time if it doesn't break the bank.

"Look at this one," Bill pointed out. "It says, 'Processes to avoid P2P software from being downloaded in *2005*?' What planet is she on? Nobody was aware of this in 2005. There wasn't one IT expert who breathed a word about this then."

"And I see she likes to save the best for last. 'Match LabMD's security measures to current industry standards for healthcare information ISO 27799, the HIPAA Security Rule, and other applicable industry standards.' *Other applicable industry standards?* Has she ignored everything I've said? I don't get the point of all of this. There are no FTC standards; there is no law; HIPAA was not violated; and we have given all this to them already! How much work is this for you, Bill?"

"I don't know yet. It's frustrating. We have already told the FTC all of this in one way or another. It looks like Dana is asking for third-party documentation for anything and everything."

Luckily, Bill is all about organization and process. It's natural for him; it's how he thinks. In this case, his loyalty wasn't taken for granted. Still, it meant enduring two weeks of working until eight at night. This resembled a non-stop project out of an episode of TV's *CSI*. In fact, this exercise was eerily like Kelley Drye having us get ready to go to trial against the FTC before being in the judicial system. Each submission was a submissive bow to the King, hoping he would find mercy and let us out of the tower.

"This had better work," I repeated with a heavy sigh.

I only went along with this because I was at my wits end. I saw no option other than war, but I was willing to play one more round of nicey nicey to see if the FTC would go away. I was the King with a bag over my head. It's hard to rule from that position. I trusted my lawyer to guide us to a winning conclusion. However, if the bag came off and I discovered we'd been exploited, there was going to be hell to pay.

## The First Invoice

I spent most of my days running on empty. Keep in mind that the only people who knew about this in the company were still only Bill, Tom, Phil, our billing manager Anne, and me (Elizabeth had moved to Arizona). I didn't know what the employees thought about their managers silently scurrying around for unknown reasons.

It was the beginning of May 2011 and, like clockwork, I saw the first invoice from Kelley Drye arrive in my mailbox. I fought the huge desire to rip it open, but instead picked it up and walked calmly back to my office, shutting the door. I guessed about $5,000.

I tore open the envelope and dug through the pages until I found the amount owed. Sure enough, it was $5,374.80—for just over 12 hours of work. My guess was a worst case scenario, and my greatest fears were coming to fruition. Bill number one, which included the dispute over how many lawyers would be in the room when I was in DC, had blown through that number. The shock didn't wear off quickly.

I walked into Carpenter's office.

"Guess how much the bill is for March with Kelley Drye?"

"Seven grand?"

"Close. $5,400."

"Let me see that." I handed it to Carpenter's outreached hand. "Hard to see if they're charging the one sixth of an hour minimum or two sixths, but we'll have to watch that," he said. "There wasn't much action in March."

"We kept a saddle on them in April. And we won't get the April bill until June," I calculated. "The month of May is the heavy lifting. If we do most of the work in May, we can keep these lawyers under control financially.

"You know, over half that time invoiced was for our first meeting. That's when I was unceremoniously told to play it her way or pick up my retainer check. Having Kristin in attendance when I asked her not to be cost an extra grand. I guess that's chump change to Kelley Drye."

On May 2nd, Alain Sheer contacted our lawyers in Washington, asking when we would have something ready. Dana told them a portion would be ready in two weeks, on May 16th, with the final portion complete by the end of the month.

In the meantime, I was scheduled to go to Washington DC for the 2011 American Urological Association annual meeting the morning of Saturday, May 14th. The largest urology meeting in the world, it moves each year to various cities throughout the United States. LabMD typically has a booth in the exhibit hall, and we do the usual marketing, networking, and dog-and-pony show. Because of this, I told Dana I'd be in DC and could come into her office.

"No. That won't be necessary. I think we'll be fine, but if we need you, we'll call," she snapped.

"Okay" was the best response I could come up with, given my shock. Her tone and brevity made me feel, once again, that she'd be happy if I'd stand in the corner while they do their job—another common strategy in the legal game. *How could I sit on the sidelines while she crafted my fate? She seemed perfectly capable of attending our funeral while playing bingo on her iPhone.*

"I'm paying the bill, and I want to be in the game," I told Phil with finality, but I respected Dana's wishes.

By May 3rd, Bill and Tom had taken Dana's broad descriptions to heart and practically killed themselves preparing everything.

Then Phil alerted Kelley Drye with the following e-mail:

From: Phil Carpenter
Sent: Tuesday May 3, 2011
To: Dana Rosenfeld
Subject: Initial Responses

Dana

Please find attached our initial thoughts to the questions you presented. Many of the points require some elaboration, and we will discuss them in detail during our call. We will talk to you in a few moments.

Thanks!
Philip Carpenter, Esq.

We e-mailed Kelley Drye our 538 pages of supporting documents and thoughts—the first round of lawyer/client tennis. My belief and frustration that this round of legal play was big waste of money was still lingering. But I'd just have to "get over it" and understand this was about survival, not fair play. The FTC wields the power to drain a company dry; truth has nothing to do with it. This might seem fruitless, but I decided it wasn't nearly as painful as a consent decree or years of litigation. I even rationalized getting along with Dana, hoping she knew better than I did. After all, she was my lawyer; I relied on her. I was filled with self-doubt about ever agreeing to go along with this plan. *"You'd better let it go and make lemonade out of lemons, you're already committed, no reason to keep torturing yourself by second guessing all the time,"* I told myself, even though I was sick to my stomach thinking that this was just going to play into the FTC's plan of breaking our backs through financial bleeding so that we would have no choice but to eventually succumb in order to survive.

While I find the "let it go, move on, and focus on your core goals" mentality morally repugnant, it's how I had experienced many corporations and legal professionals. There's an intelligence to it I don't always disagree with, depending on the battle. But in *this* battle, I knew LabMD was being dragged through the mud.

I'd told Kelley Drye repeatedly about my frustration with the partnership of Tiversa, Congress, and the FTC. Dana dismissed it by saying things like "it doesn't matter" and "that's a separate issue" and "the FTC doesn't care; the file got out, that's it!" I still believed the first moves made by Tiversa and the government were hugely relevant, and I was baffled by how my own lawyer constantly argued the opposite. Everyone in DC had become the enemy. A giant organism with virtually connected tentacles, I had to slowly back away from it to get to safety. Ultimately, I wanted to nail them all.

Specifically, I felt boxed in by two tentacles of the Beltway beast—my law firm and my government. I again harkened back to my ninth-grade civics teacher Mrs. Lewandowski. She told me there were two types of fair: taxi fare and a fair with rides. If I spent too much time waiting for another type of fair, I would be sorely disappointed. She saved me from wasting a lot of time waiting for ships to come in.

Disgustedly, I went along as I watched Bill demonstrate loyalty and professionalism that was a gift. In the meantime, I kept making lists, reading, and researching.

*We're living in a horror movie. Nobody is going to believe me—they're going to think I'm blowing this out of proportion.* By now, we had learned not to be surprised by anything the FTC did. It was the same old script: stone faced, without emotion or logic, the FTC was trapped in their own world, incessantly repeating their mantra, "Congress has given us broad authority." They lumbered through our world, crushing our operations as they clumsily kneeled down, their eyeball peering through our window.

## Bringing in a Third Party

Dana still wanted LabMD to hire an outside company to perform an objective analysis of LabMD, claiming the FTC would like that step. But based on my former hesitations, "objective" is not a word I'd use to describe such companies. Try "exploitative." Those that don't live in the real world value the hot air of committees, consultants, and institutions. They don't know any better; it was, of course, only logical that the FTC would be the first to sign up for such 'reliable' fodder. So in the spirit of compromise and to "justify" ourselves to the King, I reached out to an outside IT support professional who had already helped us maintain our networks. As we grew the company, we'd moved IT operations in-house, but Allen Truitt was still our main go-to guy outside the company. Seeing his cell number still logged in my phone, I called him.

"Allen."

"Yes?"

"Hey, Daugherty here, Mr. Truitt."

"Hey, Mike! How ya doin'?"

"Great. What have you been up to?"

"Well, I sold the company to a group in Birmingham, and I'm working with those people now."

"Oh, well, congratulations! I hope you made a fortune. Good for you."

"Well, we did okay, but the day-to-day is much easier. I can focus on what I like."

"I take that as code for 'you don't miss managing a bunch of people all day long.'"

"Yeah, well. So what's going on?"

"Allen, I need help with a problem. Sounds hard to believe, but the FTC is investigating our data security practices."

"What? Why?"

I told the eighth person on the planet my story, reassuring him I'm not making this up as I knew it sounded like a movie.

"Mike, this is terrible! I can't believe it. Wow. I mean, you guys were set up."

"So, the bottom line is this, Allen: I need you to review what your practices were, memorialize them, and sign an affidavit that we can turn in to the FTC. Can you do that?"

"Sure, I'll come in. I may need to check with Birmingham, but I don't see any issues there. I can come in next week. Then I'll e-mail you specific options for us to work out."

When Allen came in, once again I recounted our song and dance. He was kind enough to submit an affidavit that said the following:

## ALLEN TRUETT'S AFFIDAVIT[3]

The undersigned affiant, Allen Truett, being first duly sworn, hereby deposes and says:

1. I was the primary technical liaison to LabMD, Inc. ("LabMD") from August 2003 to March 2007 (the "Contract Period") . . .
2. Automated Technologies, Inc. ("APT") also helped LabMD to design its network and provided recommendations on hardware, software, and network configuration . . . including providing information on current network security, such as firewalls and anti-virus protection.
3. All new equipment and software was implemented and tested by APT during the Contract Period using industry standards to ensure that the equipment and software was functioning properly during the Contract Period.
4. To the best of my knowledge, APT staff did not identify LimeWire on any LabMD computers during the Contract Period.
5. The security measures taken by LabMD during the Contract Period were consistent with those being used by other APT customers of a similar size and security needs profile.

I was glad to have this affidavit, but I worried submitting it would make the FTC say, "Well, we can't nail them there, so let's keep digging until we find something else." Meanwhile, back at base camp, Bill, Phil, Anne, and Tom were metaphorically reshuffling the chairs on the deck while simultaneously managing the operations of a cancer detection center. Our spirits had been cracked. Still, we quietly conserved energy for the next stage and sent more documentation to Kelley Drye. After Kristin dove in with her analysis, she came up for air with the following e-mail:

In a message dated 5/10/2011 Kristin wrote:

From: Kristin A. McPartland
Sent: Tuesday May 5, 2011
To: Bill Barnett
Subject: Questions regarding screenshots

Bill

I have some technical questions regarding the screenshots showing the LimeWire stub installer and installation. Could we have a brief call tomorrow morning to walk through the documents? I can be available at your convenience.

Thanks,
Kristin

About an hour later, at 5:50 p.m., I e-mailed her this response:

From: Michael Daugherty
Sent: Tuesday May 5, 2011
To: Kristin A. McPartland, Bill Barnett
CC: Phil Carpenter, Dana Rosenfeld
Subject: Re: Questions regarding screenshots

We all have questions about that stub installer. And I don't know if Bill has the answers or not. Could you e-mail a question or two giving us a hint? We have been mulling over that installer stuff for several weeks looking for an answer as to where it came from.

Mike Daugherty

After 6 p.m. she e-mailed the questions.

From: Kristin A. McPartland
Sent: Tuesday May 5, 2011
To: Mike Daugherty, Bill Barnett
CC: Phil Carpenter, Dana Rosenfeld
Subject: Re: Questions regarding screenshots

Thanks, Mike. My only question on the stub installer is the same one that you have. Is there any indication of how it was installed without the program actually being installed? Also, how do you know that it is related to LimeWire (it's not evident on the screenshot, at least to my eyes).

I also have questions on the screenshot showing the installation in 2006, including:

1. The Windows Firewall was run at the same time as the LimeWire installation. Does this mean that the firewall caught the installation, e.g., the user would have to click a box or otherwise override the firewall to permit installation?
2. It looks like the LimeWire application was run again on 4/18/08. Is there any indication of what was done then? Was the program just accessed and run? What happened with the icon on the same date/time? Was it moved?
3. There is an entry for "Copying" of a file on the same 4/18/08 time and date. Does this indicate that a file was copied by LimeWire at that time?
4. "Buy LimeWire PRO" appears as an Internet shortcut on 4/25/08. What does this refer to?
5. LimeWire appears to have been uninstalled on 4/25/08. Is that correct? If so, why/how was it detected and uninstalled? I thought it wasn't uninstalled until after Tiversa notified you in May 2008.

I think these questions will be easier to answer by phone than by e-mail but let me know how you'd like to proceed.

Thanks,
Kristin

Bill bellowed, "What is she doing? A fact-checking expedition? You think the FTC is going to give a hoot? Why are we having to explain the program to her? We didn't write it. Why are we doing the FTC's work for them? If the FTC doesn't already understand LimeWire, why are we here?"

I was ticked at the questions as well. "No way are we going to give her verbal answers so she can just ask again or say she forgot. Answer those in writing. Why does Kelley Drye need to know all of this? And if the FTC doesn't even understand how this stuff works, then why are they investigating? The burden is not on us. *She* is fact checking. Bill, keep a leash on this with written documentation so they can't come back and say we didn't tell them."

After my outburst, I read Bill's answers and said to him, "She doesn't even get the basics. What is going on here?"

The next morning, Bill gave Kristin a follow-up call about the detailed answers he e-mailed her. We were concerned. Why did we have to make our lawyers experts in this software, all the while running up the billable hours? We concluded we'd have to try harder to keep them in a box.

Around lunchtime, Kristin e-mailed this:

From: Kristin A. McPartland
Sent: Wednesday May 11, 2011
To: Mike Daugherty, Phil Carpenter, Bill Barnett
CC: Dana Rosenfeld
Subject: LabMD First submission to FTC_v3.DOC

As discussed on our call this morning, attached please find a draft submission to the FTC. As you'll see, I have structured the exhibit numbers to show both the actual submission exhibit number and the number used on LabMD's Excel spreadsheet for ease of document identification during the editing process. Please also note that there are a number of comments and a few outstanding document requests embedded in the text. I suggest setting up a call tomorrow to go over this draft and the remaining questions. I am available at your convenience.

Thanks,
Kristin

It was all I could do to complete this reassembly of the facts, contain legal costs, and keep my staff from going off the rails. I had no idea what the Kelley Drye lawyers would do next until they did it, and by then it would be too late. The fuse had been lit. We all wondered about what happened to Kelley Drye simply sending the letter and us filling in the blanks.

It wasn't until later that day I got a chance to review the third version of the letter. If we could have just been told this is what was needed so we could have done it ourselves, it would have been much faster—and cheaper. Their behavior made me feel trapped. I did not have the resources to fight Dana. Every time I tried, I was dismissed!

After I read the letter, I fired off the following:

From: Mike Daugherty
Sent: Wednesday, May 11, 2011 5:16 PM
To: Kristin A. McPartland, Phil Carpenter, Bill Barnett
CC: Dana Rosenfeld
Subject: Re: LabMD First submission to FTC_v3.DOC

We are reviewing still but feel compelled to clarify that Tiversa was unable and INCAPABLE of providing screenshots. LabMD took all referenced screenshots of LABMD's Rebecca's desktop to educate the FTC. The FTC gave us the disk with only the file

on it. Tiversa only gave LabMD the file they took and refused all additional assistance unless we retained them.
Mike Daugherty

I walked into Bill's office. He looked as frustrated as I felt, being the poor guy who had to suddenly play tech support to our lawyers.

"Sorry, man. It's more surprises. This wasn't what I'd agreed on, but we're in the middle of it now. I think they're covering their own asses on our company's dime."

Bill said, "I try to make sure she understands. She's just being literal and checking every single minor detail. But it appears she'll only rely on what can be footnoted or proven in writing."

I attempted to rationalize our situation with Bill. "This is boiling down to a strategy disagreement here. I get that we don't want to look like we don't have credibility, but the level of her questions is concerning. And they're repetitive. We just have to get through this. Please be patient."

On May 12th, Bill sent out his status list to make sure everyone knew what needed to be done.

From: Bill Barnett
Sent: Thursday May 12, 2011
To: Mike Daugherty, Phil Carpenter
Subject: FTC current task lists

1. Sending clean, LabMD taken screenshots to Kristin for Tiversa and FTC-provided aging file.
2. FTC letter modifications—finish more changes and adding more info about what has been done since the incident.
3. Add'l docs sent by Mike last night, which to scan and send to Kristin—discuss later
4. Data intelligence company letter from Mark—ready for review later today
5. Do we need modifications to Allen affidavit—change item 7, add more info about medical facilities and offices he worked

with at the time, his background and experience—add to letter vs. opinion presently in letter

6. Peter Carlton affidavit—schedule time for questions, get signed and notarized.

After that, we had a conference call focused on affidavits and "human documentation" not "hardware or software" documentation. Kristin was to speak with our former employee Peter Carlton about his meeting with us back in March so an affidavit could be drawn up. We were sure he'd oblige, especially if it meant he didn't have to go in front of the FTC and be interviewed under oath for God knows what.

The morning of Friday, May 13th, Bill started out by e-mailing a revised "To Do" list over the progress of Kristin's work. By now, the written aspect was completely intentional. We didn't trust the firm one bit; we thought they would say anything. Bill said:

1. Bill bullet point affidavit for walkaround processes
2. FTC letter modifications—finish more changes and adding more info about what has been done since the incident.
3. Add'l docs sent by Mike last night, which to scan and send to Kristin—discuss later
4. Data intelligence company letter from Mark—ready for review later today
5. Do we need modifications to Allen affidavit—change item 7, add more info about medical facilities and offices he worked with at the time, his background and experience—add to letter vs. opinion presently in letter
6. Peter Carlton affidavit—schedule time for review, get signed and notarized.
7. Add Bill's resume to submissions
8. Handbook version on Rebecca's desktop approved list of Web sites for each dept
9. Jeremy—confirm when were PCs locked down?
10. Any files shared that are LabMD information files from billing mgr pc
11. Change name on 2007–2008 policy manual (ask Bill what this is regarding)

Bill and Phil were both in full court press on this issue, Bill doing the technical and Phil reviewing the legal. Their fuses were smoldering, ready to light. The details, questions, and documentation seemed irrelevant. We'd given so much of this to the FTC already, and they didn't even ask questions about most of it. Why, suddenly, would the FTC pay attention?

Feeling like he was slamming brakes on a car that couldn't stop, Bill went into full documentation mode regarding Kristin. He e-mailed me this question:

From: Bill Barnett
Sent: Friday May 13, 2011
To: Mike Daugherty, Phil Carpenter
Subject: Quick question—FTC letter discussion yesterday with Kristin

Yesterday, during our conversation with Kristin, we all had notes on our sheets and she was making changes. I was going to ask her if she had a revision based on yesterday's conversation or should we put one from all of our notes together first? Or just wait to see what she has later today?

I found out from Kristin we wouldn't have another version of the letter to look at until Monday, the deadline date. I told Bill to wait. Then Bill and I went back and forth on the phone with her. She worked hard and was always pleasant to talk to. However, we were frustrated with how this was all over the place at the last hour. Plus she was talking to Chris and Allen about affidavit issues while revising the letter for the fifth time. Some of her questions were so basic; we knew they'd already been addressed.

Everyone was ready for the weekend break.

When I woke up Saturday morning, scurrying to make my flight to DC, I checked my e-mail. Round five from Kristin. It read:

From: Kristin A. McPartland
Sent: Saturday May 14, 2011
To: Michael Daugherty
Subject: RE: LabMD First Submission to FTC

LabMD was notified by Tiversa, a private company, on May 13, 2008 that a file appearing to contain LabMD patient information was available on the P2P file sharing site, LimeWire. As the screenshot attached as Exhibit 13/15 shows, the file was apparently accessed by Tiversa on February 5, 2008.

Site? Did she just call LimeWire a site? They are making my staff run around proving a murder mystery and she just called LimeWire a site? By now they can't keep their basic facts straight? Tired and stressed under the looming shadow of the FTC, this was not helping our already shaken confidence. I was pissed. I fired off the following:

From: Michael Daugherty
Sent: Saturday May 14, 2011 8:26 AM
To: Kristin A. McPartland, Phil Carpenter, Bill Barnett
CC: Dana Rosenfeld
Subject: Re: LabMD First submission to FTC_v5.DOC

We will work on this this weekend but there is no such thing as a P2P site called LimeWire. This is foundational. We will provide you with an accurate description before Monday morning. LimeWire is not a Web site and we have to be completely impossible to misunderstand here, because this letter will be part of civil litigation against Tiversa as described in the letter we sent them that you have in your possession.

Mike Daugherty

Dana e-mailed back Saturday evening:

> From: Dana Rosenfeld
> Sent: Saturday May 14, 2011 6:23 PM
> To: Michael Daugherty, Kristin A. McPartland, Phil Carpenter,
> Bill Barnett
> Subject: Re: LabMD First submission to FTC_v5.DOC
>
> This is obviously an inadvertent error and will be fixed. As
> you know, Kristin was working late into the night to get this
> out to all of us so we could review this weekend. Please pro-
> vide any comments and the additional information requested
> asap.
>
> Thanks,
> Dana

Inadvertent error? At $390 an hour? I bet those words just roll off the tongue like she is on autopilot. In three sentences, she dismissed our concerns, made some excuse, and then told us to hurry up. How much benefit of the doubt am I supposed to carry around? I was getting tired of fighting three fronts at once, Tiversa, the FTC, and Kelley Drye. My fuse was burning down and was closer to the bomb.

At the convention over the weekend, I had my hands full. Being in the urology world for 25 years, these annual meetings are like second homes to me—a welcome reprieve. But the reprieve was short-lived. The wheels came off quickly, with Kristin still on a fact-checking expedition in a way that made us kowtow to the FTC.

By now, Carpenter didn't think these lawyers were bringing any-thing to the table. We would give them the facts in writing and they'd still be omitted from the drafts or be wrong. Bill insisted he told her certain information repeatedly. Then Kristin would question something and everyone would lose their tempers. They insisted they had, once again, already told her—in writing. Due to this, we weren't confident in the results. If we dared question anything, the lawyers responded like an attack of locusts. At our wits' end, we all watched helplessly. Has every company going through something similar just rolled over in the face of the bully tactics and the looming expense?

I walked into my hotel room at 4:00 p.m. on the 16th, about an hour and a half before the deadline. I returned calls from Phil and Bill, who were both furious. Why, this late in the game, did the lawyers keep finding errors in the versions they'd already responded to? I needed to get everyone to hold onto the handrails and get this ride over with. In an attempt to relieve tension, I had them participate in a conference call. After listening to various repetitious questions and concerns, I lost my temper.

"Okay. *What the hell* is going on? Everyone listen to me." Phil and Bill knew I meant Kristin. "Make it happen. Hammer it out. Kristin, what is it you need to know?"

Kristin answered by asking for an explanation of a technical point. It wasn't a bad question. The timing of the question was the problem.

"Bill and Phil, what about that?"

Phil and Bill answered Kristin's question easily, but they were ticked that they'd already given her the information. *Two more rounds of this game to go. They'll get over the hump and worry about who was wrong later.*

"Okay, then I'll jump off this call and you'll iron out the wrinkles. Get it done. Any questions? Good. Good-bye."

When I spoke to Phil a few moments later, he made it sound like everyone could see the finish line. I felt grateful. *Bill and Phil are committed, and LabMD is fortunate to have such passionate people on board. I don't need this crap!*

Of course, the letter went out at the very last moment—only three seconds left on the clock. But as long as it took us, we knew it would take the FTC longer. Everyone simply needed to turn off their brains and recover. If Round Two ended up like Round One, we needed to rest up for an impending fight.

Round Two would have to focus on what we had done to "tighten up" our practices since we first learned of the "incident." The theme would be "What has LabMD done for the FTC lately?" This would be broken down into three areas:

1. Administrative Safeguards
2. Physical Safeguards
3. Technical Safeguards

Administrative Safeguards focused on who was doing what and what new policies were in place. (See previous mention of required policies on inhaling, exhaling, toilet flushing, eye batting, smiling, walking, kitchen sinks, and any other policies the FTC may or may not deem relevant.)

Physical Safeguards focused on how we had the place locked down. Believe it or not, we installed a 16-camera video recording system that recorded every area except closets and bathrooms. This scared our staff members, who felt as if they were being recorded 24/7, and they were. But their behavior wasn't the reason for the surveillance. Unfortunately, we couldn't tell them why, which really did a number on morale.

Technical Safeguards focused on what hardware and software changes we'd made—without guidelines or suggestions from "The Deciders." We had to go above and beyond. A marketplace for advanced security software barely existed for companies with fewer than 1,000 employees. That meant we'd have to "buy up," which gave us yet another argument for whether any of this was "reasonable" in the FTC's eyes. But given the crickets I'd hear when I brought up these issues, my DC lawyer had trained me not to mention such hopeful commentary.

The software we installed, WebSense, wasn't cheap. Installing it was a staged process: Think of trying to install a new track on an existing roller coaster packed with riders *without* stopping the roller coaster. Once they heard about our "little problem" we had a hard time getting calls returned.

Our final submission went out Tuesday, May 31, 2011, as we still danced for the FTC as if in a Broadway-esque audition. The FTC agents in the audience were looking up over their reading glasses, rubbing their chins, and puffing on their pipes as they blurted out, "We don't know exactly what we're looking for, but we'll know it when we see it. Keep in mind, few will make the grade."

The most exciting thing about the week after that Memorial Day? We wouldn't have to hear from the FTC or Kelley Drye for weeks. I popped open a beer and turned on Sports Center.

*"Your time is limited, so don't waste it living someone else's life.*
*Don't be trapped by dogma—which is living with the results of other people's thinking.*
*Don't let the noise of other's opinions drown out your own inner voice.*
*And most important, have the courage to follow your heart and intuition.*
*They somehow already know what you truly want to become.*
*Everything else is secondary."*

—STEVE JOBS

# CHAPTER 20
# Summer—Slow, Hot, with a Few Bugs

I turned to the new month of June feeling like I'd just submitted a final exam back in the day at U of M in Ann Arbor. I only wanted to sleep, recover, and stop having my cage rattled. Still trying to keep the company on track and make growth plans with the FTC looming over the organization, I didn't know if I'd be able to give our new managers the attention they needed to be successful. June was like living with a terminal disease going into remission. The FTC wasn't messing with our day-to-day lives for now, but we all knew in the back of our minds, it lurked out there and threatened to come roaring back any moment. *They love that trick.*

On Monday morning, June 13th, I pulled into the office in a good mood, eager to focus on LabMD work. I strolled in, plopped my briefcase on my desk, and walked into the break room.

"Good morning!" I sang out in the direction of the billing department.

"Morning," rang back a chorus of voices.

After I got my orange juice, I detoured through the IT department on my way back to the administration area. "Good morning!" As I cut right, my eye caught the tall stack of weekend mail in my tray on the corner of my assistant's desk. I scooped it up, walked into my office, and dropped it in front of my computer, ready to start purging the 30 or so envelopes.

A pall cast across the room as I saw the return address on the cream-colored envelope. Kelley Drye. From the envelope's thickness, I immediately identified it as the invoice for May. I slid my finger under the flap and ripped it. *Okay, about $15,000. Prep yourself, Mike.* I shuffled the papers—about seven of them—toward the back to get to the bottom line. Then I went "deer in the headlights." My senses turned off except for my fixated vision on the number: $30,162.45. *This can't be. Somebody pull the plug right now and put me out of my misery.*

I took a deep breath and read through the pages of charges. Kristin billed for 57.80 hours and Dana billed for 11.70. What was Kristin doing taking one and a half weeks of solid work to write two letters that had so much input from our in-house counsel? I groaned. I know what she was doing—documenting her tail off as if she were the one turning in a term paper.

I refused to fly off the handle. I had to conserve my energy. I channeled my anger into strategizing against the enemy, or was I actually in shock and denial? *Let's pretend this didn't happen right now.*

Two days later, I wrote a check for the invoice. Paying it quickly should remove my mental anguish from the assault LabMD was undergoing. But two days after that, I knew I'd have to deal with this sooner or later. I wasn't ready to have my peace and quiet obliterated by another battle with my law firm, but I felt betrayed and realized I'd better deal with this right away.

Mentally ready, I walked into Phil's office to show him the detailed invoice.

"Guess what?" I teased.

"What?"

"The May invoice from Kelley Drye is here already. So, would ya like to guess how much it is, just for fun?"

"Eighteen thousand?"

"Nope—more."

"Twenty . . . okay . . . twenty-five thousand?"

"Nope—more."

"Whaaaaaaaaat? *Thirty* . . . ?"

"Bingo! $30,162.45"

"That is complete crap. Let me see that," he said. He reached across the desk, needing to see it to believe it.

"Oh my God! What was she doing all that time? Six hours? Eight and a half hours?"

As Phil started to digest what had bowled me over just days before, I was suddenly hit with a rush of adrenaline.

"I forgot to pull the check from Mary's stack for mailing!"

"What?"

"The Kelley Drye check—I printed it but meant to hold it. I think it went out!" I said as I ran down the hall to check with Mary. It had gone out the day before.

Suddenly, I did a 180 and called Dana's number as I walked back to Phil's office. I left a voicemail: "Dana, this is Mike Daugherty. Please give me a call back about the invoice. We sent a thirty-thousand-dollar check in error. I hadn't planned on the check going out until we had spoken as I have questions about the invoice. Please give me a call and hold that check if you're able to get to it in time. It hasn't arrived at your office yet. Thanks."

"Well, I don't like this invoice one bit. It's insane how many hours it took," replied Phil.

"I know. That's exactly what I'm upset about. However, do you actually think Dana will give me a straight answer about this when she's more than happy to disagree with me? I'm not going to get in a debate until all of our ducks are in a row. At what point did we ever authorize them to work all those hours performing background checks? The directive was to give us the outline and we would fill in the blanks. If they wanted to check everything because they don't believe you, our lawyer, then they could have either withdrawn from the case or done it on their own dime. They were covering *their* asses, not ours. But to them, it's just thirty grand—poof." I blew an imaginary puffball out of my open palm and walked out of his office. *Why am I not surprised that here I stand, in another invoice battle with a law firm? It isn't like they weren't warned. Why do they not believe me?*

That day, I went to lunch alone to get my bearings. The dominos were still falling. Evelyn was gone, this law firm was moving forward in headstrong fashion, and my eyes were forced off growing the company to deal with this threat. I resolved to become even more self-reliant since no one outside the company was bringing anything to the table. *But how am I going to stop this bloodshed?*

This was no ordinary situation. I had another problem on my hands. (As if the FTC weren't enough.) The Kelley Drye lawyers were too expensive. I couldn't have lawyers going rogue. They didn't know better, but they thought they did. With the submissions turned in, the question of this firm being fired wasn't a matter of "if," but rather "when."

What's more, Dana's invoice represented another slap across my face that served to strengthen my determination. Landing on top of this big mess would take a while, but landing there I would. I had tried not to fight back for so long, no matter how many pokes in the eye Tiversa and the FTC gave me. This invoice somehow crossed another line. Where other people might buckle, I found myself stronger, more determined, and clearer of mind.

With the damages so great, my response would have to be proportionately big.

Then I heard that contrarian voice of the beltway sociopath whispering in my ear, filling my head with doubt: *Don't cut your nose off to spite your face. The FTC is so much bigger than you. It isn't even a contest. Don't let this consume you. A consent decree isn't so bad. It really isn't. Sign the papers and get back to running your business. Your company needs you. Quit being so stubborn.*

Truthfully, I wanted to line up all those lawyers who sang me that lullaby and ask them, "Why did you become a lawyer? Is this your version of defending people or are you covering your ass again? Is this all just one big game? Does standing for nothing make it easy to say anything?"

Later in the day, Dana laid her paper trail of "concern and cooperation" in an e-mail. But it's what wasn't on paper that worried me.

From: Dana Rosenfeld
Sent: Friday June 17, 2011
To: Michael Daugherty

Mike,

I understand you have some questions about our recent invoice. I am tied up today but am happy to discuss it on Monday. Let me know what time works best for you. In the meantime, we've given instructions to our accounting department not to cash the check.

Dana

As I awoke from my recovery slumber around July 1, I thought it best to discuss the invoice directly with Dana and called.

"Dana, Mike Daugherty here."

"Hi, Mike."

"Hi. I just wanted to briefly discuss the invoice and let you know that Phil is going to review the invoice with you. He will have specific questions organized."

"I will be happy to discuss it with him."

"Good. We have questions about the quantity of the hours and what specifically was done. In the meantime, I will send a check for fifteen thousand dollars."

"Mike, that's fine. If you want to split the balance into two payments, I'm fine with that."

At this point, I *consciously* made no comment. I suspected Dana was steamrolling me, trying to interpret my silence as an agreement. But I didn't agree to send the second payment. Dana could assume whatever she wanted to, but she and Phil would have to talk first. Until that happened, a discussion with me was a waste. I find most lawyers don't take non-lawyers seriously, so she could take it up with one of her own.

## Follow-up Questions from the FTC

Before long, we were back in the game with Kelley Drye and the FTC. Dana e-mailed on July 7th that "Alain and Ruth called to ask a few factual follow-up questions." Dana had this annoying habit of crossing out everyone's formal name and then handwriting their first name when communicating by letter. I thought this was a disingenuous attempt to imply "I'm so tight and chummy with the powerful FTC," when the last thing I wanted my lawyer to be with "Alain and Ruth" was all "tight and chummy." I really detested all of them and their ways. *None of this is about friendship. You people have no evidence, no standards, and are fishing around until we break. Let's cut the crap, shall we?*

Right out of the gate Dana listed the six questions from the FTC. Question number one: "Did the file-sharing event take place at the 1117 Perimeter Center location or at the Powers Ferry Road location?"

*Come again? Are you serious? You mean these government lawyers who have drained us dry, made us make six submissions that involved thousands of pages of documents, including diagrams, and burned through thousands of dollars in legal fees are so detached and lazy, they don't know what address we were at in 2008? They have to actually ask us this? My "you won't believe this" file is overflowing.*

Their questions were basic and chilling. Only a government lawyer would mindlessly dwell for days on such tedium—and why shouldn't they? Their clock never ends, their money never runs out, their accountability is non-existent, and their games help justify their self-righteous existence . . . all in the name of "the consumer," but to hell with the "taxpayer."

After spending much time and effort over the past 18 months being cooperative and informative, these questions were insulting. *What address were we at? They don't know that?* I couldn't get over that question. Plus the other questions on the list again showed their indifference to what they were doing to my company. They weren't professional. There was neither stability nor leadership. Did they have so much power they were removed from any requirement for competency?

Seeing that the FTC was serious about nailing LabMD to the wall, I got more serious about hauling their butts into court.

The passive aggressive crap from Dana was adding up. Dismissing Ben Wright, ignoring my Tiversa arguments, the ridiculous invoices for fact checking during the submission prep, and the dismissive attitude in reviewing our invoice questions—all this resulted in a contemptuous feeling for the entire organization. The tipping point was reached when one of Dana's e-mails contained the following comment:

> "Could you provide any more detail on #2? If you don't have an answer from ... outside expert yet, could we provide an approximate date when LabMD will have more information? At the least, we should identify the forensic expert and think about providing a copy of his contract and resume. *This would show that LabMD is taking this seriously and devoting resources to pinpointing the source of the incident.*"

Congratulations! THAT is the wrong thing to say. Show that LabMD is taking this seriously? You mean to tell me the FTC doesn't think we're taking this seriously? We don't require any more evidence of their stupidity. Perhaps we should walk through their front doors in rags with chains around our ankles, begging for mercy from the King. When Dana left the FTC, did she forget to turn in her uniform? If Dana wants to ignore the Tiversa involvement and the fact that we know how the FTC got the file, then she'll have to live with the facts she currently has in her pipe and smoke them. Such unmitigated gall and I'm paying for this.

I was so furious, I hit Dana back with this e-mail lecture:
This is all going to run to the definition of reasonable. The FTC's definition seems to be very elastic indeed. This is a disgusting experience ... and when it is over, I'm going to broadcast it on high. Thank goodness we have the Congressional record, otherwise everyone listening would just chalk it up to emotion and fantasy on our part ... but there our file is, in black and white, in the Congressional Testimony ... I can't wait to find

out what Congress thinks about having been given converted property as an 'example.' . . . LabMD, being innocent and not thinking like a crook, was clueless about what was happening to us. This guilty until proven innocent stuff has got to come to an end.

I am going to turn the tables on everyone involved in this . . . all in due time . . . and that isn't puffery. I have to defend this organization, our patients, and industry. We are being judged by those with power but no knowledge. That is one dangerous and expensive combination. I hope the FTC ties this up soon . . . because I am going to have to come out of my corner swinging very soon. I would like not to have to drag them into this while we are still 'under the microscope.' When they are 'done,' will they tell us or just make us stew for months on end?

I slammed the send button, rubbing the story I had been screaming for months right in her face. It was all intended as documentation, with a question at the end, forcing her to acknowledge and reply. Two can play this game. I was hitting the balls harder, and I waited for her return shot.

I must have struck a nerve because Dana's reply was laced with little commitment and plenty of innuendo.

I cannot say for sure, but I think we are likely to hear back from the FTC within a few weeks after we provide the requested information about whether they will close the matter or want to move forward to consent negotiations. If they decide to close it, I would caution you against making negative public statements about the FTC or its process. They can reopen an investigation at any time.

After I read it, I laughed out loud. *Wow.* "*They can reopen an investigation at any time.*" *Another FTC trick that I will duly note. Is my lawyer warning me or threatening me? Why is it that lawyers can be in such a rush to tell you how you can lose but not as eager to describe how to win? So far I see a one trick pony whose ride is not taking me where I want to go. I'd love to have a higher opinion of lawyers, but it's behavior like this that lets me know I'm right on the money. Dana's worthless to me now. The FTC can tell it to the judge.*

I was so frustrated I was about to explode. I felt victimized and helpless by this overarching system of lumbering government indifference that was marching forward, crushing everything in its path. There had to be a way to stop it.

I had to take some sort of action so I could at least blow off some steam. I needed a of sense control. All I knew to do was go out and try to learn more. I banished myself into Starbuck's isolation and started searching, searching, searching the internet. Hungry for anything that I might have missed . . . I only knew to go back to the drawing board. It was that or go crazy.

Most of what I saw was a rehash of the past or irrelevant. Four items popped out that were validating to me, but I was sure would be meaningless to DC lawyers. I was a bit embarrassed that I hadn't seen these sooner, but I didn't know it was out there until I found it.

The first was a press release from Tiversa released May 28, 2009. *Two years ago . . . how did I miss this?*

This was a slickly worded propaganda piece filled with false bravado. Highlights:

"Tiversa today announced the findings of new research that revealed 13,185,252 breached files emanating from over 4,310,839 sources on P2P file-sharing networks within a twelve month period . . . The research is based on data in an ongoing study by Tiversa, whose patent-pending technology monitors roughly 450 million users issuing more than 1.5 billion searches a day. The files analyzed included only those identified on behalf of Tiversa's existing customer base . . ."

*Research for what? I'm sure if Tiversa would have said "For the US Government" they would have gotten more attention.*

*Breached? Are you saying that a breach is something that is vulnerable? Everything is vulnerable.*

*Monitoring 450 million users? Does Tiversa have 450 million customers?*

*1.5 billion searches a day? That's quite a big number. Tiversa calls this "monitoring"? Sounds like surveillance to me. Hey Tiversa...who is watching you watching us?*

*Only identified on behalf of Tiversa's existing customer base? What does that mean? Are the files you're monitoring the property of your customers?*

"Tiversa might see the Protected Health Information (PHI) of tens of thousands being disclosed by a hospital or medial billing company . . . Findings released in February 2009, in a collaborative research study (Data Hemorrhages in the Health-Care Sector) between Tiversa and The Tuck School of Business at Dartmouth College highlight these same risks by focusing on the exposure rate of sensitive data in the healthcare industry."

*Tiversa might see the PHI of tens of thousands? And my lawyer doesn't think this is applicable to my situation with the FTC. Great. What is this small company in Pennsylvania and a Business School in New Hampshire doing hovering over all these files? Something tells me they aren't "trying to help." I'm shocked that nobody else is shocked.*

"Also identified was a 1,718-page document from a medical testing laboratory containing Social Security numbers, insurance information, and treatment codes for thousands of patients . . ."

*Okay, as if it didn't already, this means war. You sneaky snake. How dare you, Tiversa, hold up our property as a means to scare others so you can close more business.*

"Tiversa provides P2P Intelligence and Security Services to corporations, government agencies, and individuals based on patent pending technologies . . . Tiversa detects, locates, and identifies exposed files in real-time, while assisting in remediation and prevention efforts."

*Oh, I get it. Tiversa goes out and finds "exposed" files. It would be very interesting to find out what their definition of "exposed." is. Then they find the owners and try to "educate" them into hiring Tiversa. Nasty. And the US Congress sat there and lapped it up like dogs. The FTC couldn't care less about the means to achieve their illusory mission. This is outrageous . . . and dismissive and patronizing lawyers sing out, "Doesn't matter." It matters, all right. It matters to me.*

The second article was a glimmer of hope from the *Columbia Journalism Review* criticizing Bloomberg and *Business Week*'s story on Wikileaks. Titled "Bloomberg and *Business Week*'s Problematic WikiLeaks Story: Red flags aflutter as the news outfit runs with seriously questionable evidence."[1]

Turns out a Bloomberg reporter, Michael Reilly, also had the unfortunate luck of encountering Robert Boback. Like the US Government, he also took Boback's banter hook, line, and sinker, and promptly got spanked for it by his fellow comrades in the media.

Highlights from the criticism:

"How many red flags can we count in this Bloomberg Business-Week piece on Wikileaks? . . .

First the headline: Is Wikileaks Hacking for Secrets?

Second red flag is the subhead: Internet security company Tiversa says Wikileaks may be exploiting a feature in peer-to-peer file-sharing applications to search for classified data . . .

Huh? Who the heck is Tiversa? It ain't exactly McAfee or whatever.

The third red flag is all the weasel words in the key paragraph explaining the "evidence." Hmm. So a P2P security company says Wikileaks "appears to have" hacked into military computers and "may have" used P2P to do it. What's wrong with this picture? . . .

Neatly enough for Tiversa, *BizWeek* plays along with the cloak and dagger stuff . . . and cut to PR executives high-fiving.

Fourth red flag: It's essentially a one-source story.

Fifth sorta-kinda red flag (once you've seen two or three in one piece, it's good to start suspecting everything in it) is that two of Tiversa's advisors have awfully tight ties to the US military and federal government. Wesley Clark, the former NATO commander and four-star general is an advisor, as is Howard Schmidt, who worked for the feds for three decades . . .

The piece raised questions from Forbes' Andy Greenberg . . .
Greenburg confirms that Tiversa is working for the US Government,

which is Wikileak's sworn enemy, and he blows apart Bloomberg's piece with this reporting:

In fact, in a phone interview with me today, Boback sounded distinctly less sure of his firm's deductions than he did in the Bloomberg piece . . . 'Can I say that those are Wikileaks? I can't.' . . .

Bloomberg and *BusinessWeek* shouldn't have run with this one. It looks for all the world that they may (to borrow a word) have published a smear."

Third was just for pure entertainment value. For some reason the thought occurred to me that I had not looked up Robert Boback on LinkedIn. When I found his profile, I found his background to be a bit surprising. He had a BS in Biology and then became a chiropractor. *A chiropractor? The guy that has made my life a living hell is a chiropractor? Congress is listening to a chiropractor about data security? Where are the credentials?*

The fourth discovery was video[2] from a prior interview that Boback gave to what looked like a local Pittsburgh television station. His words had a much different meaning to me than the rest of the viewing audience.

*Boback: The Marine One document was actually discovered last summer and we found that during the course of our normal business. We weren't looking for it, it just came into our systems because it matched a set of criteria that we were prefer . . . uh . . . we were looking for for our clients . . . in protecting our clients. That document, it was clear that it was very sensitive. We immediately contacted the defense contractor following what we use at Tiversa as a duty of care policy. When we come across someone's information, it's . . . we feel it's our responsibility to return that to those individuals.*

*Interviewer: Even if you're not tracking it for the client you're working on?*

*Boback: Even if we're not tracking it. We want to do the right thing at Tiversa. It's not uncommon for us to have this happen, so therefore we return that to the company who the document belongs to and that's free of charge. There's no . . . there's literally no strings attached to this. We give that back. We give any identifying information to help them solve the problem. If, in turn, that good faith is returned and they want to do something with Tiversa down the road, so be it, but that certainly is not our rationale for doing it, so in the Marine One case, we actually, uh . . . returned this to this defense contractor in Maryland, highlighted the problem to them. They immediately contacted the Defense Department, also the White House, who in turn contacted Tiversa.*

How many more times did I have to be outraged by everyone else dismissing this information as if it wasn't applicable to the FTC situation? I thirst for more info. I immediately picked up the phone and called Bloomberg. I was told, "Oh yeah. These guys at Tiversa are a piece of work. They basically have three business models, Fortune 500, Government, and what I call "shakedown." The shakedown part is that they call up the owners whose files they have scooped up, usually financial institutions, if they want to hire them. Some do, some don't. If the target doesn't bite, Tiversa usually just moves on to the next guy. You are the first medical facility I have ever heard them playing this on. Questionable practices, to say the least."

Oh, how I wish I had known this earlier, but then again, in the words of countless lawyers that I have discussed this with, "Doesn't matter."

Over the next few weeks, the FTC had a few more questions about things they could not read and certain screenshots. Phil and Bill cleaned up the last few details, and we got back to business while we waited for our verdict. At this point, I couldn't care what the FTC did. My mind was made up. Either the FTC would let us go or I'd fight in court. At first, I resisted signing a consent decree due to reputation damage. But after cooperating with these people over the past 20 months, that reason had become only the tip of the iceberg. The curtains need to be ripped out of their windows.

On the 19th of August, Dana let us know that the FTC had called and wanted a face-to-face meeting. *More lawyer fees.* The FTC agents and Dana agreed to meet in the early afternoon of August 24th, then Phil and I would debrief with her after the meeting.

After almost two years, I was so used to this type of game, it becomes easier to keep the issue in the back of my mind and go on with my normal duties until the magic hour arrived. I fully expected the FTC to turn down all of our ideas and go right for a consent decree. This would be the moment when Dana Rosenfeld might finally understand that I held that waste of a government agency in complete contempt and wouldn't sign a thing, come hell or high water.

On top of that, ready to unload on her, I had put up with dismissive e-mails, insubordination, disorganization, mistakes, and ridiculous bills she refused to review in the end, plus her trickery in playing word games when we had never come to a payment agreement. I couldn't wait for the day Kelley Drye ceased to darken our doorstep.

While lost in these thoughts, I received an e-mail from Dana that said:

We are back from our meeting. Would like to call us together? Kristin is here in my office.

I replied that we would call at 3:15 p.m.

At 3:10 p.m., members of my staff and I assembled in my library, a small room with a round glass table. Across from me was Phil, to my right was Bill, and to my left was our paralegal Louise. We moved the phone to the center of the table to be equidistant from the speakerphone. I dialed the number with a sense of doom.

"Hello, Dana. This is Mike."

"Hi, Mike."

"Dana, you are on speakerphone and we have Phil, Bill, and our paralegal Louise in the room. Is Kristin there?"

"I'm here!"

"Hello ... okay ... hit it."

"Well, I will get right to the point. The FTC denied our requests for a closing letter, and they want to begin negotiations for a consent decree. They understand that LabMD is a small company, but they feel that, due to the severity of the data, a decree is warranted."

I kept cool as a cucumber as I asked conversationally, "And how, exactly, did they come to their decision?"

"They have a point system. It takes into consideration the size of the company, severity of the breach, response time to correct, other circumstances, etcetera. While they appreciate that LabMD is a small company, they're concerned that the time to respond was too long, and the fact that it's medical information with diagnosis codes makes it too severe.

"The FTC isn't satisfied that LabMD's safeguards were reasonable at the time, although they said our current situation is very good. The FTC uses a sliding scale in what they analyze in making their decision. LabMD's small size is a positive. However, the sensitivity of the data— date of birth, Social Security number, diagnosis codes—is very bad and could allow someone to figure out that a person had cancer. They state that LabMD had an 'invitation' for misuse due to the company's poor training methods and ability for managers to have free rein over their workstations even a day after our notification. LabMD's reaction to the issue was insignificant, too slow, and not comprehensive. LabMD used inside people and not outside experts. I have asked for a closing letter instead of a consent decree. That is a public letter and a comparative slap on the wrist. I doubt it will fly. We'll hear back in a week."

"Invitation for misuse, huh?" I responded, frustrated. "An invitation but no specifics? They don't have a damn thing if that's the best they can come up with. Dana, here we go again.

"First, the file never got out and they know it, or they would be stating the file got out. If they could have nailed us on that, they would've got out their hammers long ago. The file did not get out. There was no breach. That's why they're using the language 'invitation for misuse.' That is disgusting behavior on their part. They are on a witch hunt and have been the entire time. They have no standards. But they don't get to make things up as they go along. Does everyone else let them rewrite history?

"Second, they have no idea about how fast or slow we responded, because Dana, they got the file from a con artist and they have declined our invitation to come down here. They can't judge speed unless they understand the system. Since they think they get to do whatever they want, this doesn't matter to them a whiff. Did they address anything about how they got the file?"

To that, Dana responded, "I believe the FTC found the file themselves."

Stunned and angered, I wanted to set her straight. "No, Dana. They got it from Tiversa while in front of Congress and compelled it directly from them. It's right in the testimony. Testimony, Dana, as in under oath, before the United States Congress. The FTC is lying through omission." My voice was loud and direct.

The wheels had come off the cart. Not only was the FTC basically admitting they didn't have any proof of a breach since they weren't putting that on the table, but our own lawyer hadn't paid attention to me or what we'd sent her. It was all "roll along to the executioner's block" with her.

"I will check with Ruth and get back. I'm just reporting back to you what they said," she replied sheepishly. I couldn't tell if she was actually on the defense or holding back curse words, but I bought none of her excuse-making. In fact, I was enjoying Dana falling off her high horse for the first time. Did she actually think I'd roll over? Evidently, this must have come as a surprise to her. While I was sounding like I was circling the FTC in my conversation, I was actually circling Dana and Kristin.

I launched back into them. "Alain told Evelyn long ago, Dana. In the very beginning. I don't think it's in writing. Ruth wasn't the one to tell us. Ask her where it came from. They're all a bunch of poker-playing cons. Hold on a second."

I hit the mute button and shouted, "Dammit, Dana should know this . . . She either hasn't read what we sent her or doesn't believe us or doesn't care. Is she afraid to burn her personal FTC bridge?" Everyone sat there dead silent, observing the stark red color of my face.

I unmuted the phone.

"Dana, Tiversa downloaded our file. We're not going to pretend that didn't happen, or that the FTC doesn't know it, or that it's not relevant. Tiversa had the file and then wouldn't tell us anything else unless we signed a services agreement. We have the e-mails. You know we have the e-mails. That meant $475 per hour and a guesstimate of $40,000."

"Mike, if we can show that, then the FTC would be interested in it."

*Funny. That wasn't your opinion last spring when you sent me an e-mail blowing off Ben Wright.*

"Dana, it isn't like I haven't been saying this the entire time. They knew before we did all the government agencies that paid for this search. The FTC was sitting there right with Tiversa, Dartmouth and Clark at the 2007 Oversight hearing. Give me a break!"

I decided not to further debate this master wordsmith game player. Dana had all along used dismissal as her line of first defense. If that didn't work, she went to playing stupid, like a fox. If that didn't work, she went to apologizing and spewing out meaningless crap. That's how she played her endless game of running in circles. My opinion was nothing is going to change by this time.

But her plan wasn't working. What would she do next?

"We know they know where it came from. Let's move on." I got aggressive as if going in for the kill. Pounding the point over and over, I wouldn't let her out of the corner this time. She had to address this head on.

"The FTC will have to argue a case," I said. "Where are they going to get the standards that let them argue their case? They have no standards, Dana. What standard are they going to allege we broke? In a legal sense, they are screwed. Where are the standards?"

What came out of her mouth next had us all dumbfounded. We slumped in our chairs as the words spewed out. Her defensive explanation:

"The FTC has posted standards online. They have continually been updated."

"What? You are saying that IT standards for security are dictated by the Federal Trade Commission and they are posted online? Oh please. That won't cut it. Dana, the congressional testimony itself from Robert Boback talked about the lack of FTC action on this issue. They can't rewrite history. Forget it.

I stood up out of my chair, making everyone in the room lean back in theirs. I leaned over the table with my mouth one foot over the speaker and launched, "You know what, Dana? Number one, there were no standards on the Web site in 2008. Number two, what they posted, those are not clear standards. The FTC does not set clear standards. They should not be entitled to set standards. I feel like I'm being seduced into a big web by a black widow spider. I won't go!"

Everyone remained dead quiet. Seconds passed. Phil had a shocked but gleeful look on his face as if he were wondering *did Mike just call Dana a black widow? Mike just called Dana a black widow!*

I was done with the game. I played it, it failed, next. I lowered my voice and slowly, calmly said, "Send me those standards, Dana. I want them via e-mail from you. I'm not signing a thing. I want written proof of exactly what you are referring to as those standards the FTC is relying on. I need them today."

"Okay. I will find them and e-mail them."

"Thanks. Now, finally, as I have said before and from the beginning, I'm not signing anything. Let's talk specifically about the FTC 'telling it to the judge.'"

Dana, as if wearing full FTC regalia on their educational video started in, "Well, Alain and Ruth will have to get permission to litigate, and then they will file a suit with an administrative agency or else outside in federal court. They have the choice and they have the options. The FTC appoints its own administrative judges and can choose to take that ruling or not."

*Really! What is this, a Shakespearian play set from the 16th century? Did Congress really load them this full of bullets?*

"This can get expensive and very time consuming, Mike. But if you're going to litigate, I can't help you there. I am not a litigator, and I have to work with these people."

With that comment, I wanted to burst out laughing. Man, I hate it and love it all at the same time when I am *this* right. I was in no way shocked that she would *bail* when we show our steel spine. And she's supposed to be *defending us?* No way am I letting her out that easy leaving her free of me, her fly in the ointment, to fight the FTC on my own. I wasn't going to give her the satisfaction of having me out of her life. I was certainly going to fire her, but when it was best for LabMD, not her. I had to set it up to protect the company first, so I started to strategize the timing of her termination.

I was now into killer instinct survival mode. Dana and I were like two boxers dancing around the ring. It was time for me to whip out the flute and charm the snake by playing another tune. I had heard enough. I pulled back on the verbal war to keep her locked into the game so I could have time to find a replacement.

"No, Dana, we don't know if we'll take that route yet, but I need to understand that option." *Just as I now understand that you're probably going to jump ship.*

"We need to examine all our options here—whether they be to negotiate, litigate, or what. Let's sit back and ponder this for a day or two. Please e-mail me the FTC 'standards' and Phil will be back in touch."

Then I asked, "Kristin, are you still in there somewhere?"

"I'm here!"

"Wasn't that fun?"

About four seconds of silence passed. No one made a move or said a word. They might have been afraid to. I looked up at Phil and Bill and then said, "I never want to talk to her again. Ever. I have to find another lawyer." The team was all on board with that!

As we disbanded, I walked back to my desk, fuming, and slammed down my notepad. *Why does it take these people so long to get it? I'm fed up with that entire cult of narcissists. They just know they're the center of the universe. Now we can finally get to the fight and get this thing over with.*

The FTC and Dana Rosenfeld never got it in their heads that my teeth sink in deep and I don't do losing, especially not to these hollow heroes, even if they are appointed by the US Government.

At 3:39 p.m., I received an e-mail from Dana, who wasted no time getting back to me on FTC standards. However, she must have been too busy to do anything but include a link, which was to the FTC Protecting Personal Information guide. This guide was quite, shall we say, basic.

Then at 5:20 p.m., we received this:

From: Dana Rosenfeld
Sent: Wednesday August 24, 2011 5:19 PM
To: Phil Carpenter
Subject: RE: FTC materials

All,
The business guidance publication I sent you earlier was issued in July 2007. Note the sections on firewalls, detecting breaches and employee training. This guidance is based on the publications from NIST, SANS, etc., listed on the last page, and is the basis for the FTC's view regarding the reasonableness of LabMD's data security program at the time of the incident.

In addition, the FTC released information on P2P networks in 2008, http://www.ftc.gov/bcp/edu/pubs/consumer/alerts/alt128.shtm, and a business guide in 2010: http://business.ftc.gov/documents/bus46-peer-peer-file-sharing-guide-business

Finally, Kristin and I had a follow up conversation with Ruth about the source of the patient information. She stated that the FTC has information indicating that the LabMD patient information was found via LimeWire, although she would not tell us how the FTC got its copy. I asked if she was certain about this, and she confirmed that the information was in fact available on a file sharing network. Obviously this is something the FTC would need to prove if the case were to be litigated.

I hope this information is helpful.

Dana

Not 15 minutes later, our genius in-house counsel, Phil Carpenter, through no prodding of my own, slapped a saddle on those two by sending the following:

From: Phil Carpenter
Date: Wednesday August 24, 2011 5:32 PM
To: Dana Rosenfeld
Subject: Re: FTC materials

Thanks, Dana. From here, we will look at standards for the reasonableness argument. Please hold off on any further research at this time but please do let us know when the FTC gets back to you.

Thanks,
Phil

I walked into Phil's office and said, "Can you believe she has the nerve to cite SANS as what the FTC bases their publications on? Does she not get that Ben Wright teaches there? Now she's citing SANS when she told me to never communicate with Ben again, which is like saying not to call SANS. Note she uses the words *guidance* and *publications* but not once *standards* in that e-mail. I wonder where she, Alain, and Ruth are going to vacation together this coming Labor Day weekend?"

Carpenter howled at that one, but it really wasn't funny. All the cards had been thrown down on the table. Physically, these lawyers had left the FTC, but emotionally and professionally, they still had their uniforms on. Lesson to the world, when hiring a lawyer to fight against the government, make sure the brainwashing has been cleaned off. She did say she had to work with these people. It's all another trick of the Devil Inside the Beltway as they place their relationship with the agency goons ahead of their duty to defend.

"I'm so pissed that I have to fight the FTC *and* our lawyers *and* Tiversa. Between the arrogance of the bills, ignoring Ben Wright, not knowing our address, just to name a few, I need to do something. If she thinks she's getting a dime more out of us, she's crazy."

"Maybe she'll reduce the bill to get rid of us. I'm sure she probably would be happy to have us gone," Phil suggested.

"Reduce the bill? No. I want all the money back. But first, make sure she puts in writing what her recommendations are. If nothing else, I may want to frame it for the wall. I know she'll whitewash it, but I want something from her in writing.

"The game now is stall, stall, stall. They go on ice while I calm down and figure out our next move. We need a new law firm, but more important, we can't have more of the same with lawyers like these. They're masters of silence in guiding people down the gangplank. It's all settle, settle, settle with them. It isn't even that the truth is missing; it's that the truth means nothing. And they still send the bill."

"I need a shower to get the legal stench off my body."

Over time, Phil had learned to take my lawyer tirades in stride. He knew I had a point and also knew I wasn't referring to him. Certainly, not all lawyers are this way—just *many* of them—and *most* of them inside Washington.

Phil piped up, "I'll start pulling current cases that the FTC has going, Mike. Let's see what they have on their plate and how they fight these things. Then we can review those and see what patterns emerge. I can handle Ruth and Alain, anyway. There's no reason they can't call here if it comes to that. Fighting them is a different matter if it happens right away, but nothing has happened. There's no history of speed here."

"I know. That's fine. I feel as if we just wasted months of doing nothing more than handing them more evidence to turn against us, yet none of it helps or hurts. There are no standards, so I'll be interested to see what the courts think. I bet the FTC doesn't even get to court that often. They're so 'huff and puff and blow your house down' that most of the time it works.

"Let me know what you find. Going home . . . have a good night."

On August 25th, Phil e-mailed me current cases and reminded Dana that we wanted her recommendations in writing. As far as the cases went, he found nothing on data security, and I mean a big zero. As a matter of fact, a data security case has never even been tried by the FTC.

I walked into Phil's office and, as I opened that door, I felt like we were in that movie *Groundhog Day*, constantly repeating the past. "You know, this is just great, but not great. Now we know what our DC friends are all about: three parts—arrogance, power, and sadism. They push now and ask forgiveness later."

"I know," Phil replied, "but I think they have a problem on their hands. There really are no standards. Let's see what they do once we tell them we aren't playing along. I think we should slow this thing down to a dripping faucet and force them to make their moves. We need to call their bluff. If they actually do this, they'll have a very full plate, even though they probably haven't even thought of that yet."

"Yes, I bet they're so proud of themselves, saving the world and all. Must be nice to use whatever means possible with no boundaries whatsoever when you just know you're right. This is *exactly* why the founding fathers built a system of checks and balances. Absolute power corrupts. It doesn't take a genius to figure that out."

With that, Phil and I gave everyone the silent treatment until they chose to contact us. I needed normalcy and perspective. I had to take a mental and physical break to be sharp, so for the next week or so, I didn't do much. I trusted my gut and let my brain function without pressure. This was like a huge game of chess. I'd just left the game board on the table waiting for someone to call me back to make a move, whenever that was.

Then, on August 31st, Phil got the following e-mail from Dana:

From: Dana Rosenfeld
Sent: Friday August 26, 2011 4:31 PM
To: Phil Carpenter
Subject: RE: Re[2]: I had to follow-up

Hi Phil,
As I indicated when we spoke the other day, in the event
LabMD decides to proceed to litigation, you will need to
choose litigation counsel to assist you. While Kristin and I
are fully prepared and well qualified to negotiate a consent
order, as I indicated to Mike at the beginning of our relationship, I am not a litigator. Nonetheless, several of my partners
are experienced FTC litigators and could handle either administrative or federal court litigation against the FTC. As far as
I am aware, however, none have the type of IT background
or data security litigation expertise Mike seems to be looking
for. As a result, I am happy to compile a list of possible candi-
dates—both inside Kelley Drye and from other firms—for you
and he to consider. Our goal is to make you as comfortable as
possible with any decision regarding counsel you make going
forward, and the reason for my call was to make sure you
have sufficient time to consider your options. I should also
mention that it is fairly standard for companies to retain additional counsel during the litigation phase. I would, of course,
be pleased to stay involved for as long as you would like me
to, and provide support to any new counsel. Please let me
know if you have any additional questions.

Best,
Dana

Oh, I really enjoyed this e-mail from her. She knew I was onto her
and that I didn't care about "Inside the Beltway" diplomacy. *We are
prepared to negotiate consent decrees.* And that's it? I bet most people

have let her get away with that because those government people think they've written the Bible.

Right around this time, I also discovered an interesting August 26th interview of Dana in *Law360*. The text speaks for itself.

**Q: What is an important case or issue relevant to your practice area and why?**

A: A series of consent orders obtained by the FTC in the late 1990s and early 2000s set the stage for privacy and data security law enforcement for years to come. These early privacy cases held companies accountable for their privacy statements and practices. As an assistant director in the Bureau of Consumer Protection at the FTC, I was involved in developing the theories that led to these settlements. And now as a lawyer in private practice, I appreciate that these early cases were important for several significant reasons.

First they established the FTC as the leading federal agency in the newly emerging area of privacy, a role which it has continued to play to the present day. In addition, the work by the FTC resulted in comprehensive and lasting changes in the way businesses collect, use, and disclose customer information. While this process has evolved over time, and led to the passage of privacy and data security laws on the state and federal level, it was the early work by the FTC that brought attention to the practices in the first instance.

*Let me get this straight: A series of consent decrees set the stage? Law enforcement for years to come? So glad to see she is so proud of her work and embraces the Federal Trade Commission with such fervor. Wow. Wow. Wow. And judging by recent history, the FTC needs a few lessons in effectiveness. I don't think their lofty ideals, draconian measures, and smug attitude are working out for the American public. Time for a drink.*

And that was the last we heard about Dana Rosenfeld and Kelley Drye—until after Labor Day.

*"Nothing in the world is more dangerous
than sincere ignorance and conscientious stupidity."*

—MARTIN LUTHER KING, JR.

## CHAPTER 21
# Guess I'm Not Crazy After All

When I'm mad, I do things right then and there. Even when I'm not mad, I do things right then and there because I'm busy—only difference is I have a slower heart rate. In this case, I knew I needed to take care of the company first and then dump Dana Rosenfeld. But before doing anything, I went back to my main source of information throughout this entire experience—Google.

I shut my office door, sat in front of my computer, and took a deep breath. The Friday before Labor Day weekend, everyone was winding down, but I was just getting started. I brought up Google and started typing in phrases: FTC lawyers, FTC defeated, FTC fight, legal battles with FTC, Section 5 and the FTC, etc. I was impatient and on a mission, but nothing hit home. I needed to calm down, so I left early before the holiday traffic hit, put on my gym clothes, plopped on the couch, fired up the laptop, and again shut out the world. With my dogs calmly laying on the floor by the couch, it was dead quiet in my house.

I started again on Google: FTC lawyers fight, FTC investigations, winning FTC investigations, learning how to fight the FTC. No matter what I put in, the first page came up with links that usually went to the FTC Web site. *Boy, I'm going to have to dig here.* With every entry, I would go 10 pages deep. I saw a pattern of a few cases with little commentary or how-to information about dealing with the FTC. All I could find were FTC web links, companies under investigation, or advocacy groups thinking that all businesses were evil and should "fry" (based on their years of experience working on teams in corporations and government, naturally).

The digging continued. Nothing. I had to find *some* lead to *some* people who knew how to deal with the FTC, not a silent killer or a classic Beltway Big Firm, Big Billing, Big Bullshit lawyer. As I thought of the lawyers I'd encountered at the FTC and elsewhere, I got this ice-cold feeling about never finding anyone who cared about the immorality of it all.

A scene in the movie *Alien* popped into my mind. The lead characters learn that their crewmate Ash is a robot and hook him back up to get information.

| | |
|---|---|
| *Lambert:* | "You admire it." |
| *Ash:* | "I admire its purity. A survivor . . . unclouded by conscience, remorse, or delusions of morality." |
| *Parker:* | "Look, I am . . . I've heard enough of this, and I'm asking you to pull the plug." |

(Ripley goes to disconnect Ash, who interrupts.)

| | |
|---|---|
| *Ash:* | "Last word." |
| *Ripley:* | "What?" |
| *Ash:* | "I can't lie to you about your chances, but . . . you have my sympathies." |

Well, I was pulling the plug, and I was hell-bent on finding someone with "delusions of morality" to beat this current alien, the Federal Trade Commission. So far, it seemed as if everyone inside the Beltway fit Ash's description.

## "Who is Afraid of the FTC?"

I kept Googling, digging, Googling, digging . . . until finally something different from the sameness of the rambling titles grabbed my eye. Buried deep about 15 pages, I found a PowerPoint presentation. Its title was perfect: "Who is Afraid of the FTC?" by Claudia Callaway and Kathy Foster.[1] *Well, I'm not afraid. I may be frustrated, but until now, I thought I was alone in the world.*

I downloaded their presentation and opened it. It was from a talk given in 2007 by these two lawyers working in a law firm called Manatt. I read through it and wow! Nowhere had I *ever* seen such a step-by-step, easy-to-understand "guide to what they (referring to FTC agents in general) do" like I saw here. *Why couldn't I have found this two years ago?* The guide talked about who the agents are, what the path is like, and how to negotiate it. *Great. Here are my new lawyers, I hope. Goodbye, Google, hello, Manatt Web site.*

A moment of panic set in when I couldn't find either of the named lawyers listed with the Manatt firm. Then I tried LinkedIn. When I found Kathy Foster there, it appeared she'd returned to the Department of Homeland Security. *No thanks. Please tell me Claudia hasn't gone to the safety of the dark side.*

I continued searching. *Okay Claudia, where are you . . . come on, baby . . . where are you? YES . . . moved to a law firm called Kattan, but she's in DC practicing law. Get the phone . . . what's the number? I hope this lawyer thinks the way she writes presentations. If she does, we're in business.*

It was 4:00 p.m. Voicemail, of course. I calmed down, put on my professional corporate voice, and asked Claudia to return my call. *If she got hit with my adrenaline as a first impression, she may be put off.* Although downplaying my hopes the best I could, I still felt excited. This was one of the few authentic presentations I'd ever seen, not all the paranoia that's thrown out by law firms to pull in clients. I'd hit a single. But I had to suspend the game until I heard back to see if I'd score a run or not.

At 4:30 p.m. that day, my cell phone rang and I answered.

"Hi Mike. This is Claudia Callaway."

"Claudia, wow. Thanks for returning my call."

"Hello! Yes, I got your voicemail. What's going on with the FTC and what can we do for you? You'll have to pardon me, but I'm driving while we speak. I'm picking up a moonwalk for my son's party this weekend."

"No problem. Sounds like you're planning a good time. I'm so glad you called. Well, where do I begin? I saw your PowerPoint presentation, 'Who is Afraid of the FTC?' online."

"Really? Where?"

"Google. I pulled up some presentation you made, by the looks of it."

"When did we do that? That was years ago."

"Yeah, like four years ago, with Kathy Foster. You both have changed firms. I've been searching for you."

"Yes. Kathy is back at Homeland Security."

"I know. I've been doing my homework. That is one great presentation."

"Why thank you. What about it made you call?"

"Because it's the only thing I've ever seen about dealing with the FTC that's rung true with my experience so far."

"What's going on? Tell me what's happening. Are you in litigation?"

"No, not yet. I won't go along with their negotiation request. Let me back up. In 2008, we got a call from a company named Tiversa . . ."

I condensed the story into about 10 minutes and didn't lose her. She was right there with me—a new and pleasant experience. *We're actually having a conversation. No pushback, no dismissal, no patronizing tone, no cutting me off before my last word—all that out. I tried not to get my hopes up, but this attorney was easy.*

I summed it up—Tiversa, the refusal to answer questions without a "services agreement," the safety of LabMD's system, the FTC investigation, the volumes of paper, the agents' endless questions that made it seem like they were jerking us around, the stress on management, the law firm, the billing, the consent decree attempts, and the firing of Kelley Drye.

Claudia's words, "Mike, everyone is owed a defense. You do *not* have to roll over to the FTC. You don't. Don't let them push you around."

That was the moment I first came off rock bottom. She was the first lawyer that had given me hope that I could get my company, employees, and life back on track.

"Claudia, oh—you have no idea. Thank you. Nothing is worse than having to walk around for the rest of my life knowing I had bowed to these people. Every fiber of my being won't do it. They don't care that Congress was misled. They don't care that we were manipulated. They don't care about a cancer detection center. They don't care that it wasn't a breach. It *still* shocks me when I think about it. Our present lawyer won't litigate, we've just learned. Plus we don't like how we've been treated. Dealing with that firm is draining enough. These lawyers have to go. We'll fire our law firm as soon as I get someone to hand it off to. I want that lawyer to be you."

"Who is the firm?"

"Kelley Drye."

"Okay. Mike, I will be happy to tell the FTC to go pound sand. Hopefully, the commissioners aren't so shortsighted that they want to persecute a medical facility for an alleged breach that was subsidized by other government agencies."

"Claudia, I'm running down the clock to buy time. We have them all on ice right now. I need an engagement letter, and we have to fly up and meet you. What's your rate?"

It was more than Kelley Drye's, but I didn't care. I believed I would get someone to go in and actually fight. I also trusted her not to abuse the invoicing process. I think she got the message I was all lawyered out.

I conferenced in Phil and we all spoke for a few more minutes. Then we e-mailed Claudia documents to bring her up to speed. She said she'd review them over the holiday weekend. *Finally, we were locked and loaded with what I hoped was the right team.*

We got Claudia's engagement letter on the 6th of September. I was leaving for New York and then France two days later and would be away for at least a week. Carpenter had to review it and get back with any changes. Eager to get going, we set a plan to fly to Washington DC on September 23rd to meet her.

Coincidentally, I also received this e-mail from Dana Rosenfeld on September 6th:

From: Dana Rosenfeld
Sent: Tuesday September 6, 2011 10:19 AM
To: Michael Daugherty, Phil Carpenter
Subject: FW: screenshots

Mike and Phil,
Ruth Yodaiken sent this list of data security consents against small enterprises for guidance purposes. Note that two of the three—Fajilan and Nations Title—name the owner as an individual respondent. The FTC typically does this in matters involving privately held companies, and I would expect they will want to do so here. As you think about next steps, I thought this would be an important factor to consider.

Best,
Dana

My translation: *Hey Mike, just a quick note to let you know the FTC is going after you personally and that is something to "consider." Have a nice day.*

Where's the support? Where's the brainstorming? Where is the proactivity? So much was missing. I couldn't resist firing back an e-mail and calling her out on this missive.

From: Michael Daugherty
Sent: Tuesday September 6, 2011 10:42 AM
To: Dana Rosenfeld, Phil Carpenter
Subject: RE: screenshots

Dana,
Thanks. I thought Ruth was on vacation. If there are any other e-mails from the FTC at Kelley Drye regarding LabMD, we need copies, please. We have been aware of their suggestions

to "educate" due to my self-education on their machinations. The self-righteous are so smooth. I feel like I am being seduced into a web by a black widow. I love documenting every move in this process. And that Ruth and Alain . . . so helpful. Must be such a burden to think you rule the world . . . but the lack of needing to have due process, prove anything, or have any true purpose other than to taint reputations with innuendo using "consent decrees" sure does lighten their load. If LabMD is a bad example, then we have loads of company. And remember . . . we have industry experts that the FTC cites as leaders who are of the expert opinion that there was no breach. The FTC can tell it to the judge. I have had a change to my schedule and will be flying a plane to Paris next week from NYC. Back on Sept 17.

Mike Daugherty

Dana soon replied with this play straight out of the "cover your ass school of law" playbook:

From: Dana Rosenfeld
Sent: Tuesday September 6, 2011 11:02 AM
To: Michael Daugherty, Phil Carpenter
Subject: RE: screenshots

Mike
Ruth sent this last week. I was out at the end of last week or would have had her e-mail sooner. I had already sent you the Fajilan consent in a prior e-mail, and I know the FTC had discussed the Nutter matter with you earlier. The only new consent in Ruth's e-mail is Nations Title, which is a Gramm Leach Bliley case, so not directly applicable to LabMD. We've sent you all other substantive e-mails from the FTC.

We will wait to hear back from you before initiating any communications with the FTC. They may, however, contact us next week when Ruth and Alain return from vacation. We'll let them know you are out of the country.

Dana

Although I was done with Dana, I wanted one more thing—to have her write down her opinion, whitewashed or not, of why she thought we shouldn't fight in the courts. I knew her opinion would be out of the same "cover your ass" playbook, but I wanted it nonetheless.

The FTC had taught me to take my sweet time. Gone were the days when I responded to them with urgency. Then I went on vacation with the smug satisfaction that all of my enemies were in for a big surprise. Feeling relaxed, I put this game board up on the shelf for two peaceful weeks traveling to New York, Canada, Iceland, Scotland, and France.

When I got back to the office on September 19th, Phil said he had not gotten a response back from Claudia on the changes he'd requested to her engagement letter. This worried me. I needed something rock solid before I could pull the plug on Kelley Drye. With the silence deafening, I got aggressive and anxious. All my fantasies of dumping Kelley Drye and telling the FTC to "tell it to the judge" precariously hung in the balance.

I called Claudia and left a voicemail. No response. I called the next day. Again, no response. First I got frustrated, then obsessive. Having a career working in surgery and with surgeons had made me hypersensitive to promptly returning phone calls, so delays like this were pet peeves of mine.

Then I called her firm's main line and asked for the managing partner's office. Evidently that broke the ice with more force. He must have had someone call down to her office immediately, because I suddenly got a tidal wave of phone calls and e-mails. With my call to the partner, I had no intention of getting everyone so excited, but I had a law firm to fire and a government agency to answer to. (New lesson learned about dealing with law firms: If you want to rock the boat a bit too much, call the managing partner!)

Claudia and Phil finally spoke on Wednesday the 21st. Then he came into my office and stood in front of me. "We're okay," said Phil, "but I really want that engagement letter signed. I don't want to go through this all over again with another firm."

"I know. Claudia is as cool as a cucumber. She doesn't seem to get that we feel like adopted beat-up puppy dogs."

"Yeah, well, a signed engagement letter is not a big request. We need to have one when we're there on Friday. I'd love to have this little detail taken care of. It shouldn't be a big deal."

"I know," I replied. "And I'd like to have the big detail of telling the FTC to take a hike taken care of. All in due time. If Friday goes well, we pull the trigger on Kelley Drye on Monday. In writing. No more than a sentence. Dana won't be surprised. She might even have the champagne on chill waiting for the big moment."

## Reprising Dana

Thursday afternoon, September 22nd, Phil and I flew to Reagan Airport in DC, landing at 6:23 p.m. on Delta. I had my cell phone turned back on the moment the wheels of the jet landed on the runway. At Reagan, cell reception can be shoddy, so I thought I'd better make sure all was fine before we deplaned.

As the new messages filled up my screen, my heart stopped when I saw one from Dana. *Did her spies tell her we're in town and going to another firm?* Then I opened it—her unknowing grand finale. She answered our latest request for the risks of going to litigation with the FTC. It said:

From: Dana Rosenfeld
Sent: Thursday September 22, 2011 5:34 PM
To: Michael Daugherty, Phil Carpenter
Subject: RE: Following up

Phil and Mike,
While litigation is always an option for any company facing the prospect of an FTC consent order, I would not recommend such an approach here for several reasons. As we have discussed, there are no examples of privacy/data security matters that have been litigated with the FTC. This likely is because it

is particularly difficult to challenge the FTC's allegations when sensitive information that was within a company's possession appears to have been compromised in some way. In addition, it is very costly to litigate, and the results are always uncertain. Moreover, in our experience, when companies begin to litigate but later conclude that for whatever reason, they'd prefer to settle, the FTC often will not agree to the same deal they would have in the first instance. At this point in the process, we've gained some goodwill and are in a position to try to shape the order to lessen the compliance burdens as much as possible. And it's always helpful to bring incidents like this to a close and allow you to focus on the growth of your business rather than something that happened years ago. I'm happy to discuss this further with you next week when you are back in the office.

Regards,
Dana

This was a gift from the heavens letting me know we were making the right move.

We got to Claudia's DC office bright and early. The conference room was stocked with breakfast and bagels. I was glad to meet Claudia's cordial assistant, Miss Jones, so I could show her I was capable of perfect behavior when not under duress. The room was set up with an easel so I could use visual aids in going over the story for the five hundredth time.

In walked Claudia with a member of her team, Christina Grigorian. I had an immediate flashback to the first day at Kelley Drye. *Why is it so many law firms have teams of lawyers who will only travel in packs? If they're so good, why do we have to go through this?* However, I decided not to raise that battle. This team was clearly on my side.

Due to attorney-client privilege, I will describe the meeting simply as a great personal and professional success. Both Claudia and Christine were skilled, responsive, and respectful. No false promises and no saber rattling. I felt defensive tension leave my body.

The plan we made was all about defending LabMD and making the FTC prove its case. The "you're guilty until proven innocent" days were over. Christina would reach out to the FTC agents to let them know a new law firm was in town. That should hit them from left field. Then they will schedule a meeting with the FTC to get up to speed. That should help educate our new team and kill time. After that meeting, we'll regroup for the next step.

With that, all hands were happily on deck except for one thing—we still didn't have Claudia's signed engagement letter. We pressed for it. We wanted that issue settled. This was post-traumatic stress from working with other law firms.

## Dumping Dana

On Monday, Phil e-mailed me a proposed termination e-mail to Kelley Drye. I was always trained that endings should be brief, like the one Anne Boleyn had. This was too long. Then he sent me an updated version, which he called Dana E-mail Take 2. This was also to pass my approval, but he inadvertently sent it to her as well. That was fine, just not the pretty ending we wanted.

From: Dana Rosenfeld
Sent: Monday September 26, 2011 3:17 PM
To: Phil Carpenter
Subject: RE: LabMD Case

Phil,
I am in receipt of both e-mails. We will work with our IT folks to make copies of our file. Please note, however, that since Evelyn handled the original productions, we do not have any of your initial FTC submissions other than what she sent to us. In addition, you were previously provided with copies of all the submissions we made to the FTC, including disks containing the documents. The only remaining materials are e-mails between us (me and Kristin with you, Mike, and Bill) and our

e-mails with the FTC. We can have these loaded on disks and sent to you or your counsel, but I'm not certain at this point how long that process will take. I'll let you know once I have an estimate from our IT staff. Will your new counsel be reaching out to Alain and Ruth to let them know of the change in counsel or would you like me to do that? To whom would you like us to send these materials? Finally, I would appreciate if you would let me know when I can expect payment of your outstanding invoices.

Regards,
Dana

I printed this off and walked into Phil's office with it.

"Evidently you ruined her Sunday," I told him. "I love her last sentence about the bill. Maybe she will answer some questions about their practices, but I doubt it. Her FTC DNA sure didn't leave her bloodstream when she left government work. Phil, only answer her other questions and ignore the last one. I'll handle her on the money issues."

"Sounds good to me."

"Nice one hitting the send button too early."

"I know! Sorry."

"Harmless error. Luckily."

That same day, Christina was to reach out to the FTC, introduce herself, and ask for a meeting. Of course, government phone tag can eat up days on the taxpayer's dime, and true to form, the meeting between our new law team and the FTC wasn't scheduled until October 5th, 2011. After the meeting, we conferenced in for a post mortem.

"Hello, everyone. Are both Christina and Claudia on?" I asked.

"Yes, we're here."

"Okay . . . spill it."

Christina started off with, "Well, I think they're not sure exactly what's going on. They asked what happened to the other counsel, and we told them we weren't clear on it. They want to move ahead with discussion of starting negotiations. We let them know we'd need time to review everything. They want to meet again in two weeks."

"We're coming to town for this one," I chimed in.

"Of course. That's fine. Now, Mike, you're running the show, but you may want to think it over if you want to be in the room."

I laughed out loud. "What—are you afraid I'm going to speak as freely with them as I do with you? Come on! Can't I have any fun? I know it's smarter if only Phil goes. But why can't I be there to stare them down and maybe give them a few verbal jabs? I at least have that coming."

"Whatever you want to do," Claudia replied cautiously.

"No, Claudia. I'm looking at Phil, and he doesn't want me in there, either. You people are such chickens. I may come to town, but that's fine. We have strategic planning in Las Vegas that week. The only day open is Friday, October 20th. We'll come in from Vegas that afternoon. I don't want us around there on West Coast time all jet lagged."

"Okay. I'll check on that day with Alain."

"Anything else?" I asked.

"Not really," replied Christina. "I think we sort of caught them off guard and they're wondering what's going on."

"Good. They need to stay circled and confused," I said.

The next day, we planned our flights and confirmed an appointment for 2 p.m. on October 20th—no muss and no fuss. We're finally letting the FTC know we've been nothing but cooperative, but we are not rolling over without due process. The agents will have to work hard to make us a notch on their bedpost. Phil and I had a lunch meeting to discuss strategy. My mood was dead serious, which he picked up on immediately.

"Phil, we've mulled around taking action against Dartmouth and Tiversa before, but we were willing to let every outrageous act on their part pass if the FTC would go away. But the FTC isn't going away. This morning, it hit me with crystal clarity. The time to strike is now."

"Okay . . . why?"

"What Dartmouth and Tiversa have done has just passed the point of no return because the FTC is moving forward. The damages are too severe. They've dragged me into this game and aren't used to pushback. It's hardball time. The public needs to know. Let the people decide. I know it sounds corny, but the people are all we've got."

*Vicomte de Valmont: Now, yes or no? It's up to you, of course. I will merely confine myself to remarking that a "no" will be regarded as a declaration of war. A single word is all that's required.*
*Marquise de Merteuil: All right. War.*

—FROM DANGEROUS LIAISONS BY
CHRISTOPHER HAMPTON (SCREENPLAY)

# CHAPTER 22
## Now It's My Turn

The violation I felt when I found our patient file in the Congressional Record and *Wired Magazine* was always fresh in my mind. The hypocrisy and entitlement of posting our intimate property without our permission or knowledge was an outrage. The effort to exploit a medical facility, while cloaking it as a patriotic act, fuels my fury to this day.

But what do I do about it and when do I do it? Do I sue? Do I call the police? Do I call the media? Going to court is an expensive judicial casino, the police don't take white-collar walk-in reports seriously, and the media would use it for their own ratings and then spit us back out on the street. So how do we get the FTC off our backs and never have Tiversa, Dartmouth, or anyone in the US government pull this stunt on anyone ever again? And how do we somehow get back all our money and lost opportunity?

Slowly, I was turning the tables. I had waited for more than three years as I observed appalling, even amoral behavior. *Time to unleash my fury on them all.* The antagonists had committed different sins, so each required different strategies. Kelley Drye was fired—check. Tiversa and Dartmouth needed to be sued—in process. But what to do with the FTC? A complicated issue.

I always believed the FTC knew from day one that Tiversa downloaded our file but I couldn't be sure. The FTC *was* at the 2007 Congressional hearing, sitting with Wesley Clark, Robert Boback, and Johnson from Dartmouth. The Tiversa and Dartmouth suit made sure FTC agents knew what we believed happened, but not for a millisecond did I think they would actually care.

The surprises were just beginning.

I harkened back to 2008 when I held the naive belief that I would be respectfully treated by an agency of the US government. Boy, had I ever changed. My experience has taught me that agency lawyers are self-proclaimed legends with too much power. The words "Congress has assigned us broad enforcement powers" come dripping off their tongues like a looping recorded message. It's used to start every speech, comment, and defense—like a hall pass from the legislative branch to go where they want, when they want, and how they want. As the poster children for asking forgiveness later, they exploit an asleep-at-the-wheel, gridlocked Congress. But this kind of self-policing game certainly shouldn't work. In my view, the lights needed to be turned on so people could see how our government actually works. The public has the right of access and interest in judicial and government proceedings. *Vampires cannot live long in the sunlight.*

So, with that strategy in mind, I asked Phil to craft the lawsuit against Tiversa and Dartmouth as a narrative not only for the courts, but for the Federal Trade Commission and the citizens of the United States. Let the government agencies, Congress, the judiciary, and the court of public opinion all have a crack at this. Let's hear the opinions of others regarding Dartmouth's digging through medical data and slapping our file in their research paper. Let's see what they think of Tiversa's "pay or no play" program.

Phil, Bill, and I had our LabMD "plan and review" strategy meeting for fiscal 2012 set up for Las Vegas beginning October 16th until October 19th. We'd discuss growing our business—something we hadn't found much time for, given all the animals scratching at our door. Phil would have a near-final draft of the lawsuit ready for Las Vegas because we wanted the lawsuit filed *before* we met with the FTC on October 20th. That gave him fewer than two weeks to write this critical legal motion. So for the next 10 days, Phil spent half his time in the office and half his time at home in peace and quiet, crafting our first shot over the bow. "If you won't give me a draft before we leave, give me *something* to read on the plane on the way out to Las Vegas," I implored. When Phil agreed, I felt like a kid counting the days until Christmas.

This "Christmas" arrived on October 16th as we boarded a Delta flight to Las Vegas. Phil handed me the draft so I could settle in and read it during the flight.

"Okay, it's *not* done—but here's what I have so far."

"Can I mark it up?"

"Yes."

Almost jumping up and down in my seat, I smirked, "Oh, I can't wait." I settled back and the world disappeared. Seatback up, seatbelt buckled, all electronic devices in the off position. I dove into the lawsuit wording before the plane pushed back from the gate.

In spite of how long this had been going on, holding an actual lawsuit seemed odd, like it had an otherworldly feel. *This really happened. I can't believe it. This ever-morphing and expanding absurdity is forcing me to attack it to make it go away. Where am I going? I don't know, but I'd best not look down because nerves won't help right now. It's a leap of faith and full steam ahead at the same time.*

The body of the suit was exquisite in its simple way of just telling the story—no muss, no fuss as he laid out the facts:[1]

- Defendants accepted federal funds from the National Institute of Standards and Technology, the United States Department of Justice, the United States Department of Homeland Security, the National Science Foundation, and other federal/state/local governments in furtherance of its activities, including those activities described herein.

- As early as 2007, Defendants worked in concert and intentionally to search the Internet and computer networks for computer files containing personally identifiable information.

- During the 2007 Committee Hearing, Defendant Tiversa admitted that it "developed technology that would allow it to position itself throughout the various P2P networks" and view all searches and information available on P2P networks.

- During the 2007 Committee Hearing, Defendant Tiversa admitted that its proprietary software allowed it to process 300 million searches per day, over 170 million more searches than Google was processing per day.

- Defendants Johnson and Tiversa intentionally searched for, down-loaded, and opened patient-generated spreadsheets containing details of medical treatments and costs, government applications for employment containing detailed background information, social security numbers, dates of birth, places of birth, mother's maiden name, history of residences and acquaintances, schooling history, employment history and other data which, according to Defendant Johnson, "could be used to commit medical or financial identity theft" as part of the Initial Search.
- The Johnson Paper included a "redacted excerpt" of the 1718 File.
- The 1718 File was created on a LabMD computer.
- The 1718 File was stored on a LabMD computer.
- The 1718 File was the personal property of LabMD, Inc.
- Numerous other computer files containing PHI and PII (Personal Health Information and Personal Identity Information) were intentionally searched for, downloaded, and opened by Defendants Tiversa and Johnson as part of the Johnson Paper.
- During an interview following the publication of the Johnson Paper, Defendant Johnson publicly admitted to intentionally searching major computer networks to locate computer files containing PHI belonging to certain top 10 publicly traded healthcare firms across the United States.

I sat in my seat, disquieted. Even though I'd been living this saga for almost four years, it was quite astounding to read about it point by point. *Wow, this is powerful. Truly powerful. No wonder I have had to live in denial most of the time. It is too outrageous to acknowledge every day.*

I simply had to sit with it. Then, after looking out the jet window awhile, I reached under my seat for my writing tablet and wrote down what I believed to be the motivations of the players who'd created this fiasco. Part coping mechanism trying to understand my abusers, part strategy planning, I had to repeat the obvious yet again.

- Tiversa has a data security product it wanted to promote. Its principals build a team of highly respected government and industry advisors to give them a platform of credibility and access to powerful people at the top of government and industry.

- General Wesley Clark has a stake in Tiversa and, thus, self-interest in its success. He uses his status as a four-star general to open doors and to arrange introductions. Howard Schmidt is also on the Tiversa Advisory Board and is Obama's Head of Cybersecurity.
- Their relationship gets Tiversa access to power players inside the Beltway and academia so it can build relationships with potential clients.
- The team of Dartmouth, Tiversa, and Clark attend a Congressional hearing in 2007, testifying about the functionality and power. At some point, they gain government funding for a research project.
- The team starts downloading millions of files, looking for the most sensitive documents.
- Upon taking LabMD's property, Boback calls LabMD, refusing to give us specific details unless his company is retained.

*Tiversa and Dartmouth ignored our 2010 questions and never provided answers. We still wanted to know why Tiversa put OUR file in front of Congress as an example. Was it because we wouldn't pay them? How many other files of US companies are they sitting on? Were any of the files they gave to the government owned by their paying clients? How much property belonging to others do they have? What would happen to all of the "treasure" they hauled in if they got bought out by the Chinese or the Russians or the Iranians?*

*This dangerous situation is going on right under the noses of the dumb and blind United States government—and with its tacit approval and funding. Congress clearly doesn't get it but that doesn't mean the FTC can come after me.*

I got up and walked back to Phil's seat. Surrounded by strangers, I didn't want to say too much. With a sincere look, I handed him the draft and said, "Phil, this is amazing. To read all of this in one place, it seems like it happened to somebody else. My shock continues. Well done."

"Oh, thank you, but there's more to do."

"I know, but so far, very good."

We landed in Las Vegas for three days of meetings. Getting our company to move forward with this huge unknown hanging over us was a formidable task. The variable costs of legal fees, public impact, length of battle, potential dirty tricks, and who knows what else the FTC had up its sleeve made our foundation shaky.

Then Bill got sick as a dog with a terrible flu. What had been planned as a group brainstorming session turned out to be a review session instead with no final resolutions. We landed back in Atlanta on Wednesday, October 19th and filed the lawsuit in the Fulton County Courthouse that day: LabMD vs. Tiversa, the Trustees of Dartmouth College, and M. Eric Johnson.

In a blur of warp-speed travel, Phil and I turned around and landed in Washington DC on Thursday morning. Hopping into a cab, we sped away to the offices of Katten Muchin Rosenman, LLP, where we were warmly greeted by Claudia and Christina.

"Good morning," chimed Christina. "Are you guys jet lagged?"

"I'm okay, but Phil is toasted," I replied. "I've never been to Las Vegas or had to adjust to that before. It really takes a toll."

"You've never been to Las Vegas?" Christina asked, a bit incredulous.

"No. I was blown away by the strip. It's great! I call it the people zoo," I said.

"Good morning," Claudia chimed in as she walked into the room. "How was the trip?"

"Good morning—great. Vegas, Atlanta, DC in 20 hours. Where are we going for lunch? I'm starving."

"Is Thai okay? We love this place around the corner and then we can make the 2 p.m. at the FTC."

No sooner had we walked in than we were walking out to enjoy lunch at a Thai restaurant and discuss the plan for today's meeting with Alain and Ruth.

"We filed the case vs. Tiversa and Dartmouth yesterday," I told our lawyers.

"And tell me again why you chose state court over federal?" Claudia asked.

I sensed friendly concern in her voice. These outside (Claudia) versus inside (Phil) counsel conversations seemed to have everyone walking on eggshells, not wanting to start an internal disagreement, especially with me on the phone. I preferred to hang everyone's ego at the door and get on with the bottom line.

"State court has a longer discovery schedule. We need the time. Also, the state law is what has the most teeth," I answered. The discovery time allowed for the gathering of evidence.

"I just don't want you to get hit with a bad judge. Federal is usually a better draw." said Claudia.

"Are we giving the FTC agents a copy of the suit?" I inquired.

"Heck no!" answered all three in unison.

"They can go look that up for themselves," Phil added.

"Okay, so while I sit in Starbucks waiting for you to come out, what's the overall plan?" I asked. "We'll listen to what they have to say," replied Claudia, "and then I'll tell them, when the time is right, that we aren't authorized to enter into any negotiations for anything. We want to keep them on their heels. This will be the first time for pushback."

"Perfect," I responded. "Make them work for every inch of the playing field. If it comes to it, feel free to call their bluff and tell them I'm not signing anything. I've been holding my breath for too long. Let's get on with it."

"There isn't much to do other than get in there," Claudia responded. "The cards will hit the table, and we'll see how they react."

"Okay, well let's get on with it. Take notes! I don't want to miss a word. It just kills me I can't be in there staring into their eyes, but I understand."

As we left the restaurant, I pointed out the coffee shop where I'd be waiting, and they agreed to meet me there afterward. *How far we've come since my last visit to the FTC. My freshman year of the DC game was over.* Unlike 2010, I was no longer shocked by the FTC holding justice as an afterthought nor the indifference of this town. *Washington DC is filled with bad actors just playing their part.*

My calmness . . . I was proud of it. I'd come to realize that any type of emotion was a waste of energy in this place. Nobody at the FTC cared about any moves I'd make. Things moved so slowly, it was hard to get a pulse. *Who would've ever thought I'd find myself here, cool as a cucumber, unfazed by these hollow heroes?*

I opened the door to the shop, ordered a large skinny pumpkin latte, sat down, and fired up my laptop. I mentally left this artificial America and got back to my real life.

After an hour of catching up on every e-mail, every to-do list, and every phone call, I looked at my watch. Bored! So I picked up the *Washington Post* and read it, then moved on to a local Washington magazine. *Where are they?* About 10 minutes later, Phil sent me a text saying they were on their way. *Did the FTC agents get mad? I hope so. Am I a pain in their tail? That would be good. Is the Mike Daugherty hassle index going through the roof? I can only hope. Oh come on guys, hurry up.*

I looked up to see the three of them walking through the door with friendly smiles on their faces. *I've waited this long; I can wait a little longer.* So I greeted them with "Get your coffee and let's all sit down. I don't want to start until we're all settled in." A complete lie. If I'd have been thinking, I would've had their orders already placed and coffee waiting.

They sat down soon enough, and finally I said, "So, spill it."

"Well, I don't think they're very happy," Christina said.

I burst out laughing. "Fantastic!"

"Yes, they think the world revolves around them," Phil added.

Claudia started, "We let them go at it first. The usual talk. Section Five and reasonable practices. The file got out. The issue is if the practices were reasonable. I let them run for a few minutes. Then I asked Alain, 'What standards do you have for what is reasonable?' He, of course, didn't like that and wouldn't answer the question. He just came back with, 'What standards did LabMD use?' At that point, I told him, 'Just a minute. *You* are bringing the action against LabMD, not the other way around. If you're making a case against

LabMD and its security practices, you must have some standard to base that on.' He just repeated, 'What standard did LabMD base its practices on?' It was going nowhere, but he got the point."

"I'm so relieved that somebody finally told the FTC we're not going to do the legal rollover," I replied. "I so wish I'd been sitting there when you told him that."

"Well, there's more. Ruth and Alain started to press again for consent decree negotiations."

"Yeah, Ruth said it was as if LabMD had just left the file lying out in the hallway for someone to pick up and walk away with," Christina said in a mocking voice.

"Oh really. Right. Again, based on what evidence? Have they ever had to actually use evidence?"

"So I told Alain and Ruth we had no authorization to enter into any negotiations. LabMD would not negotiate anything."

"That's *great!* Then what happened?" This was exciting—like being ringside at a boxing match.

"Hey, we have to keep it down," Claudia warned. "You never know who's listening around here."

"Oh yeah. Right . . . okay . . . go on."

"Things got a bit animated. Not that bad, but Ruth seemed genuinely pissed off. Alain was more cool."

"Yeah, Ruth was not happy at all," Phil chimed in.

"That's odd. I didn't know she cared so much. How touching,"

"Alain said they're prepared to file a lawsuit against LabMD this week."

"Great! I can't wait. Then we can get it out of kangaroo court central."

Claudia continued. "I told him, 'No you aren't. You know you have to go to your commissioner to get permission to do that. Do you really think the FTC wants to sue a cancer detection center given the circumstances surrounding how you got this information? With Tiversa getting it and plastering it up in front of Congress? You have nothing on LabMD and you know it. There's no 'there there.'"

"That is *phenomenal.* I love that! Great, Claudia. Thank you. Finally." I meant that with deep gratitude and huge relief.

"You are so welcome. Then I said, 'We were hard pressed to believe that the commissioners were going to allow this. Furthermore, we have just served a suit against Tiversa and Dartmouth.' That seemed to pique their interest. After that, there was no more to say. They know you aren't even coming to the plate, and they said they're going to sue you next week. The lines are drawn in the sand. It's time to call their bluff. End of discussion."

"That would be the fastest move that organization has ever made. Good luck there," I added.

Then I paused and took it all in like a breath of fresh morning air. "Wow, this is awesome. I wonder what they'll do next. We have to move this out of the agency realm. I say we drag it out, drag it out, drag it out. Let their knees get bloody as they stretch it down the field. What's next?"

"Well, I certainly doubt you'll see a lawsuit next week. They don't know what they'll do at this point, I'm pretty sure. Per your strategy and desires, if they sue, they sue. If they don't, you wait."

"Fantastic. I'm the fly in their ointment. I want to drive them nuts for what they do to small businesses. They finally know I'm not rolling over. They'll have to recalculate what they're fighting for, but their egos get so involved, I'm sure they won't take this lying down. Bullies never do. Okay, great work. GREAT WORK! Let's get back to Reagan airport, Phil, and head home."

And with that, we walked to the parking ramp with Claudia and Christina and said our appreciative goodbyes. This time when I hailed a cab, unlike the last, I wasn't in shock nor was I disillusioned. *David had just hit Goliath on the ankle.*

*"It had long since come to my attention that
people of accomplishment
rarely sat back and let things happen to them.
They went out and happened to things."*

—Leonardo da Vinci

# CHAPTER 23
# Sometimes You Have to Smack Them in the Face to Get Their Attention

So we waited yet again. The legal balls were rolling down the hill. Tiversa, Dartmouth, and its Professor Johnson had been sued. The FTC had been told we would not enter into a negotiation. Now we had to sit back and see who did what. I imagined with glee Boback, Tiversa, and the Dartmouth team reading the lawsuit, sphincters tightening with every page, blindsided by this move. Their arrogance probably made them think of us as meaningless little Georgia shopkeepers.

At the same time, I was about to learn if the legendary wrath of the sleeping giant, the FTC, would be stirred. Reacting to their puffed-up legend of relentless revenge would only play into their propaganda warfare and weaken my resolve. I refused to pay attention to it. *This is what probably drove Dana Rosenfeld nuts about working with me.*

As a veteran of the Washington regulatory game, Dana knew full well it wasn't about truth and justice. I couldn't get through her head that I *knew that as well and didn't care.* I was going to make it about truth and justice, period. With our Constitution fading away over the horizon, someone had to try and pull it back into view. If fighting this was my small part to play, so be it. It became my conscious choice to announce my findings to the world.

I had met lawyers who described FTC agents as vengeful zealots. They said these people would defy logic and pursue those who don't bow to the FTC's power just to show all others what lengths they would go to. Even if they ultimately lost their case in a legal fight, their overall objective was to send a message to anyone else who may consider pushing back. The message: Think twice before standing up to the FTC.

This reputation appalled me all the more. Had the agency been a private enemy going to war against me, that would have been one thing. But this was *my country* kicking me around the room. I love my country and felt a duty to take on this disease-riddled beast. This is what Congress created; this is what our president must manage. If they're both asleep at the wheel, government agencies won't get fixed unless someone sheds light on them. *On with it, then. I may lose a few battles, but I will not lose the war.*

With this in mind, I waited. I returned to my daily practice of pushing the FTC and Tiversa down into my subconscious so I could refocus on my business. I had become used to the low-level but constant tension caused by its presence. I was dug in for the long haul. They could not break my focus. Like a tumorous growth that one has for years, upon removal, while it may seem odd, I actually may miss them one day, be it in three or 20 years after they have gone. For now, the removal was dependent on the FTC's exposure.

Strategy questions simmered in the back of my mind for weeks. *How do I get this taken seriously? This can't be seen as a screaming rant where I picket outside FTC offices. I have to take a much more sophisticated strategy, making these agents put down their cards for all the world to see. I must keep it classy and respectable, especially since one of the Devil's favorite tricks is to attack the accuser's reputation. This will be down-and-dirty warfare.*

November came and went, and no sooner had Thanksgiving passed than the responses to our lawsuit arrived from Tiversa and Dartmouth. Dartmouth struck first, filing on November 23rd, 2011. No surprise—they immediately moved the case to federal court. Federal courts, as Claudia had mentioned, have a reputation of better, more consistent judiciary than state courts. We expected that and were fine with it. We hoped we'd benefit from the judge lottery as well.

After reading the response from Dartmouth, I boiled it down to one argument. Location, location, location. Craftily written, without denying any violation of law outside the state of Georgia, they went for the "cyberspace never-never land" argument that none of their actions occurred in Georgia:[1]

- The Complaint Should Be Dismissed Because The Court Lacks Personal Jurisdiction Over Defendants Dartmouth And Johnson.
- Legal Standard For Exercising Personal Jurisdiction
- The Defendants Are Not Subject To The Long-Arm Jurisdiction Of Georgia.
- Defendants Have Not Committed Any Tortious Act Or Omission In Georgia.
- Defendants Did Not Commit Any Tortious Injury in Georgia and Any Limited Activities of Defendants in Georgia Are Wholly Unrelated to Plaintiff's Alleged Injury.
- Defendants Do Not Have Sufficient Contacts With Georgia.
- Constitutional Due Process Prohibits The Court From Exercising Personal Jurisdiction Over The Defendants.
- To The Extent The Court Does Not Dismiss The Plaintiff's Complaint, The Case Should Be Transferred To The United States District Court For The District Of New Hampshire.
- The Complaint Should Be Dismissed Because It Fails To State A Claim Upon Which Relief Can Be Granted And Is Not Pled Properly.
- Plaintiff's Claims Under The Computer Fraud And Abuse Act Should Be Dismissed.
  a. Plaintiff's Claims Are Time-Barred.
  b. The 1718 File Was Not Accessed Or Used "Without Authority."
- Plaintiff's Claims For Violation Of The Georgia Computer Crimes Statute, O.C.G.A. § 16-9-93, Should Be Dismissed.
- Plaintiff's Claims For Trespass Should Be Dismissed.
- Plaintiff's Claims For Conversion Should Be Dismissed.
- Based on the foregoing, Defendants Dartmouth and Johnson respectfully request that this Court dismiss Plaintiff's Complaint with prejudice or, in the alternative, transfer this matter to the United States District Court for the District of New Hampshire and that the Court grant to Defendants Dartmouth and Johnson any and all other relief deemed appropriate.

We anticipated Tiversa wanting to get out of Georgia. The Georgia Statute has the most teeth for playing around computer networks without a license, so that's where the punishment would be the harshest. Although most states have almost no cybercrime laws, Georgia's statute has been on the books since 1991. The main points of the Georgia Computer Systems Protection Act[2] are:

A. Computer Theft

Any person who uses a computer or computer network with knowledge that such use is without authority and with the intention of:

1. Taking or appropriating any property of another, whether or not with the intention of depriving the owner of possession;
2. Obtaining property by any deceitful means or artful practice; or
3. Converting property to such person's use in violation of an agreement or other known legal obligation to make a specified application or disposition of such property . . .

shall be guilty of the crime of computer theft.

B. Computer Trespass

Any person who uses a computer or computer network with knowledge that such use is without authority and with the intention of:

1. Deleting or in any way removing, either temporarily or permanently, any computer program or data from a computer or computer network;
2. Obstructing, interrupting, or in any way interfering with the use of a computer program or data; or
3. Altering, damaging, or in any way causing the malfunction of a computer, computer network, or computer program, regardless of how long the alteration, damage, or malfunction persists . . .

shall be guilty of the crime of computer trespass.

C. Computer Invasion of Privacy

Any person who uses a computer or computer network with the intention of examining any employment, medical, salary, credit, or any other financial or personal data relating to any other person with knowledge that such examination is without authority shall be guilty of the crime of computer invasion of privacy.

The laws and courts in this country are woefully behind in understanding or properly regulating the improper use of technology, but in Georgia, I believe we're ahead of the curve. That being said, there are very few cybersecurity cases on the books for judges to refer to. They are not computer engineers, so one of the defendant's strategies may be to confuse the judge. However, I didn't look at this only as a technology case. Based upon review of Georgia Statue and the underlying facts I have already mentioned, it sounded like a theft case to me. I read the computer theft statute to say that nobody can use a computer or network to take possession of data without authority. Well, there is no way I would ever have given Tiversa or Darmouth authority to take confidential medical or personal data. So, if I, as the sole owner and CEO of LabMD did not give Tiversa authority to download LabMD's file, who did? Who could? The malware, LimeWire, created the criminal opening. Tiversa created technology to exploit the openings created by the malware. Tiversa should have been aware of the confidential nature of the information when they opened a port and entered our workstation and downloaded our file.

Furthermore, I could not imagine a Judge would say anyone like Tiversa, a private enterprise, had the right to copy private medical and personal information, distribute it, throw it up before Congress and not be held accountable.

I sat in Phil's office reading our lawsuit against Tiversa and Dartmouth again, shaking my head in disgust. Then I said, "Isn't this nothing more than a flat-out case of theft? Those files were and are LabMD's property. Medical files. No one SHOULD go digging in the trash and shaking doors. What's more, even if you go out looking for files, you SHOULDN'T get to read them and publish them. Vigilante activities are uncalled for. Exactly who do they think they are? I can't believe all of those congressman sat there listening to testimony and not one of them thought to question the technology Tiversa used to take private data.

"It goes to show how the powerful don't understand technology. If Tiversa and Dartmouth had gone out and picked up five thousand wallets with cash and ID in them and dropped them on the congressional table, wouldn't someone have asked them specific details regarding how they got it? But not a peep out of this crowd. And these guys want to regulate the Internet? Until they educate themselves, God help us all!"

Tiversa and Dartmouth and Johnson didn't stumble upon LabMD's property; they said they went *looking for it* with unique, powerful, and government-funded tools. *Since when can a private company act as a government agent? That's bone-chilling behavior. Big brother writes a check to private enterprise and academia, who then go out and bring back a treasure trove of others' property, and the FTC starts rewriting history and attacking small businesses. That's like Queen Elizabeth I sending Walter Raleigh to loot Spanish ships, but that was well before the US Constitution existed!*

A lawyer friend of mine reviewed the brief and said, "I understood this case would all boil down to whether or not the judge understands that our network and workstation were opened in Georgia. If he gets that, they're toast. If he doesn't, then we move the same case to another jurisdiction."

"Oh, that's such legal gamesmanship when everyone turns into a statue and kills logic. How can it *not* have happened in Georgia? We're here. The file was here. There's no proof it was ever shared. Nothing on that computer shows that any of those files were ever uploaded anywhere. How can they say it happened in Pennsylvania? And if they use software to remotely open our door locks, that's not a Georgia burglary?

"I do not want to move this case out of Georgia. LabMD is a Georgia company. Georgia law has teeth and that file was here. Let them prove otherwise in discovery. That seems to be the only way we'll ever get them to give any information," I emphasized.

My friend replied with trepidation, "Mike, it will depend on the case law and the judge."

"Oh right, I forgot, the judge lottery. Welcome to Vegas. What's this trade secret argument they're trying to make?"

"That's their Hail Mary pass. They're attempting to argue that medical files are trade secrets and so aren't covered the same way. They cite law that says the trade secret law trumps other laws. Then they cite a law that identifies a medical file as a trade secret. Therefore, they're saying the law we cite is not applicable because the medical file is a trade secret. They're reaching. Boy, are they ever reaching. Good sign if they have to dig that deep for excuses."

Validating his trepidation, I moaned, "The legal system in this country is so screwed up! The lawyers and judges *spend* millions and *make* millions splitting words and turning their meanings upside down. Is there no common sense?

"Well, I'll wait and see how this unfolds. Why waste my energy now? Oh yeah . . . Happy Thanksgiving," I added with a laugh.

"Happy Thanksgiving."

The Wednesday after Thanksgiving, Tiversa's response arrived. Its arguments differed from Team Dartmouth's, but not by much[3].

- The Complaint Should be Dismissed for Lack of Personal Jurisdiction.
- In the Alternative, the Complaint Should Be Dismissed Because It Fails To State a Claim Upon Which Relief Can Be Granted.
- Plaintiff's Claim For Violation of the Computer Fraud And Abuse Act (Count I) Should Be Dismissed.

- Plaintiff's Claim is Time-Barred.
  a. LabMD Fails to Allege the Requisite Elements of a Claim under the CFAA.
  b. Plaintiff's Claim For Violation Of The Georgia Computer Crimes Statute
  (Count II) Should Be Dismissed.

- Plaintiff's Claims For Conversion (Count III) and Trespass (Count IV) Should Be Dismissed For Failure to State a Claim Upon Which Relief May Be Granted.
- Plaintiff's Claims for Conversion and Trespass Are Preempted by Georgia's Trade Secret Act.
- Plaintiff's Claim for Conversion Fails Because Copying is Not Conversion.
- Tiversa conducted the search of the P2P network at issue in Pennsylvania, and its effort to reach out from Pennsylvania to solicit business from LabMD failed. Georgia's long arm statute and federal Due Process requirements mandate dismissal of Tiversa for lack of personal jurisdiction because no act, omission, or transaction occurred in Georgia. Moreover, the Complaint fails to state a claim upon which relief can be granted for the simple reason that Tiversa merely searched for and found information that was publicly available to everyone back in 2008 and continues to be available to anyone who accesses the P2P network today.

I looked up at Phil and said, "I like that they claim the file wasn't in Georgia but admit they did download it. How can they not admit that anyway, with all their testimony? So now they're going for the 'publicly available' angle. Does the public have Tiversa's technology? Are they actually saying if we mistakenly made the file vulnerable, the file is then theirs for the taking? Really? Wow. That won't fly."

"They're also trying to call a medical record a trade secret. That's a stretch. Overall they put forth what I fully expected them to argue. They're in a box. You shouldn't just open up medical files because you found them on the street when you know what they are. We're going to hear 'it was in the public domain' and 'LabMD extended everyone authority' all day long. It appears to me they don't have much to defend themselves with, so they're playing a lousy hand the best they can."

Phil said, "Right, because everyone knows that a medical chart is free for just anyone to rummage through. I can't wait for them to tell *that* to a jury. 'Yeah, we looked for it knowingly, read it, tried to get LabMD to pay, they wouldn't, and we put it up before Congress.'

"Funny coincidence, the FTC wanted the file right after that. Washington DC, the land of the amazing coincidence," I said with contempt and dripping sarcasm. "Now what do we do?"

"We show the judge this occurred in Georgia. That's clearly where this battle is going first," Phil repeated.

"That means we call in an expert like Scott Moulton?"

"Hopefully Scott can explain how Tiversa and Dartmouth entered Georgia. I hope the judge doesn't believe in ghosts."

And with that, I called Scott right then and there. He travels all over the world teaching computer investigation and forensics. Luckily, he lives in Atlanta. Among his many talents, he handles complete forensic data collection and preparation of evidence for legal cases. He speaks on data recovery, forensics, and audits, plus he identifies internal security issues and is a licensed private detective.

The first available day for all of us to meet was December 14th, so I marked my schedule and cooled my jets for a while.

The ball dropped back in our court. We had to reply to Tiversa and Dartmouth's motions to dismiss, and we had until mid-January to complete them, according to agreed-upon extensions. In the meantime, with December filled with client and employee parties and family matters, I had precious little time to play catch-up ball.

First on my neglected to-do list was to fire off a letter to the managing partner at Kelley Drye to express my extreme displeasure. I was reminded to get to this because the latest billing alleged a balance due of more than $24,000.

"You know, they're right, we should deal with this invoice," I sneered. With that, Phil sent the managing partner a note resembling a comment card that needed lots of paper.

Dear Mr. Callagy,

As General Counsel for LabMD, Inc. ("LabMD"), I am writing today to dispute the invoices received to date for services rendered by Kelly

Drye & Warren, LLP ("KDW"). The engagement letter executed by LabMD on March 17, 2011 ("Engagement Letter") outlines KDW's obligations and duties with respect to its representation of LabMD. Based upon KDW's complete and utter breach of several fundamental provisions of the Engagement Letter, LabMD hereby requests that all fees paid to date be returned to LabMD within twenty (20) days of receipt of this correspondence and that any outstanding balances be credited to bring LabMD's balance to zero. Failure to do so will leave LabMD with no other choice but to file a fee dispute complaint with the District of Columbia Bar and pursue all other available legal remedies to resolve this matter.[4]

The laboratory world has a constant sense of urgency as human beings are waiting for their results. The legal world certainly does not have the same need for speed, from the courts on down. Those people live on another planet when it comes to time management. I did not watch the clock.

## LabMD's Christmas

Ahhh . . . mid December, one of my favorite times of the year. People in our client offices are more relaxed, everyone is more social, and our company Christmas party is an event our employees rave about.

We always like to give our clients a personal-touch, small-business-feel gift every year. By regulation, we're not allowed to spend a ton of money, so in Marietta is a "mom and pop" right-out-of-the-good-old-days store called the Marietta Candy & Cake Co. we love. For about $2 a dozen, we order 500 dozen chocolate chip cookies, wrap them in red boxes stuffed with holiday confetti, and slap on a pretty bow. Instead of sending a basket that gets lost in the crowd, we hand each person a box as a thank you. It's the intimacy of fresh-baked cookies and the personal touch we want to convey. As a small business, we want each person involved—from the receptionist to the surgeon—to feel important.

To thank those who work at LabMD, my favorite way is the annual Christmas party. Looking forward to an escape from lawyers, Tiversa, Dartmouth, and the FTC, I put on a happy face and hosted a blow-out party at Maggianos in Buckhead. We doubled the room size from before. With its high ceilings, dark mahogany paneling, with Christmas lights and wreaths surrounding a dance floor, the room was beautiful! We brought in the out-of-state employees, hired a DJ, and set up a gift table. The bar opened at 6 p.m. with appetizers—jumbo lump crab cakes and marinated shrimp with breadcrumbs. The jingle is in the mingle and the energy took off on its own. It was the employees' night. People walked in the door wearing suits and ties, fancy dresses, spiked heels, and bling. Because half the staff wears scrubs every day, it's especially fun to watch this Christmas runway show.

As we sat down at our tables with unassigned seating, the feast continued. Out marched the restaurant staff with a family-style banquet, laying on each table salads, beef ravioli, tenderloin medallions, veal parmesan, and lobster cannellini (mouthwatering crepes stuffed with lobster meat and Italian cheeses, topped with sherry cream sauce and breadcrumbs). We made the gift theme this year "wine and jewelry" and conducted a lottery deciding who got first pull and proceeded with the gift-giving.

Then, with colors flashing and mirror ball spinning, the DJ started the music. People quickly split into two worlds—those who like to dance until midnight and those who'd prefer to be home in bed. For those in the midnight crowd, the room turned into a midtown nightclub. We did the electric slide and wobble as well as "party rock." Although I'd only partaken of one alcoholic drink, I didn't act very presidential on the dance floor. I wanted everyone to feel free enough to rock and roll that night, myself included. Although it was fun watching people dance their tails off, the rather-be-in-bed crowd simply sat at their tables watching us as if we were animals at the zoo. This made me unsure we'd repeat the nightclub portion of our evening in the future. I wanted everyone to have a good time! I know I did!

For me, this evening was a touchstone of my vision of what LabMD should be: hardworking, hard-playing, committed people employed in a healthcare setting. They're a great group. I was glad I wouldn't let the ghost of the US government get to them; it was *my* job to deal with the barbarians at the gate. Walking to my car, relaxed yet refreshed from the fun of the evening, I sighed. *That was good.*

## Cyber Detective

The December 14th meeting rolled around—time to get down to business with Scott Moulton's help. His hourly rate made us eager to cut out the casual conversation. After the brief "how ya doing?" talk, I walked up to the white board, marker in hand.

"Okay, here's the deal, Scott. We're suing Tiversa and Dartmouth for violations of the Computer Fraud and Abuse Act for exceeding their authorization to enter our network as well as violating the Georgia Computer Systems Protection Act."

"Now explain how you can prove our point, Scott."

For the next 90 minutes, Bill and Phil and I went back and forth with Scott, asking question so we all understood everything. We knew that Tiversa and Dartmouth didn't want this lawsuit in Georgia. Instead, they wanted it in New Hampshire or Pennsylvania, where Dartmouth and Tiversa are respectively located. But those states simply don't have laws with teeth like Georgia has. Also, it just makes sense. People, even many trained lawyers, assume the Internet is a Never-Never land in outer space without laws or jurisdiction. Cyberspace is not Never-Never Land.

While tying things up, Scott said, "I wish I would've been in on this from the beginning. I would have told you to ignore that letter from the FTC."

"There isn't a lawyer on the planet who would've recommended that!" I said.

"But it's the truth. If the federal lawyers knock on your door, they already believe you're guilty. The investigation is just a formality."

That comment struck me as a cold lesson. Scott was exactly right.

"I wouldn't have believed that before," I said, "but I believe it now. You're right, but ignoring the first letter from the FTC never occurred to me or any lawyer. What do you need to get your affidavit done, Scott?"

"I need to put together the facts and type them up. It won't take long because I've been through this before. I should have something within the week."

"Okay, great. Phil will work with you directly on this."

With Scott set up to knock out his work, it was time to take advantage of this temporary pause in the game and put up my feet. Fate chimed in with one of her favorite lines, "Not so fast."

*"Give 'em the old Razzle Dazzle*
*Razzle Dazzle 'em*
*Show 'em the first rate sorcerer you are*
*Long as you keep 'em way off balance*
*How can they spot you've got no talents?*
*Razzle Dazzle 'em."*

—"RAZZLE DAZZLE" FROM *CHICAGO*,
BY FRED EBB & JOHN KANDER

# CHAPTER 24
# The FTC that Stole Christmas

I can't stand crowded holiday flights. As a spoiled road warrior who usually never checks bags, I find Christmas travel magnifies all the negatives of commercial flying. Long lines, long waits for bags, full flights, and short tempers (starting with the airline employees). I try my best to slide in between the masses, praying I'm not within 100 feet of a screaming baby.

In 2011, Christmas fell on a Sunday, so I flew to Detroit on Thursday night, December 22nd, and arrived there about 8 p.m. *Even being this close to Christmas, thankfully things worked out pretty well.* Pulling boxes and bags off the carousel, I loaded them on a cart and called my parents, giving them the "all clear" as they waited in the cell phone area of Metro Airport. *Detroit's new airport efficiency ain't bad!*

We arrived at my parents' home by 10 p.m., then I unpacked, organized the gifts that still needed wrapping, and sat down with my folks for a chat before bed.

"How's business, bud?" my dad asked.

"Pretty good, Dad. Things are solid," I said, careful to protect my parents from the worry and anger I'd been feeling. "Not really much to report. Things are just humming along."

"Well, that's good."

My father is a retired homicide detective with the City of Detroit, so I've been no stranger to police officers, attorneys, and judges all my life. He would like this story, but on balance, he was suffering from recurrent prostate cancer. If I spilled the beans, he had a lot of time to sit in his chair, stewing over what the federal government was doing to his son. Because I didn't want him to waste energy doing that, I lied by omission. So I spent our time lying on the couch, watching the news, and eating frozen Snickers bars as if it were 1976. *That's what going home was all about for me. I needed to recharge.*

Friday, my mother started the morning with her usual questions.

"Orange juice, Michael?"

"Yes, please."

"Eggs?"

"No."

"Toast?"

"No, thanks."

"Are you sure?"

"Yes, Mom. I'm fine." I don't want to start eating like crazy. We'll have enough of that tomorrow and Sunday. Oh yeah, remember that tomorrow morning I have my interview for my Nexus card at the US/Canadian border in Detroit—9:00 a.m. After that I'm done with everything I have to do."

"That's fine. I assume you'll be here for dinner tonight."

My body had arrived home for Christmas, but my mind was still preoccupied with work. Christmas wouldn't start for me until the lab closed on Friday—always something popping up with e-mails and phone calls. My BlackBerry, iPad, and laptop had shrunk my world so I could leave Atlanta and still be at work. But it also meant I could leave Atlanta and *not* get away from work.

After working out and showering, Dad and I went out to lunch where all dyed-in-the-wool, true-blue Detroiters go—the Coney Island. But first, I picked up my niece Laura, 15, and nephew Patrick, 12, from my sister and brother-in-law's place a mile away, so I could hear the sounds of Christmas cheer—or in this case, the bantering of two adolescents who live to torture each other. Ah, home sweet home.

Actually, with Patrick growing up, there was less pointless bickering and teasing now than in previous years. Laura was turning into a beautiful woman, which was annoying to me (why should she have boys calling before she turned 30?). I thoroughly enjoy being the uncle who can call it like I see it. Usually, that means Patrick gets the brunt because he's got a mouth on him ... like his Uncle Mike. My favorite comments go something like this: "You know, I don't have to leave either of you any money when I go just because I don't have children. There are plenty of fine charities that more than deserve it." Or "I hear you don't believe in Santa Claus any more. He's very happy about that. He never liked your behavior, anyway." Or, if I'm *not* kidding around: "I'm doing you a favor telling you what you're doing is annoying. In the real world, people won't tell you; they'll just turn around and walk away."

After our "healthy" meal of Coney dogs, chili, milkshakes, and fries with cheese (I didn't have the shake or fries, dietary considerations and all), I went to Caribou Coffee to knock off a few hours of work before our lab's Christmas shutdown took full effect. Hypnotized by my laptop and latte, three hours seemed like 30 minutes. By 4:30, it was time to hang it up for the weekend.

I hadn't been in the house three minutes when I compulsively looked at my BlackBerry, finding a text message from Phil. "Call me. FTC."

*Oh great. These bastards do love their petty torments. What bugs me is that nobody else will believe it; they'll just think I'm pissed off.* I walked out of the house, pacing up and down the driveway in the cold with the phone to my ear as I waited for Phil to pick up.

"Hello, I'm sorry. I'm sorry I have to ruin your Christmas weekend. The FTC just sent you a CID."[1]

"What's a CID?"

"It's a civil investigative demand. It means you have to sit for a subpoena, but it's a government subpoena on steroids."

Wound up and pissed off at first, I burst out laughing. "I love this. I really love this. It proves what a bunch of petty children they are. I asked them to come to Atlanta. 'No.' Dana asks them if they need anything else. 'No.' They're so self-righteous, they never thought in a million years anyone wouldn't negotiate with them. Then they bellow about how they're going to sue. This is the best they can come up with? A CID? Good. These bastards want to play 'drag it out,' so let's play 'drag it out.' I'm recording all of this wasteful taxpayer gamesmanship by these career bureaucrats and lawyers. I'm not surprised at the stupidity of some people. What does surprise me is their vast numbers."

"I'm sorry, Mike. I didn't want to ruin your Christmas, but I *had* to tell you."

"Oh please. Ruin my Christmas? I was made for this. I love this stuff. Think of all the poor people who have to put up with this. Don't think that teeny weenie Alain Sheer didn't snicker when he sent this off today. Congress needs to view this Frankenstein agency in all its reality. Of course, members of Congress won't do it unless their constituents or the media rip their eyelids open.

"Don't worry, Phil. Now I have something to do in case I get bored this weekend! E-mail me that damn CID. Talk to you later."

"Okay. I'm sorry, Mike. Look on the bright side. They did *not* file a suit. They don't have a case. They're resorting to games. This is their temper tantrum. It's a childish government temper tantrum. We can deal with it on Monday."

"Okay. E-mail Claudia and Christina. Let's meet on the 27th via phone. Rack it up. Win or lose the battle, they're going to lose a leg. Until they have a photo of me on the wall of the FTC to throw darts at, I'm a failure.

"You know me. I blow up and calm down fast. I'll be fine. You absolutely did the right thing telling me. Have a Merry Christmas!" I added with a humorless laugh.

Phil knew me well enough to know I don't only talk when I'm this mad. My energy quickly leaves the emotional world and turns to action—big, laser focused action. And boy, does this crowd ever deserve the big action they've got coming their way.

Standing alone in my driveway, I calmed myself down as the sun was setting and looked straight up into the sky. In the quiet of the cold Christmas eve, feeling the chill of the wind blow across my face, I quietly pondered what had just happened. *What type of human being sits in our nation's capital and does this stuff? And at Christmas! As Evelyn once told me, 'When someone shows you who they are, believe them.' Duly noted. War.*

I sat on the ground for a minute to gather myself, knowing I'd have to go inside and do some great acting. I could see my mother working in the kitchen through the window. I have a hard time lying to anyone—especially my parents. But for their own peace of mind and Christmas weekend, I had to. *These are arrows I don't ever forget. Innocent until proven guilty? That's just circle-and-confuse gamesmanship with these self-deluded bureaucrats. Get ready to dance now.*

And with that thought, I walked into the house, heart rate calmed down, a smirk on my face. I was an actor, a planner, a son home for Christmas, and a patient soldier lying in wait, willing to do what it takes to drive the enemy completely nuts. This called for patience and perseverance. And what better time than Christmas to lie on the couch Googling the FTC and data security practices to my heart's content? In the grand scheme of things, this was only one giant game of chess—with the US government on the other side of the chess board. I could handle that. I bore easily. I would make this as fun as possible.

"Hey, Mom."

"Are you done with your calls?"

"I think so. Things should be calm now that it's after five. The physician's offices are ghost towns."

"Chris and Gerry should be here soon." Chris and Gerry are my sister and brother-in-law who were flying in from Phoenix.

"Did their plane land?"

"Yes. Your father is still at the airport but should be getting home soon. Then we'll eat."

"Okay, great," I said as I plopped on the couch and started my iPad. Opening Google, I entered "FTC CID Data Security." *My 72 hours of research and reconnaissance had begun.*

The research and articles I found with loads of time to read—right under my family's nose—were quite empowering. I realized I wasn't alone—quite the contrary. My senses were invigorated as I dug and dug until I discovered article after article, e-mailing it to myself and Phil Carpenter.

This gave me time to think. I laughed, realizing that Alain Sheer had huffed and puffed back in October but did not follow through. *The FTC didn't file a lawsuit, and if these agents believed they had the goods, they would have. All they have is their usual tools of broad investigation and other petty torments and they won't give up. They think they're on a crusade to save the world and the law doesn't apply to them. I'm sure Congress didn't intend the FTC to be this way. But the current FTC, under Chairman Jon Leibowitz's watch, is what happens when Congress is asleep at the wheel and bully tactics silence the masses.*

I vowed to remember three foundational assumptions:

1. These people don't care about the Founding Fathers' intent.
2. If you believe they'll fight fair, you're a fool.
3. What kills a vampire is direct sunlight.

With that, my plan solidified. Drag this out, go into a mental hibernation of infinite patience, document their every move, shine a light on their actions, and let America know. *Why, this is the opportunity of a lifetime. I won't whine about it; I'll turn this around and ride it—and hopefully drive them right into the ground.*

The next three days were filled with shopping, dinners, watching TV, sleeping, and family gatherings, with Internet research in between all of it.

One amusing discovery is that annual FTC brochure where they parade all their "victories" out in a three color brochure. In the 16th century, they put heads on spikes to scare the commoners, but evidently, in current times, they use a yearbook.[2]

My favorite "Eureka!" was a paper I found from Michael D. Scott, Professor of Law and Director of the International IT Law Summer Program in London. His 60-page paper was titled *The FTC, the Unfairness Doctrine, and Data Security Breach Litigation: Has the Commission Gone Too Far?*[3] on August 20, 2007.

On the evening of December 26th, I went to bed around 10 p.m. Away from my parents, I could concentrate without worrying about anyone reading my screen over my shoulder. I fired off the following to my battery of attorneys:

All:

Loads of research done by me all this weekend. I'm going to shine a light high on this . . . but from a "legal" perspective, here's a great argument from Michael Scott's paper[2] (attached) at Southwestern Law in LA, should they dare to let a judge opine on their actions. They seem to have morphed back to what's gotten them into trouble in the past, which is doing whatever the hell they want to, as if rules are for the little people. (Why does everyone just roll over to these bullies?)

I quote: "The FTC recently began to apply the unfairness doctrine to situations in which a company has suffered a data security breach. The Commission has held no hearings, solicited no public comments, engaged in no rulemaking, nor issued any policy statements or guidelines on when, if ever, the unfairness doctrine can, or should, be applied to data security breaches. Instead, the agency merely began filing complaints against companies that suffered such breaches. The application of the unfairness doctrine to data security breaches constitutes a significant shift in how the Commission has used the doctrine in the last few years."

Speak to you all on the conference call line at 10:30 a.m. eastern. I will have to sneak out because I don't want to worry my family, so if I am a minute or two late, hang in there.

Happy Holidays!
Mike

It's the little things that matter. The timing of the CID still stung. Forgive? No. Forget? Never.

*How do I win this? The legal process is one slow, expensive game but there are other ways to skin the cat. The FTC agents hate my guts, so let's shine a light on what they do when they hate someone's guts.* Lumbering organizations like this aren't good at turning on a dime or making constant small adjustments. I was brainstorming and writing down thoughts: media, book writing, magazines, political organizations. My approach was get to the courts, and in the meantime, figure out other ways to hit them where it counts. *I need to outrage Congress, and the way to do that is to outrage the public. This phone call tomorrow will have me being the leader, not the follower. The only person that really has skin in the game is me.*

As I turned out the light and went to bed, for some odd reason, I felt like a million bucks. Better clarity than confusion. Fine with me. And to all a good night.

I woke up the next morning needing to drive to Ann Arbor to copy some documents at the FedEx Kinko's on North Campus and have a quiet place to talk on my cell—but not a coffee shop. Because it was starting to sleet outside, I knew the normal "I have to go see a friend" would not fly with my mother.

"Why do you have to go now, Michael?" she asked. "Look at it outside."

"I know. But I have to get some things done for work. If it weren't for that, I wouldn't go, but the traffic will be light and it's only 10 miles. I'll be fine." Lie lie lie lie lie . . . man, I hated that.

"Can't you wait until later? Can't you wait until after lunch?"

"No, I'll be fine. I'll call soon."

As I slid on my jacket and wrapped my scarf around my neck, I kissed her goodbye and felt like a lying sneak walking out the door.

With huge snowflakes falling—half ice and half snow—driving on the M14 freeway was dicey as the salt trucks hadn't made it out yet. I didn't care. Growing up in Michigan, I knew how to drive on this stuff. Plus, I couldn't wait to finally talk to someone about these latest developments. I'd been living two lives the past three days and I didn't like that. Too much effort!

I arrived in Ann Arbor just before 10:30 a.m. and sent an "A OK" text to my mother's cell phone. Then I dialed the conference call line. Everyone was already on.

"Hi, I'm here."

"Hello. Did you have a great Christmas, Mike?"

"I did, actually. We saw *Mission Impossible* last night. Ate too much. My family is worried that I have an iPad addiction. All I did was surf the web about the FTC, but they didn't know the subject matter. I hope you all had a fine time as well."

"That's funny," chuckled Christina with her bubbly laugh. *Christina always has such a sincere disposition. I really like her personality. These lawyers are so supportive and respectful. Makes me a much better client, I'm sure.*

"We did, Christmas was great," they all chimed in, sort of on top of one another.

"Okay, so Merry Christmas, have a CID. Now what? I want to know all legal options in this game."

"I had read that Michael Scott paper[3], Mike," said Claudia. "Very interesting commentary. I say we make the FTC people work for it, because that's exactly going to be their problem if this ever gets to court."

"Yes, but what's the algorithm? We have to have a multiple-step plan. What are our options?"

Phil offered, "First thing is appeal, and we have only three days to do that."

"Business days or calendar days?"

"I don't know. I have to find out."

"I want to get this out of the hands of the FTC and into the judicial system. What does that road look like?"

We continued our strategy discussion, laying out various options. Basically, the courts don't rule favorably against anyone fighting a government agency until all internal government agency "administrative appeal" avenues have been exhausted. In this case, that meant file a notice of appeal, file a motion to quash the CID, then wait for a reply. That was just for starters. The hilarious thing, not surprisingly, was knowing the FTC commissioners act as their own judges for these motions to quash and *you can't attend your own hearing*. Doesn't that seem less than objective? And are they likely to overrule their own employees? If an internal administrative judge presides instead of the outside courts (which is the FTC's choice, not the defendant's), and the agents get a negative ruling, they can also choose to ignore that. Hence their wear-you-down power keeps going. No wonder most companies just roll over. I can't make this stuff up . . . our Congress did. I wonder if they had a party after they burned the Constitution?

This would have been amazing to me three years before, but I'd come to fully understand that Congress and the politicians from both parties have stripped the checks and balances of government by creating these centralized enforcement agencies. Congress doesn't pay attention to what happens when it makes laws with such weak boundaries nor do they care about the repercussions to the innocent when they award "broad authority." As a result, the courts have their hands tied with such untethered laws, and few people ever alert Congress about the overreaching behavior that results. This makes the administrative agency's "self-policing" judicial system a farce. *Now I understand why so many lawyers spoke of the FTC like they're out of an episode of the Sopranos. Who needs this?*

After much discussion, our plan to navigate the FTC's kangaroo court pattern formulated as follows. We'd file an appeal within days, letting them know we won't go along with this, then file a motion to quash the CID by mid-January, and wait for the commissioner assigned to this area to rule—in this case, Commissioner Brill. With Brill's lack of business experience and her carefully developed perspective from the cushy insides of academia and government, we knew that after she rolled the issue over in her head for (maybe) two seconds, we would lose. I also realized that any attempt to attend my own hearing would go nowhere, but we wanted to document the request to prove a point. Likely they didn't want to be discomfited by having to look me in the eye. After all, they didn't seem especially keen on fair play or accountability.

After that first exercise in judicial futility, we would then appeal Commissioner Brill's totally predictable decision, moving the motion to quash to the entire five FTC commissioners and request a hearing. (All commissioners are appointed by the president, by the way. No more than a party majority of one, so with President Obama in the White House, we had three Democrats and two Republicans. I have become an expert.)

Fully anticipating we'd lose, the sham would be nearly over. After we get our rejection letter months later, then, depending on the outcome, we'd examine our options at that point in time.

"Look, folks, we all know what the outcome is going to be," I said. "Let's not kid ourselves. The road out of FTC hell is to get to the courts. They've never tried a data security case in court, so nobody has slapped these bullies down. These people have zero interest in logic, fairness, and due process. They keep repeating that mantra 'the FTC has broad powers assigned by Congress' like they're in a cult. If the law said jump off a bridge, they'd be putting clips on their noses and waving goodbye to mommy as they belly flopped into the Potomac."

Three seconds of silence.

"Can't I even get a laugh from you lawyers? This is billable time. Laugh."

"Okay, chuckle, chuckle," Claudia contributed.

"Thank you. Okay, anyway, so we're going to appeal right away. Phil can do that—right, Phil?"

"Oh yeah. I can knock that out in no time."

"Mike, we have a great associate, Julian Dayal, who can craft the Motion to Quash. Plus his time is less expensive than ours. He's a phenomenal writer. Let me put together a budget and he'll create something excellent. He's fantastic and aggressive."

"Okay, that sounds fine." I agreed to look at it after hearing the words "put together a budget." *Professional.*

I continued, "So we're on 'Operation Run the Clock.' I want to throw every trash can in front of them I can. Every objection, every request. Make them work for this. It's all drop shots, moon balls, and slow pace. Make them crazy and drive them where they won't want to go: anywhere that will hold them accountable. There's no 'there there,' as Claudia said to them months ago. This is an FTC temper tantrum, which means the agency won't back down. We need to navigate our way through this travesty and end up in the judicial system. We are heading to two courts: Federal and Public Opinion. That's the plan."

"Mike, your instincts have been right all along. We're here for you," Claudia said.

*What did she just say?*

"Thanks. Okay. I guess we'll hear from you about Julian, and Phil will be in touch with a copy of the appeal."

"Right, I'll copy you on this, but I have it handled," Phil said.

"All right. Talk to you in a week or so. Happy New Year!"

And we all hung up.

I called Phil right back.

"Okay, she said 'budget.'"

"I know. I want to keep an eye on this. We're under a time crunch so we're going to need help, which is fine, but I don't want another invoicing explosion like we had with Kelley Drye."

"Oh believe me, I don't either, but at least this firm is all about fighting back and there's no internal conflict around what we're doing. I'm so sick of lawyers who think I'm deluded because I want to defend myself against these purveyors of constitutional misinterpretation. They're rampant. I can't believe this cancer our country must suffer. I'd better shut up. Don't want to get up on my box again."

"Fine, fine, fine. Okay, I'm in the office today, so I'll get on this."

"Thanks. I'm going home now to let my family know I could handle the roads okay. Bye."

Well, this was not exactly the way I expected 2011 to end, but it was par for the course. Thankfully, we had a plan. The road was long, but at least the folks at the FTC knew I was gunning for them.

*"The executive branch has grown too strong, the judicial branch too arrogant and the legislative branch too stupid."*

—Lyn Nofziger

# CHAPTER 25
# More Than Mere Formalities

I heard a fool on television say, "Policy is the structure for dreams." Spoken like someone who needs a reality check and has never chased a dream or experienced the downside of bureaucracy. Most government agencies work out of the same playbook to some degree: The FTC's moves look like this:

Slow down the investigation with exquisite patience to mentally wear down the victim

Self-police so that accountability is rare

Utilize a huge battery of wholesale lawyers

Deny hearing attendance to defendants

Run the judicial clock with the administrative court

Reputation Assassination

Consent Decree press releases that are loaded with fine print

It was time to take control of the game. While Phil and Julian went to work, I did what they needed me to do; I left them alone. Phil filed the notice of appeal while Julian worked his wicked pen on the Motion to Quash. Phil had to reply to the Eleventh Circuit Court with our response to Tiversa's and Dartmouth's Motion to Dismiss. With all these plates spinning, there wasn't much for me to do until, low and behold, Kelley Drye sent a response to the stinging complaint I sent in December. Those big-firm souls couldn't contain themselves. They automatically fired up a mixture of righteous indignation combined with circle and confuse strategy.

## BYE BYE KELLEY DRYE:[1]

Dear Mr. Carpenter:

I am a member of Kelley Drye & Warren LLP ("Kelley Drye"), as well as Kelley Drye's Firm Counsel. Firm Chairman John Callagy has forwarded to me for response the letters to him from you and Michael Daugherty, dated December 8, 2011.

We take strong exception to your statements regarding the quality and zealousness of Kelley Drye's representation of LabMD, but do not believe it would be productive to address each and every one of your statements, given your obvious hostility, as reflected most clearly in the insulting and derogatory letter from Mr. Daugherty. However, we would like to address certain of your more extreme charges . . .

*(whining, bridge burning, flame throwing, puffery, rewriting history, memory loss, blah blah blah . . . and in conclusion)*

In short, Kelley Drye represented LabMD diligently, competently and zealously, and Kelley Drye's invoices were fair and reasonable. Nonetheless, we are willing to make some accommodation, in order permanently to conclude our relationship and settle any outstanding issues. Accordingly, for those reasons, we are willing to relieve LabMD of its obligation to pay the $24,108.40 in billed fees and expenses that our records show currently are outstanding. If you reject this offer, we reserve all of our rights, including, without limitation, the right to seek recovery of all outstanding billed fees and expenses, as well as all amounts incurred but not billed, plus interest, and all legal fees and other costs of collection (as set forth in our engagement letter with LabMD). Please confirm that you are agreeable to this compromise.

Very truly yours,
Steven P. Caley

I chuckle every time I read this. If Dana Rosenfeld had anything to do with writing this letter, then she has a bright future in litigation even though she insists she doesn't litigate, as she evidently will argue anything. I didn't have time to further ponder Kelley Drye as I was preoccupied with more pressing matters, but this sure was fun.

## Who Runs the Show at the FTC?

The FTC had five commissioners. With a Democratic President, there currently were two Republicans and three Democrats. My focus was on the Chairman Jon Leibowitz, who I would assume set the tone of the organization, and Julie Brill, who, I discovered, was the Commissioner over my "non-public investigation." These were the two that were behind this "as forgiveness later" fiasco and I was not heartened by what I discovered about either one of them.

*Jon Leibowitz:* Sworn in as a commissioner of the FTC on September 3, 2004, and designated chairman on March 2, 2009, by President Barack Obama, Mr. Leibowitz has a long history of being addicted to the Kool-Aid-induced delusion that government solves all problems. He thinks government is the good guy and he's not afraid to overreach. If anyone needs checks and balances, it's Mr. Leibowitz. While he just resigned his post effective February 15, 2013, he set the tone that resulted in the data security witch hunt that scarred LabMD. His culture of "enforcement without standards" permeated the FTC. This guy wanted to save the world and little things like standards, facts, and details were not going to get in his way.

This commissioner's background has a history of snuggling up with bureaucracy. During the Clinton Administration, he worked in various positions in the Senate, capping his time there with left-wing ideologues Paul Simon and Herb Kohl. Then Mr. Leibowitz sought refuge as VP for Congressional Affairs for the Motion Picture Association of America. He had left the DC nest for the Hollywood Elite faster than you could say "George Bush is President." No surprise there—birds of a feather flocking together and all. However, Mr. Leibowitz bounced back across the Potomac when he was sworn in as an FTC commissioner. (President Bush had to appoint a Democrat.) Leibowitz was pent-up with anticipation and ripe to save the world—all on the taxpayers' dime but far removed from their view.

Patiently waiting to finally fly through the sky, Clark Kent—er, I mean, Mr. Leibowitz—finally earned his tights and cape when President Obama appointed him FTC chairman. This set the stage for the Big L to save the world from all those nasty businesspeople raping and pillaging the country since 1776.

He never understood that slicing open the body to snoop around might kill the patient. Enjoying the fine art of instilling fear, Mr. Leibowitz is a living example of exactly why the Founding Fathers placed checks and balances on power.

Lesson learned: Be very afraid of ambitious government lawyers hungry to make their mark on Washington like a dog is eager to make his mark on a hydrant. They are so lost in their own theater they don't know they are acting.

*Julie Brill:* Happy was my day when Julie Brill was not selected to fill Leibowitz's shoes. Replacing one lifelong institutionalized lawyer with precious little time outside of government with an even greater zealot does not a solution make. After all, those without experience in certain areas, like children, may suffer from magical thinking.

Ms. Brill has accrued more than 20 years as a state antitrust and consumer protection regulator, most of which was spent in the economically powerful and racially diverse state of Vermont. Except for two years as an associate lawyer in New York, she's gone from cradle to school to government. No private business experience. No technology training. No other industry work. This woman has never left the mother ship, so how can she know what goes on beyond her still-attached umbilical cord?

In interviews with Ms. Brill, her descriptions of herself and the FTC are telling. Her favorite words appear to be *regulator, regulator, regulator, regulator, enforcer, enforcer, enforcer, enforcer* . . . and then, after coming up for air, *state regulator, no-nonsense,* and my personal favorite, *"small but mighty."* I keep digging for such linguistic nuggets as *fair, objective, due process,* and (revealing my naive optimism) *constitutional.*

Like all government lawyers, she can sling outlandish comments around with a believable voice, solid eye contact, and steely cool smile. In one published interview, she called the FTC a *transparent agency.* (I checked and it was not stand-up comedy night.)

How can an investigative enforcement agency bursting at the seams with salaried government lawyers be transparent? Investigators need to be fair and honest, not transparent. Yet Ms. Brill wouldn't even allow me to *attend my own hearings* regarding LabMD's Motion to Quash. (Bullies can't look their victims in the eye.) Is it too time consuming to allow the accused to have a voice? Too inconvenient? Too messy?

Headstrong and unwilling to read a tea leaf, Ms. Brill believes what she says. Case in point: When presented with the question about pay-for-delay pharmaceutical settlements in which the FTC has met with a number of setbacks in both courts and Congress, she remained unfazed. "I believe that some pay-for-delay deals result in a large amount of consumer harm, and we should not let the setbacks . . . deter us from continuing *to do the right thing.* . . ." (emphasis mine)

Excuse me? Evidently, Julie Brill thinks she has been anointed "Commissioner of Doing the Right Thing." Her self-righteous justification for squandering taxpayer dollars and inflicting harm on the economy comes as no surprise. It's time for this regulator to reread her employee handbook, immediately followed by the Constitution. Nowhere does it say "stretch the laws until pushed back by Congress or the courts."

Ms. Brill thinks her narrow career focus gives her the right to manage and communicate with the wide variety of industries in which she has no experience. Her speech to the NYU School of Law in September, 2011,[2] tells the true tale:

> We focused on a local issue: big errors by big companies that impacted people in small towns across Vermont. . . . I now work to develop the law that frames the world in which you will start your legal career—as you will someday end up working on the law that frames the world of future students. Find your own small world in which to practice law, where—if you look hard enough—you will discover issues that have great significance for us all. And in those small worlds, find some heroes, just as I found Bill Sorrell, Roy Cooper, and Louis Brandeis. You will all have the foundation to do what you set out to do—not just because you will have

a law school diploma—but because you will have studied at this unique place, where commitment to public service is at the core of this institution. Some of you will go in and out of public service, or find ways to serve the public while at the same time pursuing other career paths. The important thing is that you give back in some way, and make a difference on a small scale or a large scale. If precedence serves as any indicator, many of you will dedicate your entire careers to answering Brandeis's call to become a 'people's lawyer.'

Buried deep beneath her seductive public service propaganda are these scary comments: "I now work to develop the law" . . . "people's lawyer" . . . "Public service is at the core of this institution." . . . Where are you, Julie Brill, China? Do you have any comments at all about *private industry* being able to serve the public in any way, shape, or form? Or do you have that classic adolescent attitude that all companies are evil until proven good? I think I know which way your bias blows.

Her sinister and calculating long term goal is to use FTC settlements to create common law. She should not be allowed to build a library of consent decrees that she can use to try to twist the law the way she sees fit. Brill wants to use her pulpit to create these common laws and then jam them down our throats because she thinks she's doing the right thing. Too high and mighty to go through due process, she exploits her power. Why deal with the annoying and time consuming three branches of government when a steam roller is so handy?

Rather than convincing Congress to pass laws, Ms. Brill would rather rule the world to fit her warped perspective by developing common law via a string of consent decrees that hide behind the skirts of administrative judges. This is fine in her mind because she knows she is right. Dangerous.

Lesson learned: Zealots come in all shapes and sizes. Frozen smiles, narrow career paths, and regulatory pep rallies are all bad signs. I now see their pattern of behavior.

- Broad, long, and unclear request letters
- Tactics of circling and confusing
- False show of concern

- Threats of impending litigation
- Monotone voice like an old, lifeless professor
- Lingering stony silence and intentionally selected words
- Attempts to trip us up with questions aimed to box us in
- Slow response times meant to unnerve us so we'd pay the ransom
- Show of consent decrees to see what others before us have succumbed to

## VS. Tiversa and Dartmouth

The Tiversa and Dartmouth's motions, our next deadlines, were filed on January 13th, 2012. Our main points: This injustice occurred in Georgia and the invaders came in and downloaded the file, opening up a port on our workstation. (Our complete response, noted later in this chapter, rested on arguments from this affidavit written by our technology consultant, Scott Moulton.)

### AFFIDAVIT OF SCOTT A. MOULTON[3]

. . . I have reviewed the Complaint and supporting exhibits filed in the above-referenced action. After reviewing Exhibit B to the Complaint, I learned that Defendants Tiversa and M. Eric Johnson, with Defendant Dartmouth's knowledge and consent, searched peer-to-peer ("P2P") networks and randomly gathered a sample of shared files related to health care and health care institutions. Defendant Tiversa's servers and software allowed Defendant Dartmouth and Defendant Johnson to sample for files in the four most popular P2P networks (each of which supports the most popular clients) including Gnutella, Aries and e-donkey . . .

. . . When a user makes a search request on the P2P Gnutella network, the search goes through an Ultra-peer and checks the listings on the computers connected to the Gnutella network. When a file is found that the user wants to download and a request for the file is made, the file comes directly from the Internet Protocol ("IP") address of the computer where the file is physically located because Ultra-peers only have the file listing and not the actual file . . .

. . . When a user seeks to download a file from the P2P Gnutella network, the P2P Gnutella network software program opens a Transmission

Control Protocol / Internet Protocol ("TCP/IP") port at the site where the file is located . . .

. . . TCP/IP is a way of connecting to a host computer. In order to connect to a host computer, the computer seeking access to the host computer sends a command to the host computer to open a port at the host site and to transfer data from the host site. Opening a TCP/IP port to connect to a host computer at another location is the same as physically being at the host site to take action on the file. When Defendants Tiversa, Mr. Johnson, and Dartmouth College searched for the May 13 File, they opened a physical TCP/IP connection on LabMD's computer, located in the State of Georgia.

The point we would drive home to the court was this: Government can't hire private enterprise to go snooping through computer files under the smoke-and-mirror defense that the files were "out there anyway" and in the "public domain." The FTC, Tiversa, Dartmouth, and Johnson all hope the judge gets confused and won't see the man behind the curtain. This isn't complicated. It's simple. They knowingly searched for and downloaded private health information. Then they read it. Then they kept it. Then they posted it in the Dartmouth study. Then *Wired Magazine*.

LabMD's response to Tiversa, which can be read in its entirety in the endnotes,[4] is summarized in this Introduction:

### LABMD'S RESPONSE TO DEFENDANT TIVERSA'S MOTION TO DISMISS

Defendant's request to dismiss Plaintiff's complaint trivializes the gravity of the situation by comparing the intentional downloading of highly sensitive, private medical information containing medical conditions of LabMD's patients to the simple downloading of music or client lists of a company. Defendant does not dispute that: (1) it intentionally searched computer networks fishing for sensitive computer files containing highly confidential personally identifiable health information ("PHI") and personally identifiable information ("PII"); (2) it downloaded computer files it knew contained PHI and PII; and (3) with knowledge that the downloaded files likely contained PHI and PII, it opened and viewed certain computer files. Instead, Defendant argues it is not subject to the jurisdiction of this Honorable Court and the downloading of the 1,718 File was "authorized." Such arguments are specious at best.

Our response[5] to Dartmouth and Johnson made the following additional points:

### LABMD'S RESPONSE TO DEFENDANT TRUSTEES OF DARTMOUTH COLLEGE AND M. ERIC JOHNSON'S MOTION TO DISMISS

While Defendants intend to reduce the personal jurisdiction question to a question of where Defendants' computers were physically located, such argument grossly misstates the nature of P2P technology. Additionally, Defendants, acting in conspiracy with Defendant Tiversa, had minimum contacts with Georgia. These elements are certainly enough to subject Defendants to this forum.

Defendants' argument regarding authorization is also without merit. Defendants do not dispute that LabMD, Inc., did not authorize the file to be shared. Additionally, and more importantly, Defendants were keenly aware that downloading and, more importantly, viewing of any computer files possibility containing PHI or PII could never be authorized. Indeed, the entire basis of Defendants' testimony before the United States Congress and Defendants' publications was that the types of files it was finding on P2P networks were not intended to be shared.

As if it's okay to go searching for medical files and read them. This is another example of the US government's sense of entitlement over all things belonging to its citizens. Didn't members of Congress "get" what Tiversa and Dartmouth were doing? I don't know what Kool-Aid they were drinking, but an introduction by the former four-star general Wesley Clark probably had an effect. *Having power without knowledge is scary. It also seems to be pandemic in Washington.*

We sent our responses and went back to our usual business—waiting. Before long, we heard that our case drew a senior status judge.

"Senior status" refers to a form of semi-retirement for United States federal judges. After these judges reach a certain combination of age (65) and years of service (15) on the federal courts, they're allowed to assume senior status. One fewer year of service is required for each additional year of age. A senior status judge receives the full salary of a judge but works part-time. This means defendants might as well sit down with a pot of coffee and a good book because their wait for a ruling from the court just got longer. Being a senior judge is considered a "good gig." When a very prominent attorney in Atlanta learned who our judge was, he wasn't happy. "That guy is going to look for any way to punt this case. He thinks he knows everything about technology because he was the first to sport a calculator. He doesn't like to work. This is not good news."

With our response checked off the list, we had one more to dragon to slay early in January—reviewing the Motion to Quash, crafted by Julian under the watchful eyes of Claudia and Christina. Julian did a fantastic job. After spending so much time with DC lawyers who tiptoed through the tulips dealing with the Feds, Julian went right for their throats.

What follows is a summary of the Motion to Quash.[6]

In April 2009, Dartmouth College published a paper entitled 'Data Hemorrhage in the Health-Care Sector.' The paper was based upon activities "conducted in collaboration with Tiversa" using Tiversa's proprietary technology and was financially supported by a US Department of Homeland Security Grant Award issued under the auspices of the Institute for Information Infrastructure Protection. According to the paper, Tiversa and Dartmouth began their project by "looking for files from top ten publicly traded health-care firms" that were available on P2P networks.

As part of the initial search, Tiversa and Dartmouth manually reviewed 3,328 computer files downloaded from P2P networks, many of which contained PII and PHI.[7] Following their initial search, Tiversa and Dartmouth undertook a Second Search ("Second Search") lasting approximately six months. During the Second Search, Tiversa and Dartmouth downloaded close to four million documents, including over 20,000 medical patient records. Tiversa described the evolving technology it used for the second search in a 2009 hearing before the United States House of Representatives Subcommittee on Commerce, Trade and Consumer Protection ("2009 CTC hearing"). Tiversa testified that, through the use of its proprietary software, it "can see and detect all previously undetected activity" and "where an individual user can only see a very small portion of a P2P file sharing network, [it] can see the P2P network in its entirety in real time." Further, Tiversa "processed as many as 1.6 billion P2P searches per day, approximately 8 times that of web searches entered into Google per day."

To showcase its technology during the hearing, Tiversa performed a "live demonstration" whereby it intentionally searched for and downloaded over 275,000 tax returns. On July 29, 2009, Tiversa appeared before the United States House of Representatives Committee on Oversight and Government Reform and testified further about the technology it used to perform the Second Search. According to its testimony, Tiversa deployed newly developed P2P search technology allowing it to penetrate even "the most technologically advanced" computer security, despite the presence of "firewalls and encryption." It was with this technology, and during the Second Search, that Tiversa and Dartmouth downloaded the 1,718 File, a copy of which Tiversa produced at the 2009 CTC hearing.

The FTC's timing here proved to be troubling. The 2008 download of the 1,718 File was explicitly reviewed by at least two congressional committees (none of which recommended taking any course of action against LabMD). And yet, in the three years since the download of the 1,718 File was publicized to Congress and elsewhere, the FTC has taken no action. It wasn't until LabMD declined to engage Tiversa's "security services" for the sixth time and then sued Tiversa for computer fraud, computer crimes, conversion, and trespassing that the FTC was compelled to issue the present CID. This unusual timing only serves to incentivize organizations to pay off Tiversa (as non-payment appears to coincide with the opening of an FTC investigation).

This Motion of Quash was a ray of light breaking through the clouds. For a while, I allowed myself the luxury of hope—that is, hope that truth would win out. But after years of holding my breath, believing I was the only one swimming against the tide while getting "advice" from so many "big time" lawyers, how could I live in delusional naiveté believing the FTC would take this seriously? Reminding myself of the plan we'd formed the day after Christmas, I knew this Motion to Quash was more a message of defiance to the FTC than any belief that we would actually stop its game. LabMD was perceived as a cog in the FTC's wheel. But in the early stages of my plan, we aimed to get out of this FTC kangaroo court.

Internal administrative motions are required before any outside courts can rule. Commissioner Julie Brill (the commissioner overseeing this process) wasn't going to do anything but deny our Motion to Quash. How can it be deemed objective when the appeal goes to the same commissioner who runs the investigation? *Asking Julie Brill to quash a CID was like asking a parent to testify against their child. How can a lack of fundamental objectivity and fairness actually go on in the United States of America? LAZY LAZY LAZY.*

Again, we waited. January came and went. No time for LabMD's annual planning meeting. No extra funds to launch new projects. Then the invoice came for the Motion to Quash and exceeded $15,000. When we received it, we realized we'd never seen a budget. But because Julian did such a valuable job, I just let it slide. The Kattan team of Claudia, Christina, and Julian had earned their fee.

February and March were "normal" at LabMD. (Thankfully, Bill could manage operations on his own.) We welcomed the addition of Mark Seknicka as our new IT manager after Tom's retirement. Mark, a primary player in the 2011 update of our network, slipped in without effort. The consummate professional with an unbelievably strong background, he was a joy to have on the team.

Riding the federal merry-go-round, we knew this stage of the game required filing motions back and forth to each other—a form of boring, slow government tennis. The "broad powers awarded to the FTC by Congress" (they tell you that ad nauseam) have allowed the agency opportunities to be petty and disrespectful. One annoying power play is not being required to let the investigated party know if and when the investigation is over. Once they have darkened your doorstep, they can make you wonder for years what, if anything, is going on. It's unbelievable what past and current Presidents and Congress have allowed the FTC to do. (Push back on this and they act like you want the government to retire the military). To work there you must suffer some form of emotional death so these tactics roll off your back. This form of "under the radar" harassment is one of the FTC's specialties. It is what the government agency tactics have become in this country. No class, no boundaries, no dignity, no respect.

Not that I was expecting a frequent status report about what was going on. However, I knew once we finished with the kangaroo court portion of our battle, I'd be wondering about the next move as I recalled Dana Rosenfeld's bone-chilling comment, "The FTC can reopen their investigation at any time."

I felt compelled to increase the numbers on my side. After four years of the same mantra ringing in my head—"this can't be real" and "people won't believe this"—I changed my tune and asked, "What's the most effective way to bring more foot soldiers onto my side of this battlefield?" At this point, I only had faith in the court of public opinion; all other courts were a seat at a blackjack table.

## The Power of the Pen

The next morning, I got in early and met Phil in Bill's office. When he walked in, I announced to both of them I was going to write a book.

"I have to take some sort of action to try to get the Feds to leave us alone. I trust the court of public opinion more than I trust government agencies. I firmly believe we need more accountability" People need to know. A story like this may sound like a television drama, but what's so unusual about this case is all the congressional testimony and documentation. This is a terrible reflection of the overreach of the US government and an example of how power corrupts. This needs to stop, LabMD needs to get our money back, and the President and members of Congress need to put a saddle on those wild horses at the FTC, if not *all* government agency behavior. And I need to keep my sanity. Maybe this will help."

Both of them stared back blankly, paused, and then said, "Okay," very slowly.

Evidently, they didn't know what to make of my announcement. After a good 15 seconds of a pregnant pause, Phil said, "Nothing can go out without a solid legal review!" *I knew this was good advice, but I just wanted to do something without lawyers involved. Oh well.*

I looked at Bill with my eyes, imploring, "I need your support again. I can't do it without you." Then I said, "I'm going to take Monday, Friday, and Saturday off most weeks and write when I'm out of the office."

"We can work with that," Bill responded professionally and dutifully.

I cracked up. "I'm sure I'll be missed." *He's probably thrilled I won't be diverting his attention for three days every week. And this new challenge will certainly take silent, granular concentration to get it done right.*

As I started my adventure as an author, I thought of it as a necessary CEO move to defend my company. A macroeconomic defense, moving away and above, attacking the beasts from the opposite side where they'd least expect it, so huge was their arrogance and lack of accountability. We were anchored to the Feds and they wouldn't let go, plus the internal system was stacked against us. This story would be compelling to anyone who cared about how our government behaves and the topic was timely. And if nothing else, writing a book would allow me to channel my energy while battling this "cancer" and turn it into something positive. *This book talks about what government agents do when they think nobody is looking. Let's make them accountable. It's worth a shot.*

With that, I started to study book writing and publishing. I flew to California and took a course on self-publishing from guru Carla King at the San Francisco Writer's Conference. I met authors, agents, publishers, and editors. I started to network with my newly discovered world of thinkers and creative souls. This was a joy. I felt free, empowered, and exhilarated. *The book had to be good. Failure was not an option.* I was all ears.

This was also the first time I'd taken the step of letting anyone in the world know what had been going on with LabMD since 2008. While cautious and wary in my explanations, I found most people who heard them weren't appalled at what our government was capable of. It seems as though most people think our government is corrupt. Liberals choose to see corrupt wars and social policies; conservatives choose to see corrupt government size and spending habits. The common comment was "corrupt."

Through these new San Francisco connections, I was introduced to Stephanie Chandler. Stephanie was CEO of Authority Publishing, a company she started in 2007. Stephanie was a businessperson who entered into publishing after a successful career in corporate technology sales. I thought she would "get it" about the technology and corporate worlds colliding with government and "get it" she did.

"I think this story could be huge," she told me.

I never allowed myself to believe it would be easy, so that was nice to hear, but rolled off my back.

"I need your help and guidance. I need a developmental editor. I don't have time for mistakes," I told Stephanie.

I hired Stephanie's company for developmental editing and coaching. My new adventure with destination unknown had begun.

In the meantime, outside of the hours spent writing, thinking, organizing, and planning, the days and weeks were passing. In early

April, I said to Phil, "Hey, it has been three months since we filed that objection to Julie Brill."

"Don't jinx it!" Phil laughed.

*Me and my big mouth!*

On April 19th, this notification arrived from Julie Brill.[8]

RE: LabMD, Inc.'s Petition to Limit or Quash the Civil Investigative Demand; and Michael J. Daugherty's Petition to Limit or Quash the Civil Investigative Demand

Dear Ms. Callaway, Ms. Grigorian, and Mr. Dayal:

On January 10, 2012, the Federal Trade Commission ("FTC" or "Commission") received the above Petitions filed by LabMD, Inc. ("LabMD") and its President, Michael J. Daugherty (collectively, "Petitioners"). This letter advises you of the Commission's disposition of the Petitions, effected through this ruling by Commissioner Julie Brill, acting as the Commission's delegate. For the reasons explained below, the Petitions are denied.

We were under no illusions, regarding this round as merely a formality. We had our response at the ready. Next, we'd move for a full FTC commissioner review. Let the entire world see the FTC argue how they think they can investigate whatever they want out of curiosity; that I can't attend my own hearings; that they can enforce rules they make up on their own. The FTC is a totalitarian animal shielded by the broken branches of our government tree. Our government, formed with the intent to deter government tyranny, has found a crack in the wall that our founding fathers built.

First, we wanted to point out the FTC's inability to police itself, as they can't help themselves from overreach. Second, we knew this group wouldn't allow me to be present at my own hearing, so numb was it to fair play. And when it came to denying my presence, they made our prediction reality. Third, we were slowing down the clock, throwing every trash can in their way and intentionally checking off every necessary legal step so we could get out of their grasp and bolt to the judicial system.

Given that, we immediately fired back a request for a full hearing by all five FTC commissioners. With it (still intact) was my original request to be present at the hearing.[9]

Dear Mr. Clark:

I am writing to you as counsel to LabMD, Inc. and Michael J. Daugherty. Please be advised that we are requesting a review of the LabMD, Inc.'s Petition to Limit or Quash the Civil Investigative Demand and Michael J. Daugherty's Petition to Limit or Quash the Civil Investigative Demand by the full Commission pursuant to 16 CFR 2.7.

Philip Carpenter, Esq.

Once this hit the mail, I went back to what had become second nature—waiting—and went back to my quiet new lifestyle of book writing. By midsummer, enough time had passed that friends and family had noticed my absence. "Where have you been?" and "Is everything okay?" became common questions.

"Oh, I've been slammed with work. It's just crazy over there. And then the travel," I'd reply. I didn't want to drain the writing process, so I kept everything inside, only sharing it with my laptop. This resolve lasted quite a while.

It became clear I needed more days away from the office, and then time to calm down and close out the world like a leaf coming to rest on the ground. The slightest breeze would disturb me until I got settled in. Instead of the three days at work, four days writing, I soon turned to week-long stretches in cities outside Atlanta.

## Freedom of Information Act or FOIA

Whenever there was a lull in the action I would have time to reflect. I can't explain why it took so long, maybe there was too much going on distracting me, but I finally insisted that we file a Freedom of Information Act with the Feds to find out the specific circumstances surrounding the funds given to Dartmouth and Tiversa by government agencies. I knew it would take forever, regardless of how long the Feds said it would take, but we needed to get the ball rolling.

On May 15, 2012, Phil honed in on the Department of Homeland Security and filed our request. We asked for anything and everything that had to do with Dartmouth getting money to execute their study. Not trusting the integrity of the agency players, I thought we were throwing a message in a bottle into the ocean. One day it may come back and surprise us.

Just as I was getting settled into my writing process, the FTC responded to our request for full commission review in the lightning-quick time of eight weeks.

In the response we received June 21st, the Democrats on the Commission, Leibowitz, Brill, and Ramirez, voted to move ahead, the Obama-appointed Republican (Ohlhausen) abstained, and the last man standing, the only one not beholden to the current Administration (Republican J. Thomas Rosch) dissented. For the life of me, to this day I don't know why Ohlhausen would abstain. Politics? I had no clue.

Playing right into our spotlight, they held the hearing without notifying us. Classic. In fine form letter fashion, they then let us know our request was denied. It read:

It is ordered that the April 20, 2012 letter ruling is affirmed;

It is further ordered that LabMD's and Mr. Daugherty's request for a hearing is DENIED;

Nice that Congress allows them to not let you attend your own hearing. Another slice from their "death by a thousand cuts" strategy, the FTC was behaving according to plan and beautifully displaying its arrogance. However, we didn't expect the dissent from

Commissioner Rosch. That was a bonus! It shed light on the fact that when we get to court, we'll have a good argument, especially as the FTC seem to be squabbling a bit. Commissioner Rosch summed it up well:[10]

> I do not agree that staff should further inquire—either by document request, interrogatory, or investigational hearing—about the 1,718 File. Specifically, I am concerned that Tiversa is more than an ordinary witness, informant, or "whistle-blower." It is a commercial entity that has a financial interest in intentionally exposing and capturing sensitive files on computer networks, and a business model of offering its services to help organizations protect against similar infiltrations. Indeed, in the instant matter, an argument has been raised that Tiversa used its robust, patented peer-to-peer monitoring technology to retrieve the 1,718 File, and then repeatedly solicited LabMD, offering investigative and remediation services regarding the breach, long before Commission staff contacted LabMD. In my view, while there appears to be nothing per se unlawful about this evidence, the Commission should avoid even the appearance of bias or impropriety by not relying on such evidence or information in this investigation.

Please allow me to translate this lawyered-up government agency jargon. What I thought Commissioner Rosch was telling his fellow commissioners is: "This stinks big time. If you aren't careful, the FTC will look biased and corrupt by conspiring with other government agencies, Tiversa and Dartmouth, in this appalling display of constitutional indifference."

Yet if it weren't for Tiversa and Dartmouth, LabMD wouldn't be in this boat. However, keeping in line with the arrogance displayed, I knew the FTC would keep on trucking. No way would Julie Brill, an institutionalized lawyer who needed an oxygen tank to leave the professional bubble she's always lived in, admit she didn't have reason to snoop around. Way too smug for that. Anyone who runs roughshod over protocol while operating a totalitarian regime like the FTC would be the last person interested in enforcing the checks and balances of the US Constitution. I knew exactly who I was dealing with.

To continue my plan, we'd have to get to court. I imagined the FTC commissioners grabbing my ankles, trying to drag me down as I got closer to the judiciary.

On Friday morning, June 22nd, I was in the conference room when Phil walked in and said, "The FTC called. It's Alain Sheer. Let's go call him back."

"Well, that didn't take long!" I chortled.

I sat across from Phil's desk as he dialed the phone.

"Alain Sheer."

"Hello Alain, this is Phil Carpenter at LabMD, how are you?"

I always bristle when lawyers are friendly with each other.

"Fine. Let me get Ruth. Hold on. Well, she may miss the beginning here. I'll start. I assume you have the commission's decision?"

"Yes, we do."

"Well, do you intend on complying?"

Phil responded, "If you mean are we going to sit for the CID now, I don't ... "

I started flailing my arms in the air and mouthing, "No, no, no!"

"Oh, here's Ruth," Alain chimed in.

Then I was mouthing, "Mute the phone."

"Alain, hold on a second."

"What?" Phil asked me.

"Don't fall for that entrapment crap from him. We have this guy's number. Don't even go near answering his question of whether we're going to comply or not. We *are* going to court. He wants to trip us up on some other charge now, like not cooperating. Don't take the bait!"

"I got it. Don't worry."

"Alain. Hello there, Ruth."

"Hello," Ruth said, more matter-of-fact-like than I'd heard her before.

The game playing quickly began.

"So, as I was saying, are you telling us you're refusing to cooperate with the FTC's CID now that the full commission has made its decision?"

"Alain, you and I are both lawyers and I think you know our position very well. We have certainly been cooperative with the FTC and don't want any characterizations alleged of LabMD not being cooperative. At the same time, you understand our position hasn't changed on the jurisdiction matter."

Ruth chimed in, taking control and seemingly agitated, "Well, either you're going to comply or you aren't. The commission has affirmed the CID."

"LabMD's position is as it has always been. We still maintain this is a jurisdictional issue and the FTC doesn't have the authority to request, or enforce, a CID. We very much are waiting for the courts to make that decision, not the commission itself."

"Well, I suppose that means you aren't going to sit for the CID."

"It means exactly what I said—that we want the judicial process to continue and are eager for the courts to make that decision on LabMD's position."

"I suppose there's nothing else to discuss then," Alain said with a bit of a bite. Ruth mumbled something in the background.

"Alain, that is our position," Phil said, trying to keep a friendly tone.

"Okay, we'll be in touch." He hung up.

"Ah, poor folks. Isn't it a tough day for the FTC when the victim fights having his head put on the block? I'm such a pain," I growled. "I didn't want us to take the trap, Phil. Alain was trying to trick you into saying you refused to be cooperative. They want to create different charges now. We have to walk carefully here. They're ticked off about not getting their way. They have no boundaries. I just had to say these things for my own sake."

"That's fine. I got it. We didn't get trapped. The next step will be interesting."

"Do you think they'll drop it?"

"Not a chance in hell. These guys lose all perspective and go crazy. They last thing they're going to do is drop it. They don't like to have their supremacy questioned in the least."

"Oh well, okay . . . back to the conference room. Thanks."

*This is pretty cool. We know exactly who they are. We are totally onto their game, and they couldn't entrap us. Not only that, but it only took all of five minutes, and I'm not rattled. Back to work. A guy could get used to this.*

The next day came another attempt to ensnare us,[11] this time in written form via FedEx, of course. After reading it, I said to Carpenter, "Phil, you tell that SOB to never communicate with us other than in writing ever again. We aren't going to let them play any more verbal entrapment games. I do this all the time with unethical communicators. It goes like this, 'in the interest of avoiding any misunderstandings by either party, we think it best that all future communications be strictly in writing.' We are fully entrenched in enemy mode now. There is no further need to pretend we are not at war. Shut them down."

With that, Phil fired off this missive:[12]

June 29, 2012

Mr. Alain Sheer
Senior Attorney, Division of Privacy and Identity Protection
Bureau of Consumer Protection
United States Federal Trade Commission
Washington, D.C. 20580

Dear Alain:

I am writing in response to your June 27, 2012 correspondence following your impromptu call. As the call was rather last minute, I did not take a verbatim transcription of our conversation and cannot attest to your characterization of the conversation on the phone. In order to avoid this issue in the future, as it appears that the FTC is concerned with certain representations made by LabMD, Inc. and Mr. Michael J. Daugherty (the "Parties"), I respectfully request that all future communications be in written form.

With respect to the Civil Investigative Demands ("CID") issued to the Parties on December 21, 2011, I refer you to their respective Motions to Quash which outline, in great detail, the factual and legal basis upon which the Parties believe the CIDs are invalid and illegal. For purposes of this letter, the Parties renew and incorporate their arguments regarding the invalidity of the CIDs herein as though stated in their entirety. As such, it is not possible to make any representations about the CIDs or compliance with the same since they are a nullity by law. I trust this letter addresses all of your questions.

Philip Carpenter, Esq.

Playing nicey nicey with the FTC was over. These people never "play nice;" they just smile while loading their guns.

"It used to be, everyone was entitled to their own opinion, but not their own facts.
But that's not the case anymore. Facts matter not at all.
Perception is everything."

—STEPHEN COLBERT

# CHAPTER 26
# The Endless Climb Up Judicial Mountain

Waiting. On the one hand, the FTC agents think this entire issue is a big deal. On the other hand, it would never occur to them to actually get something done that didn't require an annual calendar. Those of us in private enterprise view their glacial pace with bemusement and frustration. These people scream fire and then saunter their way to the extinguisher. But when one head of the beast went to sleep, the other woke up. Finally, after almost a year, we received a response from Judge Forrester from the United States District Court, Northern District, Atlanta Division. After over four years of this ordeal, I was about to learn there were more shocking lessons regarding our judicial system.

## Can't See the Forrester for the Trees

On August 15, 2012, Judge Forrester, after a ten month wait, finally ruled there was no jurisdiction in Georgia. This meant we had a year to refile the case in Pennsylvania. He stated Tiversa did not solicit business regularly in Georgia and the event did not occur in Georgia even though he accepted LabMD's assertion that Tiversa opened a port and entered LabMD's workstation. After becoming an expert in this over the past few years, I could not believe my eyes. It took me hours to review the ruling.[1]

Here are key quotes from Judge Forrester's ruling with my reply to follow:

- According to the Johnson Paper, Johnson and Tiversa initially searched peer-to-peer networks looking for files from the top ten publicly traded health-care firms and randomly gathered a sample of shared files related to health care.

*Evidently the court is not the least bit concerned with Tiversa and Dartmouth's unauthorized taking possession of medical files. A private company funded by the Feds goes opening ports to take medical files . . . is anyone home? This is not okay. The court skipped right over the issue of whether this was a theft case. This is not a sexy technology case.*

*Did the court understand that we're not playing finders keepers here? Just because you take someone's property does not mean you get to control its distribution. The court evidently thought, "Oh well." What is it about saying the word computer that made the court's head go spinning? By jumping over the elephant in the room, the court set a dangerous precedent.*

- Defendants accessed LabMD's computers and networks, which must have been connected to the peer-to-peer network, and downloaded file.

*Once again, I think it is time for a judicial class in computer technology. LabMD's computers and network was NOT connected to a P2P network. A P2P network is NOT a singularly enclosed system of computers run by one organization. Only one LabMD folder on one workstation was accessible by Tiversa. A peer to peer network is a descriptive term.*

*The judicial skimming over what is really going on here is disturbing. The court blew a golden opportunity to assist victims because the court took everything at face value rather than breaking a sweat and cracking a book. Even government funding does not justify taking property you know not to be yours. The entire world knows you are not allowed to be digging around for other's medical files and so should the court. Nap time is over. Now Forrester runs back to bed by wordsmithing traditional jurisdictional analysis so he can boot the case out of his courtroom with creative interpretation of the word "regular".*

- These limited contacts between Tiversa and LabMD—one telephone call and eight e-mails—are insufficient to establish that Tiversa *regularly* solicits business in Georgia. The word "regular" is defined as

"recurring, attending, or functioning at fixed or uniform intervals."
WEBSTER'S NEW COLLEGIATE DICTIONARY 992 (9th ed.
1990).

*First of all, is Forrester really citing Webster's dictionary in a legal ruling? Seriously? Okay, the word "regular" can also mean "periodical." According to my contacts at Bloomberg, Tiversa regularly contacted companies whose file they had taken in order to solicit business. What would the court prefer, a pattern of every Monday at 8 a.m.? Would that suffice? Is regular all about a schedule? I guess this means you can call every now and then and try to solicit business. Of course, the next judge could see it differently as the roulette wheel readies itself for another spin.*

- Georgia courts have not specifically dealt with personal jurisdiction in the context of peer-to-peer file sharing, but have established precedent in similar contexts . . . the Georgia Court of Appeals addressed whether personal jurisdiction existed over a South Carolina resident who had stalked a Georgia resident by sending harassing e-mails to her, her friends, and her colleagues . . . the court found the *conduct* giving rise to the offense occurred at the physical place where the defendant typed in and sent his e-mails. The court held that the defendant did not engage in any conduct in Georgia when he sent e-mails from out of state . . . The court similarly found personal jurisdiction lacking under subsection (2) of the long-arm statute where a defendant stalked a Georgia woman by calling her from his out-of-state home. "Although the injurious consequences would have been felt in Georgia, it is undisputed that [the defendant] never came to Georgia so as to commit an act here. Therefore, applying the Long Arm Statute as interpreted . . . , we agree with the trial court that [plaintiff] has alleged no acts by [the defendant] giving the Georgia courts personal jurisdiction over him . . ." Id. At 772.

*When I read this I was fit to be tied. This is the type of judicial fairy tale writing that makes me avoid the courts with as much vigor as I do a Las Vegas casino when I'm on a tight budget. Since the courts haven't dealt with this specifically and evidently wasn't in the mood to break a sweat, presto chango, downloading medical files is now the same as harassment. Yeah, like beating you in the face is the same as calling you names.*

*Tiversa opened a port and entered our workstation, the court accepted that and Tiversa did not dispute, and Forrester still considered this similar to a stalking case. I guess this means that if you plant a bomb in Georgia, drive over to South Carolina, send a signal from Greenville to detonate, Georgia will be just fine with that. Does that mean if Tiversa was in Tehran this would be occurring outside the United States? The soul of the law needs logic and reason, not someone to punt the ball because they don't want to be in the game.*

*This is NOT a stalking or harassment case. Hello. Property. Physical. Possession. Distribution. This is not a case about hurting our feelings.*

I called Phil and left a voice mail. "Don't even get me started, just start prepping the appeal."

By now, the summer of 2012, I was beyond disillusioned with the entire game, but refusing to lose hope in my country. Nothing surprised me. Nothing stopped my resolve of letting my fellow Americans know about this system screaming for repair.

So . . . we waited again as I got back to writing my book. After what the Northern District Court just handed us, it became the only place I could put my energy and feel like I had a snowball's chance in hell of making a difference. I sequestered myself as much as possible. In late August, I told my family I was taking an executive course rather than secretly writing a book, and I spent a week at the Executive Residences at the University of Michigan, Ross School of Business, only 20 miles away from their home.

Michigan alumnus and playwright Arthur Miller once said, "[The University of Michigan] was, in short, the testing ground for all my prejudices, my beliefs and my ignorance, and it helped to lay out the boundaries of my life." He hit the nail right on the head. Back in Ann Arbor, regressed to my student mentality, I could focus, shutting out the world for hours. Because it was after the summer term but before fall classes began, the place was empty. I was able to knock out 30,000 words in a week.

Satisfied with my progress so far, I returned to Atlanta to check in on the mother ship. Then, on August 31st, I had to fly my plane up to Wisconsin for its annual service. Battling a vicious headwind, I landed short of my destination to refuel—just north of the Illinois/Wisconsin border in southeastern Wisconsin. I parked the plane by the fuel pump and hopped out as a kind gentleman at the operations base started to fuel up my plane.

I'd been flying for about three hours, so when I turned on my BlackBerry, I expected e-mails to start rolling in. The phone dinged four times. "You have four new messages. Message one: Hi Mike, it's Louise."

Louise Locke is a dear friend I studied with at Michigan. A whip smart lawyer, we get along because we both debate and mouth off with wild abandon. While I still see her as the friend who worked the desk at the dorm, she was now an extremely successful employment lawyer and partner at Jackson Lewis. She stated her message pointedly.

"I'm sure you know the FTC is suing you. I'm sure you probably know that. Okay, bye."

"What? For what?" I said out loud.

I quickly dialed Louise, hoping she'd pick up while I paced the tarmac as the wind gusted all around.

"Hi, Mike."

"I don't know anything, Louise. What about?"

"Oh, sorry. Well, it was in *Law360*. They're suing you to sit for a CID."

"That's hilarious!"

"Mike, this isn't hilarious," she said in a dead-serious, professional tone.

"Hold on, let me conference in Phil."

I put her on hold and called him, giddy with excitement.

"Hello."

"Phil, I have Louise Locke on the other line. She said the FTC just sued me."

"What! I haven't received anything."

"Well, I'm going to conference her in. Hold on."

"Okay, Kathryn and Phil, are you both there?"

"Yes," they confirmed.

"What's going on?" Phil asked.

"Well, we get *Law360*, and they have a story about the FTC suing Michael J. Daugherty and LabMD for a CID."[2]

"We haven't been served or notified or anything," Phil complained.

"This is fantastic!" I laughed.

"Mike, seriously, this isn't fantastic. You should take this more seriously," Louise scolded.

"Mike, it isn't a good thing," Phil confirmed.

"Oh, jeez. You lawyers don't get it. Fine. Fine. I know it isn't great, but they're showing their true colors, chasing a mirage. Their actions speak for themselves. Okay, I'll act scared and sullen so you two will be happy."

Pausing for three seconds while hearing silence on the other end, I continued.

"I'm going to boomerang their every move. However, I do need to point out they did it AGAIN, dropping their bombs on a holiday weekend. They *do* like to pull wings off of butterflies!"

Ignoring my pesky commentary, Kathryn told Phil, "Anyway, looks like you'll have to go to federal court in Georgia and speak to a judge about this."

"Great. Georgia, huh? Great. Keeps the costs down and we may have a fair shot at a judge who has been polluted by the Beltway mentality," I said.

"Thanks, Louise. We'll dig into it," Phil chimed in.

We hung up and I called Phil right back.

"Wow. Please find out and let me know, but don't call me. I'll call you. I need to get upstate and then I can deal with this. I want my head clear while I fly."

"Okay. Fly safe. Sorry you found out this way!"

"Oh, it isn't like we didn't expect this. We're finally going to the judiciary. It has to be better than dealing with these administrative grunts. Talk to you later."

I flew to the Cumberland airport, dropped of my plane, and my mechanic and friend Jim Barker drove me to the Minneapolis airport for my commercial return to Atlanta. I tried to be conversational, but it was too tempting to bury myself in my iPad to read the filing Phil had e-mailed me. The FTC wanted an emergency hearing with the judge. *Emergency! They're so cute. Suddenly it's an emergency when we're challenging their authority. Well, to them I suppose it would be an emergency!*

Exhilarated, I finally felt like I was drawing them into our web. As I got to the gate and sat down in a remote corner, I called Phil.

"So what news do you have?"

"Well, it looks like we have Judge William Duffey. He's a Bush appointee, formerly with King and Spalding, and was also with the US Attorney's office. That may mean he'll pull the government line. We haven't been served yet. I don't get what's going on. Also, someone from the media has called the company. Some guy from *Law360.*"

"Hmm. Well, this may be it," I said hurriedly as I rolled my carryon luggage toward the gate. "This may be the media break. We'll see. Tell Bill that *nobody* talks to the media. Take down their information and we'll decide what to do later. We'll have to prep the staff, but I don't want to scare them. Nothing might happen. We're in the middle of the political conventions and elections, but we have to be prepared. Let's discuss this tomorrow. We're starting to board."

I landed in Atlanta, looking forward to another holiday weekend of research and strategy, thanks to the FTC. *Fine with me. What goes around comes around.*

The funnel was narrowing. Judge Duffey was a no-nonsense, intense judge known to have high expectations of lawyers—a breath of fresh air. The more I learned about him, the more I realized he was no fool and nobody's tool.

We looked forward to our day in court.

On Tuesday, September 4th, a reporter called our office and reached Phil. Turns out the *Atlanta Business Chronicle* got wind of the lawsuit and planned to run a story. *Oh, boy.*

"Here we go," Phil said. "They want to talk to you on the phone."

"Should I?" I asked.

"Well, if the story is going to break, yes, you should talk to them because you want your side represented."

"Okay, then tell them I want to be there face to face. I can be in their office in the morning."

"Okay, that's fine."

And with that, I called around to see what I could learn about the *Atlanta Business Chronicle.* The word was that the editor was a fair guy. Phil and I showed up wearing suits and ties at 9:30 a.m. the next morning. We quickly learned they'd done their homework on all the cases, including the suit versus Dartmouth and Tiversa. As a matter of fact, the look on the editor's face was one of empathy. This felt strange. *This had been a secret for years and now total strangers would learn about it. Was I in store for praise, damnation, or being ignored?* Recognizing a fatalistic attitude, I resolved to stay within myself.

There wasn't much to say except to make sure they had their facts straight, which they did. Then they took some photos of me and off we went, preparing to inform our staff about what had been going on since 2008—and telling them what may or may not happen if the story should spin out of control.

By Wednesday, September 5th, we still hadn't been served notice. How confusing. It was even more confusing when we got a call from the FTC's lawyer saying the judge had signed an order saying we were to be in court on September 19th. The Feds have unique rules. They can serve you verbally. *Nice to know. Not surprising. Moving right along.*

The story came out at 6 a.m. on Friday, September 7th, headlined "Atlanta Medical Lab Facing Off Against FTC."[3] It was fairly good. It didn't discuss who was on the advisory board at Tiversa, which I think makes it suspect, but overall, it was a pretty balanced article. It even included the concerns Commissioner Rosch brought up in his dissent.

What amused me were the FTC's comments. It was like watching a dress rehearsal for when I really take the agency to task. Because its favorite tool, silence, wasn't available, the agents moved on to their second option, acting. "What are you talking about?" seemed to be their main pitch. As the article stated:

> The FTC says its staff cannot make a proper recommendation without testimony from Daugherty and LabMD. 'This is completely routine,' the FTC's Melman said. 'This is just how administrative agencies go about carrying out their mission of investigating whether there are unlawful practices.' Melman said it's unusual to have to file a petition in federal court to start an investigation. She said the last instance was about a year ago.

Note to the FTC and Congress: "Completely routine" is completely the problem. It's all too routine to steamroll small businesses and be indifferent to the carnage you wreak. Regarding the statement "this is just how administrative agencies go about carrying out their mission," please state what that means. To us, it means, "Get over it, people. This is just how we do it around here. I don't make the rules. Oh well."

Finally, my favorite was the way the spokesperson slithered along the ground, leaving the impression that an investigation hadn't been started yet with the 'unusual to have to file a petition to start an investigation' mumbo jumbo. *More lying through omission from your federal government.* In the fall of 2011—a full year before—we had asked if there was anything else the FTC wanted. The agents said they had all they needed. What is this crap they are trying to sling about needing to file a petition to start our investigation? Hands in the cookie jar: lid slammed.

If Ms. Melman had been given a shot of truth serum, she may have said something to the effect of this: "We told LabMD and Daugherty we were done, but that was when we were going to start consent decree negotiations, and we assumed they'd just roll over. Now we know they aren't going to take our slander, we can't have that kind of "fair play" and "due process" going on around here. If everyone tried to push back like Daugherty is, we would have a real mess on our hands, so we're making an example out of him. We're painting a picture of Daugherty not being cooperative while never mentioning everything he has supplied us to date. Yeah, we aren't adverse to getting in the mud and rolling around if we have to. It's what we do. Most people just go with the flow. What's his problem, anyway?"

On Friday morning, we scheduled a meeting with the entire company, splitting the staff into two halves during 30-minute blocks, hosting a pizza lunch. Our out-of-state employees were contacted via phone. For each group, I summarized the story. I saw everyone shaking their heads in disgust and let them know the ground rules if we had an issue. I wasn't expecting one, but I wasn't taking any chances. In fact, the discussion was relatively anti-climactic.

Our sales reps didn't express concern. Unlike 2008, the world was now immune to the alarm of data leaks. Nevertheless, I instructed them to freely give out my personal cell number for anyone who had any questions. My phone never rang.

The outpouring of contempt from staff and clients for Washington shenanigans was greater than I'd expected. Plus this FTC matter being received as a "non-issue" was a refreshing validation of our clients' faith in our employees and company. We could move right along without hiring a crisis management firm that came with a big retainer. I didn't plan on this good news, so I regarded this entire experience as a bonus.

The next event was our hearing at the Federal Court in Atlanta on September 19th, 2012. Phil wanted another set of eyes during the hearing, so we asked our outside local counsel at Balch and Bingham to sit with us. We had our arguments briefed; they parroted our January 2012 Motion to Quash. It stated the FTC had no jurisdiction to dig this far down and enforce an action, therefore the CID had no merit.

Once the hearing started, Judge Duffey and the FTC representative did all the talking, with Phil saying maybe 10 words. I enjoyed watching the FTC have its "holier than thou" wings clipped by a federal judge, win or lose. My favorite comments from the transcript follow, the link to the entirety is in the endnotes.[4]

DUFFEY: So thank you for coming. I assume you traveled from Washington. I got you out of town, and it's always a good town to get out of.

FTC: These are meant to be summary proceedings, and we really appreciate the Court's attention to that fact. *(My comment: This is an arrogant dig by the FTC, as summary just means, 'Judge, just sign off so we can move forward.' We knew this attitude would anger the Honorable Court.)*

DUFFEY: I don't think the FTC is saying this, but that's because you are a trustworthy lawyer, but there might be other lawyers who are maybe a little more loose with the granted authority that's given.

DUFFEY: And to think that at that point when a complaint is brought, for somebody to say, wait a minute, that goes way too far, that's not within their jurisdiction, but they have already spent a quarter of a million dollars complying, the court might say, you know, that's right, I don't think that that's what the Section 45 grants to the FTC.

MR. KAPPLER: Well, but, Your Honor, I think you can take some comfort from the perspective that, again, you are acting consistent with what Congress intended in the first place, which is flexible, broad authority.

DUFFEY: Let me just explain something. I'm not here to be comforted. I'm here to do my duty as a judicial officer to interpret the law.

I'm trying as politely as I can tell you that ... I am not enforcing these CIDs today.

DUFFEY: But I'm also real good about doing it in a way in which I am comfortable that I'm following it with integrity and properly.

DUFFEY: I think you are just arguing to hear yourself argue right now.

DUFFEY: And you need to look at your colleague who is nodding his head, I think trying to give you a signal that we ought to talk about the process and move on.

DUFFEY: You know, the day that you become appointed an Article III judge, then you can decide what is or is not necessary. But you are an advocate now.

MR. KAPPLER: Yes, your Honor.

We walked out of there knowing we'd been heard by an honest judge who took it all seriously. Finally, the ground leveled out a bit. Judge Duffey would look at the law, not the parties, and make his decision. *I couldn't have asked for anything more at this point.*

And so we wait, again, like playing slow motion tennis. You hit a lob and it hangs in the air so long, you can leave the court and go about your life until the return shot drops in—in 60 to 180 days.

Back to the book and LabMD. During the fall of 2012, I isolated myself in England, New York City, and Florida for various stretches of time. While I focused primarily on writing the book, the pre-publication preparation needed my attention, too: Web site development, blogging, tweeting, Facebook, editing, good reads. It was like starting a new company. In fact, I soon realized I *was* starting a new company: LabMD's defense subsidiary against the intrusive army of government employees.

In the meantime, my secret life of fighting dragons was unraveling. I balanced protecting my parents from unnecessary worry and having them find out from someone other than me. Filled with dread, I kept putting off the inevitable. Then October brought their annual pilgrimage through Atlanta on their way to South Florida for the winter. This would be my moment.

I called my friend Jaime, the general manager at Chops, one of the best restaurants in Atlanta, who had read the *Atlanta Business Chronicle* article.

"Jaime, I'm bringing in the parents to let them know about this over dinner. Don't spill the beans when we get there. How about six this Friday?"

"You got it, boss. Friday at six it is. Your parents, eh? I look forward to meeting them."

"Have the Scotch ready!"

My parents arrived Friday afternoon, beating Atlanta traffic and getting to my house hours before I arrived there after work. As I walked in the house, I yelled, "Hello!" and out came the dogs, then Dad, and then Mom.

"Hey Bud!"

"Hi, Dad," I said as I kissed and hugged him.

"How's my boy?"

"Great, Dad. Hi, Mom."

"Hello, Michael," she said as I kissed and hugged her.

"How was the drive?"

"Fine. We had a bit of traffic in Knoxville, but it was fine."

I dropped my briefcase on the chair and took off my jacket.

"How's business, Bud?" Dad asked me.

"Fine. Are you guys ready for dinner? We have reservations at six at Chops. With traffic on Piedmont being heavy, we need to leave soon."

"Can you take our bags upstairs?"

"Sure." I lifted the two suitcases and made my way up to the guest bedroom.

My dad looked good, but I knew battling advanced prostate cancer over the past two years had taken its toll. He had times of extreme fatigue and, while he put up a good front and his weight was normal, he didn't have the stamina or energy he used to. *This was all the more reason to have a great steak and scotch before finally dropping the news.*

Nervously, I rushed to get to the restaurant because I wanted my announcement to be over with. Every time the FTC pierced my private life, another ounce was added to my resolve to let Americans know what the real agency was like. *Tonight my resolve gets a triple dose. I imagined the smug indifference of Julie Brill as she adjusted the crown on her head, so proud of herself as she smashes the china while running after the bull. She'd say something classic like, "I'm sorry Mr. Daugherty feels that way; however, we're here to protect the consumer." Someone pull her battery pack!*

Jaime came over, holding the menus to his face, and blocking his mouth from my parents' view, asked, "Do they know yet?"

My eyes widened and I smiled as I told my parents, "Jaime wants to know what you want from the bar."

"Beefeaters on the rocks with anchovy olives," my father said, as if he couldn't wait.

"I'll just have your house merlot," my mother demurred.

"I'll have iced tea, unsweetened," I ordered.

"So how's business, bud?" Dad asked me again.

"Fine, Dad." I wasn't chatty.

I had printed off the story from the *Atlanta Business Chronicle*, tucking two copies into my suit jacket breast pocket. First, we ordered the seafood tower appetizer and dinner. I was moving my leg up and down when my Dad asked again, "How's business, Bud?"

I rubbed my forehead. *Holy cow! He has asked that three times already. Do they already know?*

And then it hit me. *Michael, use his question as a segue.* With humor, I said, "Dad, you've asked me that three times. Do you think I'm under government investigation or something?"

"What? No!"

And before they could figure out what I was talking about, I laughed and smiled. "Well, I *am* under government investigation. The FTC has been crawling over me for almost three years. It has hit the media. Here's an article for you, Mom. Same article for you, Dad. This sums it up and will be the fastest way for you to find out what's going on. Read it and then I'll answer your questions."

They both looked completely dumbfounded. Now my parents aren't naive, believe me, so they know all about the stupid things the government is capable of. However, the first words out of my mother's mouth were something I wouldn't have expected in a million years.

"Oh, Michael! That's such a nice picture of you in the paper."

I burst out laughing. The perfect thing to say because it slammed the FTC back to its insignificance in the eyes of my parents. Then Dad looked at me and asked, "Michael, are your hands in the cookie jar?"

"What?"

"Are your hands in the cookie jar?"

"No, Dad, no! My hands aren't in the cookie jar."

"Good, because it'll take an honest man to beat these people. They're a bunch of dirty crooks."

"I'm writing a book about it. Want to see the cover?"

I took their continued dumbfounded stares as a "yes."

"Here it is."

My mother chuckled while my dad beamed proudly and said, "Man, I hope I live long enough to see this."

The evening continued with a few questions, but overall they were fine. I didn't really know what to expect; this stuff only happened in the movies. Before long, my father went off with old war stories about the FBI and the culture of corruption. I actually think he was proud of me.

I looked over at Jaime and mouthed the words, "They know." So he came over to the table and said, "When Michael's book comes out, we're going to frame the cover and the story, and we'll put it up on the wall here."

The next morning, I left for the gym while my parents were still asleep. When I returned, I found my mother reading the Duffey court transcript on her iPad.

"I can't tell who's winning," she said.

"Well, Mom, Judge Duffey is giving them as much crap as he legally can, but I don't know who will win."

Then my father said, "Do they realize you have built this company all by yourself over the last twenty years?"

"Dad, it's been sixteen years and these people couldn't care less about that. They've been living in their own bubble so long, they have no clue what reality is. They're just one gross, lumbering organism."

He shook his head in disgust as we headed out to the Waffle House for breakfast before they hit the road for Florida.

## Searching for a Way Out of the Forrester

I drove to the office to find an e-mail from Carpenter with our appeal brief. The deadline to file our appeal to the Eleventh Circuit Court of Appeals was upon us.[5] Again, I will quote and comment on the main points.

- "The applicable case law supporting the District Court's decision is not well settled such that there are novel legal concepts which require oral argument."

*I felt the Forrester ruling was lazy and dangerous. Ignoring the fundamental fact that medical files were searched for and taken with full intent and acknowledging the Georgia Courts had not dealt with jurisdiction in this context made me think this judge was looking for an out. His silence was deafening about property. We badly needed to look at the appellate court face to face. But sometimes these people don't want to look you in the eye.*

- While in Huggins, the offense was stalking, a personal injury claim, the conduct which gives rise to LabMD's claims in this appeal is a damage to property claim. The causal connection between LabMD's alleged damages and Appellees' conduct is Appellees' unauthorized . . . taking of LabMD's personal property which was located in Georgia.

*For the life of me, what was Forrester thinking? How can you say that stalking is the same as taking another's property? Bizarre. Surely, this is so basic and obvious, the Eleventh circuit would roll their eyes at Forrester's factually divergent and deeply flawed analogies. Otherwise they would be validating the argument that using technology in one state to take property in another would force the victim to try the case in the perpetrator's state. That would be handing the perpetrator a big fat loophole.*

- "Appellees (Tiversa/Dartmouth) freely admit to intentionally searching computer networks trolling for computer files with PHI and PII. Johnson and Tiversa . . . intentionally commit any action in Georgia and knew they were searching Georgia computers. Johnson and Tiversa used the data downloaded during the Initial Search to intentionally search for computer files on computer hosts that Defendants "had found other dangerous data" previously (the "Second Search") . . .
- Second, given Johnson and Tiversa's description of the technology in question, they had direct knowledge that their conduct reached Georgia. Tiversa's patented EagleVision X1 TM technology globally indexes Internet and file-sharing networks in real-time. Additionally, during the 2009 CTC hearing, Tiversa testified that between February 25, 2009, and April 26, 2009, it had "downloaded 3.908.060 files" from P2P networks, some of which contained PHI and PII and [It] has processed as many as 1.6 billion P2P searches per day, approximately 8 times that of web searches entered into Google per day . . . This unique technology has led some industry experts (*Information Week*) to refer to Tiversa as the 'Google of P2P.'"

*Well, that ought to have the appeals court judges sitting up and taking notice! So much for "we didn't know." They went looking, knew where they were looking, and claim to search more than Google. It's always great to make it easy on the appeals court by using your adversary's words against them. These were not opinions, these were documented facts.*

I thought the appeal was obvious, damning, and supported by fact. I gave Carpenter a high five and the green light to file the appeal.

After having to deal with Tiversa, the FTC, and annoying law firms, I was stunned that the courts had screwed this up so badly. I was so relieved that we would get to a high court. I could not wait to get back on track with our litigation against Tiversa, Johnson, and Dartmouth.

The briefs from the defendants, now known as the appellees, were standard fare that you can read in their entirety in the endnotes,[6] should you so desire. As they had gotten a favorable ruling from Forrester on jurisdiction, but Forrester had not ruled on the merits of the case, the appellees were still going to get sued someplace. Now we were just fighting location. Of course they were going to argue why Forrester got it right. I did read their brief as more circles and confusion, capitalizing on the court's lack of technological education. My two favorites:

In this case, Tiversa did not do or fail to do anything within the State of Georgia. The lone act that gives rise to LabMD's entire Complaint—the download of the 1,718 File—occurred not in Georgia, but in Pennsylvania, where Tiversa's offices are located and it performs its P2P network searches.

*So they admit it. I felt some sort of relief. At least that won't be on the table when we finally get to rumble. Tiversa and Dartmouth keep trying to argue that when a file is in the "public domain" it's fair game to go look for it. Well, there's no such thing as a public domain for purposes of snooping on the Internet for other people's property or sensitive private data. Show me a law, court case, or legal authority that has ever said that someone like Tiversa or Dartmouth has the right to snoop for, interrogate, or exercise dominion over anything like LabMD's medical file. Forrester has evidently never been to this circus because he didn't see the elephant staring him right the face.*

*Or perhaps he isn't blind. Perhaps he's just semi-retired, unmotivated and underestimated the magnitude of this issue. When we drew him after the case was moved up to Federal court, a lawyer told me, "This is not good. I know Forrester and he won't pay attention. He will look for any way out. He needs to be hit between the eyeballs. I'm sorry, Mike, this is bad news."*

In each instance, the technology involved—whether it is telephone call, an e-mail or Web site transmission, or a search on a P2P network—would cause some ultimate "physical" connection with a recipient in Georgia. Yet the courts construing subsection (2) of the Georgia Long Arm Statute have found that personal jurisdiction requires that the defendant be physically located in Georgia when a tortuous act is allegedly committed.

*And appellees can send their thank you note to Forrester for this 37,000 foot view of technology. Circling and confusing the courts by moving the court's attention to technology rather than possession of property, the appellees exploit nothing less than this chronic case of judicial laziness. God forbid the Eleventh Circuit also takes the bait. One lazy ruling, if the courts don't step up and get to work, will result in our all being more vulnerable to abuse. The uphill battle would just get steeper. Now we wait.*

## Cease and Desist

Deep into writing my book, I started to build my social media presence and tell our story. This did not go over well with Tiversa, who fired off a cease and desist letter. Referenced on my website for a full read, Tiversa's lawyer goes on that our accusations are false, our security is lax, and the files were publicly available. They sure did want to harp on that publicly available line. Would anyone else agree that a file stored on a medical facility's private computer was publicly available? We never gave anyone outside the company authority to enter our computers. Malware or not, I was not buying Tiversa's position.

My favorite line was, ". . .You also described an FTC investigation of LabMD. We were previously unaware of any such investigation." They called in 2008 and said they were giving the file to the FTC. Should I really believe this group by now?

## Judge Duffey Renders His Decision

The publicity ball started to slowly roll. The US Chamber of Commerce picked up the story and ran a headline that said, "FBI Says, Expect to Be Hacked; FTC Says, Expect Us to Sue You."[7] It got almost 40,000 hits. Evidently the government messing around in cybersecurity before the ink was dry on how things worked interested thousands of people. Good news. Plus I was invited to join the US Chamber of Commerce Council on Small Business. More good news.

As Thanksgiving approached, I said to Phil, "Judge Duffey is taking a long time. On the one hand, that means he's looking for a way out and I hope he found it. On the other hand, he may not be able to find it."

"Yes. Fast would be better for the FTC. This is complicated. That's generally good for us, but you never know."

I guess Judge Duffey didn't want to ruin my Thanksgiving turkey because, on the morning of Monday, November 26th, he released his decision.[8] At first glance, it looked like he gave the FTC a big win, saying LabMD had to sit for the CID. We weren't surprised. However, he did seem to split the consequences. This argument wasn't about the FTC enforcing anything yet; it was about whether or not they could investigate.

Judge Duffey's main points weren't meant to be taken lightly. His ruling read: "It is well-settled that the role of a district court in a proceeding to enforce an administrative subpoena is sharply limited; inquiry is appropriate only into whether the evidence sought is material and relevant to a lawful purpose of the agency." This meant *there was not much he could do at this point.*

"Section 5 does not specifically identify data security and consumer privacy as areas in which the FTC has jurisdiction to regulate." This meant *be careful what you wish for if LabMD pushes this all the way. The FTC has never been tested in the courts on this.*

"With regard to administrative subpoenas issued by the FTC, the Supreme Court has stated: Even if one were to regard [a] request for information . . . as caused by nothing more than official curiosity, nevertheless law enforcing [sic] agencies have a legitimate right to satisfy themselves that corporate behavior is consistent with the law and the public interest." *This meant the Supreme Court had stated that government agencies can ask for information just because they want to—a scary issue indeed.*

*"When everything seems to be going against you, remember that the airplane takes off against the wind, not with it."*

—Henry Ford

# CHAPTER 27
# No Summit in Sight

## November 27, 2012

The ink on Judge Duffey's order was barely dry when Alain Sheer sent an e-mail asking if we were going to comply. He probably was so excited he couldn't stand it.

> From: Alain Sheer
> Sent: Tuesday, November 27, 2012
> To: Philip Carpenter
> Subject: November 26, 2012 order
>
> Hi, Phil. In light of the Court's November 26, 2012 order enforcing the Commission's CIDs, please let us know immediately if you intend to comply with the order so that we can schedule investigational hearings. The CIDs require the company to produce documents and the company and Mr. Daugherty to respond to interrogatories 10 days before scheduled hearings. Please confirm receipt. Thanks. Alain

Phil let Alain know that we were considering an appeal and needed more time as Phil needed to address a personal matter that would take him out of the office. Mr. Kappler, the lawyer that presented the case before Judge Duffey, responded back, giving us until January 17, 2013, but if we were going to appeal they wanted to know by December 7, 2012.

## Where is our FOIA?

In the middle of all this commotion it occurred to me that I had not heard about our FOIA request. I certainly didn't expect them to move quickly, but it had been over six months. I had called the phone number and left several messages over the past weeks and finally received a call back in early December. The lady that called was a very kind person so I'm going to keep her name a secret, but she told me that this was a big request with over three thousand five hundred pages. It was the holiday time and if I would take the request in chunks, the lawyers would move through it faster. I trusted her and agreed. She told me that the first wave would be out by Christmas. I thought I would believe that when I saw it.

Reading a judge's order can be like deciphering the Dead Sea Scrolls—an enormous task. I had to put them down and reread them over three days. Phil did the same.

One line kept jumping out at us, "Section 5 does not specifically identify data security and consumer privacy as areas in which the FTC has jurisdiction to regulate." This was a very powerful line. We considered it a sign to the FTC that said, "Look, I can't stop you from making Daugherty sit for your CID but I am going to send you one big hint. I am not sure you have jurisdiction over this area, but that is not what is before the court, yet." If we appealed Judge Duffey's ruling, we risked losing a very good judge and a line that has been drawn in the sand for the FTC. The Court of Appeals was, shall we say, not always paying full attention. We won the judge lottery. We didn't want to throw him back. Duffey is sharp. If the FTC actually filed an action against LabMD, we would be back in front of Duffey. We liked that a lot.

We decided to pay attention to the war and give up on this battle. I said yes to sitting for the CID. Phil e-mailed the FTC news of their good fortune:

From: Phil Carpenter
Sent: Thursday December 6, 2012 3:19 PM
To: Burke Kappler
Subject: RE: LabMD, Inc.

Burke—Thank you for your extension in this matter. I am back in the office and both LabMD and Mr. Daugherty will proceed

with the CID process without appeal or request to stay. We are prepared to offer Mr. Bill Barnett as the LabMD representative. To that end, I wanted to check to see if we can provide our written responses by January 17th as proposed and schedule the CIDs for the following week. Can you let me know if this is acceptable?
Philip Carpenter, Esq.

With the FTC "back in business" vs LabMD, the cogs of "justice" started their slow grind once again.

We would sit like good boys as the government snapped our leash. The dates were February 5 and 6, 2013. The stage was set. I put it in the back of my mind and enjoyed the holidays.

Almost five years after Tiversa had darkened our doorstep I had become a legal beagle, reading court cases looking for a crack in the wall. I never gave up hope. Part of fighting was gaining knowledge. In early January, 2013, I discovered a Second Circuit US Court of Appeals ruling[1] that was a gift from the heavens.

"This appeal calls on us to decide whether a court in Connecticut may properly exercise long-arm jurisdiction over a defendant who, while domiciled and working in Canada, is alleged to have accessed a computer server located in Connecticut to misappropriate confidential information belonging to her employer."

*This was great. It came out on December 26, 2012, which was after we filed our appeal, so we needed to get this to the Eleventh Circuit Court right away.*

"While it is true that Deiter physically interacted only with computers in Canada, we do not believe that this fact defeats long-arm jurisdiction...It is not material that Deiter was outside of Connecticut when she accessed the Waterbury servers. The statute requires only that the computer or network, not the user, be located in Connecticut . . . This conclusion is reinforced by the fact that [statute] was enacted as part of a statutory scheme intended to prohibit unauthorized persons from using computers or networks with intent to, among other things, cause a computer to malfunction, alter or erase data, or copy computer data or programs."

*This was just fantastic news. The court is focusing on the intention of the law. The Georgia Computer Protection Act had the same intention.*

"For the reasons stated, we reverse the judgment of the district court and remand for further proceedings."

*A miracle.*

"Hey," I said to Carpenter, "where the heck is the Eleventh Circuit decision to our appeal, anyway?"

"I take this as a good sign that they are considering the appeal carefully."

"We need to get this Second Circuit ruling overturning the District Court over to them. It is almost directly on point."

"I know. I'm on it."

And with that, on January 21, 2013, LabMD filed a Motion to Supplement Brief to add the Second Circuit opinion.[2] Three days later, one word came back from the court: Denied.

I was disgusted that they would not look at a conflicting opinion. We hypothesized that they probably had already ruled but not yet published their decision. Or perhaps they just didn't want to be bothered. These are the tricks and turns of the judicial system that only experience teaches you. Sort of like learning just because someone tells you they love you, it doesn't mean they mean it.

Being in sales for years, I never took promises too seriously, especially from the government, but I had built a rapport with this lady at the FOIA office, so I decided to chase her about the missed deadline.

"Oh, I am so sorry. We're just so busy. It won't be long now." I was at a loss at what to do other than keep calling. Getting angry may backfire. I decided to keep up the chase with a smile.

## Dirtier Dirty Tricks

January 10, 2013 marked our three year anniversary in dealing with the Federal Trade Commission. I had learned to forget that this was my government I was dealing with. Now I believed they capitalized on their victim's naiveté, a war tactic to exploit patriotism and lower their guard. This point of view was cemented when the following arrived on January 31, 2013:

From: Alain Sheer
Sent: Wednesday January 30, 2013 3:23 PM
To: Phil Carpenter
Cc: Ruth Yodaiken, Burke Kappler
Subject: follow-up to voicemail . . .

Hi Phil:
This morning's voice mail: The reason for the voice mail was to tell you that we are going to use as exhibits at the hearings next week documents the Sacramento, California Police Department found in the possession of an alleged identity thief . . . These documents are 37 LabMD, Inc. "Day Sheet—Transaction Detail" reports from 2007, 2008, and 2009 and copies of a few checks from patients to LabMD.

We are going to send copies of the documents, and a password to open them, to you by separate e-mails. We redacted Social Security numbers, last names, bank account numbers, and certain other information from the documents to meet our policies for handling personally identifiable information. LabMD's ongoing obligation to preserve documents includes these types of documents. Please call if you have questions.

Alain

This time my confusion was over in milliseconds. I knew if it came from the FTC, something must be dirty. I found myself looking at reports with very single entry on every single line blacked out except random numbers. These were not account numbers. These looked like transaction numbers. Even though the FTC was playing their own version of *Wheel of Fortune* leveraging patient information, it wasn't long before we figured out exactly what these reports were.

Billing employees would print these off their workstation so they could have a list of all the payments received that day. It was used to balance with the daily deposits. These reports were never saved to any media. There were a few hundred names. The most recent list was from 2009 but most were older. These were then packaged and saved in a locked cabinet. Our investigation showed there was no way these would ever be on a computer or available after 2009. The sheets of paper may have been taken but not via a computer download. Of course, the FTC to this day gives LabMD no assistance. Why weren't we ever notified as soon as this was discovered? Did the FTC sit on this for their own interests?

"Phil, please call the Sacramento police and find out what the hell is going on. Why didn't they contact us?"

Within 30 minutes he called me with the following scoop:

"I got in touch with the woman who is investigating the case. She said there was some sort of identity theft arrest from a house in Sacramento and when they hauled the computers out of the thief's home, they found our file on a computer drive. There was nothing else. When I asked her why she didn't call, she said they didn't know who LabMD was, so they checked Google. That showed them LabMD vs FTC, so they just called the FTC instead. Once I started asking further questions, she stopped talking."

"And the FTC has been sitting on this for how long?"

"Over four months."

"That's nice. What a coincidence. So let me get this straight. The FTC has known about this and never told us until less than a week before we sit for the CID? Looks to me like they're using private health information for intimidation instead of letting us take the proper steps. They're violating patient notification laws."

"Looks that way."

"I'm not surprised. They really must be desperate to sink this low. This is a psychological warfare tactic to knock us off our game. I can just see them dancing around their office thinking they really have us now. It won't work." And it didn't work. I was furious. This may be a game to the FTC, but this was not a game to me. How dare they sit on this information for their own strategic purposes.

The FTC lawyers flew in from Washington DC in time for the CID. I hoped they flew coach.

Tuesday morning, Bill was ready for his time with the FTC. I decided, as did everyone else, it would be better if I didn't come along. I didn't want to make Bill nervous or have him looking over at me.

With what Carpenter told me, I can sum up Bill's day in one sentence. It was more of the same rehash, this time verbally. The horse had been beaten so many times there was no horse left to beat, but swing away the FTC did, keeping Bill under oath until well into the evening. I did my best not to watch the clock. By six p.m. it was impossible. I knew if I got all fired up, it would just play into the FTC's psychological warfare tactics, so I just kept breathing and moving forward. I didn't care what mile of this race we were on, I was not going to quit.

My turn came Wednesday morning, February 6. It didn't last three hours. It was boring. It was a rehash. It was over in time for lunch. Nothing new, more of the old, and questions still begged to be answered, "Are they going to sue me or not? I wished they would just get on with it. Don't they have bigger fish to fry?"

On Wednesday afternoon after our lunch, and while still enjoying the natural buzz from having the CID behind us, Phil notified me that he had some news he'd been holding until we were done with the hearings. Turns out that the Eleventh Circuit denied our appeal on the fifth of February, but Phil didn't want to tell me so I could keep my focus on the FTC.

I had become so used to Justice Mountain being steeper than one could imagine that I was numb. No longer surprised at the spin masters that haunt the halls of each branch of our government, I just wanted to read the damn ruling so I could have my latest meal of judicial shock, dismay, and disgust. The Eleventh Circuit Judges Carnes, Barkett, and Edmondson did not disappoint.[3]

"In preparing the article, Johnson and Tiversa searched peer-to-peer networks looking for computer files containing data that could be used potentially to commit medical or financial identity theft."

*I about fell over. Not again. Don't tell me that these judges are so numb to what is staring them smack in the face it never even occurred to them to question whether Tiversa and Johnson had any business even looking for medical files. This trio of focus just hopscotched over the morality and fairness of it all. Where is the warrant to search for files? Why are they okay with a private entity doing this? What is wrong with these judges? The Eleventh Circuit erected a wall blocking our need to explain this critical issue by not allowing us oral argument. They didn't even comment on the very appropriateness of this action. Power without knowledge and asleep at the wheel, chalk up more judges that history will prove to be lazy fools that do not have the backs of the people.*

For purposes of personal jurisdiction under Georgia's Long Arm Statute, Georgia courts have ruled that when a defendant uses the telephone or e-mail to contact a Georgia resident—defendant's conduct occurs at the place where defendant speaks into the telephone or types and sends his e-mail . . . For the long-arm statute, we see no meaningful distinction between the technology used to place telephone calls or send e-mails and the technology used in peer-to-peer file sharing. In all cases, the technology causes the transmission of information along telephone or electronic lines between an out-of-state defendant and a Georgia resident.

*I'm sorry, but what a bunch of old fart idiots. The appeals court equates downloading our computer data as being the same as harassment! Unbelievable. So now the legality of surveilling and taking someone else's property is technology dependent? It's okay to remotely download medical information and Georgia doesn't care? Do you seriously think that was the legislative intent of the Georgia Computer Protection Act? Boy, did my lawyer ever call it the day we filed this case, "When it comes to involving technology to a court, their heads go soft and their logic flies right out the window. You have to hit them right between the eyes that this is a theft case."*

*The judiciary's favorite game after a bad decision was blaming the legislature. They will bemoan that the law was poorly written and that they aren't responsible for that. God forbid that the judiciary would ever be held responsible. I wasn't buying it this time. Just because courts don't understand technology doesn't mean they get to punt the ball, do no research, prevent oral argument, and confuse lazy opinion with fact. E-mails don't steal. Phone calls don't steal. Taking others' property is taking others' property, even if Star Trek technology is a true story. What an embarrassment . . . and a tragedy.*

*I was breaking all the rules . . . shattering the code of silence among judges and the control they have over lawyers. I felt like John McEnroe yelling at an umpire. Instead of yelling, "Chalk flew up! The ball was clearly out! You must be joking!", I was yelling, "They downloaded our file! They admit it! What difference does it make how it was taken? Who are you people? I can't believe you're missing the obvious. You scare me to death and frustrate me to no end, so comfortable are you in your judicial numbness. You are the pits of the world!"*

*I would have been fined by the court like McEnroe would have been fined by the tournament. The ruling was terrible. The ball was still out.*

*Not forgotten, trust me, and don't you forget the risks, either, should you ever venture to climb Justice Mountain.*

Furious beyond belief, yet not hopeless, I asked Phil what we could do.

"Do we have to appeal to the US Supreme Court? We have a conflicting opinion from a different circuit."

The look on Phil's face was as if I'd asked him to run another five miles after a marathon.

"That's a long shot. A real long shot. And it's expensive, and they probably take two percent of what is filed."

"But this is timely. We have conflicting Appeals Courts, we have a hot topic of cybersecurity that affects the public," I pleaded, as if I were begging him to tell me I would soon wake up from this nightmare.

"The Second Circuit ruling hangs its hat on the fact that the Connecticut long-arm statute specifically mentions computers. Georgia's does not. The only thing that may be worth a shot is to ask the Eleventh Circuit for a rehearing and to send a certified question to the Georgia Supreme Court for their opinion. After all, this is about the interpretation of Georgia state law. They may bite, but doubtful. Cyber security is a big issue and it's no secret that the courts are lagging and struggling with this issue. I did show this to some law professors. They both agreed that this is a very bad ruling, but what to do, realistically?"

"Do something to document their arrogance. Send the letter. I'm sure they'll deny it. That isn't the point. I want to educate others how tough it is to get their attention. No oral argument, no viewing the recent conflicting ruling of the Second Circuit, and now watch them refuse to ask the state court about state law. I guess we're going to Pennsylvania to refile. What a mess. We're going to lose the power of the Georgia Computer Protection Act. Pennsylvania doesn't have anything like it. What a mess!"

On February 27, 2013, Phil filed the petition for rehearing and motion to send a certified question to the Georgia Supreme Court.[4]

I knew the Eleventh Circuit would not want to be pestered. I wanted that in writing.

The day after Phil mailed to petition, we got an e-mail from Alain Sheer.

From: Alain Sheer
Sent: Thursday February 28, 2013 5:40 PM
To: Phil Carpenter
Subject: RE: LabMD, Inc.

Hi Phil . . . Has LabMD notified, or is it planning to notify, the individuals listed on those LabMD documents the Sacramento police department found that their personal information was disclosed to alleged identity thieves? Please let us know by close of business tomorrow.

Alain

I found this latest missive to be darkly amusing. *Oh how innocent and concerned the FTC acts once they extract their ration of blood. Nice try, Alain... and interesting timing. You sit on this for months so we don't think patient confidentiality is your main concern. How about entrapment? And since you won't give us anything more than a number where are we to notify these people? And how? YOU have all the information. Have you called them?*

Phil replied . . . on Monday afternoon:

From: Phil Carpenter
Sent: Monday March 4, 2013 12:45 PM
To: Alain Sheer
Subject: LabMD, Inc

Alain,
Based upon the limited and redacted information that was provided by the FTC and the even more limited information provided by the City of Sacramento, LabMD is taking all

necessary and required steps to address the situation. Since the City of Sacramento will not discuss what information it has with respect to LabMD based upon "an ongoing investigation" and since the FTC is unwilling to do so either, our due diligence is extremely limited. Should the FTC and/or the City of Sacramento wish to disclose all of the information at its disposal, including un-redacted documents, LabMD can make a fully educated decision. However, with the current impediments imposed by the various agencies, LabMD can only try its best to do the right thing.

Sincerely,
Phil Carpenter

Within the hour, Alain returned this e-mail lob:

From: Alain Sheer
Sent: Monday March 4, 2013 1:16 PM
To: Phil Carpenter
Subject: RE: LabMD, Inc.

Hi Phil.
We take your e-mail to mean that the company has not sent notice to the consumers identified in the Sacramento documents, and that it does not plan to do so. If that is not the case, please let us know right away. The redacted copies of the documents we provided on January 30, 2013, include information that together could be used to identify affected consumers, such as first name, billing number, and payment date. In addition, the materials include print dates of the Day Sheets, which the company has testified it maintains. You have not asked for unredacted copies of the Sacramento materials, but if you need unredacted copies to provide notice, please let us know and we will find an appropriate way to provide them to you.

Thanks,
Alain

*What a boring game of chess with patients as pawns. We asked them right away. They are more concerned with games than patients.*

The petty attempt to trap us continued as Phil replied:

From: Phil Carpenter
Sent: Monday March 4, 2013 2:00 PM
To: Alain Sheer
Subject: RE: LabMD, Inc.

Alain,
Please find [our] February 1, 2013, letter wherein we requested unredacted copies of the City of Sacramento's materials. I trust this will clear up the incorrect statement contained in your earlier e-mail that "you have not asked for unredacted copies of the Sacramento materials."

Phil Carpenter

*How are we to contact patients when the two different governments won't give us the required information? What are we supposed to tell the patients, "We got a number that may or may not be yours, so call your Senator?"*

Alain hit another shot after the first one failed, sending this e-mail:

From: Alain Sheer
Sent: Monday March 4, 2013 3:09 PM
To: Phil Carpenter
Subject: LabMD, Inc.

Hi Phil. In our February 1, 2013, response to [LabMD's] letter, we confirmed the expectation that we need written confirmation from the company that the Sacramento documents are the company's documents (that is, created and maintained by the company) before we can provide copies without redacting the sensitive consumer information therein. No written confirmation has been forthcoming. If you can provide written confirmation now, we will provide unredacted copies of the documents to you.

Thanks,
Alain

That did it. Phil got sick of this government gamesmanship and fired off the following:

From: Phil Carpenter
Sent: Monday March 4, 2013 3:32 PM
To: Alain Sheer
Subject: RE: LabMD, Inc.

Alain,
I believe the FTC is now being uncooperative and refusing to help. I am not sure what further assurances you need here, as you asked Mr. Barnett over one hour's worth of questioning regarding the documents under oath. I do not want to alter the testimony the FTC took, and if his sworn statement under oath is not enough, then please let me know what would be enough. Quite frankly, I find it troubling that the FTC would send us redacted documents, ask a LabMD representative to testify about those same documents, and then refuse to provide clean copies without written confirmation that the documents are company documents. Additionally, my request for FTC help goes beyond what we received in your e-mail. We are asking a broader question as to any documents you have, not just the ones you e-mailed to us. I remain clear as day that we are asking the FTC to assist us in our investigation, which would include documents which you have not provided to us which might assist us in helping all involved.

How low and unprofessional would the FTC go? We knew pretty low. Only a government lawyer would play this game. Now Alain decided to send a formal letter. At least we were having a great time demonstrating that we were going to push back to abusive government trickery.

So here comes the cherry on the sundae: Alain e-mails a letter stating that they would not produce the documents unredacted until Bill Barnett signed a statement stating that the documents were LabMD's.

Here are my favorite parts:

> "On January 30, 2013, we provided you with redacted copies of all the LabMD documents we received from the Sacramento Police Department . . . You noted that Mr. Barnett's recent testimony should suffice to establish that the documents are LabMD's. However, his testimony is not final until he signs the transcript . . . we ask for a clear written representation that the redacted copies provided are LabMD's . . . we do so only as part of our effort to protect consumers from identity theft and other harms by applying uniform procedures when disclosing sensitive consumer information."

If this wasn't such a destructive process, this would be a comedy. The FTC starts off the letter by calling the documents "LabMD documents," they e-mail them to LabMD, they have LabMD marked on them, they ask if we alerted patients, and now the FTC can't be sure the documents are LabMD's until we sign that they are, in fact, LabMD's. God help us all.

My response to Phil: "I am not having Bill sign anything. They can wait until we have to approve the testimony formally. Until then, let them bask in their own petty stupidity or they can call Judge Duffey. I'm sure he'll have a few choice comments for them." And that was the last time we heard from Alain Sheer regarding his little scheme cloaked in faux concern for our patient's information security.

## Alerting the Patients

We weren't sure what responsibility we had to alert patients since we weren't sent anything but sheets of paper blacked out except for a random number. However, we weren't going to let the petty torments of the US Government get in our way.

Even though this occurred before notification laws came into play, we learned about it after. So we assumed we had sixty days from our first learning about this. That would place our deadline by the end of March. Then I shopped around for notification policies and purchased insurance for the potential victims. The company told us to expect about a fifteen percent call back and acceptance rate. This event was so far in the past that it may be less. We sent out the letter and manned the phones on March 27, 2013. My favorite excerpt from the letter sent to the patients was:

> On January 30, 2013, LabMD, Inc., received an e-mail from the United States Federal Trade Commission ("FTC") indicating that it and the City of Sacramento Police Department have documents which may contain your personally identifying information. The documents contain names, social security numbers, and chart numbers. To date, we cannot determine the full scope of information, as neither the FTC nor the City of Sacramento will release documents that have not been blacked out in certain areas for our review.

> On January 30, 2013, LabMD immediately began investigating this matter and contacted both agencies. The e-mail LabMD received from the FTC indicates that the information contained in the documents may have been used for identity theft purposes, although they refuse to provide any additional detail to LabMD.

The phone calls came in for 48 hours and ended right at a fifteen percent response rate. Our clients were impressed at our thorough efforts and empathized with a rogue employee. Since we did not have over 500 patients from a single area, we were not required to alert the media. We contacted Health and Human Services and dutifully reported our situation. Their response was balanced without alarm. We never heard back from them again.

Bill signed his testimony and it was sent back to the FTC. To date, LabMD has not received the unredacted patient information from any government agency.

Things seemed to be moving at a faster pace now. The CID was over, we had the Sacramento Surprise behind us, and were anxiously waiting our next disappointment from the Eleventh Circuit Court. The first week of April, 2013, brought the pleasant surprise of a first response to our FOIA request regarding the government dollars that went to Dartmouth and Tiversa.[5] It started with a phone call. The nice lady said that the first shipment could be e-mailed if I wanted. I accepted. The opening letter was not exactly what I had been told. No surprise there.

"A search of the Office of Cybersecurity and Communications for documents responsive to your request produced a total of 322 pages. I have determined that 56 pages of the records are releasable in their entirety, 27 pages are partially releasable, and 239 pages are withheld in their entirety pursuant to Title 5 U.S.C. 552 (b) (4) and (b) (6), FOIA Exemptions 4 and 6."

This made me wonder what happened to the other three thousand pages. Would I ever see those? What is so critical that 239 pages had to be completely redacted? So while the talk is "freedom of information," the walk is "slow the game down," "break the rules at will," and "silent as she goes." Now that I was fluent in speaking government jive, I was certainly not surprised.

One of the most amusing lines in the letter was regarding FOIA exemption 6, which was laced with hypocrisy.

"FOIA Exemption 6 exempts from disclosure personnel or medical files and similar files the release of which would cause a clearly unwarranted invasion of personal privacy." I wondered if there was barely a hand slap if this policy was not adhered to.

What were the main points that I learned from what little had been shared? There were a few surprises and even less answers.

- The Trustees at Dartmouth were awarded a maximum 24.3 million dollars for a 2.5 year performance period starting in 2006.
- The name of the project was Cyber Security Collaboration and Information Sharing.
- Tiversa's name was not mentioned in any unredacted submission to me.
- Most of what was given was boilerplate contract language
- I have no idea where the other three thousand pages are or what is in them.
- Nothing has been turned over to me since April, 2013, and all phone messages since have not been returned.
- The Federal government has returned to their familiar lair: dead silence.

This was classic US government behavior. Blatant disregard for FOIA rules, they dare you to chase them and sue. Their agenda is to ignore you. If that doesn't work, they slowly drain you dry. By the time you're close to getting what is legally yours, you may be dead. Not only does this slow down the specific requestor, it chills the nerve of most others. So much for transparency, but they get away with it as long as people bury their heads in the sand. The Feds aren't picky, so don't think this couldn't be you. Indifference equals validation.

On May 9, 2013, the Eleventh Circuit Court of Appeals sent a two sentence decision regarding our Petition for Rehearing and Motion to Send Certified Question to the Georgia Supreme Court.[6]

Motion Denied.

Motion Denied.

And that was the end of that.

## If by Rudyard Kipling

If you can keep your head when all about you
Are losing theirs and blaming it on you;
If you can trust yourself when all men doubt you,
But make allowance for their doubting too:
If you can wait and not be tired by waiting,
Or, being lied about, don't deal in lies,
Or being hated don't give way to hating,
And yet don't look too good, nor talk too wise;

If you can dream—and not make dreams your master;
If you can think—and not make thoughts your aim,
If you can meet with Triumph and Disaster
And treat those two impostors just the same:.
If you can bear to hear the truth you've spoken
Twisted by knaves to make a trap for fools,
Or watch the things you gave your life to, broken,
And stoop and build 'em up with worn-out tools;

If you can make one heap of all your winnings
And risk it on one turn of pitch-and-toss,
And lose, and start again at your beginnings,
And never breathe a word about your loss:
If you can force your heart and nerve and sinew
To serve your turn long after they are gone,
And so hold on when there is nothing in you
Except the Will which says to them: "Hold on!"

If you can talk with crowds and keep your virtue,
Or walk with Kings—nor lose the common touch,
If neither foes nor loving friends can hurt you,

If all men count with you, but none too much:
  If you can fill the unforgiving minute
  With sixty seconds' worth of distance run,
Yours is the Earth and everything that's in it,
And—which is more—you'll be a Man, my son!

# CHAPTER 28
# Discovering More Than
# I Bargained For

The Eleventh Circuit's four-word decision knocked the wind out of me. Until jurisdiction is sorted out and discovery starts, specific answers regarding Dartmouth and Tiversa must wait. To date, neither organization has responded to our 2010 inquiry. Simply put, the courts enabled them to buy time.

If there isn't existing law to support a decision, judges often seem to throw logic out the window rather than face having a ruling overturned on appeal. I'm sure many a lawyer and judge will think I'm being a spoiled sport about the rulings. So be it. I'm reminded of my father's words about lawyers suspending logic—only a judge or lawyer could look at this conflict and not admit to seeing the fundamental problem.

As this book goes to press no decision has been made on which legal avenue to take. One option is to refile the suit in Pennsylvania, but that state does not have Georgia's strong computer protection laws. The courts took away a strong line of defense from LabMD and anyone else caught in this predicament. Victims are forced to travel to states where perpetrators reside, legislators shout that courts need to be more reasonable in their interpretations, and judges bemoan terrible laws they are given to interpret. Once again I was caught in the middle of government finger pointing. The calm indifference and "oh well" attitude was infuriating.

The other option is to appeal the Eleventh Circuit's ruling with the U. S. Supreme Court. This is an expensive long shot. Only about five percent of appeals get picked up by the court but LabMD has a few things going for it.

First, this is a national legal issue that needs interpretation from the top. Most lawyers and judges I have spoken to agree that the judicial system is woefully inadequate in rulings regarding cybersecurity.

Second, there is potential conflict between the Second and Eleventh Circuit rulings on jurisdiction. The Supreme Court has been known to accept cases to settle disagreements between lower courts.

Third, the Supreme Court needs to overturn prior courts' equating phone technology with more modern computer technology. Let's enter the 21st century, shall we? What difference does it make what technology is used to take away others' property?

Both trips up the judicial mountain are chocked with expensive and potentially disheartening surprises, but one way or the other I intend to continue the climb.

June 2013

I knew it was only a matter of time before we had to absorb another snap from the government whip. I had to take advantage of the interim quiet. Things were becoming difficult on the business front.

In spite of the media's reporting our FTC battle, our physician base was solidly behind us, but their volume of testing was slowly shrinking. This was due to government and private insurance reimbursement cuts and the stagnant economy forcing patients to compromise their health maintenance by skipping non-emergency visits. FTC's attack on LabMD had tied up the time, money, and manpower needed to create new markets, go after new business, and counter the trend. For the first time in twelve years we were slipping into the red.

While reviewing our next-step strategy, I noted that with no standards and questionable practices the FTC had secured over forty consent decrees regarding data security practices over the past several years. Corporations had rolled over left and right. I know of no cases like ours where there is no evidence that data is anywhere but in the hands of those involved with the US Government.

After reading about one of the consent degrees, I reached out to the victim's attorney. Afraid of the FTC's wrath, he requested anonymity. However, he expressed shock and a sense of betrayal at the opportunistic tone in the FTC press release announcing the decree. I told him I wished I could've assisted them in their struggles and extended my condolences.

When I started the book in early 2012 I knew it was possible the events would be dismissed as a "one-off" or that I would be relegated to the back of the line as a conspiracy theorist. But I am not a conspiracy theorist. If anything, I'm a buffoonery and corruption theorist. And in that regard, and with impeccable timing, Washington DC began to resonate with one scandal after another: Benghazi, then the AP, James Rosen, the IRS, bureaucrats parading through Congress with memory loss and pleading the fifth, and finally, Snowden blowing up NSA secrets. The rising tide of revelation gave me the strength to keep digging until I got to the bottom of this.

To that end I hired yet another lawyer. Her job was to put together the pieces of the P2P story from start to finish, using publicly available documents, appropriate contacts, and resources to explain how this all got so out of hand. Her requirement was anonymity. I would own the copyright.

In July of 2013 the report arrived. It revealed in great detail not only why LabMD got entrapped, but how the FTC had engineered the fiasco in the first place. It was much, much bigger than just me or LabMD, and I read it over and over to let the truth fully sink in. *Oh my God, I have nailed them.*

What follows is an example of what happens when power is allowed to run unchecked.

## THE FTC: NEGLIGENCE, INCOMPETENCE, AND COVERING UP AT AMERICA'S EXPENSE

In June 2002, Hewlett Packard Lab researchers and computer scientists Nathaniel Good and Aaron Krekelberg published *Usability and Privacy.*[1] The following should have been dealt with before the lions left their cages:

> The excitement around P2P systems has been encouraged by recent innovations that foster easier sharing of files, such as downloading simultaneously from multiple sources, and the sharing of many different file types as well as improvements to the usability of these clients . . . If sharing is enabled, the files that you download are available to be downloaded by other users. While facilitating file sharing and searching, the systems do a poor job of preventing users from sharing potentially personal files . . . By providing several different locations and interfaces to manage file sharing and not connecting their information, users are not made aware of what files are being offered for others to download and are not able to determine how to successfully share and stop sharing files. Ambiguity and assumptions about recursion and types of files being shared allow users to make dangerous errors, such as sharing an entire hard drive. Finally, the confusing multiple purposes of the My Media interface cause users some confusion about what is actually being shared. Given the potential violation of user privacy and the current abuses that we noted above, it should be a top priority for file sharing applications to look into usability for security applications, and design their applications accordingly.

Clearly this report specifically states that these are design flaws. They even specified what the design flaws were. This report identified two features in file-sharing programs known to dupe users into inadvertently sharing the contents of their *My Documents* folder and its subfolders. Search-wizard and share-folder features would share folders, making them automatically vulnerable and open to searching. One would think our brilliant government lawyers would then look at design.

The FTC ignored the conclusions until 2003, when hearings on inadvertent sharing and *Usability and Privacy* were held by two committees of the US Congress, the House Committee on Oversight and Government Reform, and the Senate Judiciary Committee.

After this hearing, program developers including LimeWire promised to eliminate the search-wizard and share-folder "features" condemned in *Usability and Privacy*. In a subsequent hearing on May 15, 2003 before the House Committee on Government Reform, staff investigators confirmed that thousands of users of file-sharing programs were inadvertently sharing data files from popular finance-management software that would contain account numbers and detailed records about a user's finances.[2] At a June 17, 2003 hearing before the Senate Committee on the Judiciary, legislators repeatedly warned developers that unless they eliminated features that caused users to share existing files inadvertently, their programs would compromise national security:[3]

- "In government agencies, employee use of P2P networks could . . . disclose sensitive government data to the enemies of this country."
- "If the user is a government employee . . . sensitive government information could be made available to those unfriendly to the United States."
- "For government users . . . confidential memos, Defense Department information, law enforcement records, all could be available to any Internet user with some free software and the desire to go looking."[2,4]

After the hearings, the developers of LimeWire, BearShare, Morpheus and eDonkey claimed they had moved swiftly to prevent inadvertent sharing of users' personal or work files. On September 29, 2003, they published a *Code of Conduct* in which they pledged[5] never to incorporate deceptive search-wizard or share-folder features in *future* versions of their programs by imposing upon themselves the following obligations:

- "[Our] software and associated user instructions shall conspicuously require the user to confirm the folder(s) containing the file material that the user wishes to make available to other users before making such material available, and"
- "[Our] software and associated user instructions . . . shall be designed to reasonably prevent the inadvertent designation of the content of the user's . . . principal data repository . . . as material available to other users."[2]

Members of both the House and the Senate recognized that these claims of remediation and prevention had to be investigated and confirmed before the President, Pentagon, Department of Defense, consumers, and companies like LabMD, just to name a few, would be fully protected against inadvertent sharing of sensitive personal or work files. They entrusted the critical task of conducting this critical follow-up investigation to the nation's recognized experts in consumer-protection and deception-prevention—the Federal Trade Commission.

Congress was still under the naive assumption the child they spawned would obey.

## The FTC bungles it

The FTC's first mistake was choosing to *work with* the developers of LimeWire rather than *investigate* them and *analyze* the software. The FTC, arrogant in its belief that others would jump simply because it gave the order, was unaware for *two more years* that developers of file-sharing programs—like its working partners at LimeWire— were perpetuating and exacerbating the problem of inadvertent sharing. The FTC's partners were breaking their promises, violating their own *Code of Conduct*, and incorporating deceptive search-wizard and share-folder features into 2004 and later versions of their programs right under the nose of the clueless watchdog.

On June 17, 2004, the FTC's first report of its follow-up investigation on inadvertent file sharing accepted the developers' claims as true: "the risk of inadvertent sharing appears to have decreased . . ." But the FTC was wrong. By June of 2004 the risks of inadvertent file-sharing had actually *increased*, because despite the developers' assertions, the dangerous search-wizard and share-folder features that *Usability and Privacy* had identified in 2002 had since been implemented in many other popular file-sharing programs, including LimeWire.[1]

The FTC's oversight of inadvertent file-sharing in 2004 was plagued by serial incompetence. For example, to determine whether developers of file-sharing programs had kept their promises to eliminate user-interface features known to cause inadvertent sharing, the FTC didn't analyze the software. Instead, they downloaded and examined representations from the *Web sites* operated by the developers of the ten most popular file-sharing programs, including LimeWire.[2] Basically, they focused on disclosure rather than design and function. Only lawyers think like this.

To make matters worse, the FTC's decided to have its staff review only ten sets of 2004 Web site disclosures. No study or evidence published from 2002 through today has attributed even one episode of inadvertent sharing of personal or work documents to a misleading, missing, or inadequate "disclosure" made on one of these rarely-visited Web sites.

The FTC staff did not try to determine whether any of the representations and disclosures they had downloaded from www.limewire.com violated the FTC Act's prohibitions against deceptive or unfair practices. Instead, the staff examined LimeWire's Web site disclosures for oxymorons such as "facially deceptive" representations.[2]

Apparently the FTC couldn't detect anything facially deceptive about the answer the developers of LimeWire gave to a frequently asked question about data security:

> Q: Are there security risks associated with using LimeWire?
>
> A: As long as you don't share your entire hard drive, you shouldn't encounter any significant security risks using Gnutella [a large P2P network].[2,6]

This answer is wrong ... LimeWire was perfectly willing and able to share your hard drive while you remained clueless.

In 2004 the FTC admitted that its cursory investigation of inadvertent file-sharing had not *really* determined whether any of the developers of any of the ten most popular P2P file sharing programs had or were committing deceptive or unfair practices that violated the FTC Act.[2,7] Once again, the FTC announced it had decided to *work with* the developers of the Kazaa, Grokster, Morpheus, Bear-Share and LimeWire file-sharing programs in order to help them improve some of the not-facially deceptive Web site risk disclosures the FTC had reviewed.

This was another FTC decision that proved to be disastrous. It did not know if the developers of LimeWire were committing deceptive practices prohibited by the FTC Act. Working with LimeWire on that basis was a risk the FTC's consumer-protection experts *chose* to take.

The FTC rolled the dice and our security was the bet. If it turned out their new partners were committing prohibited practices known to cause dangerous breaches of national, military, corporate, and personal data, a glaring conflict of interest would divide the institutional interests of the FTC from the public interest in halting said practices. If the FTC later enforced the FTC Act against LimeWire, then the FTC would be admitting that it had recklessly facilitated violations of the FTC Act that it had corrected only belatedly—years after it had done more avoidable harm to Americans.

This means the FTC made a deliberate decision to treat additional compromises of national, military, corporate, and personal data security as the collateral cost of avoiding responsibility for its mistakes.

From 2004 through 2009, the FTC praised and worked with LimeWire even after more FTC studies and Congressional hearings had documented more LimeWire wrongdoing. Once the FTC began to work with the developers of the P2P file-sharing programs LimeWire, BearShare, eDonkey, Kazaa, and Grokster in July of 2004, it would never again find fault in the contemporaneous or subsequent actions of any of the program developers with whom the FTC had *chosen* to partner.

However, there were cracks in the facade:

- On March 12, 2005, the Web site *See What You Share* reported that criminals were again mining file-sharing networks for inadvertently shared data. It also reported that pedophiles were searching file-sharing networks for hard-core child pornography—and for inadvertently shared data about particular children.[2,8]

- The security company Blue Security reported on April 19, 2005 that inadvertent sharing had become so widespread that spammers were systematically data-mining file-sharing networks to find inadvertently shared email addresses.[9]
- On May 5, 2005, CBS *Marketwatch* reported that BearShare users were again inadvertently sharing "tax returns" and "private medical files and private bank statements." A BearShare spokesman said, "As I understand it, a new version will be coming out literally in a matter of days that will seek to close any possible vulnerabilities of this."[2,10]

In early 2005, the Department of Homeland Security (DHS) reported another long-foreseen consequence of continued inadvertent sharing of sensitive files. DHS warned all federal, state and local agencies involved in homeland security that government employees or contractors using file-sharing programs had repeatedly compromised national and military security:

- "There are documented incidents of P2P file sharing where Department of Defense (DoD) sensitive documents have been found on non-US computers with no protection against hostile intelligence services."
- "There is a military investigation . . . in which classified material has been wrongfully disclosed using P2P."
- "Multiple organizations have ongoing investigations into disclosure of sensitive or classified material due to P2P."[2,11]

## The FTC Doesn't Heed the DHS Warning

Instead of protecting Americans and American interests, the FTC chose the path of self-preservation, regaling Congress with glowing reports about the improvements and progress made by working with LimeWire. And they would have gotten away with it but for another government agency.

Fortunately, the United States Patent and Trademark Office (USPTO), another federal agency with relevant research authority, noticed inadvertent sharing of sensitive personal, work, and government files was becoming increasingly common and dangerous. USPTO authorized a comprehensive study to determine why this supposedly solved problem was recurring. In late 2006, USPTO released a 79-page analysis of the causes of inadvertent sharing entitled *Filesharing Programs and "Technological Features to Induce Users to Share"* (also known as the *USPTO Report*).[11]

The *USPTO Report* concluded that available public data strongly suggested that the developers of file-sharing programs like LimeWire *intended* to induce or dupe users of their programs into sharing files unintentionally because many of the files thus shared would be the sort of media files that drove developers' business models and profits.

The *USPTO Report* also updated and expanded the user-interface analysis done in the 2002 study *Usability and Privacy*. It examined 2004 to 2006 versions of the LimeWire, BearShare, Kazaa, eDonkey, and Morpheus programs to determine whether their developers had removed and remediated the effect of the share-folder or search-wizard features that *Usability and Privacy* had found to cause inadvertent sharing of *My Documents* folders and subfolders. It also identified three more deceptive features in these programs: (1) inadequately disclosed redistribution features; (2) partial-uninstall features; and (3) coerced-sharing features, like LimeWire's "Individually Shared File" feature.[2]

Better yet from LimeWire's perspective, users tricked into sharing their *My Documents* folders and its subfolders would share entire *collections* of media files—all of their images, all of their videos, and their entire collections of popular music—often, many thousands of audio files. This made LimeWire's library bigger and more desirable to the marketplace and *that*, my fellow victims, is why LimeWire couldn't seem to get it right.

The *USPTO Report* should have made the FTC's collective jaw drop. Instead it was the final thread that sewed the FTC's lips shut. In painstaking, screenshot-illustrated detail, the *Report*—without ever directly criticizing the FTC—made it brutally clear that the

FTC and its staff had been duped into sheltering, praising, and working with piracy syndicates so malicious that they treated widespread breaches of national, military, governmental, corporate, and personal data as acceptable side-effects of schemes intended to trick people into inadvertently sharing entire collections of popular movies and music.

The *USPTO Report* exposed wrongdoing in late-2006-to-early-2007 that the FTC could have identified, halted, and redressed in mid-2004 had they *competently* conducted the follow-up investigation of inadvertent file-sharing demanded by many members of both houses of Congress. It showed LimeWire had been causing inadvertent sharing of sensitive personal or work files by knowingly violating its own *Code of Conduct*.

The *USPTO Report* revealed what the FTC would have discovered had they actually looked at the software. LimeWire's share-folder was even more deceptive than Kazaa's feature noted in *Usability and Privacy* in 2002. Offering the example of a LimeWire user trying to stop sharing files in her *My Music* folder, the *Report* detailed how LimeWire had turned this share-folder into a deceptive one-way ratchet:

> In short, the user is told that this is a "Save Directory"—and left to figure out that in LimeWire, "save" means "share recursively," a procedure that can repeat itself indefinitely. This is actually worse than the Kazaa share-folder feature: The user receives not even a hint that a folder selected as the "Save Directory" will be shared—much less shared recursively.
>
> Realizing that she has now become a copyright-enforcement target, the user re-opens the "Saving" menu and sees that LimeWire provides a way to correct her mistake: There is a "Use default" button below and to the right of the "Save Directory."
>
> She clicks the "Use default" button and is relieved to see that the "Save Directory" is instantly reset to the empty default "Shared" folder created by LimeWire. A user might think, "Problem solved!" But nothing has changed: LimeWire is still sharing all files stored in the user's "My Music" folder and all of its subfolders. Share-folder features like those

used by LimeWire, BearShare, Morpheus, and eDonkey exhibit a behavior that can be called "librarying": A folder shared through the share-folder feature will remain shared *even if the share-folder feature is reset to its default setting or used to select a different folder to store downloaded files.* A librarying share-folder feature is a one-way ratchet: Successive uses of it can only cause users to share *more* files and folders—never less."[2,11]

Even when pressure from the House Oversight Committee finally forced LimeWire to remove the sinister search wizards, LimeWire still perpetuated their effects. New versions of LimeWire without search wizards did nothing to halt or verify any *My-Documents*-folder sharing afflicting users upgrading from prior versions of LimeWire. If you didn't uninstall your old version and start fresh with the latest version of LimeWire, the hydrant was still open.

Though the *USPTO Report* had exposed deliberate wrongdoing by LimeWire that had caused widespread and serious threats to data security, the FTC did absolutely nothing.

As a result, on July 24, 2007 the House Oversight Committee was forced to open its *second* investigation and hearing on the causes and consequences of inadvertent file-sharing. This time, an FTC witness, Mary Engle, was sitting right beside a long-time partner at LimeWire, CEO Mark Gorton, when he begrudgingly acknowledged that LimeWire was causing even some of its most sophisticated users to inadvertently share—not just sensitive personal or work-related documents—but hundreds of *classified* government documents:

> LimeWire can be part of the solution by improving the functioning of our program. I also think companies like Tiversa can be part of this solution by providing technologies which allow notice and monitoring of the networks.
>
> *Mark Gorton, CEO LimeWire*
> *Committee on Oversight and Government Reform*
> *House of Representatives, 110th Congress, 1st Session*
> *July 24, 2007*

Tom Sydnor, the lead author of the *USPTO Report*, then testified that widespread inadvertent sharing of personal and work files had recurred in 2007 for the same reasons it had occurred in 2002: developers of programs like LimeWire had violated their own self-imposed *Code of Conduct* by deploying search-wizard and share-folder features just as deceptive as those condemned in *Usability and Privacy*.

By contrast, the July 24, 2007 testimony of the FTC witness, Mary Engle,[12] was off-topic, irrelevant, and evasive. In prepared written and oral testimony she barely acknowledged that the *USPTO Report* even existed. Nor did she address the other central topic of the hearing— the question of why inadvertent sharing of personal and work files, a problem supposedly resolved in 2003, was still recurring on a far more massive and destructive scale in 2007. Instead, acting as if all was well, she recited the FTC's efforts to work with LimeWire and other file-sharing program developers, and summarized FTC enforcement cases that had nothing to do with inadvertent file-sharing. When her evasions were criticized during questioning by the Committee, she merely stammered that the FTC was still studying the months-old *USPTO Report* and that it might bring an enforcement action based upon its conclusions.

> ...the FTC staff recommended that industry do a better job of informing consumers about the risks of P2P file sharing. Over the past 3 years, we have periodically reviewed the risk disclosures provided on major P2P software Web sites and found that these disclosures have steadily improved. We also reviewed P2P Web sites to determine if they were a source of spyware ... In July 2003, the FTC issued a consumer alert warning consumers about these risks, including the risk of inadvertently sharing sensitive files and of receiving spyware, viruses, copyright-infringing materials, and unwanted pornography.
>
> *Mary Koelbel Engle, Bureau of Consumer Protection,*
> *Federal Trade Commission*
> *Committee on Oversight and Government Reform*
> *House of Representatives, 110th Congress, 1st Session*
> *July 24, 2007*

Well, I am definitely not a technology expert and can't really offer views . . . I think the kind of attention that this hearing is putting on this issue is extremely important. The more consumers and businesses and especially Government agencies know about this problem, the more they can take steps internally to prevent further breaches.

On the side of intellectual property protection, setting aside for data security, I think we have seen the industry innovate on its own to make legal methods of downloading more available, and it is helping in that area.[13]

*Mary Koelbel Engle, Bureau of Consumer Protection,*
*Federal Trade Commission*
*Committee on Oversight and Government Reform*
*House of Representatives, 110th Congress, 1st Session*
*July 24, 2007*

Mary Engle's blasé and bureaucratic response prompted Oversight Committee Chairman Henry Waxman to raise the profound problems revealed by the *USPTO Report* and his Committee's hearing with FTC Chairman Deborah Majoras. On November 13, 2007, Chairman Majoras responded to Chairman Waxman.[2,14] She noted that as a result of the hearing, the FTC was reviewing the possibility of law enforcement action. The FTC thus admitted that its three-year partners at LimeWire might have been committing deceptive or unfair practices that had violated the FTC Act. But alas, the FTC continued to sit on the sidelines as widespread breaches of national, military, corporate, and personal data security continued. When cornered, the FTC representative rolled over like a cowering dog.

## The FTC Covering Up and Playing Dumb

That did not prevent the FTC from yet again working with LimeWire to remediate inadvertent file-sharing. Somehow Chairman Majoras had concluded that if the last attempt to work with LimeWire to remediate inadvertent file-sharing had ended in disaster and had in fact *exacerbated* inadvertent sharing, then the FTC should remediate that disaster by *continuing* to work with LimeWire to remediate a new barrage of LimeWire-caused inadvertent file sharing. As Majoras put it:

> Following this Committee's hearing in July [of 2007], the FTC staff began a dialogue with the [file-sharing] industry to explore ways to do just that. The staff will *continue* to examine the major US P2P file-sharing programs and *work with* their distributors on enhancing safeguards and warnings. The staff will also work with industry to better educate consumers about the risks of inadvertent file sharing.[14]

Chairman Majoras repeated the same, failed experiment by working with LimeWire to reduce inadvertent sharing by replacing LimeWire's now-discredited *Code of Conduct* with a new set of completely optional *Voluntary Best Practices for P2P File-Sharing Software Developers To Implement To Protect Users Against Inadvertently Sharing Personal or Sensitive Data.*[2,15]

Predictably, the FTC's renewed work-with-LimeWire scheme perpetuated inadvertent sharing for two more years. During 2009, the FTC's attempt to work with LimeWire to remediate a problem that LimeWire was obviously *trying* to cause failed miserably. Stories about widespread and dangerous episodes of LimeWire users inadvertently sharing sensitive personal or work files kept coming to light.

For example, April 9, 2009, *CBS News* reported that inadvertent file-sharing had disclosed to Iran the plans for Marine One, President Obama's helicopter.[2,16] *Today Investigates* also reported that citizens of New York State were inadvertently sharing over 150,000 tax returns on peer-to-peer file-sharing networks.[2,17]

On July 29, 2009, after more than seven years of FTC incompetence, the House Oversight Committee had to hold its third hearing on inadvertent file-sharing, *Inadvertent File-Sharing: How It Endangers Citizens and Jeopardizes National Security.*[2,18] Chairman Edolphus Towns opened the hearing by condemning

LimeWire's long history of deliberate wrongdoing that had been allowed to continue because the "Federal Trade Commission took a see-no-evil, hear-no-evil approach to the file-sharing software industry."[2,18]

This House Oversight Committee's hearing *again* documented that more, dire, widespread compromises of national, military, corporate, and personal data were *still* being caused regularly—not as a result of inadvertent file-sharing generally—but as a result of inadvertent sharing of sensitive documents caused by past-and-then-current versions of the LimeWire file-sharing program. The cited examples of recent LimeWire leaks were nothing short of appalling.

> "The Social Security numbers and family information for every Master Sergeant in the Army have been found on LimeWire. The medical records of some 24,000 patients of a Texas hospital were inadvertently released. Most of the files are still available on LimeWire. FBI files, including civilian photographs of an alleged mafia hit man, were leaked while he was on trial and before he was convicted. We were astonished to discover that a security breach involving the Secret Service resulted in the leak of a file on LimeWire containing a safe house location for the First Family."[2,18]

Once again, the FTC's work-with-LimeWire approach had perpetuated the problem, sheltered the culpable, and endangered millions of American consumers and businesses whom the FTC was supposed to protect.

The Oversight hearing revealed that the FTC's partners at LimeWire were violating their *Voluntary Best Practices* just as badly as they had once violated their Code of Conduct.

Jesus wept.

Mr. Sydnor, the lead author of the *USPTO Report*, then published *Inadvertent File-Sharing Reinvented: The Dangerous Design of LimeWire 5* in 2009.[2,19] This new study analyzed the design of

LimeWire 5 and whether it complied with the *Voluntary Best Practices* that the FTC had helped LimeWire to develop and legitimize. It concluded that LimeWire 5 was a dangerous, defective program that violated most of the critical obligations imposed by DCIA's *Voluntary Best Practices*:

> "Concerned officials should *not* risk their own reputations by trusting LimeWire—again. By default, LimeWire 5 is a dangerous program that seems *intended* to make it too easy for consumers to share *all* of the files stored in their *My Documents* folder and all of its subfolders—including their entire collections of family photos, home movies, scanned medical, identifying, and business documents, popular music, and even, perhaps, *all* of their documents. Moreover, LimeWire 5 can be this dangerous *because* it violates *eight* of the most critical obligations imposed by DCIA's LimeWire-drafted *Voluntary Best Practices*.[20] LimeWire appears to take self-regulation no more seriously in 2009 than "it did in 2003."[2]

> You call for regulation, saying that Congress is the only entity with the power to step in here. I think it has already been established that there are hundreds of companies from outside US borders that we do not have legal jurisdiction over, so it is going to take more than congressional enforcement, new laws, to try to solve this problem.
>
> If I were you—and obviously I am not—I would feel more than a shade of guilt at this point for having made the laptop a dangerous weapon against the security of the United States. The 9/11 Commission reported that the central failure was a failure of imagination. Mr. Gorton, you, in particular, seem to lack imagination for how your company and its product can be deliberately misused by evildoers against this country.[13]
>
> *Representative Jim Cooper, Democrat, Tennessee*
> *Committee on Oversight and Government Reform*
> *House of Representatives, 110th Congress, 1st Session*
> *July 24, 2007*

## Frankenstein Goes on a Rampage

Six years after the FTC began working with LimeWire on improved disclosures and *Best Practices* that were supposed to reduce and remediate inadvertent sharing, the House Oversight Committee's *third* hearing had proven that inadvertent sharing of sensitive personal and work files caused by LimeWire was *still* rampant and that the FTC's two-year effort to work with LimeWire to develop *Voluntary Best Practices* had failed.

It became obvious that the FTC's strategy of see-no-evil, hear-no-evil had been not only a failure, but dangerous. Their strategy of zipped lip silence was crumbling as well. When silence didn't work, the FTC decided to make a scene in an overacting attempt to cover up years of horrible past behavior.

For their third magic trick to divert the spotlight from its serial incompetence, the FTC put on a show of aggressive and overreaching enforcement of the FTC Act—not against its long-time partners at LimeWire—but against socially productive businesses that its LimeWire partners had harmed.

This is a chapter right out of the political playbook titled, "Create a diversion/find a scapegoat."

- In January of 2010, the FTC published a misleading guide to file-sharing programs entitled *Peer-to-Peer File Sharing: A Guide for Business.*[2,21] In it, the FTC concealed nearly a decade of studies and evidence showing that programs like LimeWire had been designed to trick users into inadvertent sharing sensitive files. Instead, the FTC blamed inadvertent sharing on the mistakes of program users: "People who use P2P file sharing software can inadvertently share files. They might accidentally choose to share drives or folders that contain sensitive information . . ."

  The FTC did not explain how someone could fairly be said to choose anything "accidentally." This inane phrase succeeds in avoiding more accurate, legally relevant terms like duped or deceived . . .
- In January of 2010, the FTC sent out non-public inquiry letters, then issued a public press release alleging that the FTC Act *had been violated*

by up to 100 of LimeWire's many corporate victims—including LabMD. According to the FTC, widespread, recurring episodes of inadvertent sharing via LimeWire resulted from the unfair data security practices of LimeWire's innumerable *victims*, not the-ever-changing array of deceptive features deployed by LimeWire.

- Several months later, the FTC quietly sent a letter that terminated its 2007 investigation of, and its working partnership with, LimeWire.[2,22] Predictably, that letter ended with the FTC reciting the same caveat upon which its working partnership with LimeWire had begun: "This [closing of our investigation] is not to be construed as a determination that a violation of the law did not occur." After six years, many published studies and many public hearings, the FTC thus claimed it just did not know whether its longtime partners at LimeWire LLC had violated the FTC Act by committing deceptive practices that caused inadvertent sharing.

In late 2010, pursuant to a court order, the developers of LimeWire were forced to acknowledge with a post on their web site that all prior versions of their program were intended to induce mass piracy and so likely to cause inadvertent file-sharing and that they should be immediately uninstalled.

LIMEWIRE IS UNDER A COURT ORDER DATED OCTOBER 26, 2010 TO STOP DISTRIBUTING THE LIMEWIRE SOFTWARE . . . IF YOU HAVE DOWNLOADED LIMEWIRE SOFTWARE IN THE PAST, FILES ON YOUR PERSONAL COMPUTERS CONTAINING PRIVATE OR SENSITIVE INFORMATION MAY HAVE BEEN INADVERTENTLY SHARED AND YOU SHOULD USE YOUR BEST EFFORTS TO REMOVE THE SOFTWARE FROM YOUR COMPUTERS.[23]

The FTC's six-year working partnership with LimeWire ended with the FTC claiming while it still had no idea whether its longtime LimeWire partners had ever violated the FTC Act, but it *was sure* the FTC Act had been violated by LimeWire's innumerable corporate victims.

Even more alarming, I got a call from Bob Boback on Wednesday night that he had found on the peer-to-peer net the entire Pentagon's secret backbone network infrastructure diagram, including the server and IP addresses, with password transcripts for Pentagon's secret network servers, the Department of Defense employees' contact information, secure sockets layer instructions, and certificates allowing access to the disclosing contractors' IT systems, and ironically, a letter from OMB which explicitly talks about the risks associated with P2P file-sharing networks.[13]

*General Wesley Clark*
*Committee on Oversight and Government Reform*
*House of Representatives, 110th Congress, 1st Session*
*July 24, 2007*

Fortunately for the targeted LimeWire victims, another FTC blunder made its final, cynical attempt to shift the blame backfire in the most appropriate way possible—*inadvertently* . . .

In 2011 the FTC filed *Federal Trade Commission v. FrostWire LLC*, a public complaint against the developers of a P2P file-sharing program called FrostWire, alleging that in two versions of their program, the developers had deployed different deceptive features that could cause users to share files inadvertently.[2,24]

- The FTC complaint alleged that a version of FrostWire for Android smartphones contained a deceptive feature in its setup process that would scan the user's phone for media files and share them by default. In other words, it contained precisely the sort of media-files-only search wizard the *USPTO Report* had warned that developers might use to replace the previous search wizards that had caused inadvertent sharing of both media and non-media files.
- The complaint alleged that a desktop version of FrostWire contained a deceptive Individually Shared Files feature that could cause users to share downloaded files even though the Sharing interface in FrostWire would show *no* files or folders were being shared.

Unfortunately for the FTC, the FrostWire program is an open-source clone of LimeWire. Materially indistinguishable versions of the features that the FTC condemned in its 2011 *FrostWire* enforcement action also were deployed in LimeWire throughout the 2004-2010 period when the FTC was praising and working with LimeWire's developers.

This exonerates LabMD from wrongdoing.

The attack on this "Clone of LimeWire" confirmed by default the FTC's partners at LimeWire had been violating the FTC Act from at least 2004 through 2010. And that the FTC either knew or should have known LimeWire was committing illegal, deceptive practices that caused inadvertent file-sharing.

By the time the FTC started their non-public inquiry in 2010,[25] a LabMD employee had installed LimeWire on a LabMD computer, making one file, and only one file, vulnerable because of LimeWire's corrupt business tactics, Tiversa's monitoring technology on steroids, and the FTC's utter lack of ethics—not because LabMD had unfair data security practices that violated the FTC Act. The FTC had made itself complicit in the deceptive practices perpetrated by its working partners at LimeWire.

Consequently, the FTC enforcement action against the deceptive practices of FrostWire finally proved conclusively that the FTC is incompetent and corrupt: Throughout the six-year period in which the FTC had been working with LimeWire, it had been assisting, praising, and defending a corporation that was simultaneously causing inadvertent file-sharing by deploying deceptive features outlawed by the same FTC Act that the FTC was supposed to enforce. By 2010, the FTC thus had no right to claim that any private business had acted unfairly by failing to defend itself against the deceptive practices of LimeWire that the FTC itself had recklessly—and then culpably—been enabling and defending for six years. But it decided to anyway, playing the sinister projection game of deflection by going after innocent American businesses.

In an effort to conceal their incompetence, the FTC continued to lie to the government and public. By attacking LabMD, draining us through their harassing and overreaching investigation, and perhaps bullying other companies into signing consent decrees, the FTC has been unfair and deceptive. By attacking the victims of P2P malware in order to bury their incompetence in preventing great damage, the FTC lied to the world. In doing so, they compromised national security and placed us all in grave danger. We will see how long the FTC will continue to bully whistleblower LabMD into silence and submission.

Not surprisingly the FTC continued to play the only card left in its hand.

From: Alain Sheer
Sent: July 22, 2013, 3:58:29 PM
To: Phil Carpenter
Subject: FTC staff recommendation

Dear Mr. Carpenter,
Commission staff has recommended that the Commission issue a complaint against LabMD alleging that the company's information security practices violate Section 5 of the FTC Act. If you would like an opportunity to submit the company's views in writing to the Commission or request meetings with Commissioners before the Commission acts on the recommendation, you should contact Janis Kestenbaum an attorney advisor to Chairwoman Ramirez, immediately.

Alain Sheer
Division of Identity Protection
Bureau of Consumer Protection
Federal Trade Commission

When we did not contact Ms. Kestenbaum, we received this:

From: Janis Kestenbaum
Sent: Monday, July 22, 2013 05:53 PM
To: Phil Carpenter
Subject: Meeting with FTC Commissioners

Mr. Carpenter:
Below I've listed the contact information for the legal advisors to all the FTC Commissioners. The Chairwoman, who I work for, could meet with LabMD the week of August 5. That week may work as well with the other Commissioners, but please be in touch directly with their respective advisors.

Also, as a point of information, outside counsel often make written submissions before meetings with Commissioners to explain why they believe a complaint should not be issued. You are free to provide something in writing in addition to, or instead of, meeting with the Commissioners. But a written submission is by no means required—I just wanted to make sure you are aware of the option.


Chairwoman Ramirez
Advisor: Janis Kestenbaum
Commissioner Brill
Advisor: Shaundra Watson
Commissioner Ohlhausen
Advisor: Anna Davis
Commissioner Wright
Advisor: Beth Delaney

Regards,
Janis


Janis Claire Kestenbaum
Senior Legal Advisor | Office of Chairwoman Ramirez
Federal Trade Commission

We remained silent, only to receive this:

From: Janis Kestenbaum
Sent: Thursday, July 25, 2013 1:12 PM
To: Phil Carpenter
Subject: Re: Meeting with FTC Commissioners

Mr. Carpenter,
Touching base to see if LabMD is interested in arranging meetings with FTC Commissioners. If so, I recommend that you reach out to the legal advisors below (and me, for the Chairwoman) immediately. The week of August 5 works for the Chairwoman and I expect it works for the other Commissioners as well though you would need to confirm that with the individuals below.

If you have any questions about the process, please don't hesitate to let me know.

Regards,
Janis

So we replied with this:

From: Phil Carpenter
Sent: Thursday, July 25, 2013 1:16:39 PM
To: Janis Kestenbaum
Subject: RE: Meeting with FTC Commissioners

Janis ~ LabMD is evaluating all of its options. In order to decide the best course of action, we need to see the recommendation and the draft complaint. Can you please forward them by the close of business by Friday. It is impossible to have an intelligent conversation or write a letter without information regarding the basis of the FTC's recommendation. Please let me know if the FTC will provide us with this information.

Philip Carpenter, Esq.
General Counsel for LabMD, Inc.

Phil explained to me the government agency speak:
"It's in their operational manual. It actually happens all the time in government work. The Commissioners are quasi-legislative, so

it's actually a checks and balance thing to prevent the agency from having too much power and setting the agenda. I think it's a waste of time. They won't tell you the truth and will just go through the motions. I say skip it."

I skipped it. We really did not expect the FTC to reply to our question. Imagine our bemusement when we received this email from Alain.

From: Alain Sheer
Sent: Tuesday, July 30, 2013, 4:22:16 PM
To: Phil Carpenter
Cc: Janis Kestenbaum
Subject: documents re: Commission office meetings

Dear Mr. Carpenter:
We are providing the attached draft complaint and draft notice order (the "draft documents") in response to your request to have these documents to prepare for meetings with Commission offices. We are providing the draft documents solely to facilitate such meetings. The draft documents are non-public documents and are subject to change. In providing the draft documents to you, we reserve all applicable rights and privileges.

Alain
Non-Public

## RESPONDENT'S SECURITY PRACTICES

At all relevant times, respondent engaged in a number of practices that, taken together, failed to provide reasonable and appropriate security for personal information on its computer networks. Among other things, respondent:

(a) did not develop, implement, or maintain a comprehensive information security program to protect consumers' personal information, including sensitive medical information. Thus, for example, employees were allowed to send emails with such information to their personal email accounts without using readily available measures to protect the information from unauthorized disclosure;

(b) did not use readily available measures to identify commonly known or reasonably foreseeable security risks and vulnerabilities on its networks. By not using measures such as penetration tests, for example, respondent could not adequately assess the extent of the risks and vulnerabilities of its networks;

(c) did not use adequate measures to prevent employees from accessing personal information not needed to perform their jobs;

(d) did not adequately train employees to safeguard personal information;

(e) did not require employees, or other users with remote access to the networks, to use common authentication-related security measures, such as periodically changing passwords, prohibiting the use of the same password across applications and programs, or using two-factor authentication;

(f) did not maintain and update operating systems of computers and other devices on its networks. For example, on some computers respondent used operating systems that were unsupported by the vendor, making it unlikely that the systems would be updated to address newly discovered vulnerabilities; and

(g) did not employ readily available measures to prevent or detect unauthorized access to personal information on its computer networks. For example, respondent did not use appropriate measures to prevent employees from installing on computers applications or materials that were not needed to perform their jobs or adequately maintain or review records of activity on its networks. As a result respondent did not detect the installation or use of an unauthorized file sharing application on its networks.

11. Respondent could have corrected its security failures at relatively low cost using readily available security measures.

12. Consumers have no way of independently knowing about respondent's security failures and could not reasonably avoid possible harms from such failures, including identity theft, medical identity theft, and other harms, such as disclosure of sensitive, private medical information.

## PEER-TO-PEER FILE SHARING APPLICATIONS

13. Peer-to-peer ("P2P") file sharing applications are often used to share music, videos, pictures, and other materials between persons and entities using computers with the same or a compatible P2P application ("P2P network").

14. P2P applications allow a user to both designate files on the user's computer that are available to others on a P2P network and search for and access designated files on other computers on the P2P network.

15. After a designated file is shared with another computer, it can be passed along among other P2P network users without being downloaded again from the original source. Generally, once shared, a file cannot with certainty be removed permanently from a P2P network.

16. Since at least 2005, security professionals and others (including the Commission through its business education materials) have warned that P2P applications present a risk that users will inadvertently share files on P2P networks.

## SECURITY INCIDENTS

17. In May 2008 a third party informed respondent that its June 2007 insurance aging report (the "P2P insurance aging file") was available on a popular P2P network through LimeWire, a P2P file sharing application.

18. After receiving the May 2008 notice that the P2P insurance aging file was available through LimeWire, respondent determined that:

   (a) LimeWire had been downloaded and installed on a computer used by respondent's billing department manager (the "billing computer");

   (b) at that point in time, the P2P insurance aging file was one of hundreds of files that were designated for sharing from the billing computer using Lime Wire; and

   (c) Lime Wire had been installed on the billing computer no later than 2006.

19. The P2P insurance aging file contains personal information about approximately 9,300 consumers, including names, dates of birth, SSNs, CPT codes, and, in many instances, health insurance company names, addresses, and policy numbers.

20. Respondent had no business need for Lime Wire and removed it from the billing computer in May 2008, after receiving notice.

21. In October 2012, the Sacramento, California Police Department found more than 35 Day Sheets and a small number of copied checks in the possession of individuals who pleaded no contest to state charges of identity theft. These Day Sheets include personal information, such as names and SSNs, of at least 500 consumers in different states. Many of these consumers were not included in the P2P insurance aging file, and some of the information post-dates the P2P insurance aging file. A number of the SSNs in the Day Sheets are being, or have been, used by people with different names, which may indicate that the SSNs have been used by identity thieves.

## VIOLATION OF THE FTC ACT

22. As set forth in Paragraphs 6 through 21, respondent's failure to employ reasonable and appropriate measures to prevent unauthorized access to personal information, including dates of birth, SSNs, medical test codes, and health information, caused, or is likely to cause, substantial injury to consumers that is not offset by countervailing benefits to consumers or competition and is not reasonably avoidable by consumers. This practice was, and is, an unfair act or practice.

Proceedings on the charges asserted against the respondent named in this complaint will be held before an Administrative Law Judge of the Federal Trade Commission, under Part 3 of the Commission's Rules of Practice, 16 C.F.R. Part 3 (2012). A copy of Part 3 of the Commission's Rules is enclosed with this complaint, and the Rules are also accessible on the Commission Website at FTC Rules (16 CFR Parts 0-999).

This is not the end of the story, this is just where we hit pause and catch our breath.

While writing this last page, I received Bill Barnett's resignation. I am happy he found a green pasture. But there are no regrets here. If not for this whole extraordinary experience, I would never have met such interesting, brilliant, and, yes, sometimes powerful people. I would never have learned firsthand that with creative tactics you *can* fight city hall. I would have never had the honor of communicating this story to so many other Americans who love our country. And everything I have experienced fuels my fire to fight.

The story has transcended my own personal troubles. It's clear that a pandemic spread of bureaucrats that place their job security over and above national security are putting our country at grave risk. What started with a phone call from Pennsylvania has turned into a call for action. I can't control fate, but I can control what I do with the cards I am dealt, and I refuse to be a victim. I am a missionary, a warrior, and a survivor.

I will never give in.

You probably already figured that out.

*"When you can't make them see the light, make them feel the heat."*

—Ronald Reagan

# CHAPTER 29
# Professional Bullies

## August 29, 2013

The day before the final print files were being sent for approval the FTC filed suit against LabMD and, of course, put out a one-sided press release. It makes one wonder if they are rushing to beat my book release date. Today I run around finishing this latest addition before the window closes to make my print deadline. In their shameless and desperate attempt to justify their own meaningless and damaging existence, what they didn't say is as telling as what they did say. These professional bullies are subjective, devious, and manipulative, which adds up to dishonest. Their release and my response:

**For Release:** 08/29/2013
## FTC Files Complaint Against LabMD for Failing to Protect Consumers' Privacy
### Commission Alleges Exposure of Medical and Other Sensitive Information Over Peer-to-Peer Network

The Federal Trade Commission filed a complaint against medical testing laboratory LabMD, Inc. alleging that the company failed to reasonably protect the security of consumers' personal data, including medical information. The complaint alleges that in two separate incidents, LabMD collectively exposed the personal information of approximately 10,000 consumers.

The complaint alleges that LabMD billing information for over 9,000 consumers was found on a peer-to-peer (P2P) file-sharing network and then, in 2012, LabMD documents containing sensitive personal information of at least 500 consumers were found in the hands of identity thieves. *BREACH OF PUBLIC TRUST #1: The FTC knows it will not look good to the public that they are moving in 2013 about 9000 patients that were taken in 2008… so they "forget to mention" it. Futhermore, the 500 patient's data from Sacramento was taken no later than 2009. These were two separate incidents and are unrelated. The FTC is trying to mislead everyone to think these are connected. The Sacramento fiasco was not a P2P issue. More wordsmith trickery as they use "Alleges exposure". This is an ego vendetta because I won't sit like a good boy.*

The case is part of an ongoing effort by the Commission to ensure that companies take reasonable and appropriate measures to protect consumers' personal data. *BREACH OF PUBLIC TRUST #2: In their propaganda piece they allow the public to assume that the FTC has a definition of standards. They also fail to mention their incompetence started this whole mess in the first place.*

LabMD conducts laboratory tests on samples that physicians obtain from consumers and then provide to the company for testing. The company, which is based in Atlanta, performs medical testing for consumers around the country. The Commission's complaint alleges that LabMD failed to take reasonable and appropriate measures to prevent unauthorized disclosure of sensitive consumer data—including health information—it held. Among other things, the complaint alleges that the company:

- did not implement or maintain a comprehensive data security program to protect this information; *BREACH OF PUBLIC TRUST #3: This gives the impression LabMD had no adequate program.*
- did not use readily available measures to identify commonly known or reasonably foreseeable security risks and vulnerabilities to this information; *BREACH OF PUBLIC TRUST #4: The FTC is now getting desperate expecting us all to see into the future with their new invented legal standard "reasonably foreseeable".*
- did not use adequate measures to prevent employees from accessing personal information not needed to perform their jobs; *BREACH OF PUBLIC TRUST #5: Snowden walked out with a thumb drive as the technologically illiterate lawyers at the FTC keep slinging it.*
- did not adequately train employees on basic security practices; and *BREACH OF PUBLIC TRUST #6: Here they go again with their sneaky word "adequate".*

- did not use readily available measures to prevent and detect unauthorized access to personal information. *BREACH OF PUBLIC TRUST #7: The FTC sat on the Sacramento information for months and still refuses to give us any background information. They may not have asked the Sacramento police for information as they don't care about the patient's data nearly as much as LabMD does.*

The complaint alleges that a LabMD spreadsheet containing insurance billing information was found on a P2P network. The spreadsheet contained sensitive personal information for more than 9,000 consumers, including names, Social Security numbers, dates of birth, health insurance provider information, and standardized medical treatment codes. Misuse of such information can lead to identity theft and medical identity theft, and can also harm consumers by revealing private medical information. *BREACH OF PUBLIC TRUST #8: The FTC fails to mention that the vulnerability was due to their incompetence that they were charged to oversee as they placed their reputation ahead of protecting the public from harm.*

P2P software is commonly used to share music, videos, and other materials with other users of compatible software. The software allows users to choose files to make available to others, but also creates a significant security risk that files with sensitive data will be inadvertently shared. Once a file has been made available on a P2P network and downloaded by another user, it can be shared by that user across the network even if the original source of the file is no longer connected. *BREACH OF PUBLIC TRUST #9: The FTC fails to mention that the software is malware, that they knew this and deflecting attention to this fact by attacking those that diagnose cancer.*

"The unauthorized exposure of consumers' personal data puts them at risk," said Jessica Rich, Director of the FTC's Bureau of Consumer Protection. "The FTC is committed to ensuring that firms who collect that data use reasonable and appropriate security measures to prevent it from falling into the hands of identity thieves and other unauthorized users." *BREACH OF PUBLIC TRUST #10: The FTC is not committed enough to analyze the software of known corrupt software vendors or admit they deceived Congress.*

The complaint also alleges that in 2012 the Sacramento, California Police Department found LabMD documents in the possession of identity thieves. These documents contained personal information, including names, Social Security numbers, and in some instances, bank account information, of at least 500 consumers. The complaint alleges that a number of these Social Security numbers are being or have been used by more than one person with different names, which may be an indicator of identity theft. *BREACH OF PUBLIC TRUST #11: The FTC sat on this information for months putting their blood thirsty hunger to attack a cancer detection center ahead of protecting the patients whose data was found in Sacramento. And what exactly does "may be an indicator" mean? If they knew damages had occurred they would scream that fact from on high. They have told LabMD nothing. We had to fight them for the list of patients. The FTC uses patient data as leverage but does nothing to protect them.*

The complaint includes a proposed order against LabMD that would prevent future violations of law by requiring the company to implement a comprehensive information security program, and have that program evaluated every two years by an independent, certified security professional for the next 20 years. The order would also require the company to provide notice to consumers whose information LabMD has reason to believe was or could have been accessible to unauthorized persons and to consumers' health insurance companies. *BREACH OF PUBLIC TRUST #12: LabMD already alerted the Sacramento patients and the FTC has never given any proof to LabMD or the public that the 9000 patient's data is vulnerable or damaged. Notice they never use the word "breach" anywhere in this press release. Manipulative assumptions replace truth and transparency. Proper words and truth are missing from the FTC.*

The Commission vote to issue the administrative complaint and notice order was 4-0. *BREACH OF PUBLIC TRUST #13: While I expect such gamesmanship from Commissioners Ramirez and Brill, the laziness and cronyism by Ohlhausen and Wright is infuriating. These are complicit exposed political people and their credibility lies in a pile of ash.*

Because LabMD has, in the course of the Commission's investigation, broadly asserted that documents provided to the Commission contain confidential business information, the Commission is not publicly releasing its complaint until the process for resolving any claims of confidentiality is completed and items in the complaint deemed confidential, if any, are redacted. *BREACH OF PUBLIC TRUST #14: And if they did release the complaint their press release would be seen as the biggest ego response trumping legal professionalism in years.*

**NOTE:** The Commission issues an administrative complaint when it has "reason to believe" that the law has been or is being violated, and it appears to the Commission that a proceeding is in the public interest. The issuance of the administrative complaint marks the beginning of a proceeding in which the allegations will be tried in a formal hearing before an administrative law judge. *BREACH OF PUBLIC TRUST #15: The FTC knows that Judge Duffey would most likely be their Federal Judge and they don't want to go there, so they will continue their sham justice and disgusting attack by marching us into the administrative courts, where they get to mock the Constitution by having the option of rejecting the court's ruling.*

The Federal Trade Commission works for consumers to prevent fraudulent, deceptive, and unfair business practices and to provide information to help spot, stop, and avoid them. To file a complaint in English or Spanish, visit the FTC's online Complaint Assistant or call 1-877-FTC-HELP (1-877-382-4357). The FTC enters complaints into Consumer Sentinel, a secure, online database available to more than 2,000 civil and criminal law enforcement agencies in the U.S. and abroad. The FTC's website provides free information on a variety of consumer topics. Like the FTC on Facebook, follow us on Twitter, and subscribe to press releases for the latest FTC news and resources. *BREACH OF PUBLIC TRUST #16: The FTC also places their reputation before the public ahead of their mandate assigned by Congress. Centralized power results in tyranny and the FTC is tyrannical.*

You have read the book. You already know how the FTC works. This is just more of the same. Raping and pillaging innocent people, allowing the public to be vulnerable, then attacking small business so they aren't held accountable for their failure to carry out Congress's intent, these deflection tactics are certainly not as low as they are willing to go to survive. This crowd has no boundaries, barriers, or depths to their fight for survival. I call on the US House of Representatives Oversight Committee to rein in their attack dog and punish them for harming and endangering the innocent.

And now another new beginning . . . the lawsuit. Stay tuned for more amoral behavior by government agencies. When being attacked in the night it is best to scream as loud as possible. Remember, to this very day, the FTC, Tiversa and Dartmouth have never told us the file is anywhere else other than in their possession. Concern for the consumer and truth go missing.

*"Now this is not the end. It is not even the beginning of the end.*
*But it is, perhaps, the end of the beginning."*

—Winston Churchill

# Fathers Know Best: The Wisdom in Respecting Our Founding Fathers

I am a changed man. I have learned a few things. I would like to share them here.

I don't for one minute believe that Jon Leibowitz, Julie Brill, Alain Sheer, Dana Rosenfeld, and the rest of the "team" stroll into their offices thinking they get paid to torture and bully people. Quite the contrary, I suspect they walk into their offices patting themselves on the back for helping save the world. The insulated are clueless.

But how do some of us get this way? Why does this dynamic occur time and time again? Why do they keep their power? How can they be stopped? It seemed like psychological warfare and survival to me. As a student of history, I looked back to tyranny and torture . . . two words that impress but may not be fully understood.

The Merriam-Webster definition of *tyranny*[1] includes: "Oppressive power . . . *esp:* oppressive power exerted[2] by government . . ." and "a rigorous[3] condition imposed by some outside agency or force . . ."

As this FTC absurdity continues to morph into a "rigorous condition," I'm not the least bit surprised. The fact that it is happening to me is continually dumbfounding.

*Understanding* helps me to mentally cope. I had to figure out what makes all these bureaucrats, lawyers, and judges act in concert with a process that's so against the foundation of fairness, integrity, and justice that our country is founded on?

## Instruments in this Orchestra of Tyranny

They went to school, they worked hard, they got caught up in their careers, they joined the machine (be it a big corporation, government, media, or academia), and then they got swept up in the power and sheer mass of it all. They justified their actions with rationalizations such as "this is how it is here" and "if I help one small defenseless person, then it's all worthwhile"—or whatever they say to themselves to keep their blinders on. This type of arrogance—*regardless of party affiliation or political persuasion*—is a fertile breeding ground for tyranny as the lack of character combined with the quest for power overcomes reason. Tyranny happens when people, organizations, or governments become drunk with power and believe they are right. Our Founding Fathers knew this better than anybody *because they lived through tyranny*. Most of us in western culture have it pretty damn good, so we don't "get it." Many appeared asleep at the wheel until we recently discovered that Big Brother is reading all our "stuff". You don't know what you got until it's gone, right?

## Intent of Our Founding Fathers

If their intent was to destroy tyranny, which was the better strategy: trying to rehabilitate the corrupt (of which there's an endless supply) or putting up barriers to entry? Barriers to entry constitutes the smarter move. That's why our Founding Fathers brilliantly and proactively split the government into the three branches—Executive, Judicial, and Legislative—creating separate entities. Why? So power would not be concentrated in one place. So the minority would have protection from the pounding power of the majority. So the centralization of power would be impossible to attain. Our Founding Fathers set up these barriers to entry to protect us from the king, the dictator, the zealot, the religious extremists, and the future Hitlers of the world. For our own safety and future it's imperative that we *understand and embrace* that intent.

Our Founding Fathers didn't stop there. To make the climb even steeper for governments to overpower and harass the people, our Founding Fathers took the Legislative branch and split it in two, creating the Senate and the House of Representatives. Taking a dim view of humans trying to centralize power, they seemed to understand all ruling classes had a mighty power lust requiring lots of pushback. Their message to anyone who wanted all the power was this: *We won't risk this rare historical opportunity to escape your heavy hands merely hoping you will "get it." We doubt you will, so we will build barriers to prevent tyranny.*

America is still a rather young country with a uniquely structured government. While freedom is a given—an inalienable right—it's still a delicate proposition, as the world's history tells us. I contend that our Founding Fathers brilliantly understood that too much concentrated power anywhere within the government was to be avoided at all costs. The enemy is the centralization of power itself.

Has this intention been forgotten? Yes.

Given my recent "dancing" with the Devil Inside the Beltway, the question burned inside me: How could my country, built on such profound ideals, morph into this current state of affairs where these government-sanctioned tactics smack our Founding Fathers in the face?

Of all the ugly experiences *I've* faced, the most startling was the cold indifference and machine-like movement of those employed by government agencies. Judging by their monotone voices and ashen faces, the principle "innocent until proven guilty" seemed to be the last thing on their minds. Their behavior begs the question, "What on earth makes them okay with oppressive operating procedures? What makes them tick?"

To learn why my interrogators took part in this inquisition, I researched the motives behind their actions.

## Torture and Tyranny

This may be surprising, but for at least three thousand years, torture was legal. In *The History of Torture*, Brian Innes points out that torture "was a part of most legal codes in Europe and the Far East. There is no mention of torture in the Babylonian or Jewish systems of laws, but there is evidence that the Assyrians and Egyptians made use of it."

In *The Instruments of Torture* by Michael Kerrigan, the author wrote:

> ... Down the centuries, regimes and institutions have developed means of torture far more sophisticated and systematic than a simple beating. This mystification of brutality has profound implications. It allows torturers to believe they are acting not out of base cruelty, but *disinterested propriety*. The idea of impersonality is central to this particular vision. The Spanish Inquisition and the Soviet KGB, for example, employed torture for what they considered the *loftiest of motives*... the Soviet 'psychiatrists' who, equating dissident views with mental instability, dosed their 'patients' with state-of-the-science, mind-tormenting drugs. The priests who served the Inquisition believed they were not motivated by personal rancor but simply acting for the general good of God, His Church, Catholic society, and even their victims. *Hence the hooded anonymity of the torturer, and the quiet-spoken, scholarly manner of the inquisitor himself.*[4] (my emphasis)

What a perfect description of the FTC. Hooded anonymity. Quiet-spoken with the scholarly manner of the inquisitionist himself. Surely this could only occur in the past, right? Certainly that was centuries ago and we've evolved, right? *Wrong.*

In a modern-day example, Kerrigan reported:

> In 1989, the American nun Sister Diana Ortiz was seized by security agents in Guatemala. She later told a Washington congressional committee that she was 'lowered into a pit where inured women, children, and men writhed and moaned, and the dead decayed, under swarms of rats.' Such a scene is a waking nightmare, almost artistically contrived,

its impact residing more in its power to unsettle and unhinge than in any physical pain involved.[4]

Torturers truly regarded themselves as strong administrators of the greater good. They were consciously skilled and knew exactly what they were doing. Their eerily familiar pattern of torture wasn't so new after all: It seems these actions are also in the playbook of the Federal Trade Commission and Department of Justice. However, having physical tools of torture pulled out of their sandbox, they employ a wide variety of psychological tools.

- Sense and exploit the vulnerable.
- Maintain a one-sided power relationship with the victim.
- Orchestrate periods of agony and respite.
- Tease out the drama.
- Carefully craft the narrative.
- Get information surrendered.
- Use them as an example to anyone else who might be tempted into rebellion.
- Demonstrate the government's authority.

These tactics are clearly in the patterns of attacks waged against me by the FTC.

- Broad, long, and unclear request letters
- Circling and confusing tactics
- False show of concern
- Threats of impending litigation
- Monotone voice like an old, lifeless professor
- Lingering stony silence and intentionally selected words
- Attempts to trip us up with questions aimed to box us in
- Slow response times meant to unnerve us so we'd pay the ransom
- Show of consent decrees to see what others before us have succumbed to

If the three branches of government continue to allow the FTC and other government agencies to run amok playing these thinly veiled games, they will become a mockery—*if people don't wake up to their tactics and stop them. We must force Congress to stop allowing this to happen. Nothing makes Congress crazier than ringing telephones coming at them from all directions. Seriously, start calling their offices. It makes them crazy.*

## They Congratulate Themselves

As bureaucrats run around DC thinking they're saving the world, the opposite is often true. These self-righteous cowards are regulatory oncologists administering government "chemotherapy."

Like medicinal chemotherapy, government chemotherapy is toxic to both good and bad targets. Always arguing they are strapped for funds, regulatory agents sacrifice the good to ensnare or intimidate the bad . . . and they are just fine with that. Circumventing due process, they wear you down *via* the process. Our complicit judicial system allows them to snoop around for any reason, so don't look to the courts for your rescue. For the few that have survived the uphill climb to the Supreme Court, the Court has ruled that administrative subpoenas may be issued even out of official curiosity. In the real world, judges are loath to disagree with the Feds. Unless you have dotted and crossed all letters, possess a beyond rock solid case, are flush with time and cash, and won the judge lottery, you are going to lose. So there you have it, legislative, judicial, and psychological warfare wrapped up in one convenient package, and it's just another day inside the beltway, so don't expect anyone there to be shocked.

## The Walls Separating the Branches of Government Are Crumbling

Former FTC Commissioner J. Thomas Rosch said, "The FTC is accountable to all three branches of the US Government, and all three branches have been finger pointing toward each other.

Commissioners are appointed (and can be reappointed) by the President. Commissioners are confirmed by the Senate and the Commission engages in rulemaking on issues assigned by Congress, which also controls FTC funding. And the Commission sits as a trial and appellate tribunal, with our decisions subject to review by the federal trial and appellate courts."[26]

Agency employees love to spew their frightening mantra and license to kill: "Congress has awarded us broad powers." No members of the Judicial or Executive branch effectively hit back at Congress. It's this lack of direct oversight of the FTC that has made possible another perfect storm for injustice.

Congress created this mess in 1914 by ignoring the necessity of checks and balances to power, making the FTC *both prosecutor and judge*. How would you like your prosecutor to build the case against you and then run up and sit behind the bench? This move has laid the fertile ground for tyranny to spawn. Because Congress makes the laws and the courts only interpret them, the situation ties the judicial system in knots—*until and unless the Supreme Court has the insight to declare this arrangement unconstitutional*. Don't expect that to happen anytime soon.

The Supreme Court has repeatedly rejected claims that the lodging of legislative, prosecutorial, and judicial functions in one agency allows possible violation of constitutional due process.

Those who expect the judicial system to rescue them from being mauled by the FTC are out of luck. Sure, they can search for justice by buying a ticket to the US Judicial Court and Casino and spending a fortune fighting hacks. But short of being backed into a corner like I was, it's rarely worth it and it probably won't work.

These are the cards the US government dealt us. It can play this game when its citizens are confused or not paying attention. This explains why so many of the lawyers I spoke to in 2010 treated me as if I'd just been diagnosed with a terminal disease.

## Ripe for Tyranny

Challenges *have* been launched against the concentration of power within one agency but the Supreme Court just doesn't get it. In fact, the Court partially stripped the Executive branch of power via a ruling in Humphrey's *Executor v. United States* in 1935.[5] In that case, the Supreme Court considered whether Congress could constitutionally limit the president's power to remove commissioners under the Federal Trade Commission Act.

The Supreme Court justices held that Congress did not violate the separation of powers when it established the Federal Trade Commission and limited the president's ability to remove an appointee for a justified cause. In so holding, the Court distinguished between administrative officials who performed "purely executive" functions (such as postmasters) and officials who performed "quasi-legislative" and "quasi-judicial" functions (such as FTC commissioners). Referring to the former, the Court held that the president had absolute removal power, but addressing the latter, Congress could constitutionally limit the president's power.

Once the 63rd US Congress created the structure that set up the FTC, those who followed let this devilish beast grow and run. Nobody dares take on this agency today; it's too frightening. In the meantime, Congressional members will punt and blame the other guy, see no conflicting legal issues, and finally forget or dismiss the intent of the Founding Fathers. Every branch of government is complicit in this.

What type of protection from tyranny is any of this? In order to nullify government chemotherapy, I have had to put my company on maintenance mode and launch a new career. How many people can do that?

Do these people mean well? Do they even mean anything at all? It begs the question why do people with good intentions do bad things and *why do others play along with them?* On a more psychological level, rather than political, I wondered if humans were just wired to be this way.

## The Milgram Shock Experiment

As I researched the topics of obedience, psychological torture, government abuse, narcissism, and sociopaths, I came to my "bingo" moment when I discovered Stanley Milgram and his experiments in social psychology. Milgram's focus? Obedience to authority figures.

Specifically, he conducted a series of social psychology experiments that measured the willingness of study participants to obey an authority figure who instructed them to perform acts that conflicted with their personal conscience. The experiments began in July 1961, three months after the start of the trial of German Nazi war criminal Adolf Eichmann in Jerusalem. Milgram devised his psychological study to answer this question: "Was it that Eichmann and his accomplices in the Holocaust had mutual intent, in at least with regard to the goals of the Holocaust?" Stated another way, Milgram wanted to know if a mutual sense of morality existed among those involved.

Milgram's results concluded that the millions of accomplices were merely following orders, despite violating their deepest moral beliefs. His experiments have been repeated many times without significant variance in results to change the conclusion.

### How the Milgram Experiment Works

Three persons are involved: the one running the experiment, the subject of the experiment (a volunteer), and a confederate (the actor who is in on what was happening) pretending to be a volunteer. They filled three distinct roles: the Experimenter (an authoritative role), the Teacher (a role intended to obey the orders of the Experimenter), and the Learner (the recipient of stimulus from the Teacher). The subject and the actor both drew slips of paper to determine their roles, but unknown to the subject, both slips said "Teacher." The actor would always claim to have drawn the slip that read "Learner," thus guaranteeing that the subject would always be the Teacher. At this point, the Teacher and Learner were separated into different rooms where they could communicate but not see each other.

The subject (Teacher) believed that for each wrong answer, the Learner was receiving actual shocks, but in reality, no shocks were delivered. After the confederate (actor) was separated from the subject, the confederate set up a tape recorder integrated with the supposed electro-shock generator, which played pre-recorded sounds for each shock level. After a number of "voltage level increases," the actor started to bang on the wall that separated him from the subject. After several times banging on the wall and complaining about his heart condition, all responses by the Learner would cease.

At this point, many people indicated their desire to stop the experiment and check on the Learner. Some test subjects paused at 135 volts and began to question the purpose of the experiment. *Most continued after being assured that they would not be held responsible.* A few subjects began to laugh nervously or exhibit other signs of extreme stress once they heard the screams of pain coming from the Learner.

If at any time the subject indicated his desire to halt the experiment, he was given a succession of verbal prods by the Experimenter, in this order: Please continue.

1. The experiment requires that you continue.
2. It is absolutely essential that you continue.
3. You have no other choice, you must go on.

If the subject (Teacher) still wished to stop after all four successive verbal prods, the experiment was halted. Otherwise, it was halted after the subject had given the maximum 450-volt shock three times in succession.

The Experimenter also gave special prods if the Teacher made specific comments. If the Teacher asked whether the Learner might suffer permanent physical harm, the Experimenter replied, "Although the shocks may be painful, there is no permanent tissue damage, so please go on." If the Teacher said that the Learner clearly wants to stop, the Experimenter replied, "Whether the Learner likes it or not, you must go on until he has learned all the word pairs correctly, so please go on."

In Milgram's first set of experiments, 65 percent (26 of 40) of experiment participants administered the experiment's final massive 450-volt shock, though many were very uncomfortable doing so. At some point, every participant paused and questioned the experiment, and some said they would refund the money they were paid for participating. Throughout the experiment, subjects displayed varying degrees of tension and stress. Subjects were sweating, trembling, stuttering, biting their lips, groaning, or digging their fingernails into their skin, and some were even having nervous laughing fits or seizures.

Milgram summarized his famous experiment in his 1974 article,[6] "The Perils of Obedience," published in *Harper's Magazine*, as he wrote:

> The legal and philosophic aspects of *obedience* are of enormous importance, but they say very little about how most people behave in concrete situations. I set up a simple experiment at Yale University to test how much *pain* an ordinary citizen would inflict on another person simply because he was ordered to by an experimental scientist. Stark authority was pitted against the subjects' [participants'] strongest moral imperatives against hurting others, and, with the subjects' [participants'] ears ringing with the screams of the victims, authority won more often than not. The extreme willingness of adults to go to almost any lengths on the command of an authority constitutes the chief finding of the study and the fact most urgently demanding explanation.
>
> Ordinary people, simply doing their jobs, and without any particular hostility on their part, can become agents in a terrible destructive process. Moreover, even when the destructive effects of their work become patently clear, and they are asked to carry out actions incompatible with fundamental standards of morality, relatively few people have the resources needed to resist authority.

After the initial experiment, Milgram and other psychologists performed variations of it throughout the world—with similar results. Indeed, they found that the percentage of participants who are prepared to inflict fatal voltages remained remarkably constant—at 61 to 66 percent—regardless of time or place.

## That Explains It

In the FTC world I've experienced since 2008, I've learned this about obedience to stark authority: Alain Sheer obeys Julie Brill. Julie Brill obeys Jon Leibowitz and they will never break the chain. Typically, the courts punt, saying they can't change the laws of Congress. The Supreme Court blames congressional laws they are only to interpret. FTC agents investigate whomever they want, when they want, and how they want, even if they are only curious. Congress just sits there. In the course of researching this book I have run into staffers at Congress and professors at very prominent law schools that tell me they can't get anyone to talk about the FTC because everyone is too afraid.

So this sick game continues. In the meantime, those of us living in the real world are dodging side-slamming investigations and coffer-draining inquisitions. These antagonists sleep like babies thinking they are the champions of a higher calling as they run innocent Americans through a government-sponsored meat grinder.

Foolish arrogance and ignorance assumes that humans have changed enough in less than three centuries that these rules no longer apply. I am now wiser about who these people are and what makes them tick. If this happens to you, I hope you use my experience to be better prepared. Here are a few lessons I have learned over the past few years:

*DC lawyer/US Government/Big Corporate family incest.*

The Beltway has a triangle of power and I found myself outside of it. Bouncing from government gigs to law firms to corporate positions, the DC legal network is a never ending movable feast with client exploitation served as the main course. Corporations think hiring a former government lawyer gives them an inside track to quickly solving problems before things get messy. The law firms have their eye firmly on the prize of future revenue. They seduce their clients with representations of a great working relationship with XYZ government agency. Government lawyers may have a future job in corporate America in the back of their minds. (See the completely inappropriate FTC Chairman Jon Leibowitz out to dinner with Google VP in the midst of the FTC Google investigation.[7])

Well, newsflash—government agencies don't like pit-bull lawyers, so if you get sold a bill of goods about how tight Sadie Lawyer is with Bill Bureaucracy, don't expect a fighter on your team. Generally speaking, all this sweet talking negotiating nonsense is just a scheme for government lawyers to justify their existence and for corporate lawyers to run up billable time.

Now that I know better, I shuddered when I read a lawyer's article where he said one should be polite to government investigators. Of all the things to say, why pick that one? I'm not arguing rudeness, but I hate "don't piss them off" advice when it sits at the top of their list.

I would much rather hear "we think outside the box in viciously defending you from this leviathan." But I suspect that may be tough. Victims come and go. The long term loyalty triangle is between law firms, big business, and government agencies.

Many lawyers will *say anything*. It is critical you focus on what they *do* and *have done*. Silence is the devil's hiding place. If I hit the worst offenders with truth serum, here's what I think they would confess:

Little businessman, you're not with a major corporation, are you? Oh. Well, uh, welcome to the game. Fair warning, it's not for the faint of heart. We killed our conscience years ago due to what goes on around here.

What you're about to experience will change you. You'll be tougher later as you lose your innocence. Then you'll see things our way. We're all about billable time. We'll seduce you into peaceful surrender with our sanctimonious justification. Remember, nobody really wins in these things, anyway. There's no truth in the law. There's just law. Law is not a morality play. It's not good. It's not bad. It's a system that attempts justice.

So you got trapped. Tough luck, but better to pay your ransom and get out of here—our standard advice. Yeah, it's tough advice to hear. Because of all the symbolism in this town, one might assume we have a higher calling, like wanting to defend *you*. Most of us have thrown in the towel.

Cooperate please. We have to continually work with these government people but *you're* just passing through town.

Your name again? We'd like to send you an engagement letter before we waste another moment of our time. Wait a minute. Let's call it a consulting letter or perhaps an advice agreement. Anything so we can split hairs if you file a bar complaint or sue. We don't like fingerprints.

Lesson learned: Attack dog lawyer or nothing.

*The Judicial Club of America:* When Congress creates a dog agency, the judiciary is going to let it bark. Judges whine it is Congress's job to create laws and crappy laws are going to get crappy rulings. I used to give that some credence. Now I think many act in complicit concert with each other. Judges don't want to make government enemies with long memories. And how do they do it? Three simple words: plausible, reasonable, and burdensome.

Judges allow investigations to move forward with standards for cause so subjective and so low, wide open loopholes have been created, allowing agencies free rein to roll over everyone with their adolescent attitude that evil lurks under every stone. Small wonder government agencies project the attitude "to hell with civil rights." When ruling in technology, medicine, or other complex matters, what may be "plausible, reasonable and/or burdensome" is a tough call when you don't know what you are talking about. But when big power mixes with little knowledge, the courts churn out junk until the carnage of their ignorance is so big it gets their attention.

But the courts fingerwag at Congress for laws so poorly written they would not come out of a high school civics class, but they let them ride. Yes, Congress is the original sinner here, but the courts need to remember who they are ultimately working for, not who signs their checks or recommends them for their next step up the ladder.

The Department of Justice has become notorious for rogue prosecutorial overreach. Aaron Swartz and James Rosen are just two stinging recent examples. The Justice Department doesn't have to look far to find a judge to sign off on anything. They exploit opaque laws that Congress created by combining legal wordsmiths with complicit judges. They can nail anyone if they are determined enough. If their hand gets stuck in the cookie jar, they hide behind the skirts of Miss "It's All for National Security."

The underbelly of the Federal and State Judicial system has been quite the eye opener as well. I found quite the clubby atmosphere with a strong code of silence. When behind closed doors, judges can fight between themselves like children. I have seen it and heard it firsthand. However, unless the rulings are off the chart terrible, they present a strong united front. They all know who the nutcases are, but they just roll their eyes, feel sorry for the victims, and wait for the honorable nutcase to retire. Judges themselves have told me they are a notoriously lazy lot. The disengagement that is required for objectivity becomes an excuse for indifference and laziness. Blaming lawmakers is often the excuse of the lazy coward.

Being a judge is a sacred duty. I have met many truly great judges who are an honor to engage. They are class acts with inspirational integrity. There are too few of them.

The power that judges have is staggering. This is fueled by their sham system of accountability. The bar and the appeals process are jokes, so judges can get away with pretty much whatever they want.

The bar complaint system is a monstrosity. If you come across with emotion after being burned alive, strike one. Everyone listening to your complaint is a lawyer, strike two (sometimes they will add a "civilian" for the appearance of objectivity, but don't buy it). Finally, if you do waste your time and money making a new enemy, the most your perpetrator will usually get is a big hassle followed by a non-public hand slap. This boils down to nothing more than another trauma to emotionally scar over. Who needs it? But I think it is critical that everyday Americans understand what is going on here.

All this means is the judges know you can't do much about their behavior. I have seen one jump up and down in his seat, flapping his arms around like a bird, and yelling like a three year old. You can't catch that on a transcript. The real world lack of accountability has created a huge mess. So many terrible rulings that damage human lives have created a bottleneck to the appeals court.

The appeals courts are, therefore, overwhelmed. Good luck getting oral argument, if they even take your case. They are too busy . . . and tired. Just ask them. Their clerks do all the work, anyway. Appeals court judges want to rule off of the written brief so they can take their sweet time and not look anyone in the eye. So, they will look at the transcript only, strike one. Then the error must be major or nothing will happen, strike two. Then you if you win, you will just have to go back to the same judge, so strike three, you're out. During this, I assure you, these people sleep like babies.

Generally speaking, the Federal courts are much more professional than State courts. I have been in front of some fantastic judges, but you need to understand that the judicial system has been chopped into a sea of land mines. You will not be walking into the land of liberty and justice for all. The courtroom closet's cousin is the casino. There are many variables in direct conflict with the mask judges wear. You deserve to at least understand the truth before you choose to enter.

Lesson learned: Put your fear, not your faith, in judges. There is a code of silence that insulates them from accountability but for the worst transgressions. Let the scars heal and move on . . . and don't go back unless you are fighting for the greater good. Justice, like loyalty, is a gentle charade.

Lesson learned: Don't look at it. Don't listen to it. Say a prayer.

The FTC perversely terrifies industry, engages in psychological warfare, avoids the courts, and tortures its victims with slow, infinite, and expensive investigations. It drains them dry while looking askance at everyone who disagrees with it, including any and all other branches of government. These federal agents—civil servants—waste taxpayer dollars and drain away employer dollars that fuel economic growth and jobs.

As the poster agency for government overreach, the FTC is proof why the Founding Fathers limited government power. It's unfortunate, but human beings haven't changed at all over the years. When the buffet of power is laid out, agencies like the FTC push their way to the front of the line.

Government agencies have grown into unruly behemoths, long ago forgetting their initial lofty purpose. Like schoolyard bullies, they only punch when their monitors aren't looking. Building on their reputation of overpowering citizens, they now merely bank on the blink of who they have in their sights. Just as showing victims on the rack evoked cooperation in centuries gone by, now they brandish the consent decree and lawsuit. These people have become very, very good at being very, very bad. Their arrogant assumption of the common man's stupidity is beyond belief. And while it is said those with no integrity have no guilt, they are still responsible for their destructive good intentions. Hello, Congress, are you there?

But there stand our leaders in the four corners of Washington DC, looking away, hands in their pockets, whistling as they look up, pretending they don't see anything. They try to plead ignorance. Their castles are surrounded by walls manned by lawyers, lobbyists, and staffers standing guard. The problem isn't big government, it is big anything. We must realize that when we ignore this, we enable it.

It is high time all this silence by omission be considered corrupt. The judicial system does not accept "my lawyer told me it was okay" and "the dog ate my homework" as viable excuses, nor should we. Those that project random episodes of memory loss when coincidentally under oath, thus pleading the fifth, need to be held accountable. Enough is enough.

As the US Government tries to break my back by giving me too many plates to spin, I just grit my teeth, catch my breath, hunker down and keep moving forward. I won't stop to bemoan my fate or waste energy feeling like a victim. We must understand our self interest and fight for government integrity and transparency. Our country is worth the battle. Unless we fight, the fingers of the government will clench to form a fist that will come down right on top of us.

# Notes

## Chapter 1: Breach of Trust

1. US House. House Committee on Oversight and Government. *Inadvertent File Sharing Over Peer-to-Peer Networks: Hearing,* July 24, 2007 (serial No. 110-39). Washington: Government Printing Office 2013. http://michaeljdaugherty.com/wp-content/uploads/2013/07/Congressional-Hearing-july-24-2007.pdf

## Chapter 2: Blindfolded While Looking for Exits and Answers

1. US House Committee on Oversight and Government Reform. *Inadvertent File Sharing Over Peer-to-Peer Networks: How it Endangers Citizens and National Security, Hearing,* July 29, 2009. (Serial No. 111-23) Washington: Government Printing Office 2013. http://michaeljdaugherty.com/wp-content/uploads/2013/07/Congresssional-Hearing-July-29-2009.pdf

## Chapter 3: Post-Traumatic Confusion Syndrome

1. Tiversa Service Agreement. http://michaeljdaugherty.com/wp-Content/uploads/2013/07/pg21_Tiversa_Service_Agreement.pdf

## Chapter 4: The Calm Before the Storm

1. US House. House Committee on Oversight and Government. Inadvertent File Sharing Over Peer-to-Peer Networks, Hearing, July 24, 2007 (Serial No. 110-39). Washington: Government Printing Office 2013. http://michaeljdaugherty.com/wp-content/uploads/2013/07/PG33_Inadvertant_Filesharing_Over_Peer-to-Peer_Networks_Serial_No_110-39.pdf

2. *A&M Records, Inc. v. Napster.* 114 F. Supp.2d 896 (2000) United States District Court Northern District of California. 26 July 2000. *CNET.* N. p., n.d. Web. 12 July 2013. http://news.cnet.com/News/Pages/Special/Napster/napster_patel.html http://michaeljdaugherty.com/wp-content/uploads/2013/07/pg33-RIAA-Napster.pdf

## Chapter 5: The First Strike

1. Non-Public Inquiry Letter. Private Correspondence. http://michaeljdaugherty .com/wp-content/uploads/2013/07/Nonpublic-inquiry-letter_Redacted.pdf

2. Ibid.

## Chapter 6: Section 5 of the FTC Act—The Trap that Congress Laid

1. Section 5 of the Federal Trade Commission Act (FTC Act), Ch. 311, §5, 38 Stat. 719, *codified at* 15 U.S.C. §45(a). Section Five of FTC... http:// michaeljdaugherty.com/wp-content/uploads/2013/07/pg44_FTC_Act_ Entire_Section_5_Act.pdf

2. *Federal Trade Commission v. James B. Nutter & Company*, File No. 072 3108. http://michaeljdaugherty.com/wp-content/uploads/2013/07/pg49and50_ Nutter_Decision.pdf

3. *West's Encyclopedia of American Law*, edition 2. 2008. The Gale Group 12 Jul. 2013 http://legal-dictionary.thefreedictionary.com/consent+decree

## Chapter 7: The FTC Goes Fishing and Throws Back the Catch

1. Letter from Alain Sheer to LabMD. May 6, 2010. Private Correspondence. http://michaeljdaugherty.com/wp-content/uploads/2013/07/5-5Letter-1_ Redacted.pdf

2. March 2007 HIPAA Security Series, Security 101 for Covered Entities. http:// www.hhs.gov/ocr/privacy/hipaa/administrative/securityrule/security101.pdf http://michaeljdaugherty.com/wp-content/uploads/2013/07/pg64_March_ 2007_Security_Series.pdf

## Chapter 9: Trying to Lower Our Coffin into the Ground

1. AirVenture. http://www.airventure.org/

2. Summary Letter. Private Correspondence. http://michaeljdaugherty.com/ wp-content/uploads/2013/07/summary-letter-august102010_Redacted.pdf

3. Stempel, Jonathan. "Big record labels win LimeWire copyright case." Re uters. May 13, 2010. http://www.reuters.com/article/2010/05/13/us-limewire-copyright-ruling-idUSTRE64B63H20100513

4. U.S. House, Subcommittee on Commerce, Trade, and Consumer Protection. H.R. 2221, The Data Accountability and Protection Act, and H.R. 1319, The Informed P2P User Act, Hearing, May 4, 2009 (Serial No. 111-36). Washington: Government Printing Office 2013. http://michaeljdaugherty. com/wp-content/uploads/2013/07/Congressional-Hearing-May-5-2009. pdf

5. LabMD Patient File evidence, U.S. House, Subcommittee on Commerce, Trade, and Consumer Protection. H.R. 2221, The Data Accountability and Protection Act, and H.R. 1319, The Informed P2P User Act, Hearing, May 4, 2009 (Serial No. 111-36). Washington: Government Printing Office 2013 http://michaeljdaugherty.com/wp-content/uploads/2013/07/pg1_Tiversa_ Testimony_Exhibits.pdf

6. "Tiversa™ Advisory Board." Tiversa™. Tiversa Inc., n.d. Web. 05 July 2013 http://tiversa.com/about/advisors.html, http://michaeljdaugherty.com/wp-content/uploads/2013/07/PG92_Tiversa_Advisory_Board.pdf

## Chapter 10: Big Brother is NOT Family

1. Zetter, Kim. 3/2/2009. Academic Claims to Find Sensitive Medical Info Exposed on Peer-to-Peer Networks. Wired Magazine. http://www.wired. com/threatlevel/2009/03/p2p-networks-le/, http://michaeljdaugherty.com/ wp-content/uploads/2013/07/pg96_Academic_Claims_to_Find_Sensitive_ Medical_Info_Exposed_on_Peer-to-Peer_Networks.pdf

2. Johnson, Eric M. *Data Hemorrhages in the Health-Care Sector. Financial Cryptography and Data Security '09.* International Financial Cryptography Association., n.d. Web. 22 July 2013. http://fc09.ifca.ai/papers/54_Data_ Hemorrhages.pdf.

## Chapter 11: Finding Mr. Wright

1. Wright, Ben. 2013. Untitled. Subpeona BYOD Mobile Law, [blog]. http:// hack-igations.blogspot.com. [Accessed: 7/1/2013]

2. Associated Press. 3/29/2007. T.J. Maxx data theft worse than first reported. NBC News. http://www.nbcnews.com/id/17853440/#.UdMLFfnVDTo

## Chapter 13: Simmering with a White Elephant

1. Andrew Liszewski. "This Innocent-Looking Power Strip Can Hack Almost Any Computer Network." *Gizmodo*. Gawker Media, 23 July 2012. Web. 16 Aug. 2013. http://gizmodo.com/5928189/this-innocent-looking-power-strip-can-hack-almost-any-computer-network. http://michaeljdaugherty.

com/wp-content/uploads/2013/08/This-Innocent-Looking-Power-Strip-Can-Hack-Almost-Any-Computer-Network.pdf

2. Jorge Benitez & Jason Healey, *National Interest*, "Cybersecurity Pipe Dreams." July 27, 2012. http://newsle.com/article/0/45545130/

3. Lisa Sotto & Aaron P. Simpson, "Surviving an FTC Investigation After a Data Breach," *New York Law Journal*, 2008, http://michaeljdaugherty.com/wp-content/uploads/2013/07/FTC_investigation_DataBreach_Sotto-1.pdf

## Chapter 14: Round Four of Kissing Their Ass

1. Federal Trade Commission Submission Letter. Private Communication. http://michaeljdaugherty.com/wp-content/uploads/2013/07/Submission-letter-august302010_Redacted.pdf

2. The Federal Trade Commission. Annual Report: The FTC in 2010. Washington, D.C.: The Federal Trade Commission, 2010. Print. 2013. http://michaeljdaugherty.com/wp-content/uploads/2013/07/pg145_2010_Chairmans_Annual_Report.pdf

   The Federal Trade Commission. Annual Report: The FTC in 2011. Washington, D.C.: The Federal Trade Commission, 2011. Print. 2013. http://michaeljdaugherty.com/wp-content/uploads/2013/08/2011ChairmansReport1.pdf

   The Federal Trade Commission. Annual Report: The FTC in 2012. Washington, D.C.: The Federal Trade Commission, 2012. Print. 2013. http://michaeljdaugherty.com/wp-content/uploads/2013/08/ftc-highlights-1.pdf

3. "About: What is Wikileaks?" *Wikileaks.org*. Wikileaks, n.d. Web. http://michaeljdaugherty.com/wp-content/uploads/2013/07/pg146-history-of-wikileaks.pdf

## Chapter 16: Remission is Over

1. Letter from Alain Sheer of the Federal Trade Commission. Private Correspondence. http://michaeljdaugherty.com/wp-content/uploads/2013/07/Alain-Sheer-Letter-Feb232011_Redacted.pdf

2. "Attorneys and Professionals: Jodie Z. Bernstein." Kelley Drye. Kelley Drye & Warren LLP, n.d. Web. 05 July 2013. http://www.kelleydrye.com/attorneys/jodie_bernstein http://michaeljdaugherty.com/wp-content/uploads/2013/07/PG159_Attorneys.pdf

## Chapter 19: Quicksand

1. Kelley Drye Warren Draft. Privileged Attorney Client Communication. http://michaeljdaugherty.com/wp-content/uploads/2013/07/pg182_KDW_First_Submission_to_FTC.pdf

2. "ISO 27799:2008." ISO. International Organization for Standardization, n.d. Web. 05 July 2013. http://www.iso.org/iso/catalogue_detail?csnumber=41298 http://michaeljdaugherty.com/wp-content/uploads/2013/07/pg185_244_514_ISO_27799_2008_.pdf

3. Affidavit of Allen Truett. http://michaeljdaugherty.com/wp-content/uploads/2013/07/pg189_Affidavit.pdf

## Chapter 20: Summer—Slow, Hot, with a Few Bugs

1. Ryan Chittum. "Bloomberg and BusinessWeek's Problematic WikiLeaks Story." *Columbia Journalism Review*. Columbia Journalism Review, 9 Feb. 2011. Web. 16 Aug. 2013. http://www.cjr.org/the_audit/bloomberg_and_businessweeks_pr.php?page=all

2. Robert Boback. "Tiversa CEO Robert Boback." Interview by Bill Flanagan. *Our Region's Business*. WPIX TV, Pittsburgh, PA, Mar. 2009. Television. http://michaeljdaugherty.com/wp-content/uploads/2013/08/Tiversa-CEO-Bob-Boback.mp4

## Chapter 21: Guess I'm Not Crazy After All

1. "Who is Afraid of the FTC?" Claudia Callaway powerpoint presentation. http://michaeljdaugherty.com/wp-content/uploads/2013/07/pg213_Who_is_Afraid_of_the_FTC.ppt

## Chapter 22: Now It's My Turn

1. *LabMD, Inc. v. Tiversa, Inc., Trustees of Dartmouth College, and M. Eric Johnson*. United States District Court for the Northern District of Georgia Atlanta Division. (2011). http://michaeljdaugherty.com/wp-content/uploads/2013/07/pg227_Body_of_Tiversa_Dartmouth_Suit.pdf

## Chapter 23: Sometimes You Have to Smack Them in the Face to Get Their Attention

1. Dartmouth response to *LabMD, Inc. v. Tiversa, Inc., Trustees of Dartmouth College, and M. Eric Johnson*. 10 Feb 2012. http://michaeljdaugherty.com/wp-content/uploads/2013/07/pg235_Dartmouth_Response.pdf

2.  Georgia Computer Systems Protection Act. http://michaeljdaugherty.com/wp-content/uploads/2013/08/Georgia-Computer-Systems-Protection-Act.pdf

3.  Tiversa response to *LabMD, Inc. v. Tiversa, Inc., Trustees of Dartmouth College, and M. Eric Johnson.* 10 Feb 2012. http://michaeljdaugherty.com/wp-content/uploads/2013/07/pg239_Tiversa_Response.pdf

4.  Letter to Kelley Drye re: $24,000 invoice. Private correspondence. http://michaeljdaugherty.com/wp-content/uploads/2013/07/pg242_Dispute_Letter_about_24000_Invoice.pdf

5.  Computer Fraud and Abuse Act, 18 USC § 1030 (2012). Print. http://michaeljdaugherty.com/wp-content/uploads/2013/07/pg244-Computer-Fraud-and-Abuse-Act.pdf

## Chapter 24: The FTC that Stole Christmas

1.  CID from the Federal Trade Commission. http://michaeljdaugherty.com/wp-content/uploads/2013/07/pg248_CID.pdf

2.  The Federal Trade Commission. Annual Report: The FTC in 2010. Washington, D.C.: The Federal Trade Commission, 2010. Print. 2013. http://michaeljdaugherty.com/wp-content/uploads/2013/07/pg145_2010_Chairmans_Annual_Report.pdf

    The Federal Trade Commission. Annual Report: The FTC in 2011. Washington, D.C.: The Federal Trade Commission, 2011. Print. 2013. http://michaeljdaugherty.com/wp-content/uploads/2013/08/2011Chairman sReport1.pdf

    The Federal Trade Commission. Annual Report: The FTC in 2012. Washington, D.C.: The Federal Trade Commission, 2012. Print. 2013. http://michaeljdaugherty.com/wp-content/uploads/2013/08/ftc-highlights-1.pdf

3.  Prof. Michael D. Scott, *The FTC, The Unfairness Doctrine, and Data Security Breach Litigation: Has the Commission Gone too Far?* (1st. Edition 2007) http://michaeljdaugherty.com/wp-content/uploads/2013/07/Has-the-FTC-gone-too-far-1.pdf

## Chapter 25: More Than Mere Formalities

1.  Kelley Drye response to letter regarding $24,000 invoice. http://michaeljdaugherty.com/wp-content/uploads/2013/07/pg256_Response_24000_Letter.pdf

2.  Julie Brill. Speech given September 12, 2011 at New York University. http://www.ftc.gov/speeches/brill/110912nyubobabramsspeech.pdf

3. Affidavit of Scott A. Moulton. http://michaeljdaugherty.com/wp-content/uploads/2013/07/pg258_Affidavit.pdf

4. LabMD's response to Tiversa's Motion to Dismiss. *LabMD, Inc. v. Tiversa, Inc., Trustees of Dartmouth College, and M. Eric Johnson.* United States District Court for the Northern District of Georgia Atlanta Division. 13 Jan 2012. Print. http://michaeljdaugherty.com/wp-content/uploads/2013/07/pg259-LabMDs-Response-to-Tiversa-and-Dartmouth-motion-to-dismiss.pdf

5. LabMD's response to Dartmouth and Johnson's Motion to Dismiss. *LabMD, Inc. v. Tiversa, Inc., Trustees of Dartmouth College, and M. Eric Johnson.* United States District Court for the Northern District of Georgia Atlanta Division. (need URL)

6. Motion to Quash CID. http://michaeljdaugherty.com/wp-content/uploads/2013/07/pg260_Motion_to_Quash_CID.pdf

7. Johnson, Eric M. *Data Hemorrhages in the Health-Care Sector. Financial Cryptography and Data Security '09.* International Financial Cryptography Association., n.d. Web. 22 July 2013. http://fc09.ifca.ai/papers/54_Data_Hemorrhages.pdf.

   http://michaeljdaugherty.com/wp-content/uploads/2013/07/Data-Hemorrhages-in-the-Healthcare-Sector.pdf

8. Julie Brill notification regarding Motion to Quash denial. Letter. Hearing denied. http://michaeljdaugherty.com/wp-content/uploads/2013/07/pg264_Quash_Denial.pdf

9. LabMD'sResponse/FTCResponsehttp://michaeljdaugherty.com/wp-content/uploads/2013/07/pg265_Response_to_Quash_Denial_April_252012.pdf

10. Commissioner Rosch Response. http://michaeljdaugherty.com/wp-content/uploads/2013/07/pg266_Dissent.pdf

11. June 27th 2012 letter from FTC. http://michaeljdaugherty.com/wp-content/uploads/2013/07/pg268_June_272012_FTC.pdf

12. Response to FTC. http://michaeljdaugherty.com/wp-content/uploads/2013/07/pg269_Response_June_292012.pdf

## Chapter 26: The Endless Climb Up Judicial Mountain

1. Judge Forrester Ruling. *LabMD, Inc. v. Tiversa, Inc., Trustees of Dartmouth College, and M. Eric Johnson.* United States District Court for the Northern District of Georgia Atlanta Division. 15 Aug 2012. Print. http://michaeljdaugherty.com/wp-content/uploads/2013/07/Item1-August-15-2012-Judge-Forrester-Ruling.pdf

2. Rodriguez, Juan C. "FTC Sues to Get Patient Data Spreadsheet From LabMD." *Law360*. Lexis Nexis, 30 Aug. 2012. Web. 5 July 2013. http://www.law360. com/articles/374607/ftc-sues-to-get-patient-data-spreadsheet-from-labmd

3. Wenk, Amy. "Atlanta Medical Lab Facing Off Against FTC." *Atlanta Business Chronicle* 7-13 Sept. 2012: 3A+. Print. http://www.bizjournals.com/ atlanta/print-edition/2012/09/07/atlanta-medical-lab-facing-off-against. html?page=all   http://michaeljdaugherty.com/wp-content/uploads/2013/07/ pg274_Atlanta_Medical_Lab_Facing_Off_Against_FTC.pdf

4. Federal Court Hearing in Atlanta. September 19, 2012. *Federal Trade Commission v. LabMD, Inc. and Michael J. Daugherty*. United States District Court for the Northern District of Georgia Atlanta Division. 19 Sept 2012. Print.   http://michaeljdaugherty.com/wp-content/uploads/2013/07/pg275_ Federal_Court_Hearing_Transcript_20120919.pdf

5. Appeal Brief to the 11th Circuit Court of Appeals. *LabMD, Inc. v. Tiversa, Inc., M. Eric Johnson, and Trustees of Dartmouth College*. United States Court of Appeals for the Eleventh Circuit. 17 Oct 2012. Print. http://michaeljdaugherty .com/wp-content/uploads/2013/07/Item2-Appeal-Brief-to-the-11th-circuit-court-of-appeals.pdf

6. Brief in Response to Appeal from Tiversa and Dartmouth. *LabMD, Inc. v. Tiversa, Inc., M. Eric Johnson, and Trustees of Dartmouth College*. United States Court of Appeals for the Eleventh Circuit. 16 Nov 2012. Print. http:// michaeljdaugherty.com/wp-content/uploads/2013/07/Item3-Tiversa-and-Dartmouth-brief-in-response-to-appeal.pdf

7. Gilbert, Sheldon. "FBI Says, Expect to Be Hacked; FTC Says, Expect Us to Sue You." Web log post. *Free Enterprise*. U.S. Chamber of Commerce, 24 Oct. 2012. Web. 05 July 2013. http://www.freeenterprise.com/technology/fbi-says-expect-be-hacked-ftc-says-expect-us-sue-you   http://michaeljdaugherty.com/ wp-content/uploads/2013/07/pg279_Freeenterprise_com_Technology_ FBI_Says_Expect_Be_Hacked.pdf

8. Judge Duffey's decision. 26 Nov 2012. *Federal Trade Commission v. LabMD, Inc. and Michael J. Daugherty*. United States District Court for the Northern District of Georgia Atlanta Division. 26 Nov 2012. Print. http:// michaeljdaugherty.com/wp-content/uploads/2013/07/Item4-Judge-Duffey-November-26-decision.pdf

## Chapter 27: No Summit in Sight

1. Second Circuit Court of Appeals Ruling from Connecticut. MacDermid, Inc. v. Jackie Deiter. Lexis Nexis. United States Court of Appeals for the Second Circuit. 26 Dec 2012. Print. http://michaeljdaugherty.com/wp-content/ uploads/2013/07/Item5-Second-Circuit-Court-of-Appeals-Ruling.pdf

2. LabMD Motion to Supplement Brief to add the Second Circuit opinion. 21 Jan 2013. Response from court. LabMD, Inc. v. Tiversa, Inc., M. Eric Johnson, and Trustees of Dartmouth College. United States Court of Appeals for the Eleventh Circuit. 22 Jan. 2013. Print.

  *LabMD, Inc. v. Tiversa, Inc., M. Eric Johnson, and Trustees of Dartmouth College.* United States Court of Appeals for the Eleventh Circuit. 24 Jan. 2013. Print. http://michaeljdaugherty.com/wp-content/uploads/2013/07/Item6-January-21-2013-Motion-to-File-Supplemental-Brief-and-3-days-later-denial.pdf

3. Eleventh Circuit Appeal Denial. 5 Feb 2013. *LabMD, Inc. v. Tiversa, Inc., M. Eric Johnson, and Trustees of Dartmouth College.* United States Court of Appeals for the Eleventh Circuit. 05 Feb 2013. Print. http://michaeljdaugherty.com/wp-content/uploads/2013/07/Item7-Feb-5-2013-11th-circuit-denial-of-appeal.pdf

4. Petition for Rehearing and Motion to send certified question to the Georgia Supreme Court. LabMD, Inc. v. Tiversa, Inc., M. Eric Johnson, and Trustees of Dartmouth College. United States Court of Appeals for the Eleventh Circuit. 27 Feb 2013. Print. http://michaeljdaugherty.com/wp-content/uploads/2013/07/Item-8-Feb-27-2013-petition-for-rehearing.pdf

5. First response to FOIA request. http://michaeljdaugherty.com/wp-content/uploads/2013/07/Item9-First-week-of-april-2013-first-response-to-FOIA.pdf

6. Decision regarding Petition for Rehearing and Motion to send certified question to Georgia Supreme Court. LabMD, Inc. v. Tiversa, Inc., M. Eric Johnson, and Trustees of Dartmouth College. United States Court of Appeals for the Eleventh Circuit. 09 May 2013. Print. http://michaeljdaugherty.com/wp-content/uploads/2013/07/Item10-May-9-2013-11th-circuit-court-of-appeals-decision.pdf

## Chapter 28: Discovering More Than I Bargained For

1. Good, Nathaniel S. & Aaron Krekelberg, *Usability and Privacy: A Study of Kazaa P2P File-Sharing* (2002) reprinted in Proc. of the SIGCHI Conf. on Hum. Factors in Computing Systems, vol. 5, iss. 1, 137-144. This study is now considered one of the "classics" of research on the interaction between usability and security. *See generally,* Security and Usability: Designing Secure Systems That People Can Use (Lorrie Cranor & Simson Garfinkel eds., 2005).

2. Because this analysis focuses on the FTC's role in exacerbating the problem of inadvertent sharing, it is critical to note the May 18, 2008 installation date of the copy of LimeWire v.4.16.7 that was found, in 2010, to be inadvertently sharing the pdf file identified by the FTC from the *My Documents* folder of a LabMD computer. This installation date is critical even though LimeWire v.4.16.7 was

almost certainly neither the first version of LimeWire that had been installed on that LabMD computer nor the version of LimeWire that had caused the inadvertent, recursive sharing of that computer's *My Documents* folder.

When a newer version of LimeWire is installed on a computer, it overwrites and replaces any earlier, previously installed version of LimeWire. Consequently, this analysis presumes that earlier versions of LimeWire probably had been installed on the LabMD computer in question before May 18, 2008. Indeed, even though LimeWire's own distributors would admit, in 2009, that all 4-series versions of LimeWire were dangerously defective, earlier 4-series versions of LimeWire were actually far more deceptive than LimeWire 4.16.7.

Nevertheless, the May 18, 2008 installation date tells us when the LimeWire program on this particular computer had been updated from a previously installed version of LimeWire. Consequently, if the FTC had reason to know that LimeWire had deployed a deceptive search-wizard and/or share-folder features by 2008, then the FTC could have effectively and efficiently prevented the episode of inadvertent sharing that affected LabMD— as well as millions of other similar episodes that began after or were ongoing as of May 18, 2008 by executing its mandatory statutory duty to enforce the FTC Act and issuing simple cease-and-desist and injunctive orders compelling LimeWire to release a new version of its program that (1) eliminated the deceptive search-wizard and share-folder features that caused inadvertent sharing of *My Documents* folders and (2) remediated their past effects by "unsharing" the contents of any *My Documents* folders shared by previous versions of the program.

3. *The Dark Side of a Bright Idea: Could Personal and National Security Risks Compromise the Potential of P2P File-Sharing Network?: Hearing Before the Senate Comm. On the Judiciary*, 108th Cong. 8 (June 17, 2003) (statement of Sen. Orrin G. Hatch); see also id. At 67 (statement of Sen. Patrick Leahy); id. At 2 (statement of Sen. Dianne Feinstein).

4. *See, e.g.,* Staff Report of the United States House of Representatives Comm. on Gov't Reform, *File-Sharing Programs and Peer-to-Peer Networks: Privacy and Security Risks*, 1 (May 2003) ("Committee investigators found ... tax returns, medical records, attorney-client communications, and personal correspondence from P2P users [and] ... at least 2,500 Microsoft Money backup files, which store the user's personal financial records, available for download.") *reprinted in Overexposed: The Threat to Privacy and Security on Filesharing Networks: Hearing Before the United States House of Representatives Comm. on Gov't Reform*, 108th Cong. 127 (May 15, 2003);

see also Nicolas Christin et al., *Content Availability, Pollution and Poisoning in File Sharing Peer-to-Peer Networks*, PROC. OF THE 6TH ACM CONF. ON ELECTRONIC. COM. 68, 77 (2005) ("[S]tudies of user behavior show that a vast number of users are vastly unaware of the files they share.") (citation omitted).

5. P2P United, Member Code of Conduct (Sept. 29, 2003) http://www.ftc.gov/bcp/workshops/filesharing/presentations/eisgrau.pdf

6. LimeWire, Frequently Asked Questions http://www.limewire.org/wiki/index.php?title=Frequently_Asked_Questions#sec1 (last visited Nov. 14, 2007).

7. *See, e.g.,* Letter of Sept. 13, 2004 from FTC Chairman Majoras to Rep. Waxman at 2, 7 & n.20; *see also The Future of Peer-to-Peer (P2P) Technology, A Hearing before the Senate Subcommittee on Competition, Foreign Commerce and Infrastructure of the Senate Committee on Commerce, Science & Transportation* (June 23, 2004) (review of website disclosures confirmed in the written statement of Howard Beales).

8. Department of Homeland Security, *Unauthorized Peer to Peer (P2P) Programs on Government Computers* (2005), http://www.s2online.org/2006/IB%20Unauthorized%20Peer%20to%20Peer%20%28P2P%29%20Programs%20on%20Government%20Computers%20%20April%2019%202005%20V6.0.pdf; *see also* Eric Hortin, "Downloading Shared Files Threatens Security," *Army News Service*, April 22, 2004 ("Over a two-month period at the end of [2003], government organizations identified more than 420 suspected P2P sessions on Army systems in more than 30 locations around the globe."), http://www.mccoy.army.mil/vtriad_online/07232004/Shared%20files.htm

9. Blue Security, P2P Exploited to Spam Millions of Users 1 (2005) (cited in Gregg Keizer, Spammers Mining P-to-P for Addresses, Information-Week, April 19, 2005, http://www.informationweek.com/story/showArticle.jhtml?articleID=160903121).

10. *File Sharers, Beware!*, *CBS Evening News*, May 5, 2005, http://www.cbsnews.com/stories/2005/05/03/eveningnews/main692765.shtml; *see also id.* (reporting that one vigilant user warned 120 people that they were inadvertently sharing financial documents); *see also* Brian Krebs, *Extreme File Sharing*, *WashingtonPost.com*, Oct. 17, 2005 (reporting that when the author searched for inadvertently shared files on LimeWire, "I quickly found what I was looking for, and then some: dozens of entries for tax and payroll records, medical records, bank statements, and what appeared to be company books" and users sharing email "inboxes and archives"), http://blog.washingtonpost.com/securityfix/2005/10/extreme_file_sharing_1.html

11. *See Thomas D. Sydnor II, John Knight, Lee A. Hollaar, Filesharing Programs and "Technological Features to Induce Users to Share"*, at 21, 25, 27-28 (USPTO, 2006) *[hereinafter the USPTO Report]*. http://www.uspto.gov/web/offices/dcom/olia/copyright/oir_report_on_inadvertent_sharing_v1012.pdf Distributors later tried to use this inane "default-settings" argument to

convince Senators that concerns about inadvertent sharing were so "wholly without foundation" and that Senators should actually help distributors dispel "persistent and perniciously false allegations about peer-to-peer software and user security." *The Future of Peer-to-Peer (P2P) Technology, A Hearing before the Senate Subcommittee on Competition, Foreign Commerce and Infrastructure of the Senate Committee on Commerce, Science & Transportation* (June 23, 2004) (testimony of Mr. Michael Weiss on behalf of the distributors of BearShare, eDonkey, and Morpheus); *see also* USPTO Report at 29-30 (criticizing this testimony as "unresponsive").

12. US House. House Committee on Oversight and Government. *Inadvertent File Sharing Over Peer-To-Peer Networks*, Hearing, July 24, 2007 (Serial No. 110-39). Washington: Government Printing Office 2013.

13. US House. House Committee on Oversight and Government. *Inadvertent File Sharing Over Peer-to-Peer Networks: Hearing*, July 24, 2007 (serial No. 110-39. Washington: Government Printing Office 2013. http://michaeljdaugherty. com/wp-content/uploads/2013/07/Congressional-Hearing-july-24-2007. pdf

14. Letter of Nov. 13, 2007, from FTC Chairman Majoras to Rep. Waxman.

15. *See* Distributed Computing Industry Association, *Voluntary Best Practices for P2P File-Sharing Software Developers To Implement To Protect Users Against Inadvertently Sharing Personal or Sensitive Data* (2008). http://www.dcia.info/ activities/ispg/inadvertentsharingprotection.pdf

16. *See, e.g., Report: Iran Stole Marine One Specs,* CBS News (April 9, 2009) http:// www.cbsnews.com/2100-503063_162-4835981.html (reporting that Iran had downloaded the design specifications and avionics for the new version of the President's helicopter, *Marine One,* because they had been inadvertently shared by a user of a P2P file-sharing program).

17. Today Investigates, *New warnings on cyber-thieves,* at http://today.msnbc. msn.com/id/26184891/vp/29405819%2329405819.

18. *Inadvertent File-Sharing: How It Endangers Citizens and Jeopardizes National Security, a Hearing before the House Committee on Oversight and Government Reform,* 111ᵗʰ Cong. (July 29, 2009). http://www.gpo.gov/fdsys/pkg/CHRG-111hhrg54009/pdf/CHRG-111hhrg54009.pdf

19. Thomas D. Sydnor II, *Inadvertent File-Sharing Reinvented: The Dangerous Design of LimeWire 5,* (Progress & Freedom Foundation, July 8, 2009). Thomas Sydnor was the lead author of the *USPTO Report.* http://www.pff. org/issues-pubs/pops/2009/pop16.14-inadvertent-file-sharing-reinvented-limewire-5.pdf

20. *See* Distributed Computing Industry Association, *Voluntary Best Practices for P2P File-Sharing Software Developers To Implement To Protect Users Against*

*Inadvertently Sharing Personal or Sensitive Data* (2008). http://www.dcia.info/activities/ispg/inadvertentsharingprotection.pdf

21. *See* FTC, *Peer-to-Peer File Sharing: A Guide for Business* (Jan. 2010). http://business.ftc.gov/documents/bus46-peer-peer-file-sharing-guide-business

22. Letter of Aug. 19, 2010 from Mary Engle, Associate Divisional Director of the FTC's Bureau of Consumer Protection to LimeWire LLC. CEO George Searle.

23. *See* www.limewire.com

24. *See, e.g., Wikipedia,* "FrostWire," at http://en.wikipedia.org/wiki/FrostWire (last visited July 7, 2012).

25. Non-public inquiry letter. http://michaeljdaugherty.com/wp-content/uploads/2013/07/Nonpublic-inquiry-letter_Redacted.pdf

26. Thoughts on the FTC's Relationship (Constitutional and Otherwise) to the Legislative, Executive, and Judicial Branches Remarks of J. Thomas Rosch Commissioner, Federal Trade Commission before the Berlin Forum for EU-US Legal-Economic Affairs. September 19, 2009

## Afterword—Father Knows Best: The Wisdom in Respecting Our Founding Fathers

1. Merriam-Webster Dictionary. "Tyranny." http://www.merriam-webster.com/dictionary/tyranny

2. Merriam-Webster Dictionary. "Exert." http://www.merriam-webster.com/dictionary/exert

3. Merriam-Webster Dictionary. "Rigorous." http://www.merriam-webster.com/dictionary/rigorous

4. Michael Kerrigan, *The Instruments of Torture, Revised and Updated* (Lyons Press, 2007).

5. Sutherland, J., Opinion of the Court, Supreme Court of the United States. 295 U.S. 602 Humphrey's Executor v. United States [*] Certificate From the Court of Claims No. 637 Argued: 1, 1935 – Decided: May 27, 1935

6. Milgram, Stanley (1974). "The Perils of Obedience". *Harper's Magazine.* Abridged and adapted from *Obedience to Authority.* http://www.paulgraham.com/perils.html

7. Douglas MacMillan & Jeff Bliss, "FTC Chair Dines With Google Ad Exec Amid Antitrust Probe." Bloomberg, June 1, 2012. http://www.bloomberg.com/news/2012-05-31/ftc-chair-dines-with-google-ad-exec-amid-antitrust-probe.html

# Additional Links

The following are links referenced in emails in this book. Just in case they are removed from their original source at some point, there is a historical archive at michaeljdaugherty.com. The archive URL follows the current link.

Brian Krebs, "Justice Breyer is Among Victims in Data Breach Caused by File Sharing," *Washington Post*, July 9, 2008. http://www.washingtonpost.com/wp-dyn/content/article/2008/07/08/AR2008070802997.html

http://michaeljdaugherty.com/wp-content/uploads/2013/07/Washington_Breyer.pdf

John Foley, "Your Data and the P2P Peril," *InformationWeek*, March 15, 2008. http://www.informationweek.com/your-data-and-the-p2p-peril/206903416?queryText=206903416

http://michaeljdaugherty.com/wp-content/uploads/2013/07/Infoweek_P2P_Peril.pdf

Avi Baumstein, "Our P2P Investigation Turns Up Business Data Galore," *InformationWeek*, March 17, 2008. http://www.informationweek.com/our-p2p-investigation-turns-up-business/206903417?queryText=206903416

http://michaeljdaugherty.com/wp-content/uploads/2013/07/Infoweek_P2P.pdf

DISCLAIMER: Memories can't be verified to perfection since the human mind is faulty, but in telling this story, I have relied upon interviews with my attorneys, friends, and co-workers, in addition to court documents, emails, letters, journals, and other research. I have also taken certain liberties such as dramatizing, compressing, and/or combining events, times, or conversations. In some cases, names and identifying details have been condensed and/or changed to avoid unnecessary embarrassment to private individuals. This was done in an effort to move the story forward and spare readers the mundane, trivial details not critical to the story. While I may not remember word for word what was said in the conversations contained in this book, I have done my best to ensure that they capture my recollections and perceptions of what was discussed. For those who want more details and facts about the underlying basis for my story and strong opinions, you will find in the endnotes links to full versions of all documents and emails referenced in this book. In short, this is my story. It is an emotional story of years marred by torment and disgust dealing with the FTC. It is, ultimately, my personal account about events that have forever changed my life.

# Bibliography

"About: What is Wikileaks?" Wikileaks.org. Wikileaks, n.d. Web. http://michaeljdaugherty.com/content/uploads/2013/07/pg146-history-of-wikileaks.pdf

AirVenture. Oshkosh, Wisconsin. http://www.airventure.org/

*A&M Records, Inc. v. Napster*, 114 F.Supp.2d 896 (US Dist. Ct. N. Dist. Cal. 2000)

Associated Press. 3/29/2007. T.J. Maxx data theft worse than first reported. NBC News. http://www.nbcnews.com/id/17853440/#.UdMLFfnVDTo

Baumstein, Avi, "Our P2P Investigation Turns Up Business Data Galore," InformationWeek, 17 March, 2008. http://www.informationweek.com/our-p2p-investigation-turns-up-business/206903417?queryText=206903416

Benitez, Jorge & Jason Healey, *National Interest*, "Cybersecurity Pipe Dreams." July 27, 2012. http://newsle.com/article/0/45545130/

Boback, Robert, "Tiversa CEO Robert Boback." Interview by Bill Flanagan. *Our Region's Business*. WPIX TV, Pittsburgh, PA, March 2009. Television. http://michaeljdaugherty.com/wp-content/uploads/2013/08/Tiversa-CEO-Bob-Boback.mp4

Brill, Julie, New York University speech, 12 September, 2011. http://www.ftc.gov/speeches/brill/110912nyubobabramsspeech.pdf

Callaway, Claudia, and Helen Foster, *Who is Afraid of the FTC?* Powerpoint presentation. http://michaeljdaugherty.com/wp-content/uploads/2013/07/pg213_Who_is_Afraid_of_the_FTC.ppt

CBS Evening News, *File Sharers, Beware!* 5 May, 2005. http://www.cbsnews.com/stories/2005/05/03eveningnews/main692765.shtml

CBS News, Report: Iran Stole Marine One Specs, 9 April, 2009. http://www.cbsnews.com/2100-503063_162-4835981.html

Chittum, Ryan, "Bloomberg and Business Week's Problematic WikiLeaks Story." *Columbia Journalism Review*. Columbia Journalism Review, 9 Feb. 2011. Web. http://www.cjr.org/the_audit/bloomberg_and_businessweeks_pr.php?page=all

Christin, Nicolas, Andreas S. Weigend and John Chuang, *Content Availability, Pollution and Poisoning in File Sharing Peer-to-Peer Networks*. Proceedings of the 6<sup>th</sup> ACM Conference on Electronic Commerce. 68, 77 (2005) http://citeseerx.ist.psu.edu/viewdoc/summary?doi=10.1.1.182.9869

CID, Federal Trade Commission. http://michaeljdaugherty.com/wp-content/uploads/2013/07/pg248_CID.pdf

CID, Motion to Quash. http://michaeljdaugherty.com/wp-content/uploads/2013/07/pg260_Motion_to_Quash_CID.pdf

Computer Fraud and Abuse Act, 18 USC § 1030 (2012). Print. http://michaeljdaugherty.com/wp-content/uploads/2013/07/pg244-Computer-Fraud-and-Abuse-Act.pdf

Department of Homeland Security, Unauthorized Peer to Peer (P2P) Programs on Government Computers (2005), http://www.s2online.org/2006/IB%20Unauthorized%20Peer%20to%20Peer%20%28P2P%29%20Programs%20on%20Government%20Computers%20%20April%2019%202005%20V6.0.pdf

Distributed Computing Industry Association, *Voluntary Best Practices for P2P File-Sharing Software Developers To Implement To Protect Users Against Inadvertently Sharing Personal or Sensitive Data.* 2008

The Federal Trade Commission, *Annual Report: The FTC in 2010.* Washington, D.C.: The Federal Trade Commission, 2010. Print. 2013. http://michaeljdaugherty.com/wp-content/uploads/2013/07/pg145_2010_Chairmans_Annual_Report.pdf

The Federal Trade Commission, *Annual Report: The FTC in 2011.* Washington, D.C.: The Federal Trade Commission, 2011. Print. 2013. http://michaeljdaugherty.com/wp-content/uploads/2013/08/2011 ChairmansReport1.pdf

The Federal Trade Commission, *Annual Report: The FTC in 2012.* Washington, D.C.: The Federal Trade Commission, 2012. Print. 2013. http://michaeljdaugherty.com/wp-content/uploads/2013/08/ftc-highlights-1.pdf

Federal Trade Commission, Federal Trade Commission Act, Section 5, Ch. 311, §5, 38 Stat. 719, *codified at* 15 U.S.C. §45(a). http://michaeljdaugherty.com/wp-content/uploads/2013/07/pg44_FTC_Act_Entire_Section_5_Act.pdf

Federal Trade Commission, Peer-to-Peer File Sharing: A Guide for Business. Jan 2010. http://business.ftc.gov/documents/bus46-peer-peer-file-sharing-guide-business

*Federal Trade Commission v. James B. Nutter & Company*, File No. 072 3108. http://michaeljdaugherty.com/wp-content/uploads/2013/07/pg49and50_Nutter_Decision.pdf

*Federal Trade Commission v. LabMD, Inc. and Michael J. Daugherty.* 19 Sept 2012. http://michaeljdaugherty.com/wp-content/uploads/2013/07/pg275_Federal_Court_Hearing_Transcript_20120919.pdf

*Federal Trade Commission v. LabMD, Inc. and Michael J. Daugherty.* 26 Nov 2012. http://michaeljdaugherty.com/wp-content/uploads/2012/07/Item4-Judge-Duffey-November-26-decision.pdf

Foley, John, "Your Data and the P2P Peril," *InformationWeek*, 15 March, 2008. http://www.informationweek.com/your-data-and-the-p2p-peril/20690341 6?queryText=206903416

Freedom of Information Act request response. http://michaeljdaugherty.com/wp-content/uploads/2013/2013/07/Item9-First-week-of-april-2013-first-response-to-FOIA.pdf

Georgia Computer Systems Protection Act. http://michaeljdaugherty.com/wp-content/uploads/2013/08/Georgia-Computer-Systems-Protection-Act.pdf

Gilbert, Sheldon, "FBI says, expect to be hacked; FTC says, expect us to sue you." *Free Enterprise.* US Chamber of Commerce, 24 Oct. 2012. http://www.freeenterprise.com/technology/fbi-says-expect-be-hacked-ftc-says-expect-us-sue-you

Good, Nathaniel S. & Aaron Krekelberg, *Usability and Privacy: A Study of Kazaa P2P File-Sharing* (2002) reprinted in Proc. Of the SIGCHI Conference on Human Factors in Computing Systems, vol. 5, iss. 1, 137–144.

HIPAA Security Series, Security 101 for Covered Entities. March 2007. http://www.hhs.gov/ocr/privacy/hipaa/administrative/securityrule/security101.pdf http://michaeljdaugherty.com/wp-content/uploads/2013/07/pg64_March_2007_Security_Series.pdf

Hortin, Eric, "Downloading Shared Files Threatens Security," *Army News Service.* 22 April, 2004. http://www.mccoy.army.mil/vtriad_online/07232004/Shared%20files.htm

Humphrey's Executor v. United States 295 U.S. 602 U.S. Supreme Court, J. Sutherland. Certificate from Court of Claims No. 637. Argued: 1, 1935 – Decided: May 27, 1935

"ISO 27799:2008." ISO. International Organization for Standardization, n.d. Web. July 5, 2013. http://www.iso.org/iso/catalogue_detail?csnumber=41298

Johnson, Eric M., *Data Hemorrhages in the Health-Care Sector. Financial Cryptography and Data Security '09.* International Financial Cryptography Association., n.d. Web. 22 July 2013. http://fc09.ifca.ai/papers/54_Data_Hemorrhages.pdf

Keizer, Gregg, "Spammers Mining P-to-P for Addresses," Information Week. 19 April, 2005. http://www.informationweek.com/story/showArticle.jhtml?articleID=160903121

Kerrigan, Michael, *The Instruments of Torture, Revised and Updated*, Lyons Press, 2007.

Krebs, Brian, "Extreme File Sharing," *Washingtonpost.com*, 17 Oct, 2005. http://blog.washingtonpost.com/securityfix/2005/10/extreme_file_sharing_1.html

Krebs, Brian, "Justice Breyer is Among Victims in Data Breach Caused by File Sharing," *Washington Post*, 9 July, 2008. http://www.washingtonpost.com/wp-dyn/content/article/2008/07/08/AR2008070802997.html

*LabMD, Inc. v. Tiversa, Inc., Trustees of Dartmouth College, and M. Eric Johnson.* United States District Court for the Northern District of Georgia Atlanta Division. (2011) http://michaeljdaugherty.com/wp-content/uploads/2013/07/pg227_Body_of_Tiversa_Dartmouth_Suit.pdf

*LabMD, Inc. v. Tiversa, Inc., Trustees of Dartmouth College, and M. Eric Johnson,* Dartmouth response. 10 Feb 2012. http://michaeljdaugherty.com/wp-content/uploads/2013/07/pg235_Dartmouth_Response.pdf

*LabMD, Inc. v. Tiversa, Inc., Trustees of Dartmouth College, and M. Eric Johnson,* Tiversa response. 10 Feb 2012. http://michaeljdaugherty.com/wp-content/uploads/2013/07/pg239_Tiversa_Response.pdf

*LabMD, Inc. v. Tiversa, Inc., Trustees of Dartmouth College, and M. Eric Johnson.* LabMD's response to Tiversa's Motion to Dismiss. 13 Jan 2012. http://michaeljdaugherty.com/wp-content/uploads/2013/07/pg259-LabMDs-Response-to-Tiversa-and-Dartmouth-motion-to-dismiss.pdf

*LabMD, Inc. v. Tiversa, Inc., Trustees of Dartmouth College, and M. Eric Johnson.* LabMD's response to Dartmouth and Johnson's Motion to Dismiss. http://michaeljdaugherty.com/wp-content/uploads/2013/07/pg259-LabMDs-Response-to-Tiversa-and-Dartmouth-motion-to-dismiss.pdf See page 40.

*LabMD, Inc. v. Tiversa, Inc., Trustees of Dartmouth College, and M. Eric Johnson.* 15 Aug 2012. http://michaeljdaugherty.com/wp-content/uploads/2013/07/Item1-August-15-2012-Judge-Forrester-Ruling.pdf

*LabMD, Inc. v. Tiversa, Inc., M. Eric Johnson, and Trustees of Dartmouth College.* 17 Oct 2012. http://michaeljdaugherty.com/wp-content/uploads/2012/07/Item2-Appeal-Brief-to-the-11th-circuit-court-of-appeals.pdf

*LabMD, Inc. v. Tiversa, Inc., M. Eric Johnson, and Trustees of Dartmouth College.* 16 Nov 2012. Brief in response. http://michaeljdaugherty.com/wp-content/uploads/2013/07/Item3-Tiversa-and-Dartmouth-brief-in-response-to-appeal.pdf

*LabMD, Inc. v. Tiversa, Inc., M. Eric Johnson, and Trustees of Dartmouth College.* 21 Jan 2013. Supplement Brief to add Second Circuit opinion. Response from Court of Appeals for the Eleventh Circuit. 22 Jan 2013. http://michaeljdaugherty.com/wp-content/uploads/2013/07/Item6-January-21-2013-Motion-to-File-Supplemental-Brief-and-3-days-later-denial.pdf

*LabMD, Inc. v. Tiversa, Inc., M. Eric Johnson, and Trustees of Dartmouth College.* 5 Feb 2013. http://michaeljdaugherty.com/wp-content/uploads/2013/07/Item7-Feb-5-2013-11th-circuit-denial-of-appeal.pdf

*LabMD, Inc. v. Tiversa, Inc., M. Eric Johnson, and Trustees of Dartmouth College.* 27 Feb 2013. http://michaeljdaugherty.com/wp-content/uploads/2013/07/Item-8-Feb-27-2013-petition-for-rehearing.pdf

*LabMD, Inc. v. Tiversa, Inc., M. Eric Johnson, and Trustees of Dartmouth College.* 09 May 2013. Petition for Rehearing and Motion to send certified question to Georgia Supreme Court decision. United States Court of Appeals for the Eleventh Circuit. http://michaeljdaugherty.com/wp-content/uploads/2013/07/Item10-May-9-2013-11th-circuit-court-of-appeals-decision.pdf

LimeWire, Frequently Asked Questions. Last visited 14 Nov 2007. http://www.limewire.org/wiki/index.php?title=Frequently_Asked_Questions#sec1

Liszewski, Andrew, "This Innocent-Looking Power Strip Can Hack Almost Any Computer Network." *Gizmodo.* Gawker Media, 23 July 2012. Web. 16 Aug 2013. http://gizmodo.com/5928189/this-innocent-looking-power-strip-can-hack-almost-any-computer-network. http://michaeljdaugherty.com/wp-content/uploads/2013/08/This-Innocent-Looking-Power-Strip-Can-Hack-Almost-Any-Computer-Network.pdf

*MacDermid, Inc. v. Deiter.* 702 F 3d 725 (2d Cir 2012) Lexis Nexis. 26 Dec 2012. http://michaeljdaugherty.com/wp-content/uploads/2013/07/Item5-Second-Circuit-Court-of-Appeals-Ruling.pdf

MacMillan, Douglas, and Jeff Bliss, "FTC Chair Dines With Google Ad Exec Amid Antitrust Probe,: Bloomberg, 1 June, 2012. http://www.bloomberg.com/news/2012-05-31/ftc-chair-dines-with-google-ad-exec-amid-antitrust-probe.html

Merriam-Webster Dictionary. Exert. http://www.merriam-webster.com/dictionary/exert

Merriam-Webster Dictionary. Rigorous. http://www.merriam-webster.com/dictionary/rigorous

Merriam-Webster Dictionary. Tyranny. http://www.merriam-webster.com/dictionary/tyranny

Milgram, Stanley, "The Perils of Obedience," *Harper's Magazine.* Abridged and adapted from Obedience to Authority. http://www.paulgraham.com/perils.html

Moulton, Scott A., Affidavit. http://michaeljdaugherty.com/wp-content/uploads/2013/07/pg258_Affidavit.pdf

P2P United, Member Code of Conduct. 29 Sept 2003. http://www.ftc.gov/bcp/ Sorkshops/filesharing/presentations/eisgrau.pdf

Rodriguez, Juan C., "FTC Sues to Get Patient Data Spreadsheet From LabMD." *Law360*. Lexis Nexis, 30 Aug. 2012. http://www.law360.com/ articles/374607/ftc-sues-to-get-patient-data-spreadsheet-from-labmd

Rosch, J. Thomas, FTC File No. 1023099, Dissenting Statement. 21 June, 2012. http://michaeljdaugherty.com/wp-content/uploads/2013/07/pg266_Dissent.pdf

Rosch, J. Thomas, Remarks before the Berlin Forum for EU-US Legal-Economic Affairs. 19 Sept 2009.

Scott, Prof. Michael D., *The FTC, The Unfairness Doctrine, and Data Security Breach Litigation: Has the Commission Gone too Far?* (1st. Edition 2007) http://michaeljdaugherty.com/wp-content/uploads/2013/07/Has-the-FTC-gone-too-far-1.pdf

Sotto, Lisa & Aaron P. Simpson, "Surviving an FTC Investigation After a Data Breach," *New York Law Journal*, 2008, http://michaeljdaughterty.com/wp-content/uploads/2013/07/FTC_investigation_DataBreach_Sotto-1.pdf

Stempel, Jonathan, "Big record labels win LimeWire copyright case." Reuters. May 13, 2010. http://www.reuters.com/article/2010/05/13/ us-limewire-copyright-ruling-idUSTRE64B63H20100513

Sydnor, Thomas D. II, John Knight, Lee A. Hollaar, *Filesharing Programs and "Technological Features to Induce Users to Share,"* (also known as USPTO Report) 2006.

Sydnor, Thomas D. II, Inadvertent File-Sharing Reinvented: The Dangerous Design of LimeWire 5, Progress & Freedom Foundation, 8 July, 2009. http://www.pff.org/issues-pubs/pops/2009/pop16.14-inadvertent-file-sharing-reinvented-limewire-5.pdf

Today Investigates, New Warnings on Cyber Thieves. http://today.msnbc.msn. com/id/26184891/vp/29405819%2329405819

Truett, Allen, Affidavit. http://michaeljdaugherty.com/wp-content/uploads/ 2013/07/pg189_Affidavit.pdf

US Congress. House. Subcommittee on Commerce, Trade, and Consumer Protection. H.R. 2221, The Data Accountability and Protection Act, and H.R. 1319, The Informed P2P User Act, Hearing, May 4, 2009 (Serial No. 111-36). Washington: Government Printing Office 2013.

US Congress. House. Committee on Oversight and Government Reform. *File-Sharing Programs and Peer-to-Peer Networks: Privacy and Security Risks, 1: Hearing before the Committee on Oversight and Government Reform.* 108th Cong., 1st sess., May, 2003.

US Congress. House. Committee on Oversight and Government Reform. *Inadvertent File Sharing Over Peer-to-Peer Networks: Hearing before the Committee on Oversight and Government Reform.* 110th Cong., 1st sess., July 24, 2007.

US Congress. House. Committee on Oversight and Government Reform. *Inadvertent File Sharing Over Peer-to-Peer Networks: How it Endangers Citizens and National Security: Hearing before the Committee on Oversight and Government Reform,* 111th Cong., 1st sess., July 29, 2009. http://www.gpo.gov/fdsys/pkg/CHRG-111hhrg54009/pdf/CHRG-111hhrg54009.pdf

US Congress. House. Subcommittee on Commerce, Trade, and Consumer Protection. *H.R. 2221, The Data Accountability and Protection Act, and H.R. 1319, The Informed P2P User Act: Hearing before the Subcommittee on Commerce, Trade, and Consumer Protection.* 111th Cong., 1st sess., May 4, 2009.

US Congress. Senate. Subcommittee on Competition, Foreign Commerce and Infrastructure of the Senate Committee on Commerce, Science and Transportation. *The Future of Peer-to-Peer (P2P) Technology, A Hearing before the Senate Subcommittee on Competition, Foreign Commerce and Infrastructure of the Senate Committee on Commerce, Science and Transportation.* 109th Cong., 2d sess., 23 June 2004. Review of website disclosures confirmed in written statement of Howard Beales.

US Congress. Senate. Committee on Judiciary. *The Dark Side of a Bright Idea: Could Personal and National Security Risks Compromise the Potential of P2P File-Sharing Network?: Hearing Before the Senate Comm. On the Judiciary,* 108th Cong. 8 (June 17, 2003) (statement of Sen. Orrin G. Hatch), see also id. At 67 (statement of Sen. Patrick Leahy); id. At 2 (statement of Sen. Dianne Feinstein).

Wenk, Amy, "Atlanta Medical Lab Facing Off Against FTC." *Atlanta Business Chronicle* 7-13 Sept. 2012: 3A+.

*West's Encyclopedia of American Law,* edition 2. 2008. The Gale Group 12 Jul. 2013 http://legal-dictionary.thefreedictionary.com/consent+decree

Wikileaks, "About: What is Wikileaks?" *Wikileaks.org.* Wikileaks, n.d. Web. http://michaeldaugherty.com/wp-content/uploads/2013/07/pg146-history-of-wikileaks.pdf

Wikipedia.com, *FrostWire,* http://en.wikipedia.org/wiki/FrostWire

Wright, Ben, 2013. Untitled. Subpeona BYOD Mobile Law, [blog]. http://hackigations.blogspot.com. [Accessed: 7/1/2013]

Zetter, Kim, 3/2/2009. Academic Claims to Find Sensitive Medical Info Exposed on Peer-to-Peer Networks. Wired Magazine. http://www.wired.com/threatlevel/2009/03/p2p-networks-le/

CPSIA information can be obtained at www.ICGtesting.com
Printed in the USA
LVOW08*1458181113

361784LV00020B/193/P